STUDIES IN GDR CULTURE AND SOCIETY 4

Selected Papers from the Ninth New Hampshire Symposium on the German Democratic Republic

Editorial Board:

DD
287.3
.N48
1983

UNIVERSITY
PRESS OF
AMERICA

LANHAM • NEW YORK • LONDON

Copyright © 1984 by

University Press of America, ™ **Inc.**

4720 Boston Way
Lanham, MD 20706

3 Henrietta Street
London WC2E 8LU England

ISBN (Perfect): 0-8191-4016-3
ISBN (Cloth): 0-8191-4015-5

All University Press of America books are produced on acid-free
paper which exceeds the minimum standards set by the National
Historical Publications and Records Commission.

TABLE OF CONTENTS

iii

Preface

The twenty-one papers collected here are the revised versions of papers presented at the Ninth New Hampshire Symposium on the German Democratic Republic, which took place from June 17-24, 1983 at the World Fellowship Center near Conway, N.H.

The 1983 Symposium was attended by approximately sixty-five academicians and others with expertise on various aspects of GDR culture and society. Six countries were represented: the United States, Canada, the GDR, the Federal Republic, Great Britain, and Japan. The special guest of the Symposium was writer Edith Anderson from East Berlin.

By publishing selected papers from the Symposium we would make the research results of this annual interdisciplinary conference available to a wider audience in the United States and abroad and thus contribute to the understanding of the "other" German state.

Margy Gerber   (Bowling Green State University)
Chief Editor

Wolfgang Büscher   (West Berlin)
Christine Cosentino   (Rutgers University)
Volker Gransow   (Univ. Bielefeld/FU Berlin)
Nancy A. Lauckner   (Univ. of Tenn., Knoxville)
Duncan Smith   (Brown University)
Alexander Stephan   (UCLA)
W. Christoph Schmauch, ex officio
    (World Fellowship Center)

In memoriam Gordon Tracy

We would like to dedicate this volume to the memory of our friend and colleague Gordon Tracy, who died on January 13, 1984. A regular participant in the Symposium over the years, a genuine "Conwayaner" and member of the World Fellowship family, Gordon contributed much to the spirit of the Symposium with his wit and gentle humaneness. His knowledge of GDR theater and opera, and of theater and music in general, which was reflected in various papers read in Conway, won our respect.

Two essays by Gordon Tracy, "Opera of the 1960s and 1970s in the GDR" and "Adaptations of Drama and Myths of Antiquity in GDR Drama," appeared in Volume One and Volume Two of Studies in GDR Culture and Society.

Genesis and Adventures of the Anthology
Blitz aus heiterm Himmel

Edith Anderson

The anthology Blitz aus heiterm Himmel, which originally had the title "Geschlechtertausch" ("Sex Swap"),[1] was conceived so long ago that I tend to forget what it did to my blood pressure as it rode the interminable loop-the-loop to publication. It almost never got there. My file on it, recording half a decade of furious fencing with the publisher, grew to a thickness of seven inches. In February 1975 the book at last saw the light, but not for long.

All the stories were written to order by GDR authors of rank or at least respectability. The men were asked to imagine that they had suddenly turned into women. The women were given the same commission in reverse.

When I was invited to speak at this Symposium I was rather alarmed at the thought of addressing scholars. I am not a scholar; I have none of the instincts of a scholar. Reading the published proceedings of last year's Symposium, I saw that the German language and literature specialists here knew more about the literature of the GDR than I ever would, because when a book bores me I stop reading it unless I absolutely have to. This need not be the book's fault. So since the invitation was apparently extended because of the "Sex Swap" anthology I decided I would just talk about its genesis and adventures. It would be a light-hearted little paper and possibly provide some welcome comic relief.

But as I approached the last page, I found myself also approaching something inside myself that I can only call a well of tears. I hadn't known it was there. My discomfiture grew when two of the tears ac-

1

tually rose to my eyes and I had to admit that this was not such a funny subject. All these years I had suppressed something that hurt me. So I rewrote the paper the way we retrace our steps when we've lost something. Was it along here that I dropped the glove? Is that my earring glistening on the curbstone?

The idea for the anthology blew into my head as lightly as a wisp of dandelion fluff. Everything had seemed easy that day. It was June 17, 1970, warm but not hot, and a few of us were visiting a friend who had been given an old stone manor house by the local collective farm. It is no more ususal to give away houses under socialism than it is under capitalism, but a tree was growing through the ceiling and the other dwellings on the former manor were in even worse shape, so the whole collective had moved four miles down the road to new housing.

It was nice sitting on the crumbling terrace of a free house while our host, the writer Gotthold Gloger, whose birthday it was, joined the conversation through the open window of the kitchen where he was stirring a bouillabaisse. We were facing a dilapidated outdoor toilet and two disheveled sheep, which once came up and stepped on our feet to get from one patch of weeds to another. Sheep are heavy. And the wife of the playwright Peter Hacks, who was lacquering her long, beautifully kept fingernails in that improbable setting, gazed up for a moment across the scrub and said, "If this were mine I would have it landscaped like Versailles."

Why this started Peter Hacks talking about the new play he was writing, I don't know, but it was called "Omphale," after a Lydian princess who married Hercules and exchanged roles and clothes with him. While she rushed out with a spear and armor, he would be sitting around the house in a dress, weaving. "Omphale" was the dandelion from which the fluff blew.

Let me just say parenthetically that Peter Hacks is not a feminist or fellow traveler, he just likes using Greek myths, apocryphs, and miscellaneous classical allusions to express this or that passing thought and get it out of his system. But I couldn't get it out of mine.

Going back to Berlin in a car belonging to Aufbau Verlag--the other two guests had been editors from

2

that publishing house--I suggested the anthology to editor Günther Caspar, the man in charge of contemporary German literature. He treated me to his standard editorial response, the glazed look of a replete Roman wondering whether to stick his finger down his throat now or wait until after the next bowl of flamingo brains. After miles passed and I was still eagerly nagging him, he told me to send him an exposé.

That evening after lining up two friends as a fortifying nucleus, the essayist Annemarie Auer and the novelist Irmtraud Morgner, I rang up Franz Fühmann. He is one of the finest writers in Germany East or West and a man of immense courtesy and kindness. But he was so horror-stricken that he interrupted, "A woman! Why, that's worse than Kafka! That's much, much worse than waking up as a cockroach!" I think he wished he could erase those words from my memory, because some weeks later he dropped in to explain his "real" reason. "Mein liebes Kind," he called me, although I am six years his senior, "such a theme is much too serious for me to handle in a twenty-five-page story with a three-month deadline. It would take me a year to do it justice and I don't feel I can afford a year for that subject matter. It's a question of priorities, don't you see." Yes, I said, far preferring his first reaction, which, God knows, I don't hold against him. It was not only his truth, which he couldn't help, it was very close to <u>the</u> truth.

After Fühmann I phoned Hermann Kant, another person for whom I have the greatest admiration and respect. His best writing is polemical. Not only his sharp pen, his whole being is honed to political necessity, and he would never blurt out something he might regret. But he did blurt, as if stung by a giant hornet, "O verflucht! O verflucht! Ein ganz erschreckender Traum!" He added as conciliatingly as he could: "I think God knew what he was doing when he made me a man." He seemed really shaken.

It was those two conversations which gave me my first inkling that such an anthology would not necessarily amuse everybody--that there was an exposed nerve somewhere in the social fabric which might make the suavest of men kick back like a cannon. You may say, "She must have been awfully naive not to know that." Yes. I was living a rather sheltered life in a part of the world which Irmtraud Morgner, in her story "Valeska's Glad Tidings," called the best possible place on earth for women; and I know she meant that, despite ironic overtones.

So I wrote the exposé with more care and tact
than I might otherwise have employed. I also used my
suasions in letters to those authors I could not reach
by phone.

"What happens here," I wrote, "is an exploration
of the almost unimaginable: myself with the attributes
of the other sex and none of the attributes of mine.
What is the nature of that other whom I will never
meet, but who I would have been all my life by the
mere flip of a gene?

"Let us place ourselves in the skin of the opposite sex and just for once, instead of envying, re-
senting, despising it--or desiring, loving, worshiping
it--picture how we would feel if the positions were
reversed. Might this not be a salutary game for the
whole of society? For, as we all know, the enforce-
ment of the constitutional guarantee of equal rights
and the best intentions of conscientious citizens
still leave certain problems unsolved. The soul
seethes with attitudes that are centuries old; the law
dates from yesterday. Such a book is not the joke it
might superficially appear to be. It would be an attempt to cast light on regions which have been too
long in the dark, first and foremost in ourselves."

And truly a fight in the dark began which rivaled
the famous Chinese comic ballet. Adversaries who
didn't even know why they were adversaries, males and
females, publishers and publishees, rushed around an
unlighted stage in panic fear of the unknown other,
striking clumsily with long poles in the wrong direction.

It was the year in which all three of those basic
manifestoes, Millett's Sexual Politics, Firestone's
The Dialectics of Sex, and Greer's The Female Eunuch
were being copyrighted. We couldn't know that yet,
but they arrived before too long. Later someone would
send me The Dangerous Sex, by H.R. Hays, and I would
get my first really frightening insight into the degree to which men hate and fear uppity women who don't
know their place.

Meanwhile I got foretastes.

Aufbau Verlag rejected the anthology after six
weeks, allegedly because a majority of women editors

4

thought it too offbeat. This was told me by Günther Caspar with a malicious gleam in his eye. He correctly guessed that such news about women editors would confound me. If it were up to him, he said, Aufbau would have grabbed the book, such a wonderful idea, such a sure-fire hit! I immediately submitted the exposé to Hinstorff Verlag, a small house up in Rostock on the Baltic Sea, which at that time was reputed to be openminded, even bold.

The director welcomed me warmly. K. was a tall, broad-shouldered, and roseate man in the prime of life who wore very well-tailored suits and loved being gallant to women. He didn't actually wear a flower in his lapel, but my memory keeps suggesting it. He was delighted with the exposé. I think he pictured himself in a hammock with light summer reading that would be just a bit risqué. And why not? I myself still thought the idea was simply fun. I didn't see serious implications until the trouble started and got worse and worse. Over the protests of Hinstorff's editor-in-chief, who saw the implications immediately, the director signed a contract with me.

Two weeks later he began backtracking. We couldn't have men in the book. It was a women's book. I was summoned to Rostock, fare and hotel paid, of course, and greeted by director K. with a shade less enthusiasm. He had been quite content to have both sexes represented, but since his editor was so dead set against it, he now thought a bevy of ladies, God bless 'em, should more than suffice. I explained to him that the anthology, like the world, would be boring without both sexes; it would lose its point. He looked about helplessly. The editor-in-chief always managed to be away when I came. I tried to help.

"Perhaps you could just tell me one reason why you think men would harm the book."

After a rather long embarrassed pause he succeeded in beaming again. "Oh, never mind," he said, "I simply thought it was more fitting to have just women, but if you feel so strongly about it--" So I went home imagining I had prevailed, but of course his editor coached him all over again and I got another summons to Rostock. "No real man can imagine himself a woman," said K. "Are you telling me that Günter de Bruyn is not a real man?" I asked. De Bruyn's story had been the first to arrive. "No no no, of course not," he assured me, all flustered. Annoyed at always losing, he handed me the clincher. "It's women who need to be emancipated. Men are already emancipated!" I tried to make him understand that no group could be emancipated alone, that it was all of us or none of us, but there was no room in his head for such a thought. So I drew my only trump. We had a contract, I reminded him. The contract specified equal representation of both sexes. Without much hope he said we could change the contract.

For months after that I heard nothing from Hinstorff.

Originally I aimed for twelve authors, but I was having trouble rustling them up. Most of the men really did prove skittish. When Eduard Claudius, a veteran of the war in Spain, declared himself willing, I felt I had landed an immense carp, less for literary quality than for his very evident masculinity, but a few months later he told me tersely that he had changed his mind. He would give no reason. Jurek Becker, talented author of Jacob the Liar, at first seemed tickled to be in the book. "It's such a marvelous opportunity to lie to one's heart's content!" he declared. That was when Aufbau Verlag was still mulling over the idea, but they mulled too long for him and he tied himself up with a film. "Oh, I've always wanted to be a woman!" cried Paul Wiens. He was a poet and sensitive translator of poetry. But when the deadline came he hadn't got past paragraph one. Peter Hacks had gotten sex roles out of his system. Stefan Heym said yes with alacrity and was the first to complete his story, if not to deliver it. Instead he sent it to Playboy, on the grounds that such a book would never come out in the GDR anyway.

Not that it was easy with the women. For one thing, there were very few women writing at that time, compared with the number of men, which meant that there weren't many of caliber. Those of caliber, Annemarie Auer, for example, couldn't necessarily write stories, although she did provide an excellent historical epilogue. None of us had heard of Maxie Wander, because she herself wasn't sure she had; she was only writing letters and diaries then. Brigitte Reimann was already dying and knew it. She had no time to do anything but try and finish her last novel.

Christa Wolf was of course one of the first to be asked. Her spontaneous reaction was negative. "If you had asked me ten years ago, I would have said yes.

6

In those days I wished I was a man." I was surprised at such obtuseness from her. "We don't wish we were men," I said. "Well--" she temporized, "I'm sorry." She thanked me and rang off. The next day she called back. She probably very wisely feared there might be more in this subject than yet met her eye. And she found out what it was; she is a delver.

I knew Anna Seghers would say no. She had told me years before in an interview that she had no patience with women's rights preoccupations. It was their own fault if they let themselves be nobodies. If they had anything on the ball, they would be rec- ognized as readily as any man. But I didn't want to have to reproach myself for leaving stones unturned, especially a stone that precious.

She railed at me. "And who would bother writing such stuff?" she demanded. "You'd be surprised," I bluffed. "Not Christa Wolf, I bet," she said. I couldn't help gloating just a little when I told her yes, Christa Wolf too. But when Christa sent me her characteristically melancholy story it was accompanied by a note that said, "By the way, I scarcely believe anything will come of your anthology." It was dampen- ing. It was an ill omen, as things turned out, and I don't mean that superstitiously.

Even if nothing else had come of the anthology, it did start Christa Wolf, then forty-one, thinking about the women's question at last--mournfully, of course, never militantly; still it produced not only her contribution to the anthology, but a few years afterward the moving study "Der Schatten eines Trau- mes," ostensibly about the romantic writer Karoline von Günderrode, and, most recently, Kassandra, which elaborates the thesis of her anthology story, "Selbst- versuch"--namely, that for the male the price of male power is emotional impoverishment.

Sarah Kirsch turned in a most touching, gentle, and tenderly witty story, "Blitz aus heiterm Himmel." When Katharina's truckdriver boyfriend comes to see her he notices the change despite her neutral jeans, but makes no comment. He is tired out after days on the road and takes a nap first. Refreshed, he treats her with a fairness and camaraderie he was never able to show before. Whatever has to be done in the house, he pitches in without being asked. Together they stack her coal briquettes that have been dumped in the court, the usual method of delivery, and carry them

into the cellar. "Nowm a guy myself, now I geddequal
rights" (p. 204), thinks Katharina. They shower together, roaring with laughter at each other's erec-
tions, then go downstairs to repair Albert's truck.
They are as merry and compatible as ever, only more
so. Back from a trial run in the repaired truck, Albert remains seated. Katharina turns her face to him.
"'His hair can stay that way,' thought Albert" (p.
207).

My fear that authors might invent identical stories was soon dispelled. Irmtraud Morgner shared one
basic assumption with Sarah Kirsch: that true love
will overlook the partner's sex. Apart from that,
there were no similarities. One difference was that
Sarah avoided explaining how Katharina and Albert were
going to work things out sexually, whereas Irmtraud
was so explicit, even to the freckle on her heroine's
new apparatus which appeared and disappeared as it
shifted gears, that K. became terribly upset. When
Valeska was not experimenting with other women--this
could not be termed Lesbian, because she was a man--
she was magically assuming her old female form in order to sleep with the husband she loved above all.
She could effect this change temporarily by drinking
strong coffee.

K. demanded that Irmtraud at least cut the offen-
sive line, "The bedding smelled of tobacco and fish." [2]
She refused. Men could write such things, why could-
n't she? But the sensibilities of that great ruddy
hunk of manhood, the director of Hinstorff, proved as-
tonishingly maidenly. Here he needed no instructions
from his editor-in-chief. The very title "Geschlechtertausch" (or "Sex Swap") had made him shudder. It
was so blunt. Once when I remarked that a woman
couldn't go into a German saloon unescorted--well, she
could, but she would regret it--he cried out in fussy
consternation, "But who would want to? I wouldn't go
into one of those nasty saloons!" On such points he
knew his reasons, though he couldn't communicate them,
and would just keep shaking his head and making pris-
sy mouths until argument lay down and died.

Yet he made no objection to Gotthold Gloger's extremely rowdy, ingenious, and uproarious story, "The
Beet Harvest Revel." Victims of a malicious old witch,
a collective farmer and his wife wake up to find themselves displaced in one another's bodies. They look
the same as before, but he is she and she is he. Arnold in Milda's body wonders if the same unmentionable

disaster has befallen other couples and tries to reach his friend Gernot, the chairman of the collective, through hints to Gernot's wife, but she doesn't understand. The annual revelry after the beet harvest, from which men are excluded, turns into a witches' sabbath where the drunken collective-farm women dance themselves into a sweat and rip their clothes off. Milda, with loosened tongue, openly expresses Arnold's male-chauvinist views. As the other women become suspicious and gang up on her, the real Milda in Arnold's big fat body crashes through the rafters from her hiding place and crushes the witch flat. From the remains leaps a billy-goat and bolts out of sight. This breaks the enchantment. Except that Arnold no longer has his old appendix scar. Milda has it. The payoff comes when Arnold rushes to the newspaper office with written proof of his appendix operation and no scar, demanding an article that will expose witchcraft on the collective farms. No editor will touch the alarmist report, which might harm production figures, and Arnold spends the rest of his life suspecting every man he encounters of harboring a woman inside him and every woman of being secretly a man.

Gotthold had misunderstood his assignment, but the misunderstanding was a boon and his plot a stroke of genius. Actually the only one of the men who understood the assignment was Günter de Bruyn. His novel Buridans Esel had shown an amazing empathy with women and a sardonic insight into the patriarchal illusions of both sexes. "Geschlechtertausch"--"Sex Swap"--was the title of his exemplary contribution.

It is about a wish that comes true--too true. Carl and Anna, in transports of love, cry out their yearning to be even closer than lovers can get: "Oh, if only I could be the woman!" "Oh, if only I could be the man!" (p. 8). They decide that the next time they attain those blessed heights they will return to what they were. But the opportunity never presents itself. Anna comes down with a men's ailment the very next day and is hospitalized. Carl, the respected director of a department in his firm, phones his boss to tell him of the "accident." At first, his colleagues treat him with the most delicate tact and the same deference as before. But as his male image gradually dims, so does their respect, although his work was never better. Former friends leer at him and make passes. His opinions at meetings interest no one, they are regarded as faux pas, and his jokes fall flat. To get any recognition at all he has to waste

9

an unconscionable amount of time on his appearance and
he finds himself hating men who don't even appreciate
it; only with effort can he judge them on their merits
now, just as they have forgotten how to judge him on
his.

When Anna's condition is so far improved that the
doctor permits Carl to stay with her in the hospital
overnight, she tells him in the presence of the nurse
that it won't do. Carl perceives that Anna, or rather
Adam, is now deeply involved with this nurse, who, as
she massages Adam's scalp with hair tonic, consoles
Carl, "You will get your satisfaction in struggling
for the fuller expansion of women's rights. Goodness
knows there's enough to do" (p. 44).

With so many good stories, it made no difference
to me what other authors might write. The juxtaposition was what mattered. So as we needed one more man,
I wrote to Erik Neutsch. His first novel, Spur der
Steine, published in 1964, although apparently un-
touched by any editorial red pencil, was at least a
goodly chunk of ore with some precious metal inside,
if you hacked far enough. It belabored the Party for
interfering in private lives to an extent which was
ultimately uneconomical; for if you disciplined people
for the cut of their jib or who they fell in love
with, it not only made them personally miserable, it
deprived society of their potential. This criticism
was published in several editions.

Neutsch sent me a repulse so pompous, so monumen-
tal, so absurd that I made the mistake of laughing.

"Even if I did let myself in for neo-romantic
garbage," he droned on in Paragraph 4--he numbered his
paragraphs as if writing an outline for a debate--"who
would take the responsibility if I could not restrain
a certain naturalism en détail? For you see, supposing
I woke up one day as a woman, I would probably not
wonder first of all whether I had to wash the dishes,
but what had become of that which ranks me with the
male sex. And I assure you that this question alone
would occupy me for 25 pages."

Paragraph 5: "But as I see this only as a question with sexual but not social significance, I am
happy to remain a realist in that I disabase myself
[sic] of your assault ["indem ich mich Ihres Attentats
entwürdige"]. With socialist-realistic greetings," and
his signature made a big black clang, like iron runes

dropped in a junkyard.

Genuinely regretful that we would be deprived of his story--"Das Fehlende"? ("That Which Was Missing") --I wrote a few lines telling him so with a smile that seemed to madden him. According to K., he warned Hinstorff that if they went ahead with this impossible anthology, there would be reprisals from high up. K. gave me this bulletin in our new venue, the lobby of the Hotel Unter den Linden in Berlin. I can't vouch for the truth of it; he told me a great many fibs; I only know that from that time on he no longer smiled at me. He wore the face of a hurt father. I didn't know who my friends were, he said. His broad shoulders, he said, were taking the blows meant for me. "Blows from where?" I asked. "Be glad you don't know," he replied darkly.

Since there was no legal way that Hinstorff could wriggle out of the contract, they resorted to every kind of subterfuge. They delayed like the wives in Lysistrata running after mattresses and pillows. They produced--at least they said they could--a sturdy printer who was so insulted on behalf of his hometown Quedlinburg, which Karl-Heinz Jakobs had chosen as the setting for a matriarchate, that he refused to work on the book. They rediscovered the old dependable paper shortage, but since that could be disproved, paper came back and they blamed obstinate Irmtraud Morgner and her smelly coverlet. Behind my back they threw her story out.

"We will fight this," I told her, but it was too late--she had haughtily accepted being thrown out. "They can't do it," I insisted, "it's in the contract that they'd have to get my agreement." No, she was through with Hinstorff. Irmtraud considered that her action in walking off with her nose in the air was a kind of resistance, and maybe she was right. She built her story into the novel Trobadora Beatriz, which she was just finishing, and it was published by Aufbau Verlag without a single cut, tobacco, fish, and all, despite the lady editors there who were supposedly so leary of anything off-color. It appeared in several editions too, and is still going strong.

Hinstorff had begun deliberately destroying the anthology. In its house organ it had never given Blitz a word of advance publicity, but now it moved to active sabotage. The editor-in-chief published in Sinn und Form an attack on literature that fantasized about sex roles.[3] Three more authors were thrown out. Of the few who remained three were released, at their request, from the clause in their contracts forbidding them to publish elsewhere <u>before</u> the anthology appeared. Blushing and stammering, Sarah told me she earned so little that she couldn't wait any longer, and of course, her excuse was true. No one anywhere can make a living through poetry. The other two authors kept quiet about what they had done. In the lobby of the Hotel Unter den Linden I accused K. of flagrantly and repeatedly violating our contract. I demanded that he commit himself to a definite publication date once and for all.

"Why do you keep insisting on this anthology?" he asked. "Don't you realize it has been made valueless by all those authors going to other publishers with their stories?"

And indeed a West German publisher that had pestered Hinstorff for a license for two years wrote me that it wasn't interested in the book any more because it was no longer a sensation. Literary commentators in the West noted an East German curiosity they couldn't explain: authors so different from one another all bursting into print about how their sex had changed overnight.

With the support of the Writers' Union I threatened Hinstorff with a damage suit unless the anthology went straight to press. It did. It sold out so fast that I never saw a copy in a bookshop. It got excellent reviews. In a state of euphoria I threw a cocktail party for the authors and their spouses. I made Martinis by the gallon and we all had a high old time. Only Christa Wolf seemed to feel uncomfortable. It puzzled me. She looked gloomy, and every time I brought in another tray of canapes she lamented, "All that <u>work</u>! What did you do all that <u>work</u> for?" I had been <u>bilked</u>, yet here I was celebrating.

I wrote to Hinstorff asking when a second edition could be expected. It replied that no further editions could be expected. The letter was signed by a strange new name, and under it the title Director. K. had become a free-lance writer like the rest of us. The editor-in-chief had died. The stories were dispersed, the rights held by the individual authors jointly with new publishers. My rights as <u>Herausgeber</u> --that is, originator and organizer--had <u>disappeared</u> into thin air. Legally there was no more book to have rights to.

Yet something remained in some people's heads. Who can say whether, if Blitz had not run interference, Maxie Wander's volume of amazing interviews with GDR women, Guten Morgen, Du Schöne, would have been attempted and published, would have run into so many editions and been dramatized in so many theaters and on television? In any case, why a well of tears? I think it is drying up. We are confronted here with two very different national traditions. American women cannot judge the reactions of German women by their own.

With the exception of Annemarie Auer, the women in Blitz had little awareness of a women's movement as something that could be effected by them personally. The concept of solidarity among sisters had not reached them yet. The reason, I believe, is that while GDR women enjoy rights and benefits which women in the Federal Republic and the United States may well envy, they got those rights and benefits as a component of socialism without ever fighting for them.

This is not to say they don't appreciate what they have. They take it for granted, like people who think it normal to have three meals a day because they never had less. On the other hand, if men try to inflict a double shift on them or otherwise treat them as second-class human beings, they fume, and on an individual basis they often do something about it. Most divorces in the GDR are initiated by wives, and the divorce rate is high. The present generation of GDR women are a new breed on German soil. Over eighty percent have jobs, and that gives them not only income but confidence. In some ways they remind me of the women in Charlotte Perkins Gilman's novel Herland. What is lacking is any history of a militant women's movement comparable with the movements in the U.S. and England. I emphasize the word "comparable" because of course they had their extraordinary women and brave heroines, though few of these fought specifically for women's rights.

The story of Blitz, of "Sex Swap," is not a Whodunit. Who was really behind the suppression of an anthology which threatened no one and nothing is the wrong formulation, and we need hardly ask what was behind it. The ages-old patriarchate was behind it. The patriarchate is much more vigilant about its privileges than women have learned to be about their

13

rights, and this is true throughout the so-called civilized world. All other things being equal, socialism ought to be able to get rid of the patriarchate, but all other things are not equal; the world is embroiled in hot wars and cold wars everywhere and is on the brink of total catastrophe. We cannot expect people whose backs are against the wall to relax and talk sense about sex roles.

I wish I could tack on a happy ending. There is no happy ending. One must simply fight on, by whatever means come to hand.

Notes

[1] Blitz aus heiterm Himmel, ed. Edith Anderson (Rostock: Hinstorff, 1975). The anthology contains seven stories: Günter de Bruyn, "Geschlechtertausch"; Christa Wolf, "Selbstversuch"; Gotthold Gloger, "Das Rübenfest"; Edith Anderson, "Dein für immer oder nie" ("Thine Ever or Never"); Rolf Schneider, "Meditation"; Sarah Kirsch, "Blitz aus heiterm Himmel"; Karl-Heinz Jakobs, "Quedlinburg"; and an essay by Annemarie Auer, "Mythen und Möglichkeiten." The English translations in the text are my own.

[2] Irmtraud Morgner, "Gute Botschaft der Valeska, in her novel Leben und Abenteuer der Trobadora Beatriz nach Zeugnissen ihrer Spielfrau Laura (Darmstadt/Neuwied: Luchterhand, 1977), p. 425. The GDR edition appeared in Aufbau Verlag in 1974.

[3] Kurt Batt, "Die Exekution des Erzählers," Sinn und Form, 24, No. 6 (1972), 1248.

"'Weibliches' Schreiben" - Christa Wolf's <u>Kassandra</u>

Christiane Zehl Romero

> Seit ich begonnen habe--den Namen
> "Kassandra" vor mir hertragend als
> eine Art Legitimations- und Losungs-
> wort--mich auf jene Bereiche einzu-
> lassen, in die er mich führt, scheint
> alles, was mir sonst begegnet, "da-
> mit" zusammenzuhängen, bisher Ge-
> trenntes hat sich hinter meinem Rük-
> ken zusammengeschlossen, in vorher
> dunkle, unbewußte Räume fällt ein we-
> nig Licht. . . . Mit der Erweiterung
> des Blick-Winkels, der Neueinstellung
> der Tiefenschärfe hat mein Seh-Ra-
> ster, durch den ich unsere Zeit, uns
> alle, dich, mich selber wahrnehme,
> sich entschieden verändert, ver-
> gleichbar jener frühen entschiedenen
> Veränderung, die mein Denken, mei-
> ne Sicht und mein Selbst-Gefühl und
> Selbst-Anspruch vor mehr als dreißig
> Jahren durch die erste befreiende und
> erhellende Bekanntschaft mit der marx-
> istischen Theorie und Sehweise er-
> fuhren.1

These words from Christa Wolf's recent "Frankfurter
Poetik-Vorlesungen" are striking indeed: their author
lives and writes in a country where a feminist movement in the Western sense does not exist, since, officially at least, there is no need for one in socialism. "Der Klassenkampf ist das Primäre, die Dominan-
te, er ist das Übergeordnete. . . . Der Klassenriß
geht mitten durch <u>beide</u> Geschlechter," Wilhelm Girnus
in fact reminds Christa Wolf in his harsh critique of
the excerpt from Wolf's lectures which appeared in

Sinn und Form.[2] Among other things, he accuses her of sympathizing too much with the "bourgeois women's movement" or of trying too hard to please the West German audience of her lectures, but in any case of not presenting herself as unambiguously communist. "Zum Kommunisten Leninischer Prägung gehört, daß er sich immer von dem jeweilig in Frage stehenden bürgerlichen Standpunkt klar abgrenzt" (p. 1102).

As the initial quote suggests, Christa Wolf's "Frankfurter Poetik-Vorlesungen" follow the traces of the legendary Trojan princess and seer, Cassandra, who supposedly predicted the fall of Troy, but to deaf ears. Her prophecies brought her imprisonment and ostracism. According to some versions of the myth, which Christa Wolf does not pursue, Cassandra received the gift of prophecy from Apollo, who was in love with her. When she rejected him, he decreed that her predictions would never be believed.

Cassandra is one of the very few female figures who have come down to us from antiquity in a role other than that of lover, wife, mother, sister, i.e., in a role that is not totally dependent on and defined by the relationship to a man. "Kassandra die erste berufstätige Frau. . . . ? Was hätte eine Frau werden können außer 'Seherin'?" (V, p. 38), Christa Wolf muses. For these reasons the figure holds a special fascination for women today, particularly for feminists. There is even a journal that bears her name: kassandra. feministische zeitschrift der visuellen künste (editor: Monika Oellerich). However, the composite image we have of Cassandra is, like all the "Frauenbilder" our Occidental culture has provided for us,[3] the creation of men, among them great poets (Homer, who by the way makes no mention of her special gifts, Aischylus, Euripides, even Schiller) and famous archaeologists and anthropologists who have researched the time and culture with which she is associated as well as the earlier pre-patriarchal cultures of which her figure and role are a vestige.

Only very recently have Women's Studies, representing many disciplines, begun to look at such "Frauenbilder".[4] Their interest and research, particularly in West Germany, have focused on one area especially, the question of matriarchy. Crete with its ruins of the mysterious Minoan culture, in which, judging from pictorial representations, women seem to have played an important role, has become a place of "pilgrimage" for feminists. (Wolf, by the way, also went there.)

And, in general, pre-patriarchal cultures, matriarchal religions, and matrilinear succession have developed into important fields of study and into even more important sources of inspiration and utopian projections for feminists.[5]

In this context the figure of Cassandra assumes special significance and poignancy because from what myth, literature, archaeology, and anthropology tell us about her, she represents and suffers the transition from still largely unknown archaic forms of society to a form we know only too well: patriarchal society and its need for, and glorification of, war and victory. Patriarchal society has shaped all our thinking and experience, but may now itself be entering a phase of transition. Thus "sister Cassandra" invites identification and, more importantly, re-investigation and imaginative re-creation by women who sense this transition and feel an urgent need to take personal responsibility for the common future of mankind.

It is an invitation Christa Wolf has accepted--inevitably, one is tempted to say (with the knowledge of hindsight), if one looks at her development as a writer and the direction this has taken towards a more and more conscious as well as far-ranging examination of what "[a]ls Frau 'ich' sagen" (V, p. 148) has meant and might mean. In her "Büchner-Preis-Rede" (1980) Wolf said of twentieth-century woman:

> Nach den Kriegen, als sie sich in seiner Produktions- und Vernichtungs- maschinerie bewährt, als sie den Mann ersetzt hat, erfährt sie als äußer- stes Zugeständnis: Sie sei wie er. Dies wird sie ihm nun beweisen. Sie arbeitet wie ein Mann, das ist der Fortschritt. Steht Tag und Nacht ne- ben ihm an der Maschine. Sitzt neben ihm im Hörsaal, an Beratungs- und Vorstandstischen (dort natürlich in der Minderzahl). Schreibt, malt, dichtet wie er - fast wie er.[6]

The "almost" is important. Woman still feels strange and asks herself:

> Warum ihr immer noch so fremd zumute ist; warum die Empfindung nicht nach- läßt, daß in Lob und Tadel nicht sie

> gemeint ist, sondern immer noch die
> andre, das falsche Bild von ihr, die
> Neben-Frau. Und daß von ihr noch
> kaum die Rede war. (BPR, p. 327)

Now, however, under the threat of nuclear war, "zuge-geben: spät, zu spät vielleicht - erhebt sie ihre Stimme . . ." (BPR, p. 328).

The "Büchner-Preis-Rede" was an impassioned plea for women to raise their voices and be heard in the search for peace. Wolf's inquiry into the "Stichwort . . . KASSANDRA" (V, p. 7) now continues these vital concerns on a large scale.

Originally a series of lectures given as "Frankfurter Poetik-Vorlesungen," now a famous institution (Ingeborg Bachmann was a notable predecessor important to Wolf), this inquiry was published in two small volumes, Voraussetzungen einer Erzählung: Kassandra, subtitled Frankfurter Poetik-Vorlesungen, and Kassandra; [7] both appeared in 1983. Although published separately, the volumes belong together, as Wolf explains in her introduction to the Voraussetzungen, where she speaks of five lectures:

> Die erste und die zweite Vorlesung,
> zwei Teile eines Berichts über eine
> Griechenlandreise, bezeugen, wie die
> Kassandra-Gestalt von mir Besitz er-
> greift und ihre erste vorläufige Ver-
> körperung erfährt. Die dritte Vorle-
> sung versucht in Form eines Arbeits-
> tagebuchs die Verklammerung zwischen
> Leben und Stoff nachzuzeichnen; in
> der vierten Vorlesung, einem Brief,
> frage ich nach der historischen Wirk-
> lichkeit der Kassandra-Figur und nach
> den Bedingungen weiblichen Schrei-
> bens, früher und heute. Die fünfte
> Vorlesung ist eine Erzählung unter
> dem Titel: Kassandra. (V, p. 8)

In the "Erzählung," which was not read in its entirety in Frankfurt, Christa Wolf no longer speaks directly but instead through Cassandra, presenting her memories and reflections of Troy before and during the war, as they pass through the latter's mind in the last hours of her life spent at the gates of Mycenae, where Agamemnon has brought her as his booty. She knows that death at the hands of Clytemnestra awaits her and her conqueror.

As had been more and more the case with Wolf's
previous work, but now very consciously, even program-
matically, discursive and fictive prose, essay and
story are closely interrelated, formally and themati-
cally. It has been said that Kassandra is not a tale
at all but rather "ein großer historisch-moralischer
Essay," while Voraussetzungen einer Erzählung: Kassandra is really a story--of Christa Wolf's "ganz persönliche, sinnliche, fast erotisch-zärtliche Annäherung
an eine Gestalt und ihren historischen Ort."[8] There
is some justification for such classifications, but
they miss one major point: Wolf is not interested in
them. On the contrary, in these public lectures,
which are officially about poetics, she insists on
speaking very personally and non-theoretically, so
much so that the reviewer I have just quoted is taken
back: "was, das hat sie tatsächlich den Studenten
erzählt . . ."[9] She purposely blurs traditional distinctions between forms of prose writing, and experiments with travelogue, diary, letter, literary and
cultural analysis, story, and moral essays in her approach to the subject of Cassandra. "Mischform" was a
term she had used approvingly for Bettina von Brenta-
no's unusual and often maligned books.[10] Now she uses
the word "Gewebe--das übrigens, falls ich eine Poetik
hätte, als ästhetisches Gebilde in ihrem Zentrum stün-
de" (V, p. 7). The reason why she refuses traditional
distinctions is crucial: she is trying to record and
ultimately effect profound change:

> Ich mache Sie auch zum Zeugen eines
> Vorgangs, der meinen Seh-Raster ver-
> ändert hat, aber dieser Prozeß hat
> erst angefangen, und ich empfinde
> selbst scharf die Spannung zwischen
> den Formen, in denen wir uns verab-
> redungsgemäß bewegen, und dem leben-
> digen Material, das meine Sinne, mein
> psychischer Apparat, mein Denken mir
> zuleiteten und das sich diesen Formen
> nicht fügen wollte. Wenn ich ein
> poetologisches Problem jetzt schon
> formulieren darf, so ist es dieses:
> Es gibt keine Poetik, und es kann
> keine geben, die verhindert, daß die
> lebendige Erfahrung ungezählter Sub-
> jekte in Kunst-Objekten ertötet und
> begraben wird. (V, pp. 7-8)

19

Indeed, the lectures begin with a fundamental refusal: "'Poetikvorlesungen' heißt dieses Unternehmen,
aber ich sage Ihnen gleich: Eine Poetik kann ich Ihnen
nicht bieten" (V, p. 7). This is anything but the
modest or not so modest disclaimer we often hear from
the practicing writer uninterested in theoretical
questions concerning his art. It is, I believe, a
central theme in Wolf's work on Cassandra. She notes
at the outset:

> Aber den wütenden Wunsch, mich mit
> der Poetik oder dem Vorbild eines
> großen Schreibers auseinanderzuset-
> zen, in Klammern: Brecht, habe ich
> nie verspürt. Dies ist mir erst in
> den letzten Jahren merkwürdig gewor-
> den, und so kann es sein, daß diese
> Vorlesungen nebenbei auch die gar
> nicht gestellte Frage mit behandeln,
> warum ich keine Poetik habe." (V,
> p. 7)

She does in fact answer that question and not "nebenbei" at all. In the process she presents what one
might call, paradoxically, "eine weibliche Ästhetik,"
a female aesthetics, bearing in mind however Wolf's
rejection of poetics and aesthetics as she sees them:
a system of thought and norms "wie Philosophie und
Wissenschaft, mindestens im gleichen Maß, zu dem Zweck
erfunden, sich Wirklichkeit vom Leib zu halten, sich
vor ihr zu schützen, wie zu dem Ziel, der Wirklichkeit
näherzukommen" (V, p. 150). Thus "weibliche Ästhetik" can only imply an investigation, the process of
trying to understand what "'weibliches' Schreiben,"
"'weibliches' Sprechen" may be, and what role it may
and must play.

In her desire to "come closer to reality," Christa Wolf has long resisted the reigning aesthetic
norms for GDR literature--since her novel Nachdenken
über Christa T. (1968) and her essays Lesen und
Schreiben (1972), at least. In "Lesen und Schreiben,"
still using the language provided by the norms of her
society, she demands for example that the writer of
prose "muß ein mechanisches zugunsten eines dialekti-
schen Weltverhältnisses zu überwinden suchen." [11] Yet,
the full implications of what she was seeking came to
her slowly; chiefly, I would say, as a result of her
interest in other women writers, from her early and
intense preoccupation with Anna Seghers to her recent
work on Karoline von Günderrode and Bettina von Bren-

tano/Arnim. [12] It has been a more gradual change of
"Seh-Raster" than Christa Wolf suggests in the poetics
lectures. Still, it is here that she acknowledges and
explores it fully. The change hinges upon her per-
ceiving herself as a woman writer, as part of a "female tradition" which is "at last . . . emerging." [13]
In her earlier reflections on the value of literature,
she had said: "Der Autor ist nämlich ein wichtiger
Mensch," without commenting at all on the masculine
words she was using. [14] But now she has come to consciously view her rejection of poetics and aesthetics
as an essential dimension of speaking as a woman and
of refusing or at least re-examining these norms and
theories which were created without her full participation and are therefore, she argues, one-sided and
ultimately destructive:

> Daß Frauen zu der Kultur, in der wir
> leben, über die Jahrtausende hin of-
> fiziell und direkt so gut wie nichts
> beitragen durften, ist nicht nur eine
> entsetzliche, beschämende und skanda-
> löse Tatsache für Frauen - es ist,
> genau genommen, diejenige Schwach-
> stelle der Kultur, aus der heraus sie
> selbstzerstörerisch wird, nämlich ih-
> re Unfähigkeit zur Reife.
>
> (<u>V</u>, p. 115)

The story of Troy before and during the Trojan
War, as Christa Wolf recreates it around Cassandra, is
an example of the development of this "Schwachstelle."
Wolf explains:

> An einer Nahtstelle dieser konflikt-
> reichen Geschehnisse steht Kassandra.
> Tochter eines Königshauses, in dem
> die patrilineare Erbfolge gefestigt
> scheint, ohne daß deshalb die Köni-
> gin, Hekabe, die, wie manche meinen,
> aus der matristischen Kultur der
> Lokrer kommt, schon zur Bedeutungslo-
> sigkeit herabgesunken wäre; in dem
> die Übergangsform des Prinzessinnen-
> raubs durch den Freier (Paris-Hele-
> na), weil nur die Frau dem Manne den
> Thron übergeben konnte, durchaus noch
> bekannt ist. In dem die alten matri-
> archalischen Kulte neben den jungen
> Kulten der neuen Götter gepflegt wer-
> den mögen, besonders wohl von den

21

                    niederen Volksschichten. In dem eine
                    junge Frau Priesterin werden kann,
                    kaum noch Oberpriesterin.
                                             (V, p. 144)

In Wolf's view, it is a culture, "die der strikt pa-
triarchalischen der mykenischen Archaier, ihrem strik-
ten Eroberungswillen nicht gewachsen war" (V, p.
144). Its decline comes already in the period which
Wolf suggestively and topically calls "Vorkrieg"
(V, p. 76). During that time Troy in Wolf's story
changes. Women like Hecuba and Cassandra are excluded
from council meetings, and their advice is ignored;
women like Polyxena, Cassandra's sister, who was to
entice Achilles to tell her where his vulnerable spot
was and to come unarmed to the temple, where Paris
could kill him, become mere objects and self-hating,
self-abasing victims. Lies, such as the one that
Paris brought Helen to Troy--Helen, the ultimate example of woman as object/idol (in the lectures Wolf
reflects on Goethe's treatment of Helen in Faust II)--,
become official truth, part of a systematic and, of
course, falsifying interpretation of events according
to one overriding principle, the preparation for and
fighting of war. The reason the Trojans lose, according to Christa Wolf, is that they are behind the
Greeks in that development; they have not become as
ruthless as the Greeks and their supreme hero, Achilles, who in Christa Wolf's story has only one epithet,
"das Vieh," and who exemplifies the immaturity, in-
security, and cruelty which Christa Wolf attributes to
a culture in which women are nothing but objects, and
in which the intellect, as represented by Athena, has
only a father, no mother (V, pp. 144-45).

     In the story, told from the perspective of the
Trojan woman Cassandra, the Greeks, Western civilization's heroes, come off poorly. Achilles is not the
only one represented as a swaggering, insecure brute.
In a sense, Wolf, who at the "First Berlin Meeting of
Writers for Peace" (Dec. 13/14, 1981) said that Occidental literature is to a large extent "Schlachtenli-
teratur," creates something of a Gegenbild--at least
on the surface--to the Iliad, one of the most famous
examples of this kind of literature. The Iliad is,
most summaries say, about the wrath of Achilles, but
viewed less charitably, it is about the petulant behavior he exhibits when Agamemnon takes the slave girl
Briseis away from him, and the incredible slaughter
that ensues.

Wolf's negative portrayal of the Greeks in Kassandra does not mean that she is insensitive to the great achievements of Greek culture. But to her these are early examples of "ausgefallene Spitzenleistungen . . . nur durch Ent-Persönlichung zu haben" (V, p. 136). Their price is the inability to love and the need for conquest and thus, ultimately, war. The parallels to present-day attitudes and confrontations are implicitly and explicitly drawn by Wolf in the story and the four preceding lectures. Women under these conditions will always be objects and victims. At most they will be like Clytemnestra, who revenges the wrongs done her by her husband by killing him, or like Penthesilea the Amazon, who, out of desperation, has become a butcher ("Schlächterin") like the men:

> Arisbe: Und wir? Wenn wir auch Schlächterinnen würden?
> Penthesilea: So tun wir, was wir müssen. Doch es macht uns keinen Spaß.
> . . .
> Oinone: Aber so kann man nicht leben.
> Penthesilea: Nicht leben? Sterben schon. (K, p. 134)

In Wolf's story Cassandra is clearly sympathetic to Penthesilea and her fate (her dead body is violated by the victorious Achilles, who cannot bear the fact that a woman fought him): "Die Männer, schwach, zu Siegern hochgeputscht, brauchen, um sich überhaupt noch zu empfinden, uns als Opfer" (K, p. 137). But Cassandra does not agree with her. Penthesilea is no alternative, only the ultimate victim.

Is there an alternative? Cassandra, in Christa Wolf's re-creation, represents an attempt at one, albeit doomed, since the triumph of the Greeks over Troy signified the victory of patriarchal culture in the Occident. But behind Wolf's preoccupation with Cassandra stands the vital question: Would Cassandra, will Wolf, will the female tradition, at whose opposite ends they stand, be more successful now that patriarchy may be running its course, and more and more women and men recognize its "Schwachstelle," its inherent tendency towards destruction and self-destruction? Obviously there is no answer as yet, only the eloquent plea by Christa Wolf that they be given a chance and that they take it.

What is the alternative which the figure of Cassandra represents and Christa Wolf explores? It starts with Wolf's question: "Scheint es Dir abwegig, zu glauben, daß 'das Denken', hätten Frauen seit über zweitausend Jahren an ihm mitgedacht, heute ein andres Leben führen würde?" (V., p. 145) The question implies the answer: no. Wolf believes that it is important to investigate the attempts, no matter how abortive they may have been, which women in the past have made to contribute to history and thought--her own work on Günderrode and Bettina von Arnim follows that course--and, more importantly, that it is time now for women to participate and to see what changes they can make. Fruitful participation by women, however, presupposes that they develop the courage, perception, and language necessary to take part on their terms, independently of the patterns developed by men, as Wolf's rejection of poetics and aesthetics requires. In the fourth lecture, the letter to a fellow woman writer, Wolf asks:

> Sage Dir alle großen Namen der abendländischen Literatur auf, vergiß weder Homer noch Brecht, und frage Dich, bei welchem dieser Geistesriesen Du, als Schreibende, anknüpfen könntest. Wir haben keine authentischen Muster, das kostet uns Zeit, Umwege, Irrtümer; aber es muß ja nicht nur ein Nachteil sein.
>
> (V, p.146)

Indeed, I believe Wolf's career as a writer and our interest in her show that this lack of "authentic patterns" has also been an advantage. Gilbert and Gubar, well-known feminist critics and literary historians in this country, characterize the development that has energized her--and others:

> The son of many fathers, today's male writer feels hopelessly belated, the daughter of too few mothers, today's female writer feels that she is helping to create a viable tradition which is at last definitely emerging.[15]

However, Wolf also recognizes the difficulties:

> Ahnt man, ahnen wir, wie schwer, ja, wie gefährlich es sein kann, wenn wieder Leben in die "Sache" kommt; wenn das Idol sich wieder zu fühlen beginnt; wenn "es" die Sprache wieder

findet? Als Frau "ich" sagen muß?
(<u>V</u>, p. 148)

There is, as danger and temptation, the "Zwangsidee,
sich anpassen oder verschwinden zu müssen" (<u>V</u>, p.
150). Christa Wolf says categorically:

> Ich behaupte, daß jede Frau, die sich
> in diesem Jahrhundert und in unserem
> Kulturkreis in die vom männlichen
> Selbstverständnis geprägten Institu-
> tionen gewagt hat--"die Literatur",
> "die Ästhetik" sind solche Institu-
> tionen--, den Selbstvernichtungs-
> wunsch kennenlernen mußte.
> (<u>V</u>, p. 149)

Christa Wolf's rejection of a poetics is thus a
positive act, it means self-preservation for her as a
woman writer. Such an act is not only important for
the individual woman but for the whole of society as
well. For women--Cassandra is an example--who manage
to refuse the "Seh-Raster" provided them by men, can
see and say those simple truths that men, because of
their tradition with its glorification of the heroic
and of "Spitzenleistungen," cannot or dare not ac-
knowledge. Therefore we need to develop and acknowl-
edge the female tradition, "'weibliches' Schreiben."

> Inwieweit gibt es wirklich "weibli-
> ches" Schreiben? Insoweit Frauen aus
> historischen und biologischen Gründen
> eine andre Wirklichkeit erleben als
> Männer. . . . Insoweit Frauen nicht
> zu den Herrschenden, sondern zu den
> Beherrschten gehören, jahrhunderte-
> lang . . .; insoweit sie aufhören,
> sich an dem Versuch abzuarbeiten,
> sich in die herrschenden Wahnsysteme
> zu integrieren. Insoweit sie, schrei-
> bend und lebend, auf Autonomie aus
> sind. . . . Autonome Personen, Staa-
> ten und Systeme können sich gegen-
> seitig fördern, müssen sich nicht be-
> kämpfen wie solche, deren innere Un-
> sicherheit und Unreife andauernd Ab-
> grenzung und Imponiergebärden ver-
> langen. (<u>V</u>, pp. 114-15)

Christa Wolf includes this utopian vision in
<u>Kassandra</u>. There is an alternative culture in the

25

Troy she creates. Aeneas, who in the story becomes Cassandra's caring, understanding lover, and his father, Anchises, are part of it, as are many, mostly lower-class, women, "die Frauen am Skamander." This alternative culture is still rooted in matriarchal religion, particularly the cult of Cybele. People live in the everyday world caring for each other and the victims of the war, with which they will have nothing to do. It is from her growing acquaintance with this culture that Cassandra receives the impulse to develop her own perceptions of events in Troy and the courage to express them. After she has been imprisoned--significantly, in Troy's "Heldengräber"--for speaking her mind, "die Frauen am Skamander" rescue her and take her in. With them she enjoys "das höchste Vorrecht, das es gibt, . . . in die finstere Gegenwart, die alle Zeit besetzt hält, einen schmalen Streifen Zukunft vorzuschieben" (K, p. 152).

Because Cassandra has become an autonomous person in the course of these experiences, she cannot accept the fate that her lover, Aeneas, would offer her in the end, after the fall of Troy, if she were to join him in the "real" future, namely Rome. She prefers to die.

> Allen, die überlebten, würden die
> neuen Herren ihr Gesetz diktieren.
> Die Erde war nicht groß genug, ihnen
> zu entgehn. Du, Aineias, hattest
> keine Wahl: . . . Bald, sehr bald
> wirst du ein Held sein müssen. . . .
> Einen Helden kann ich nicht lieben.
> (K, p. 156)

The allusion is, of course, to Brecht, most specifically to Galilei's "Unglücklich das Land, das Helden nötig hat" (Leben des Galilei, Scene 13). But it is not a call to transform society so that heroes will no longer be necessary; rather it is a call to dispense altogether with the notion of the heroic, as men have created and loved it, in order to change society. Rejecting poetics means ultimately rejecting one of its central concepts, that of the hero and all it entails. This would effect profound change in our culture and thus "'weibliches' Schreiben" would be truly revolutionary.

Christa Wolf did a great deal of reading and research for Kassandra. Her bibliography at the end of Voraussetzungen einer Erzählung is quite extensive.

It includes many works important to Western feminist thinking and matriarchy research; to name a few: Silvia Bovenschen's Die imaginierte Weiblichkeit, Heide Göttner-Abendroth's Die Göttin und ihr Heros, and Klaus Theweleit's Männerphantasien.[16] But in the four lectures in which Wolf discusses her in part newly acquired knowledge, she makes it clear that "'weibliches' Schreiben" and her desperate--utopian--expectations for it (that it may help change and thereby save the world) do not involve the rejection of men and the wish to return to a matriarchal culture, if one ever existed:

> Jedoch bringt es der Fähigkeit zur Reife nicht näher, wenn an die Stelle des Männlichkeitswahns der Weiblichkeitswahn gesetzt wird und wenn die Errungenschaften vernünftigen Denkens, nur weil Männer sie hervorgebracht haben, von Frauen zugunsten einer Idealisierung vorrationaler Menschheitsetappen über Bord geworfen werden. . . . und Frauen, die sich auf ihre Weiblichkeit als einen Wert zurückziehen, handeln im Grunde, wie es ihnen andressiert wurde: Sie reagieren mit einem großangelegten Ausweichmanöver auf die Herausforderung der Realität an ihre ganze Person.
> (V, pp. 115-16)

Wolf's change of "Seh-Raster," her more and more consciously realized female perspective represents a continuing effort on her part to face this challenge of reality fully and responsibly. It is this strong commitment to social responsibility and the reality of social existence which give her very personal reflections such authority. Christa Wolf speaks subjectively as an individual and as a woman, but she has not totally lost the utopian belief, given her by the positive impulse which lies buried under all the "realer Sozialismus" in her society: that she must try to make a difference. This is what makes her so interesting to us in the West.

Tufts University

Notes

[1] Christa Wolf, Voraussetzungen einer Erzählung: Kassandra. Frankfurter Poetik-Vorlesungen (Darmstadt/ Neuwied: Luchterhand, 1983), pp. 130-31. All further references will appear parenthetically in the text with the title V.

[2] Wilhelm Girnus, "Kein 'Wenn und Aber' und das poetische Licht Sapphos," Sinn und Form, 35, No. 5 (1983), 1102. The excerpts from Wolf's lectures, "Aus den 'Frankfurter Vorlesungen,'" had appeared in Sinn und Form, 35, No. 1 (1983), 38-62. The subsequent issues of Sinn und Form carried an exchange between Girnus and Christa Wolf: Wilhelm Girnus, "Wer baute das siebentorige Theben," Sinn und Form, 35, No. 2 (1983), 439-447, to which Christa Wolf responded in "Zur Information," Sinn und Form, 35, No. 4 (1983), 863-66. Girnus then replied to Christa Wolf in the above mentioned critique in Heft 5. Girnus' comments occasioned a debate in Sinn und Form, with other readers coming to the defense of Christa Wolf (see Sinn und Form, 35, No. 5 [1983], 1087-96).

[3] See Inge Stephan and Sigrid Weigel, Die verborgene Frau (Berlin: Argument Verlag, 1983), particularly Inge Stephan's essay "Bilder und immer wieder Bilder . . .," pp. 15-33.

[4] Cf. Silvia Bovenschen, Die imaginierte Weiblichkeit (Frankfurt/M: Suhrkamp, 1978); Wolfgang Paulsen, ed., Die Frau als Heldin und Autorin (Bern and Munich: Francke, 1979); Marianne Burkhard, ed., Gestaltet und gestaltend (Amsterdam: Rodopi, 1980); Claudia Honnegger, ed., Die Hexen der Neuzeit (Frankfurt/M: Suhrkamp, 1977); Sara Lennox, ed., Auf der Suche nach den Gärten unserer Mütter (Darmstadt/Neuwied: Luchterhand, 1982); Inge Stephan and Sigrid Weigel, Die verborgene Frau. See also Adrienne Rich, Of Woman Born: Motherhood as Experience and Institution (New York: Norton, 1976).

[5] Cf. Elisabeth Gould Davis, The First Sex (New York: Putnam, 1971)--the German title is Am Anfang war die Frau; Heide Göttner-Abendroth, Die Göttin und ihr Heros (Munich: Frauenoffensive, 1982). Mostly however, there is a great deal of work and discussion going on that has not yet been published.

[6] Christa Wolf, "Büchner-Preis-Rede 1980," in Lesen und Schreiben. Neue Sammlung (Darmstadt/Neuwied:

Luchterhand, 1981), pp. 326-27. The title abbreviation BPR will be used with the parenthetical page references in the text.

7 Christa Wolf, Kassandra. Erzählung (Darmstadt/Neuwied: Luchterhand, 1983). Will be referred to as K.

8 Fritz J. Raddatz, Die Zeit, 25 March 1983, Literaturseite, pp. 1f.

9 Raddatz, pp. 1f.

10 "Nun ja! Das nächste Leben geht aber heute an. Ein Brief über die Bettine," in Lesen und Schreiben. Neue Sammlung, p. 310.

11 Christa Wolf, "Lesen und Schreiben," in Lesen und Schreiben. Neue Sammlung, p. 29.

12 Karoline von Günderrode, Der Schatten eines Traumes, Gedichte, Prosa, Briefe, Zeugnisse von Zeitgenossen, ed. Christa Wolf (Berlin/GDR: Buchverlag Der Morgen, 1979; Darmstadt/Neuwied: Luchterhand, 1979). See especially Christa Wolf's "Vorwort," reprinted in Lesen und Schreiben. Neue Sammlung, pp. 225-83; Bettina von Arnim, Die Günderode (Leipzig: Insel Verlag, 1980) with a "Nachwort" by Christa Wolf: "Nun ja! Das nächste Leben geht aber heute an. Ein Brief über die Bettine," also reprinted in Lesen und Schreiben. Neue Sammlung, pp. 284-318.

13 Sandra M. Gilbert and Susan Gubar, The Madwoman in the Attic (New Haven/London: Yale University Press, 1979), p. 50. On Christa Wolf in this context, see my paper "'Remembrance of Things Future'--On Establishing a Female Tradition," to appear in a volume of essays on Christa Wolf, ed. Marilyn Sibley Fries, Wayne State University Press.

14 "Lesen und Schreiben," p. 41.

15 Gilbert and Gubar, p. 50.

16 Klaus Theweleit, Männerphantasien (Reinbek bei Hamburg: Rowohlt, 1981).

Christa Wolf: Georg Büchner Prize
and Büchner Reception

Dieter Sevin

In 1980, the Federal Republic's most prestigious
literary award, the Georg Büchner Prize, was presented
for the first time to an author living and writing in
the GDR: Christa Wolf. The Deutsche Akademie für
Sprache und Dichtung in Darmstadt had once before selected an author who had worked in the GDR; Reiner
Kunze, however, had already settled permanently in the
West when he received the award in 1977. The bestowal
of this honor on Christa Wolf can be seen both as an
indication of a more objective reception of GDR literature in the Federal Republic and as a recognition of
the literary niveau of one of the GDR's foremost writers. This action by a West German literary academy
also reaffirms that the two Germanies--even after more
than thirty years as separate states with opposing political, social, and economic systems--have not developed apart to the extent that their literature can not
be understood on both sides of the heavily fortified
border. The growing number of GDR literary works published in the Federal Republic, including those of
Christa Wolf, confirm this contention; and even though
the publication of West German authors in the GDR is
still limited, this is due primarily to economic and
political, rather than cultural considerations.

That Christa Wolf should be selected for the
Büchner Prize is significant in more than the cultural-
political context. Indeed, it seems particularly appropriate that Christa Wolf, who has repeatedly made
mention of the admiration and special affinity she
feels for this nineteenth-century author, should receive a prize given in his name. In a 1973 interview
with Joachim Walther, she praised Büchner's Lenz, his
one long prose work: "Das ist mein Ur-Erlebnis mit
deutscher Literatur. Bei mir setzt die deutsche Prosa

31

mit Büchners Lenz Novelle ein. Das ist absolut mein Ideal von Prosa."[1] In her theoretical essay "Lesen und Schreiben" (1968) she wrote: "Büchners Lenz Novelle steht--hoch über dem trüben Strom konventioneller Prosa, die seitdem in deutscher Sprache produziert wurde--frisch und kühn da wie an dem Tag, an dem sie geschrieben ist."[2]

It is noteworthy that this second example of Christa Wolf's laudatory Büchner reception occurs in the context of an essay that was written not only as a theoretical treatise concerning the function of prose in our modern world, but also as a pointed attempt to justify her own novel Nachdenken über Christa T. to the functionaries in the Ministry of Culture who had great qualms about permitting its publication. Christa Wolf seems to say to them: Look at Büchner--he was not recognized in his time either. I am trying to follow in his footsteps. I am trying to create a new and timeless prose.[3]

Christa Wolf's admiration for Büchner is reflected not only in her essayistic writings but in her prose works as well, affirming his impact on her as a writer. This latter level of her Büchner reception could be referred to as productive reception. One can, for example, interpret Nachdenken über Christa T. as a novel in which the heroine struggles with existential problems not unlike those of Büchner's Lenz, even though the novel of course reflects the concrete historical situation of the new socialist German state. Both Lenz and Christa T. are unsuccessful authors: while Lenz' writings are, for all practical purposes, ignored, Christa T. is discouraged and does not dare to write. Christa T. knows that her feeble attempts to write do not correspond to what is expected; she is keenly aware that her subjective topics and sensitive style would be frowned upon by a society that embraces the literary theory of socialist realism. Nevertheless, a strong inner urge to write preoccupies her throughout her life. That she cannot write, cannot realize the vision she has of herself, helps ultimately to precipitate an existential crisis symbolized by her sickness and early death--just as the crisis of Lenz, his lack of recognition and later inability to write, contribute to his eventual insanity.

Christa Wolf's productive reception of Georg Büchner can also be observed in Kein Ort. Nirgends (1979).[4] Her frequent use of quotations to achieve a

32

greater authentication represents a striking structural similarity to both <u>Lenz</u> and <u>Dantons Tod</u>.[5] (This technique is also used in other Works of Christa Wolf, but less obviously.) Furthermore, a clear parallel exists between Lenz and Kleist, whom Wolf portrays in this work. Both figures are German dramatists who achieved little recognition in their own time. Both go through intense crises and are in the grip of dark fears, "namenlose Angst" (<u>Ort</u>, p. 86). Unable to cope both seek help: Lenz from Pastor Oberlin and Kleist from Hofrat Wedekind. Both are pressured by their families to conform, to do something they are unable to do. Lenz cannot be a practicing minister; and Kleist cannot be a bureaucrat, as the narrator of <u>Kein Ort. Nirgends</u> points out:

> Herr von Kleist wolle . . . zum Ausdruck bringen, daß er sich unfähig fühle, sich in irgendein konventionelles Verhältnis dieser Welt einzupassen. . . . Er finde viele Einrichtungen dieser Welt so wenig seinem Sinn gemäß, daß es ihm unmöglich sei, an ihrer Erhaltung und Ausbildung mitzuwirken. (p. 87)

Büchner and Christa Wolf both suggest that a better relationship with the opposite sex might have prevented the tragic end of their main characters.[6] Just as Lenz is unable to maintain a satisfactory relationship with Friederike, which might well have helped him to overcome his crisis, Kleist and Günderrode--in spite of their affinity for each other and their intellectual equality--are unable to break through the barriers which separate them. The tragedy of all these characters stems from their inability to communicate openly with each other: Lenz because of his jealousy, Kleist and Günderrode because of social and sex-related inhibitions. Confronted with enormous pressures from family and society alike and without anyone who understands or appreciates their talents, Kleist and Günderrode view suicide as a means of escape; their suicide parallels Lenz' escape into insanity.

It is no accident that Christa Wolf makes reference to Goethe's <u>Tasso</u> and the "Disproportion des Talents mit dem Leben" (<u>Ort</u>, p. 106). Her Kleist figure, expressing Wolf's own views, interprets Tasso's problems with great sympathy:

Wie, wenn nicht Tasso dem Fürsten,
besonders aber dem Antonio, Unrecht
täte, sondern die ihm. Wenn sein Un-
glück nicht eingebildet, sondern wirklich und unausweichlich wäre? Wenn
nicht Überspanntheit, sondern ein . .
. überscharfes Gespür für die wirklichen Verhältnisse ihm den Ausruf
abpreßte: "Wohin beweg ich meinen
Schritt, dem Ekel zu entfliehn, der
mich umsaust, dem Abgrund zu entgehn,
der vor mir liegt?" (pp. 106-07)

Indeed, both of Christa Wolf's major characters in
Kein Ort. Nirgends suffer from the pain of "die wirklichen Verhältnisse." They are unable to join in the
consensus and praise of the new times, as Christa
Wolf's Kleist concludes: "Ich aber, Günderrode, ich
und Sie, denk ich, wir leiden unter den Übeln der neu-
en [Zeit]" (Ort, p. 109). Their great sensitivity
leads to the abyss they tried to avoid, the final escape from suffering and especially from the agony of
not being able to fulfill what they consider their
destiny as writers.

Christa Wolf interprets Lenz' fate similarly, insisting that mankind has had to rebel ever since
against the famous last sentence of Büchner's novella:
"So lebte er hin." Why? Because it is a metaphor for
silence, for literature not written. As she points
out in her Büchner Prize address, many potential works
have remained unwritten in the history of mankind because the circumstances were not conducive to writing
or even made it impossible to be creative.[7] For this
reason, many an author has escaped, each in his or her
own way,

in ein andres Land, in einen andern
Beruf, einen andern Namen, in eine
Krankheit, den Wahnsinn, den Tod--al-
les Metaphern für Schweigen, wenn
es Schriftstellern widerfährt. Zum
Schweigen gebracht werden. Schweigen
wollen. Schweigen müssen. Endlich
Schweigen dürfen. (p. 12)

Lenz, Kleist, Günderrode, and Christa T. are examples
of such fates. Unappreciated and unrecognized, they
fall silent.

Christa Wolf, like Büchner in his time, has not

fallen silent. Like Büchner, she has written about characters with whom she felt an affinity, people rooted in real life whose fate moved them to write because it reflected concerns and anxieties of their own times. Christa Wolf writes in regard to Büchner--and the remark is valid for herself--that it would have been "unsinnig für ihn, herkömmliche Geschichten auszudenken, die man, mit mehr oder weniger Kunst und Technik, zu jeder Zeit nach Maß herstellen kann" (LuS, p. 205). Christa Wolf insists that writing, if it is to be timeless and thus reach, touch, and change its readers, must be much more: "Nicht weniger als der volle Einsatz der eigenen moralischen Existenz ist gefordert . . . jedesmal neu. Das ist der Ernst hinter dem Spiel der Kunst" (LuS, p. 205).

This moral consideration is part of the autobiographical dimension in writing, the discovery of which Christa Wolf attributes to Georg Büchner:

> Nur soll man nicht weiterhin, wie Büchners Mit- und Nachwelt, seine Entdeckung übersehen, daß der erzählerische Raum vier Koordinaten hat: die drei fiktiven Koordinaten der erfundenen Figuren und die vierte "wirkliche" des Erzählers. Das ist die Koordinate der Tiefe, der Zeitgenossenschaft, des unvermeidlichen Engagements, die nicht nur die Wahl des Stoffes, sondern auch seine Färbung bestimmt. Sich ihrer bewußt bedienen ist eine Grundmethode moderner Prosa. (LuS, p. 204)

This method is, of course, intensely reflected in Wolf's own work. She adds the decisive fourth co-ordinate, the autobiographical dimension, by interjecting herself into her novels. In fact, what Christa Wolf writes about Büchner and his novella Lenz also holds true for her own creative works:

> Mit wenigen Mitteln hat er sich selbst dazugetan, seinen unlöslichen Lebenskonflikt, die eigene Gefährdung, die ihm wohl bewußt ist. Ein Konflikt, in dem sich die tausendfache Bedrohung lebendiger, entwicklungshungriger und wahrheitssüchtiger Menschen in Restaurationszeiten gesteigert spiegelt: der Dichter vor

die Wahl gestellt, sich an unerträg-
liche Zustände anzupassen und sein
Talent zu ruinieren oder physisch zugrunde zu gehen. (LuS, p. 204)

Being awarded the Büchner Prize stimulated Christa Wolf to re-read Büchner's oeuvre. In her acceptance speech she ponders what Büchner's works mean to
her now and concludes: "Büchner wieder lesen heißt die
eigene Lage schärfer sehen" (p. 1). She reaffirms her
affinity with this nineteenth-century author, scientist, and revolutionary. Her speech represents an interpretation of Büchner's situation and her own:

> Büchners Beispiel vor Augen, beun-
> ruhigen mich mehr denn je die unter-
> gründigen Verflechtungen von Schrei-
> ben und Leben, von Verantwortung
> und Schuld, welche die Person, die
> schreibend lebt, lebend schreibt,
> hervorbringen und im gleichen Ar-
> beitsgang zu zerreißen drohen. (p. 1)

She sees Büchner's writings as an expression of the
author's sense of responsibility for the great concerns of his times and as evidence of his attempts to
cope with the issues that confront society and, ultimately, mankind.

In her Büchner Prize address, Wolf manifests a
particular interest in Büchner's female characters.
What happens to Rosetta, Marie, Lena, Julie, Lucile?
she asks rhetorically. They remain outside of the
rational systems which Danton, Paine, and Leonce
create as a defense against their inner emptiness.
Little do the female characters recognize the truth
about the man they love, which is, as Wolf points out,

> daß seine Gebrechlichkeit und die
> Furcht, ihrer gewahr zu werden, ihn
> in seine wahnwitzigen Systeme hinein-
> treibt. Daß er . . . durch erbar-
> mungslose Arbeitsteilung beraubt, ein
> Verwundeter, Zerrissener sich in die
> halsbrecherischsten Geschwindigkeiten
> hineinsetzt, um nur jene "Höllenfahrt
> der Selbsterkenntnis" nicht antreten
> zu müssen, ohne die es doch, nach
> Kant, keine Vernunft gibt. Und daß,
> wer sich selbst nicht kennt, kein
> Weib erkennen kann.

36

So trennen sich ihre Wege. Rosetta
schweigt. Liebt. Leidet. Wird als
Marie umgebracht. Folgt, als Julie,
dem Manne in den Tod. Treibt in den
Wahnsinn als Lucile. Opfert sich.
Klagt, da heißt sie Lena: Bin ich
denn wie die arme hilflose Quelle,
die jedes Bild, das sich über sie
bückt, in ihrem stillen Grund abspie-
geln muß? (p. 6)

Büchner seems to say "No" to Lena's self-analytical
question, and Christa Wolf concurs. Woman's role is
not to be confined to the support of man, his actions,
and his Denksysteme, especially not in our age, in a
civilization "welche das ihr Liebste und Wertvollste--
Geld und technische Perfektion--in irrsinnigem Kurz-
schlußdenken an die Produkte zu ihrer Selbsttötung
wendet" (p. 2). The ground on which both men and wom-
en tread has become very thin, and Christa Wolf main-
tains that women must not leave the responsibility for
survival to men because of the male propinquity for
self-destruction, a tendency which is manifested in
all of Büchner's male characters.[8]

Woman must free herself from her dependence on
man, and for Wolf it is progress when she "erfährt . .
. als äußerstes Zugeständnis: Sie sei wie er" (BPR, p.
9). But herein lies the grave danger that woman will
miss her real calling. See what you are freeing your-
self from and what you will be like, Wolf warns, if
you become like man, whom she calls "den Erhalter des
Gleichgewichts des Schreckens . . . , den Planer wirt-
schaftlichen Mißwachstums . . . , den Umverteiler des
Hungers in der Welt" (BPR, p. 10).

When woman becomes like man, who created this up-
side-down situation ("Der Zustand der Welt ist ver-
kehrt. . . ," BPR, p. 4), she is enslaved anew, as
Wolf, using the example of twentieth-century woman,
points out:

Um frei zu werden, ist sie neue Ver-
strickungen eingegangen. Um zu sich
selbst zu kommen, wurden ihr neue Ar-
ten der Selbstverleugnung abverlangt.
Sie ist besten Willens gewesen. Hat
ihre Hoffnung gesetzt in das wissenschaftliche Zeitalter. Hat seiner
Rationalität vertraut und sieht sich

dem Irrationalismus ausgeliefert. . . .
(BPR, p. 9)

By adapting herself to the male world, woman, in
Wolf's view, deprives herself of her own unique human
quality, the ability to love, which is lacking in man.
Man, enslaved by his rational systems, into which he,
fearing his inner emptiness, has withdrawn, is incap-
able of real love and is himself in need of liberation. Using Büchner's characters Leonce and Rosetta
to refer to men and women in general, Wolf writes:

> Ihre und seine Angst, denn nun teilen
> sie das schreckliche Geheimnis, das
> Tabu der Tabus: Daß Leonce unter sei-
> nen vielen Namen nicht lieben, daß er
> nur Totes lieben kann. . . . Bleibt
> also . . . Rosetta unter ihren vielen
> Namen nur die Wahl, in den toten Raum
> zurückgedrängt oder ihm gleich zu
> werden? (BPR, pp. 10-11)

Woman's role is not to become like man but instead
with her gift of love to help man free himself from
his "wahnwitzige Systeme." They should work together
to overcome the paradox that binds them both:

> . . . Sich gemeinsam, sich gegensei-
> tig zur Vernunft zu bringen--das gäbe
> es nicht? Sie beide, an das gleiche
> Paradox geschmiedet, wären nicht im-
> stande, einen einzigen richtigen
> Schritt aufeinander zu zu tun? Auch
> dieser historische Augenblick wäre
> vertan? (BPR, p. 11)

Christa Wolf's view again parallels what Büchner represents in his creative work. Not a silent and suffering Rosetta, but a maturely thinking, liberated,
yet loving, Lena is capable of helping Leonce discover
or rediscover his ability to love.

But will man listen and believe woman, will she
really have an effect when, motivated by love, she
challenges his stronghold of ingenious systems and icy
abstractions? Wolf deals with this question in her
most recent work, Kassandra, a parable of our modern
and endangered world.[9] The role of women in patriarchal society and the dangers resulting from remaining
outside the rational or, more correctly, irrational
male thinking processes are major aspects of the

work. [10]

In _Kassandra_ Christa Wolf shows what happens when
a woman opposes the irrational "rationality" of man,
as, for instance, when Cassandra opposes the murder of
helpless Greek prisoners: "Du also, Priesterin, ge-
stattest meinen Leuten nicht, Gleiches mit Gleichem zu
vergelten?--Ich sagte: Nein. Das war beinah das einzge
Wort, das mir noch blieb" (K, p. 130).   When she refuses to join the conspiracy against Achilles, the men
try once more to appeal to her rationality: "Nun, Kassandra. Nicht wahr, du bist vernünftig" (K, p. 144).
Cassandra, however, sees nothing but utter irrational-
ity in the plan, not only because it would mean the
sacrifice of her sister, Polyxena, but also because
she foresees that Achilles' death would make an end to
this terrible war impossible. Even though she hates
Achilles as much as or more than any of the men who
want to kill him do--Achilles had murdered one of her
brothers on the altar of her temple; throughout the
book she refers to him as "Achill das Vieh"--she cannot agree to the murder of a human being. Rather than
sacrifice her conviction, she is prepared to be thrown
into the dungeon by her brother and father.

What is a woman to do in the face of such brutal
methods used to silence her when she dares to oppose
men's thinking and actions? Should she silently give
in and join the warring men in her family, possibly
rushing ahead to her death, like Julie in _Dantons Tod_?
Or should she join the ranks of the women who wish to
fight all men, such as Penthesilea? This too is an unacceptable alternative in Christa Wolf's eyes.   Even
though Cassandra sympathizes with Penthesilea, she can
not condone women using the same means as men to try
and achieve their goals. Cassandra, like Christa
Wolf, one might add, disagrees with Penthesilea's interpretation of the situation of women: "Die bewohnte
Welt, soweit sie uns bekannt war, hatte sich immer
grausamer, immer schneller gegen uns gekehrt. Gegen
uns Frauen . . ." (K., p. 134). Cassandra sees the
world turning not just against women, but "gegen uns
Menschen." Penthesilea, who sees only two alterna-
tives--to kill or to be killed--, may arouse sympathy
and admiration; but her way can only lead to more
atrocities, and Christa Wolf's Cassandra must, therefore, reject her.

Shortly before her death, Cassandra clearly recognizes the dangers inherent in human nature, particularly the danger of war, and ponders the need to com-

municate her insights to future generations:

> Wann Krieg beginnt, das kann man wis-
> sen, aber wann beginnt der Vorkrieg?
> Falls es da Regeln gäbe, müßte man
> sie weitersagen. In Ton, in Stein
> eingraben, überliefern. Was stünde
> da. Da stünde unter andern Sätzen:
> Laßt euch nicht von den Eignen täu-
> schen. (K, pp. 76-77)

The ultimate frustration for Cassandra is that she is
unable to leave a warning about what she has learned.
Not knowing how to write herself, she pleads with
the woman holding her captive: "Klytaimnestra, sperr
mich ein, auf ewig, in dein finsterstes Verlies. Gib
mir knapp zum Leben. Aber, ich fleh dich an: Schick
mir einen Schreiber. . . ." (K, p. 93). Her wish is
not fulfilled. Cassandra is silenced, like many after
her, without having been given the opportunity to tell
future generations about her insights and concerns.
Her fate parallels in this regard that of Lenz and
Christa T.

   In her fictional account, Christa Wolf attempts
of course to serve as Cassandra's scribe in our time
by warning about the dangers of impending war and destruction, and pleading for a new partnership between
men and women so that they may cope jointly with the
immense problems that confront the human race. Together, man and woman might be able to change such absurd reasoning and assertions as "eine exzessive atomare Aufrüstung beider Seiten mindere als 'Gleichgewicht des Schreckens' die Kriegsgefahr" (V, p. 87).
Together they might avoid Lucile's despair and not
have to fall silent, like Lenz, who is driven to insanity "über dem Verlust seiner Übereinstimmung mit
der gemeinen Vernunft" (BPR, p. 2). Today, even more
than in Büchner's time, giving in to generally accepted, common rationality means, indeed, giving in to insanity.

   Wolf, like Büchner, however, has not resigned
herself to common rationality nor given in to the
temptation of escaping responsibility; she did not
chose one of the many "Metaphern für Schweigen." She
feels the full weight of responsibility for her own
time. She believes that it is essential for the writer to raise the pertinent questions of the time:

> Unschuldig und ohne Verantwortung
> sein--dies mag als Wunschbild in Zei-
> ten der Schwäche aufkommen; es ist
> ein Fluchtbild. In den konkreten
> Verhältnissen, in denen wir leben und
> schreiben, erwachsen werden--was auch
> heißt: sehend--, uns einmischen, ver-
> sagen, wieder aufbegehren und auf
> neue Erfahrung süchtig sind. In die-
> sen konkreten Verhältnissen ist ein
> Zustand verantwortungsloser Unschuld
> nicht vorgesehen. Heute und hier!
> heißt es da. . . . (BPR, p. 1)

Christa Wolf does not hesitate to affirm her faith in the written word:

> Die Sprache der Literatur scheint es
> merkwürdigerweise zu sein, die der
> Wirklichkeit des Menschen heute am
> nächsten kommt; die den Menschen am
> besten kennt. . . . Vielleicht weil
> immer moralischer Mut des Autors--der
> zur Selbsterkenntnis--in Literatur
> eingeht. (BPR, pp. 12-13)

This moral courage, which finds its expression in Wolf's delineation of the fundamental claims of human-ity in a disordered world and which attests to her af-finity with Büchner, makes her an author whose signif-icance transcends the geopolitical borders of the Ger-man Democratic Republic.

Vanderbilt University

Notes

[1] Christa Wolf, "Interview mit Joachim Walther," in Meinetwegen Schmetterlinge. Gespräche mit Schrift-stellern, ed. Joachim Walther (Berlin: Buchverlag Der Morgen, 1973), p. 15.

[2] Christa Wolf, "Lesen und Schreiben," in Lesen und Schreiben. Aufsätze und Prosastücke (Darmstadt/ Neuwied: Luchterhand, 1972), pp. 204-05. All subse-quent quotations from this work are from this edition, which will be indicated as LuS in parentheses in the text.

[3] See Dieter Sevin, "The Plea for Artistic Freedom in Christa Wolf's 'Lesen und Schreiben' and Nachdenken über Christa T.: Essay and Fiction as Mutually Supportive Genre Forms," in Studies in GDR Culture and Society 2, ed. Margy Gerber et al. (Washington, D.C.: University Press of America, 1982), pp. 31-42.

[4] Christa Wolf, Kein Ort. Nirgends (Darmstadt/Neuwied: Luchterhand, 1979). All subsequent quotations are from this edition and will be indicated in parentheses in the text; the title abbreviation Ort will be used when necessary for clarity.

[5] See Ute Brandes, "Quotations as Authentication: No Place on Earth," in Critical Perspectives on Christa Wolf, ed. Marilyn Sibley Fries (Detroit: Wayne State University Press, forthcoming).

[6] See Dieter Sevin, "Die existentielle Krise in Büchner's Lenz," in Seminar, 15, No. 1 (1979), 15-26.

[7] Christa Wolf, Büchner Preis Rede. Sonderdruck für die Freunde des Luchterhand Verlages (Darmstadt/Neuwied: Luchterhand, 1980), p. 12. All subsequent references will appear parenthetically in the text, when necessary for clarity, with the abbreviation BPR.

[8] As a nineteenth-century author, Büchner could of course not foresee the full consequences of such tendencies in our days. As Wolf points out: "Büchner hat so früh, und ich glaube, mit Grauen gesehen, daß die Lust, die das neue Zeitalter an sich selber fand, an ihrer Wurzel mit Zerstörungslust verquickt war. Doch die voll ausgebildete Fratze jenes Paradoxons, das Schöpfung an Vernichtung koppelt, hat er nicht erblickt, ein Wort wie 'Megatote' nicht gekannt. . . ." (BPR, p. 6). The criticical attitude which Christa Wolf has toward science as a panacea for all problems of mankind and as a cause of irrational and inhuman actions is, of course, a major concern in Büchner's Woyzeck.

[9] Christa Wolf, Kassandra (Darmstadt/Neuwied: Luchterhand, 1983). All subsequent references to Kassandra will appear parenthetically in the text with the title abbreviation K. Christa Wolf's productive reception of Büchner can also be seen in this work. As in Dantons Tod, the main character is confronted with the probability, if not the certainty of death. Both Danton and Cassandra are victims of the irration-

al atrocities which man inflicts upon man and which both are trying to prevent. Both do little to escape their fate. Wolf's prose story is narrated through the reflective processes of Cassandra, who looks back on her life and the terrible war which, at times, brought her near the brink of insanity. Insanity is a major motif in Büchner's Lenz. Wolf's use in Kassandra (p.138) of the words spoken by Rosetta in Büchner's Leonce und Lena: "Meine Füße gingen lieber aus der Zeit" (Büchner, Sämtliche Werke und Briefe [Hamburg: Wegner, 1967], I, 110) is a further indication of the extent to which, consciously or unconsciously, Wolf was preoccupied with Büchner's works.

[10] Christa Wolf emphasizes this aspect also in Voraussetzungen einer Erzählung: Kassandra. Frankfurter Poetik-Vorlesungen (Darmstadt/Neuwied: Luchterhand, 1983). For example:

> Daß Frauen zur Kultur, in der wir leben, über die Jahrtausende hin offiziell und direkt so gut wie nichts beitragen durften, ist nicht nur eine entsetzliche, beschämende und skandalöse Tatsache für Frauen--es ist, genau genommen, diejenige Schwachstelle der Kultur, aus der heraus sie selbstzerstörerisch wird, nämlich ihre Unfähigkeit zur Reife. (p. 115)

A New Irmtraud Morgner:
Humor, Fantasy, Structures, and Ideas in
Amanda. Ein Hexenroman

Sheila K. Johnson

Irmtraud Morgner's optimistic world view in Leben und Abenteuer der Trobadora Beatriz nach Zeugnissen ihrer Spielfrau Laura (1974)[1] has changed to a deep-seated concern about the world's chances for survival. Her new novel, Amanda. Ein Hexenroman (1983),[2] is an expression of this concern for humanity's future, with emphasis on women's part in shaping that future.

The global thrust of Amanda explains, in part, the interest this long-awaited novel has stirred, especially in the Western press. Initial reviews, impressionistic for the most part, have also drawn attention to the obvious parallels between Morgner's new novel and Christa Wolf's latest work of fiction, Kassandra.[3] Both books 1) have a central, "warning," female character drawn from mythology, i.e., return to prehistoric models; 2) are concerned that men are destroying humankind through war, which is seen as resulting from the prevailing patriarchal, conquering mentality; 3) condemn the neglect of subjectivity in favor of objectivity and rationalism; 4) condemn both patriarchal and matriarchal exclusivity; 5) portray women as being in a captive state, robbed of influence; and 6) view women as the embodiment of hope and potential for change. In a 1983 interview for Die Zeit, Sigrid Löffler questioned Morgner regarding the clear coincidence of ideas between her new novel and Wolf's and reported Morgner's reply: "Sie habe mit Christa Wolf überhaupt nicht darüber geredet."[4] Indeed, the ideas around which both authoresses have structured their most recent works are not unique to them--and we can be thankful for that.

Amanda was not written to expose the wrongs his-

torically done to women--although it does that too--
but rather to give an illustration of women gaining
the confidence and influence they need to help lead
humanity away from the path to self-destruction; it is
a book about "die Rettbarkeit der Welt" (p. 258). A
decade ago, Morgner's goal was "Welt zu machen."[5] The
impulse behind Amanda was more: "sie [die Erde] vor
der Vernichtung zu retten" (p. 607).

In spite of the similarities in Morgner's and
Wolf's basic concerns about humanity and its rescue
from nuclear holocaust, their literary treatment of
these ideas is vastly different. Structure and use of
humor and fantasy are primary areas of divergence.
Wolf's Erzählung focuses sharply on the central character, while Morgner's 656-page montage novel becomes
extremely complex in its various layers of time, character, and event. Whereas Wolf makes the Cassandra
myth almost biographical, Morgner's fancy flies as
freely as do her witches. Although Wolf, through Cassandra, talks about "Humor," "Lachen," and "Heiter-
keit" (Kassandra, pp. 60, 137, and 150, respectively),
Morgner actually gives the reader something to laugh
about.

The following interpretation of Amanda will look
first at Morgner's humor and fantasy, then at her
structuring devices, and, finally, at the development
of the particular ideas in the novel. Primary among
these are her ideas about history, value systems, the
role of the writer, and the future course of the
world.

Morgner's humor sets her writings apart not only
from Wolf's Kassandra, but from the larger body of
German literature by women written in the last decade
as well. It is a quality of her style and a vehicle
for her thoughts, not a gratuitously inserted element.
"Sie lachte nur bei ernsten Gelegenheiten" (p. 19),
Beatriz, the chronicler of Amanda, writes of her former Spielfrau Laura: a fitting characterization for
much of Morgner's writing in her new novel.

Like her world view, Morgner's humor has meta-
morphosed. "Mein Humor ist schwarz geworden--und
neigt zum Grotesken," she commented in a 1982 interview.[6] Honed by events--historical, political, per-
sonal--the humor in Amanda is often expressed as
sharply critical wit, satire, parody, or exaggeration;
its guises are myriad, ranging from funny and ridicu-
lous to grotesque and even gross. As in Trobadora

Beatriz Morgner still looks to laughter as a means of achieving sovereignty over adversity and adversaries, but this laughter has new undertones. The change in her concept of laughter is reflected in the motto she chose for Amanda, a quotation from E.T.A. Hoffmann: "Das Lachen ist nur der Schmerzenslaut der Sehnsucht nach der Heimat, die im Innern sich regt" (p. 5). Morgner's laughter is expression not suppression of her most profound feelings. The "Heimat" she longs for is the as yet unrealized communist society, a point which becomes increasingly clear in the course of the novel. Humor has become, in part, a survival-mechanism in her struggle toward achieving that utopia. She recently asserted that retention and cultivation of humor are for her "eine Frage des Stolzes, eine des Widerstands und des Überlebens."[7]

In a review of Amanda, Sybille Cramer cogently emphasizes the central, political role of the comic, referring to Morgner's quotation from Marx ("Die letzte Phase einer weltgeschichtlichen Gestalt ist ihre Komödie," p. 597), as her "poetologisches Programm des Komischen."[8] Cramer concludes: "Das Komische [in Amanda] hält das von der Vernunft Ausgegrenzte fest und spielt es aus gegen das logische Prinzip einer Welt, die Himmel und Hölle mobilisiert, wenn es um ihre Herrschaft geht" (p. 26). Examples will be cited below in various contexts, to show how Morgner uses humor to make some of her most serious points.

As with Morgner's humor, her fantasy, too, has a socio-critical function, a point stressed by Patricia Herminghouse in her analysis of Trobadora Beatriz. Morgner's fantasy provides, to quote Herminghouse, an "Ausblick auf zukünftige Möglichkeit" and "eine Art Verfremdungseffekt, der das Bewußtsein der Leser auf ungelöste Widersprüche aufmerksam macht."[9] Herminghouse's assessment holds true for the fantasy of Amanda as well.

In the free space for creation that Morgner's fantasy opens up, she has given her own interpretation to images from the prehistoric past. Outstanding among these are the figures of Beatriz, Arke (a Morgner invention), and Pandora. These three females, who, in fantastically imaginative ways, incorporate and reveal new possibilities for rescuing humanity today, deserve closer scrutiny.

Beatriz was subsumed by Laura in Trobadora Beatriz, but her voice, that of the poet (which she was

47

historically), is needed again, and thus she is brought back to life. In Amanda Morgner lends Beatriz the mythological form of a siren, a type of owl-bodied women known for the power of their song. She has Arke, Beatriz' intellectual complement, introduce a new version of the siren myth, one which is grounded in Morgner's condemnation of war: "In alten Zeiten lebten alle weisen Frauen ein zweites Leben in Sirenengestalt. Damals gab es noch viele Sirenen. . . . Kriegslieder konnten sie mühelos niedersingen" (p. 16). The siren Beatriz gradually assumes a purpose: to aid women (and even some men) in their struggle against patriarchal suppression, exploitation of the environment, and waging of war. Cramer offers the following convincing and textually founded explanation of why Morgner chose the siren guise for the figure which represents the writer in Amanda, i.e., most nearly resembles Morgner's role; employing Morgner's own images, Cramer writes: "Die Sirene, elementarste Bedrohung für Odysseus' Herrschaft über die Natur, für seine im Namen des Überlebens angetretene Reise in die Zukunft, wird mobilisiert gegen einen männlichen Fortschrittsgedanken, der alles, was sein Ziel bedroht, zum anderen macht" (p. 26). By emphasizing the sirens' particular strengths, i.e., their ability to persuade through song, and by giving her particular incarnation of a siren individuality and a positive purpose, Morgner revises the negative image which has been ascribed to sirens in a mythology written by men.

Morgner's partly invented, partly traditionally based mythology is transmitted to Beatriz primarily by "die Schlange" Arke (p. 13), who is a counterpart to Melusine in Trobadora Beatriz. A free-wheeling earth spirit and daughter of Mother Earth, Gaja, Arke is in tune with what is happening around the earth at all times (p. 34). She gets about by means of "Siebenmeilenflügel" (p. 212), which unfortunately have no fine-control mechanism, causing her occasionally to overshoot her landing point.[10]

Arke is Beatriz' main link to the past and present. She fulfills a necessary function because, in the course of most of the novel, Beatriz remains confined to, first, a cellar, then, a cave and, finally, a cage in the East Berlin Zoo. (Morgner's own address in the same city is Am Tierpark.) About a third of the way through Amanda, Beatriz wakes up to discover that her tongue has been mysteriously ripped out (p. 200). Although no specific perpetrators are named, patriarchal forces are suspected. Despite the obvious attempt to silence her, Beatriz keeps on "singing," on paper. And, as one visitor to her volery remarks: "det Viech frißt Papier" (p. 418). Beatriz "trains" her skills by recording Laura's biography, producing a text based on archival material brought to her by Arke and titled the "Historie von Amanda der Großen." In this text and in the fact that efforts were made to cancel out Beatriz' voice we can find parallels with Morgner, who was able to publish no new works of fiction between 1974 and 1982, but who obviously continued writing.

Pandora does not appear in Amanda as an actual character, but rather remains in the realm of ideas as she does in Goethe's Pandora, the source which, along with Peter Hacks' essay on the play, Morgner credits for inspiring her own Pandora. For Morgner as for Goethe, Pandora is a humanitarian symbol and the embodiment of hope for the future. Morgner specifically rejects Hesiod's and Plato's versions of the Pandora myth, which represented Pandora as the bringer of all the evil in the world, and, instead, turns her into the positive central symbol of her novel. She introduces the image of Pandora by means of a Delphic oracle (p. 11), which Beatriz and Arke gradually unravel. References to Pandora and "die Büchse der Pandora" recur in various contexts throughout the novel. [11] More will be said about the value system which Morgner attributes to her Pandora in the subsequent discussion of the ideas on which Amanda is based.

Not content with what her fantasy can derive from --or read into--Greek mythology, Morgner invents a Brocken or Blocksberg mythology, which is very loosely related to Goethe's Walpurgis scenes in Faust. The microcosm of the Brocken world is "peopled" by the disruptive halves of women, i.e., witches, by patriarchal dictators (an "Oberteufel" and an "Oberengel") and their male troops, as well as by a small faction of heretics, otherwise called "Genies" or "Querköpfe," among whom are some of Morgner's favorite great minds: Jakob Böhme, Bach, Goethe, Hölderlin, Büchner, Engels, Einstein (p. 501).

In Amanda, the Brocken is a nexus of the symbolic and the real. Morgner stresses its negative character as a military-riddled border area, but she also uses it as a testing ground where seemingly impossible ideas can be worked out. [12] Morgner reveals the concept behind her invention of the fantastic Brocken world in the chapter titled "Brockenmythologie":

Unmögliches, das heißt, das Mögliche
von übermorgen, . . . ist nur auf
Bergen denkbar.
Deshalb heißen diese Berge Zauber-
berge.
Und die Besucher solcher Berge wer-
den heute und morgen als Ketzer und
Hexen bezeichnet und übermorgen als
Weise.
Alle Länder der Erde haben solche
Zauberberge. . . .
In deutsch heißt der Zauberberg
Brocken oder Blocksberg. (p. 115)

The mountains where theories for change are born
have long been dominated, to employ Morgner's metaphor, by "one-man-parties" (p. 114). Arke, Morgner's
frequent spokeswoman, articulates the idea that this
condition must be changed: "Tatsächlich . . . gehört
die Eroberung solcher Berge zum Allernächsten und Kon-
kretesten, das die Menschheit fürs Überleben leisten
muß" (p. 52).

It is on the Brocken that a rebellion of witches
is rehearsed for many years (in the "Hexentheater, auf
den drei Brettern, die die Welt bedeuten sollen," p.
403) and, eventually, with the cooperative participation of the male "Querköpfe," successfully carried
out. Amanda lays out her plan for the revolt to Laura
(p. 548), and, although the details of the actual
overthrow of the patriarchal powers are never specified, Morgner's novel is strewn with statements which
confirm that it has indeed taken place--some time after the spring of 1977 and before the summer of 1980
(see the subsequent discussion of time structure), and
that the witches have gained a place at the top of the
mountain.

The following are just a few of the numerous in-
dicators that the witches have, at some point during
those years, won their initial victory on the Brocken:
Isebel, former leader of the male-hating yet male-imi-
tating feminist faction of Brocken witches, is from
the beginning of the novel (i.e., 1980) installed as
the new head of the Blocksberg Archives (p. 52), where
she gets to exercise authority but cannot cause much
trouble (p. 99). The "Oberteufel" Kolbuk and "Oberengel" Zacharias have been thrown off the Brocken (p.
245). Amanda, whose wisdom as well as her Eulenspiegel characteristics (pp. 148, 603) and her sister-
under-the-feather relationship with Beatriz are signi-

fied by the owl costume which she and her androgynous[13] witch faction wear, has assumed her new title "Blocksberg-Präsidentin" (p. 653).

The witches' "Revolution von unten" (p. 291) against the patriarchal dictators of the Brocken world is to serve as an example for women and men in the real world. Non-violent rebellion (the "Oberteufel" and "Oberengel" are not killed) is offered as a substitute for destructive political solutions, as an alternative to war. Arke's clarion cry concerning this point is relayed by Beatriz: "Der Krieg als klassisches Mittel zur Durchsetzung politischer Ziele müsse tabuisiert werden" (p. 634). The leadership role of the Brocken as the "Heimat der Friedensforscher" (p. 548) is explained by Amanda:

> Nach Fehlversuchen in der Politik kann nicht wie im Labor neu angefangen werden. Deshalb lassen sich die für die Weltgeschichte nicht länger entbehrlichen weiblichen Erfahrungswerte nur auf dem Blocksberg schnell experimentell in nutzbare Formen bringen. (pp. 547-548)

Morgner's fantasy thus provides a setting, the Brokken, in which she can present in metaphorical form her conviction that action must be taken by women in order that--here again Arke--"der Zukunft die Zukunft bewahrt wird" (p. 246).

While humor and fantasy have come to be trademarks of Morgner's fiction, having taken hold in Trobadora Beatriz after some experimentation (e.g., in Hochzeit in Konstantinopel, 1969; Gauklerlegende, 1971; and Die wundersamen Reisen Gustavs des Weltfahrers, 1972), a further area in which she has made literary contributions is that of structure. The outstanding features include montage, multiple time levels, and various spheres of action.

Amanda, Volume II of a proposed trilogy, is, like Trobadora Beatriz (Volume I), a montage of literary short forms. In the new novel we find myths, parables, media reports, interviews, dialogues in the form of playlets, extended quotations, lectures, nonsense and other rhymes, among other forms. These intersect with and interrupt the thread of Laura's biography, which stretches, in numerous episodes, from the first through the final chapter. Amanda is, however, a tapestry of a tighter weave than was Trobadora Beatriz. The free association of ideas in the latter has been replaced by a more deliberate structuring.

The most significant aspect of the structure in Amanda is Morgner's treatment of the time levels. Awareness and understanding of the two basic time planes on which the novel develops is essential to the comprehension of the main ideas. Amanda begins in the late spring or early summer of 1980, with Beatriz' rebirth (seven years after her death on March 12, 1973, in Trobadora Beatriz); it ends on New Year's Eve of the same year. Thirty of the total 141 divisions of the novel (139 chapters, a "Griechisches Vorspiel," and a conclusion, "Silvesternachspiel") develop on this first time level and have Beatriz as central figure. The other chapters unroll in a time span beginning August 28, 1933, the date of Laura's birth, and ending in chapter 139 on May 15, 1977, the day on which Laura hears the pronouncement that her last youthful ideal, her Faust surrogate, Heinrich, "ist gerichtet" (p. 651). Laura and those she encounters in these forty-four years provide the focus in 111 chapters.[14] What happens in the three and a half years between the two time planes is left largely for the reader to surmise. In a rare direct reference to that period, Beatriz writes that Laura lectured to "Junghexen" in 1979 (p. 100); this suggests that she has begun to take an active role in the witches'/women's movement. What becomes of her beyond that date is never discussed. The factors which connect the time periods lie primarily in the realm of ideas, which will be dealt with subsequently.

Morgner uses parallel time levels to illustrate two of her major concepts in Amanda. First, on the level of Laura's biography, she shows how an approach to life based on private solutions (pp. 274, 636, and 647) and individualist strategies (p. 655)--the path Laura set out on at the end of Trobadora Beatriz-- leads to a dead end. During this same first period, however, another approach to life is being tested within the world of witches, that of social revolution. By working as well on the later, second time level, that one beginning in 1980, Morgner is able to make the point that the witches' cooperative strategy has meanwhile succeeded on the Brocken and stands as a positive alternative to the failed plans of the individualists.

Within the two time levels there are further

structuring elements of three distinct but related spheres of action through which the plot of Amanda develops. One is the theoretical-abstract sphere, the realm of Beatriz and Arke, who conceive of and question ideas. This will be treated below. The second sphere is the Brocken society, where, as has been demonstrated, theory and praxis are combined to bring about social change. The third is the sphere of praxis, where significant (social) theory has only begun to be formulated; this is Laura's world of half-people, in which women are basically limited to the private sphere and men to the public. Morgner is very much occupied with the concepts of theory and praxis, the abstract and concrete, and examines them repeatedly in Amanda.[15] Her conclusion is that they must be combined in a way which ultimately reaches beyond individual goals.

A further, and related, major thesis of the novel is that, with few exceptions, people existing in the third sphere (the "real" world) have been halved by patriarchal drives to conquer and to specialize. As a countermeasure to this truncation, the women of the third sphere, represented in Amanda by a group in East Berlin, have joined together in night study sessions called "Unsinnskollegien" (p. 313), which are also attended by some Brocken whore/witches; actually, only the witches' heads--referred to on the Brocken as their "Schamteile" (p. 352) and consequently veiled--participate in the lectures, their bodies remain captive in the Brockenpuff. Despite factionalism, a division into a "hexische" and a "närrische Fraktion" (p. 313), they are able to work together. "Die beiden Fraktionen wechselten sich bei der Ausrichtung der Veranstaltungen . . . ab" (p. 313), reports the narrator, Beatriz. The Berlin women's common effort--cooperation despite differences--reflects that of the three-faction witches' world on the Brocken, where all the witches support Amanda as leader, in order to achieve their goal. In a 1982 interview, Morgner expressed her conviction that such communal efforts among women are indispensable.[16]

A central concern of the Berlin group is that women's intellectual side is unrealized. Vilma, Laura's alter ego and head of the "närrische Fraktion," relays the women's conclusion: "Da strikte geistige Arbeit weiblichen Menschen weder möglich [ist] noch erstrebenswert, [hat] die Frau als geistige Lebensform bisher noch nicht stattgefunden" (p. 353).[17] This is a negative situation which the Berlin women are commit-

53

ted to remedy. With the half-men, on the other hand, the subjective side has remained undeveloped. A representative victim, Konrad--Laura's first lover, Vilma's husband, and Amanda's number one Puff customer-- describes this state as a "Mangel an Herzensbildung" (p. 332). The men have no commensurate organization to combat their problem; like the Brocken "Querköpfe," who are led by Amanda and her witches, the half-men must look to their female counterparts in the real world to establish the precedent of becoming whole people.

The theory-based action of the second, Brocken, sphere stands as a model for the Berlin sphere. But, as the witches say in the closing lines of Amanda, with the example set, the victory is only half won: "Der ganze Sieg ist freilich auch eine lange Geschichte" (p. 656). The whole history is, of course, the preservation of humankind's future.

In the final pages of Amanda Morgner suggests how she believes this ultimate goal might be attained. Here she choses lines from a Lao-tse poem through which to express her ideas. The victorious witches accompany the birth of a new year by singing the verses. They and, by association, women in general, have gained a voice in determining the course of the future. The next step is to use that voice effectively. The plan for praxis is set forth in the initial lines of the poem, which suggest non-violent revolution and compromise: "was man stürzen will, muß man erheben / was man nehmen will, muß man geben" (p. 655). The penultimate line explains the necessity of such a strategy: "erkennen, eh sich die Dinge geklärt." The last line then explains just what is to be realized: "das Weiche besiegt das Harte . . . " Morgner's idea as incorporated in Amanda is that the one set of values, "das Harte," male values, must be replaced by another, "das Weiche," female values.

A series of questions regarding these systems of values arises at this point. Why does Morgner believe that a new system of values can give hope for the future of humanity? Where does she look for inspiration and for alternative models? What are the actual values she espouses? The answers to these questions reveal some of the fundamental ideas in Amanda.

Morgner is convinced of the necessity of a new value system because she deems the course on which the old one has set humankind to be a path of destruction of nature and of human life; she questions, criticizes, and rejects the patriarchally determined trajectory of history. Morgner expresses her fear concerning the future through several characters. Primary are those of the first sphere, Beatriz and Arke, but she also speaks through Konrad, who, as the intimate of three central figures, Laura, Vilma, and Amanda, recognizes the potential of women to change the world.18 In the course of the novel, he rejects his passionate attachment to history (p. 224) and, expressing an attitude representative of that generally held by the main characters in Amanda, explains:

> Die Geschichte ist keine Königin. Sie
> ist eine Horde Könige in Gestalt
> von Apokalyptischen Reitern, die mit
> Krieg, Hunger, Krankheit und Tod seit
> Jahrtausenden die Menschheit martern.
> Die Fortsetzung dieser Tradition,
> Meinungsverschiedenheiten mit Gewalt
> zu lösen, heißt: Atomkrieg. (p. 271)

Ten years before she completed Amanda, Morgner set as a goal for herself, "die gute Botschaft [zu] schreiben . . . , die die Frau in die Historie einführt."19 Unfortunately for their assessment of the novel, reviewers Alice Schwarzer (Der Spiegel, 6 June 1983) and Gisela Lindemann (Die Zeit, 29 July 1983) both quote Morgner's 1972 comment as if it had been made recently. In the intervening years, Morgner appears to have decided that the task of introducing women into history is not worth the effort, since history has become for her a synonym for the patriarchal tradition. History, in her present view, is the record of men's wars and men's achievements. Arke expresses this thought with laconic disgust: "Dann übernahmen die Männer die Herrschaft und führten ein, was die Menschen heute Geschichte nennen: Privateigentum, Klassentrennung, Ausbeutung, Staatsgewalt, Kriege" (p. 16).

Where do women fit into this picture of history? Arke answers for Morgner: "Und da weibliche Wesen in der Zeit, die allgemein Geschichte genannt [wird], heimatlos geblieben [sind], [haben] sie überhaupt außerhalb gesiedelt" (p. 98). Outside? "[H]istorisch expropriiert" (p. 226), is how Vilma describes what has happened to herself and other women. With very few exceptions they have been, as seen in Amanda, relegated--confined--to the private sphere, as a support system for men, and have been forced to make the best of this situation. Here, too, Vilma best represents the situation: "Die meisten Kräfte, die mir das Leben abverlangte, hab ich für Anpassung aufbringen müssen" (p. 227). She concludes with one of the novel's more delightful observations: "Aber ich hab keine Pillen gefressen. . . . Früher wurde das Hexenwesen mit Scheiterhaufen bekämpft, heute mit Scheißegaltabletten" (p. 227). Because the course of history has proved to be an accelerating slide toward annihilation, women no longer dare to be indifferent nor, like Laura, to seek "die absolute Flucht auf eine Hinterland-Insel" (p. 154). They, like the witches, must intercede now.

Where does Morgner seek an alternative to the historically instituted--male--values which her characters condemn? Having rejected history as a source of models, she turns to prehistory. Whereas history inspires fear, prehistory offers hope. It represents a time before "Schlachtenmut, Eroberungswille, Siegesgier" (p. 14) became virtues for which men were honored. Christa Wolf calls this time "Vorkrieg" (Kassandra, p. 76). There is, however, a major problem with using prehistory as a source of models for women, a problem I have cited with relation to the Pandora figure: the records of these "pre-war" times--myths, legends, sagas--have been passed down in male interpretations ("patriarchalische Bearbeitung," "Umwertung," p. 50) and must be re-evaluated and rewritten. By feminists? Morgner, through Beatriz, speaks with contempt of the bourgeois women's movement in the West (p. 561), a stand she also took in Trobadora Beatriz, and the only female labeled a feminist in Amanda is Isebel, who is mocked for her attitudes. But in a recent interview Morgner identified herself with feminists "im Sinne von Marx," quoting Marx' comment, "der gesellschaftliche Fortschritt lasse sich exakt messen an der gesellschaftlichen Stellung des schönen Geschlechts," and concluding: "Und wenn der die Sache so hoch eingebunden hat, dann kann das doch kein Nebenwiderspruch sein, oder?"[20] In her novel Morgner has Amanda criticize the double moral standard in the GDR and then comment: "Ein Sozialismus aber, der die Männervorherrschaft nicht abschafft, kann keinen Kommunismus aufbauen" (p. 549). Perhaps, then, in her role as a revolutionary from within the system Morgner can help effect a change in the condition of male hegemony. Neither Beatriz nor Arke claims to be a feminist, and they are the ones who take on the task, with a little help from friends, of reinterpreting prehistorical models such as Pandora, the Earth Mother,

Gaja, and the sirens. Not stopping at female images, they also revamp those of the traditional God/devil figures.

What do Arke and Beatriz derive from their feminine reading of prehistory? They discover the potential of personification and myth as tools to bring human beings into a closer, more subjective, relationship with each other and with their environment. The figure in Amanda who formulates ideas about personification is a mysterious character named Girgana; she gives lectures on the subject in the women's study group. In one such lecture, which Arke reports on to Beatriz, Girgana makes her central point that "die Fähigkeit zur Aneignung [der Welt]" (p. 461) has been lost and replaced by impersonal, quantitative abstractions. Girgana proposes that personification offers the ideal unification of abstract and concrete language, and that "Personifikationen unansprechbarer, Menschenleben prägender Erscheinungen können bildlich schlüssig und also brauchbar sein zur sinnlich-denkerischen, gefühlsmäßigen Bewältigung der materiellen Welt" (p. 554-55).

What are the actual values which Morgner believes must be conveyed through personification? In effect each of the figures in Amanda conveys certain values, negative and/or positive. But Morgner also specifies an actual system of values, the embodiment or personification of which is Pandora. These values are "Erdenliebe, Sinn für Harmonie und Hegen, Kompromißfähigkeit und Frieden" (p. 211), also referred to as "die Güter mit den Fittichen" (p. 83). Pandora's qualitative values are to replace the highly quantitative ones of Prometheus: "meßbare Reichtümer und Wahrheiten, Besserwissen, Sinn für Recht und Nutzen, Unbeugsamkeit, Vaterlandsliebe, Eroberungen, Siege und Wohlstände" (p. 211). The process of replacement involves Prometheus' (i.e., men's) learning to desire the values Pandora (i.e., women) represents.

Women, unlike Goethe's Pandora, are, according to Morgner, to take an active role in changing men's value system. They can do so by using the tools at hand. The ability to nurture and to make compromises are the very qualities which have been historically relegated to women's province and have been highly developed in the private sphere. Amanda proclaims: "Plötzlich wird die Fähigkeit zu Hegen . . . für die größten öffentlichen Zwecke unentbehrlich" (p. 547). Arke draws the significant conclusion: "Nur wenn die andere Hälfte

57

der Menschheit, die Frauen, bestimmte, bisher nur für private Zwecke entwickelte Fähigkeiten und Tugenden in die große Politik einbringen, können atomare und ökologische Katastrophen abgewendet werden" (p. 377).

If men--and women--, aided by personification and myth, succeed in comprehending, cherishing, and actively striving for Pandora's values, the historical practice of treating the environment and other human beings as something which must be conquered, suppressed, and ultimately destroyed can be changed. Arke makes the following prognosis:

> Nur wenn die Männer und die von Männern geführten progressiven Regierungen erkennen, daß sie die Probleme der Weltpolitik und Ökologie und ihre eigenen ohne gewisse Fähigkeiten und Tugenden der Frauen nicht bewältigen und entsprechend handeln, kann der Planet gerettet werden. (pp. 377-78)

What are the practical means of achieving the establishment of the new value system? Concrete suggestions for how women can increase their effectiveness in society are discussed by Arke, Beatriz, and other "wise women" who are also reincarnated as sirens. "Die Kunst der politischen Einbläserei" (p. 379), for example, is debated in four different chapters (52, 70, 90, and 126) and emerges as a more positive strategy than a feminism based either on the man as model or norm (pp. 98 and 413) or on "Männerhaß" (p. 425). The siren Katherine, a reincarnation of Katherine the Great, points out: "Viel Emanzipationsgerede ruft als Gegenreaktion Aggression auf den Plan" (p. 379). Persuading and convincing are presented as being ultimately more effective than actions based on force. Most significant for Morgner, the poet Beatriz decides to act on the following insight which she derives from Goethe: "Auch ein Buch könnte Mittel zur Bekanntmachung von Hindernissen sein, die überwunden werden müssen, soll die Menschheit nicht zugrunde gehen" (p. 258).

The direction of the historical past having been exposed as ultimately fatal and an alternative value system with women as its originators and implementers laid out, a question remains as to what sort of role the writer has in the process of change. One thing is certain: Morgner's writer must be a "she." Is she, however, to be a prophet, a poet, or a philosopher, or, perhaps, a combination of these?

In 1972, Morgner stated that she wanted to write the "Evangelium einer Prophetin."[21] But when the siren Beatriz asks, shortly after her rebirth, if she is to assume the role of "Rettungsprophetin" (p. 97), Arke quickly instructs her regarding the superfluity of that calling in 1980: "Von Propheten hör ich ungern. . . . Weil die Erde voll von ihnen ist. Die meisten Propheten sind Personifikationen menschlicher Vermessenheit und Liebesunfähigkeit" (p. 97). Needed instead is the poet who can find the "impossible" language to shake humanity out of its present state. This unique language is to be found in the poet who also offers a new philosophy.

Morgner believes that it is her task as a writer to aid in the general process of implementing the value system so carefully established in Amanda. One senses urgency and strong identification with her poet figure, Beatriz, in the statement: "Sirenischer Gesang [muß] diese Empfindensfähigkeit von Individuen zur Kompromiß- und Friedensfähigkeit von Völkern und deren Regierungen unnormal schnell entwickeln helfen" (p. 634). These concepts must be incorporated into new forms that reinforce the progress already made toward peace. Peace like any other prevailing force "bedarf ideologischer Stütze. Dafür haben sich Legenden und Sagen aufs beste bewährt" (p. 61). And the intelligent creation of these forms is the work of the poet-philosopher.

The new literary forms must be grounded in a new philosophy, one based on women's value system, and not on "geschichtspessimistischer Ideologie" (p. 287). In Laura's words, this philosophy should be for "Nichtfachleute. Über täglich zu bewältigende, unabweisbare, elementare Lebensereignisse" (p. 153). A further significant reason for a new philosophy is given by a member of the women's study group: "Die Philosophen haben die Welt bisher nur männlich interpretiert. Es kommt aber darauf an, sie auch weiblich zu interpretieren, um sie menschlich verändern zu können" (p. 312).

What poet is better equipped to incorporate a philosophy into her writing than one who can remember the values of the times before the incessant wars, the times of "die weisen Frauen" (p. 16). Such a poet, however, must refuse to be silenced: "Dichtern kann Schrecken die Sprache verschlagen" (p. 30). Excessive fatalism, intimidation, suppression must be overcome; if not, as Arke tells us: "Dann ist Sirene Beatriz ganz und gar mundtot gemacht, nicht mal mehr fähig, schriftlich anzudeuten, in welche Richtung sich die Menschheit in Bewegung setzen müßte, um die Güter mit Fittichen [i.e., Pandora's values] aus der Pandora-Büchse wieder einfangen zu können" (p. 360). The task of the writer is implied when Vilma calls "die ungeschriebene Philosophie" her "Königin" (p. 227). The unwritten philosophy is the one yet to be written by women. Morgner intended to break through the ban of silence. Amanda is her philosophical first step: a beginning of a female philosophy.

As we have seen, much of the substance of Amanda involves the problem of finding metaphorical language and models which can be effective in the present world situation and in the future. The poets who can dare the most in this quest for an "impossible" language suitable for "the day after tomorrow" are the women poets; they have the least to lose. They are the ones who must also decide that they are going to share, at least, the mountain tops of creativity with men, and that they will do so on their own terms.

The future generation is represented in Amanda by Laura's son, Wesselin, and it is for him that Beatriz wanted to write her book, for "den sozialistischen Fachmann Wesselin" (p. 579). Morgner's portrait of Wesselin implicitly and explicitly shows disapprobation of the limitations experienced by those born in the GDR and, at the same time, illustrates some of the advantages which are theirs. Beatriz hopes that the imperfect form of socialism, which is all Wesselin knows, will one day change, "wenn Pandora zurückkehrt und auf urkommunistischer Tradition der Kommunismus erwächst . . ." (p. 591). Here, too, Pandora is the embodiment of Morgner's hope.

In the final scene of Amanda, Morgner metaphorically crystallizes her ideas about the role of the writer and the establishment of a new value system; she also strikes a hopeful note regarding the world's future. Here, as throughout the novel, Morgner choses to convey her thoughts through humor and fantasy. Amanda ends with a New Year's Eve (1980) fireworks scene being observed by Beatriz, just freed from her cage, and a gathering of Amanda-led witches, who have brought Beatriz a new tongue and sewn it fast. The writer has regained the full power of her voice. The scene takes place in the East Berlin Tierparkschloß, and Girgana, a "Nachtwächterin" (p. 459) there plays a prominent part. She explains the significance of the setting: "Krach und Feuer sind traditionelle Mittel, um Hexen und andere böse Geister auszutreiben" (p. 654). This atavistic rite aimed at asuaging men's fears that they will lose control is then mocked. Girgana, the woman who discovered and passed on the secret of understanding the impossible, i.e., of learning to love the earth through personifying it, personifies here the triumphant woman ridiculing men who ritually--but futilely--still try to banish witches, in Morgner's metaphor, the effective half of women. And Girgana has the last laugh. To quote Morgner: "Das Gelächter wird--bezüglich, was am schlimmsten ist --besonders grell."[22] Girgana and the witches echo Laura's "unflätiges Gelächter" (p. 22) heard in the first chapter of Amanda, when she described the times in which she was living (i.e., 1971) with the words: "Närrische Zeiten im Ernst" (p. 21). Beatriz paints the final scene: "Als der Austreibungskrach sich zu infernalischem Lärm steigerte, brachen meine Besucherinnen in Gelächter aus. Am unflätigsten lachte Girgana" (p. 656). Girgana has sung her song and like others of Morgner's heroines--Vera, Melusine, Vilma, Beatriz--she can disappear from the picture. "Und sie hörte nicht auf, bis sie sich totgelacht hatte" (p. 656).

Morgner indicates what her own task as a writer is to be, when she has Beatriz answer a final question posed by the assembled witches regarding the biography of Laura which she, Beatriz, has completed up to mid-1977: "Wann wirst du den zweiten Teil fertig geschrieben haben?" (p. 656). With her brand new tongue Beatriz answers: "Demnächst" (p. 656). Morgner made the same promise in the summer of 1982, concerning Volume III, which she said will continue Laura's story and revolve around a female "Hanswurst."[23]

The metaphorical examples for shaping the future have been provided in the successful rebellion of the Brocken witches and in the value system of Pandora. Going a step farther, Morgner relates her theories in Amanda to the contemporary world situation and stresses that those women and men who have begun asserting the new value system she has outlined metaphorically have already made some progress in establishing this system:

> in diesem Europa [wird] offenbar doch
> schon begriffen, daß die Erde das ge-

meinsame Haus aller Menschen ist.
Erstmals in der Menschengeschichte
[kommt] ein Gefühl für weltweite Men-
schenabhängigkeit auf, . . . von glo-
baler Verantwortung. Erstmals [wird]
geahnt, daß es ein gemeinsames mensch-
liches Interesse gibt, das größer ist
als alle trennenden weltanschaulichen
und ökonomischen Interessen: das Über-
lebensinteresse. (p. 634)

Will the European peace movement on which she
built her hopes in Amanda last long enough to fulfill
the promise it holds to lead in "the whole victory"
(p. 656) for Morgner, for women, for humanity? The
name of that victory is Frieden.

Ohio State University

Notes

[1] Irmtraud Morgner, Leben und Abenteuer der Trobadora Beatriz nach Zeugnissen ihrer Spielfrau Laura
(Berlin/Weimar: Aufbau, 1974; Darmstadt: Luchterhand,
1976).

[2] Irmtraud Morgner, Amanda. Ein Hexenroman (Ber-
lin/Weimar: Aufbau, 1983; Darmstadt: Luchterhand,
1983). Subsequent page references given in the text
are based on the Luchterhand edition.

[3] Christa Wolf, Kassandra. Erzählung (Darmstadt:
Luchterhand, 1983).

[4] Sigrid Löffler, "Eine anmutige Spinnerin: Die
Frauen müssen die Welt instandbesetzen," Die Zeit,
17 June 1983, p. 23.

[5] Irmtraud Morgner, "Interview," in Meinetwegen
Schmetterlinge: Gespräche mit Schriftstellern, ed.
Joachim Walther (Berlin: Der Morgen, 1973), p. 54.

[6] Unpublished interview with Sheila K. Johnson,
Berlin (GDR), 13 July 1982.

[7] Morgner interview with Johnson.

[8] Sibylle Cramer, "Leben und Abenteuer der Laura

Salman. Irmtraud Morgners Hexenroman 'Amanda,'" in Lesezeichen: Zeitschrift für neue Literatur, 1983, p. 26.

[9] Patricia A. Herminghouse, "Die Frau und das Phantastische in der neuen DDR-Literatur: Der Fall Irmtraud Morgner," in Die Frau als Heldin und Autorin: neue kritische Ansätze zur deutschen Literatur, ed. Wolfgang Paulsen, 10. Amherster Kolloquium (Bern: Franke, 1977), p. 259.

[10] For examples of Morgner's having fun with this ploy, see pp. 245, 301, et passim.

[11] See pages 11, 76-77, 82-84, 96, 211, 257-58, 301, 360, 409, 576, 591, and 653.

[12] The military has removed the patriarchs and their troops from the geographical Brocken; the witches had long been on a neighboring mountain. The concept of the Brocken as a "Zauberberg" is however not tied to a physical location. Amanda explains to Laura: "der Zauberberg unseres Landes [ist] seit einiger Zeit im wörtlichen Sinne sozusagen kein Berg mehr. . . . Und deshalb verstehst du auch, daß die Bezeichnung 'Brocken' für den Ort, wo sich Kolbuk mit seinen Raben jetzt zu treffen pflegt, ungenau geworden ist" (p. 276).

[13] Androgyny as a quality was praised by Morgner in my 1982 interview, as it is in Amanda by the siren Katherine. All three sirens in Amanda are positive figures and often function as spokeswoman for Morgner.

[14] Morgner herself enjoys playing with numbers, if not with numerology. She talked about this interest in the 1982 interview, and she lets Heinrich indulge in number games and speculations in Chapter 132 of Amanda.

[15] See pages 40, 52, 97, 163, 354, 459, 461, 553, and 638.

[16] Morgner interview with Johnson.

[17] Beatriz, as chronicler in Amanda, bases much of her text on "archival materials" or on her verbal exchanges with Arke, and records such passages as indirect discourse; her use of the subjunctive (usually subjunctive II) is inappropriate out of context, and therefore indicative verb forms will be substituted

in brackets when such passages are quoted.

[18] See, for example, his conversation with Laura, p. 650.

[19] Morgner, "Interview," in _Meinetwegen_, p. 54.

[20] Löffler, p. 23.

[21] Morgner, "Interview," in _Meinetwegen_, p. 54.

[22] Morgner interview with Johnson.

[23] Morgner interview with Johnson.

Stefan Heym's Revolutionary Wandering Jew:
A Warning and a Hope for the Future

Nancy A. Lauckner

The publication of Stefan Heym's <u>Ahasver</u> in the FRG in 1981 represents a surprising event in GDR literature.[1] After a long absence, the legendary figure of the Wandering Jew has burst upon the literary scene from an unexpected quarter and in a highly thought-provoking way. His return raises some questions which I attempt to answer in this paper by carefully analyzing this new Ahasver: Why does this legendary character, whose origins lie in religious superstition, suddenly appear as the protagonist of a novel by a GDR socialist author in the supposedly enlightened late twentieth century; and what message can this Wandering Jew possibly have for the modern world? The author of <u>Der König David Bericht</u> has again drawn on the Bible and religious legend to cloak his criticism of our own times. He implicitly accuses both Christianity and communism of failure to achieve their similar goals of social justice and peace and postulates the need for a new revolution led by human beings acting as their own saviors (p. 206) to prevent the impending nuclear holocaust and to usher in "das wahre Reich GOttes" (p. 209) when peace will reign and suffering will cease.

Heym has carefully researched the legend and its history and records his findings in the novel in the scholarly correspondence about Ahasver conducted by the fictitious GDR professor Siegfried Beifuß and the Israeli professor Jochanaan Leuchtentrager, perhaps as a means of informing the reader about the legend, as Jurek Becker suggests.[2] According to the legend, Christ stopped at a shoemaker's shop on the way to the Crucifixion and asked to rest there briefly. When the shoemaker refused, Jesus cursed him to wander the world without rest until Christ's return. Heym repeatedly weaves this scene into his novel, and, in the

65

Beifuß-Leuchtentrager correspondence, explains how the stories of several well-known figures have influenced the legend. Leuchtentrager notes that Christ's cryptic remark about John, the "beloved" desciple, ("If I will that he tarry till I come, what is that to thee?" - John 21: 22) unintentionally led to the belief that John, like the Wandering Jew, would not die, whereas other persons seem to have become connected with the legend because they abused Jesus (pp. 237-38): Malchus, the servant of the high priest, seized Jesus in the Garden of Gethsemane; Cartaphilus, one of Pilate's doorkeepers, is said to have struck Jesus to make him hurry; and the mysterious Buttadeus is presumably a variant of Cartaphilus.[3] All three have appeared in numerous accounts as the Wandering Jew. The novel contains references to many chronicled "sightings" of the Wandering Jew since 1228 and particularly focuses on his alleged contact with Paulus von Eitzen, a sixteenth-century cleric, who plays a prominent role in the book and with whom "eine eigentliche Ahasver-Literatur" begins (p. 239).[4]

Thus far, Heym's discussion of the legend and its development accurately reflects the research on the subject, but his purpose leads him to embroider on the legend in some highly original ways. For example, Beifuß, as director of the Institut für wissenschaftlichen Atheismus, cannot accept the concept of a living Ahasver, since to do so would entail belief in miracles (p. 62), so he dredges up two historical eccentrics and tries to show how they may have been construed as the Wandering Jew. One, Jörg von Meißen, was a barefoot prophet who traveled through Eastern Europe preaching repentance and upon whose appearance disasters often followed; the other, Wassilij Blazhennij, was a medicant monk who warned Ivan the Terrible of God's wrath (pp. 182-87). Although Beifuß cites an actual article in the Zeitschrift des Vereins für Hamburgische Geschichte as the authority for this interpretation (p. 182),[5] it is both unusual and unsubstantiated to identify these two eccentrics as the Wandering Jew, as Leuchtentrager points out (p. 186). However, this Israeli scholar does something even more unorthodox: he claims to find startling evidence for the authenticity of the legend in one of the Dead Sea Scrolls. To support his claim, he offers a translation of the appropriate fragments of a scroll "just released for publication" (p. 96). In this passage, the Teacher of Righteousness asks to rest by the door of the Prince of the Congregation (identified as Ahasver) and rejects the latter's attempt to make him a

military leader of the poor and oppressed. When Ahasver refuses to let him rest, the Teacher of Righteousness (identified as the "Son of Man") curses him in
the words of the legend (pp. 97-98). Despite Heym's
use of many facts and phrases from authentic Dead Sea
Scrolls, scroll 9QRes does not exist. It is a brilliant invention concocted to add authority to Leuchtentrager's contention that Ahasver is real. In fact,
there is no evidence for nor reference to the legend
of the Wandering Jew in the actual Dead Sea Scrolls.[6]
Besides including such materials to confirm or dis-
prove Ahasver's existence, Heym deviates still further
from standard research by extending the legend in two
directions: his Wandering Jew is extant at virtually
the beginning of time as one of the angels who fall
with Lucifer after the Creation, and he is also present at the end of time when he participates in another
revolt at the Second Coming. Much of the fascination
of Ahasver derives from these fanciful additions to
the legend which are essential to Heym's concept of
the Wandering Jew as a revolutionary figure.

To develop Ahasver's story, Heym uses a montage
of four time levels (the time of Creation, Jesus'
time, the sixteenth century, and the twentieth century) and a level that transcends time. Usually a chapter treats only one level, and the action proceeds
chronologically on each time level, although there is
no pattern to the order in which the levels are distributed over the twenty-nine chapters. Each level
has its own plot which always includes Ahasver's revolutionary activity as a unifying strand: in each case
this revolutionary figure works to destroy the status
quo, to change man and the world, and to bring about
the promised kingdom of God.

On the time level of Creation, Ahasver narrates
the Creation and rebellion as memories, but uses the
present tense to describe the fall in progress. Here
he is one of the angels, "die Erstgeborenen, erschaf-
fen am ersten Tag . . . aus Feuer und dem Hauch des
Unendlichen" (p. 5). These attributes identify the
angels as "Geist" (p. 8), and account for Ahasver's
later appearance with a fiery trail (p. 299), which
might otherwise symbolize his hellish connections.
These angels are identified as "die Unruhe, . . . die
ewige Veränderung, das Schöpferische" (p. 5), and
these traits characterize Ahasver throughout the novel. Thus, it is significant that Ahasver views God
himself as "Veränderung" because he irrevocably
changed things by creating the world (p. 177). It is,

therefore, not surprising that "Ahasver," the name of this angel who is "Geist vom Geiste GOttes" (p. 125), should mean "der Geliebte" (p. 7), "'der von Gott Erhöhte,' oder 'von Gott Geliebte'" (p. 64).[7] Despite these characteristics, which seem to suggest Ahasver's oneness of mind and purpose with God, he is a fallen angel, banished for refusing to pay homage to Adam.

Ahasver's response to God's request to honor Adam places him on Lucifer's side in his first rebellion against God: "Ich werde den doch nicht verehren, der jünger und geringer ist als ich. . . . er bewegt die Welt nicht, aber ich bewege sie . . . er ist Staub, aber ich bin Geist" (pp. 7-8). His rejection of Adam anticipates his later refusal of Christ's request in the legendary scene on the Via Dolorosa. No mere hybris motivates this rebellion, however, as Lucifer's plea for God's understanding shows: "Dieser [Adam, i.e., humanity] . . . wird . . . aus Deiner Erde einen stinkigen Sumpf machen, er wird das Blut seines Bruders vergießen . . . und mehr Sünden begehen als ich je erfinden könnte . . ." (p. 8). Thus, Ahasver and Lucifer resist because they think man will harm and ultimately destroy the world God has created.

For his defiance Ahasver falls with Lucifer, in whose company he then appears frequently throughout the novel, and this Wandering Jew suffers his first divine curse: "die Tiefen zu durchwandern bis zum Jüngsten Tag" (p. 130). Yet, as he falls, Ahasver reaffirms his rebellion: ". . . ich bereue nicht" (p. 5). His final words on this level serve both to foreshadow his future activities and to differentiate his ideas from Lucifer's: Ahasver laments the fate of "eine so große Hoffnung. . . . Eine so schöne Welt! Ein so schöner Mensch!" but consoles himself that "[a]lles ist veränderbar," while Lucifer prepares to wait, knowing "alles wird mählich zu mir kommen, denn . . . es ist nichts von Dauer" (p. 8). Thus, the lines are drawn: Lucifer will accept the status quo because he believes it predestines the world's downfall, which he desires (p. 179),[8] but Ahasver will constantly try to change the world "'da er glaubt, sie sei veränderbar und die Menschen in ihr desgleichen'" (p. 76).[9] Although Ahasver's activity seems directed against God, he is actually trying to restore God's original plan and promises for the world and man (p. 210). Thus, Ahasver's "ganz eigenes Verhältnis zu Gott . . . , zugleich Rebell und Geliebter" (p. 156) is only apparently a contradiction, explicable by Ahasver's efforts to bring about God's purposes despite him.

The second level, Jesus' time, consists of memories which the first-person narrator, Ahasver, recounts largely in the past tense with occasional use of the present. He recalls several occasions on which he met and conversed with Jesus, each time urging him to lead a military revolt to establish "das wahre Reich GOttes" (p. 54) and rejecting him when he refused. He first meets Reb Joshua (Jesus' historical name) in the wilderness after the temptation by Satan and perceives that this man radiates "ein Licht . . . und eine große Hoffnung" (p. 53), which implicitly reflects the "great hope" of Creation (p. 9). Like the biblical Satan, Ahasver shows Jesus all the kingdoms of the world, yet his intent is revolutionary, not diabolical. After mentioning ubiquitous injustices, Ahasver pleads: "Bist du GOttes Sohn, so . . . kehre das Untere zuoberst, denn die Zeit ist gekommen, das wahre Reich GOttes zu errichten" (p. 54). They then toss Old Testament prophecies back and forth, with Ahasver declaring that the Messiah is to be a military leader and ruler, and Jesus explaining that he must be a gentle helper (pp. 54-55). Unable to shake Jesus' determination, Ahasver angrily denies his Messiahship. However, Heym has Ahasver promise to be with Jesus when the others abandon him and to let him rest at his house (pp. 55-56), thus foreshadowing the Wandering Jew's legendary sin.

Their next personal meeting occurs at the Last Supper, where Ahasver exhibits certain characteristics of John, the "beloved" disciple, by sitting beside Jesus and leaning on his chest (p. 81; John 13: 21). Disgusted by Jesus' humility, he again appeals to him: "Tue . . . nicht, als sei dein Schicksal dir vorbestimmt, sondern raffe dich auf und kämpfe" (p. 81). When Jesus refuses, saying "die Liebe ist stärker als das Schwert," Ahasver predicts the consequences in a biting indictment of the Church's failure to follow Christ's teachings and establish his kingdom: "die nach dir kommen, . . . werden zum Schwert greifen im Namen der Liebe, und das Reich, von dem du geträumt hast, wird härter regiert als das römische, und . . . das Volk wird den Nacken beugen unter den Fuß des Herrn" (p. 82). Convinced that his efforts are in vain when Jesus tells Judas to do his deed quickly, Ahasver turns his back on Jesus, symbolically rejecting him again (pp. 82-83). He even participates indirectly in the betrayal by keeping silent about Judas' plan; and, for this service, he receives one of Judas' thirty pieces of silver (p. 83), which becomes one of the Wandering Jew's identifying characteristics on subsequent levels.

His final meeting with Jesus on this level occurs, of course, on the way to the Crucifixion, and
Heym imbues this legendary scene, too, with new, revolutionary meaning. Stopping at Ahasver's house, Jesus
recalls the promise of rest there, but Ahasver tries
again to make him the awaited military Messiah. He
vows to draw his "sword of God" and fight for Jesus,
if the latter will only throw down the cross and lead
the people in battle (pp. 123-24). When Jesus responds in the words addressed to Peter at Gethsemane:
"Lasse dein Schwert in der Scheide. Soll ich den
Kelch nicht trinken, den mir mein Vater gegeben hat?"
(cf. John 18: 11), Ahasver forcibly rejects him, yell-
ing "Pack dich, du Narr!" (p. 124). Jesus then curses
Ahasver in the words of the legend: "Der Menschensohn
geht, wie geschrieben steht nach dem Wort des Propheten, du aber wirst bleiben und meiner harren, bis ich
wiederkehre" (p. 124). Although his efforts have been
unsuccessful, the rebellious angel, sure that he has
acted in the best interests of God and man, weeps at
Jesus' death (p. 126) for the great revolutionary hope
Christ could have fulfilled but did not.

The third time level, the sixteenth century, differs from the previous two in that it is narrated by
an omniscient narrator in the present tense,[10] and the
coarse, hearty language gives the effect of Luther's
German without resembling it exactly. Ahasver's activities on this level are the most difficult to analyze because his revolutionary intent here expresses
itself indirectly. Ahasver himself is more similar to
the traditional Wandering Jew on this level than anywhere else in the novel except for the curse scene.
Like the legendary Wanderer, this Ahasver appears in
several guises and in various cities; his age varies
by seemingly magical means (p. 307); the soles of his
feet bear a five-nailed cross (p. 43) and are heavily
calloused by centuries of walking (p. 204); he disap-
pears mysteriously (p. 207) but cannot die (p. 118);
his appearances are feared as omens of trouble (p.
205); and he encounters Paulus von Eitzen. Although
his frequent companion, the sixteenth-century Leuchtentrager, is not part of the legend, his presence
calls to mind the legendary view of the Wandering Jew
as a diabolical figure.[11] Ahasver differs from the
traditional Wandering Jew in ways that reflect Heym's
conception of him as a revolutionary: thus, he often
exhibits the might (p. 67), size and nimbus (p. 206)
of an angel, albeit a fallen one (p. 308); he recalls

his nationalistc fervor from level two (p. 118); and he does not repent of the behavior that earned him Christ's curse, still regarding Jesus as "'der falsche Meschiach'" (p. 49) because he failed to bring about God's kingdom by military means (pp. 118, 206).

Ahasver's revolutionary deeds, attitudes, and ideas in the sixteenth century are largely expressed through his role as Eitzen's antagonist. Unlike the chronicle of Chrysostomus Dudulaeus, which limits Eitzen's contact with the Wandering Jew to a brief period around Easter 1542,[12] Heym's version describes repeated encounters from their first meeting during Eitzen's student days in Wittenberg until his death in Schleswig. On several occasions, Ahasver is implicitly analogous to Christ; perhaps Heym intends him to be Jesus' revolutionary alter ego, an hypothesis supported by subsequent events. Although Ahasver expresses his personal hostility to Eitzen by repeatedly consorting with Margriet, the object of Eitzen's always thwarted lust, their basic antagonism concerns religion: Ahasver is the champion of God's as yet unrealized kingdom, while Eitzen, an ardent supporter of Luther's views on church and state, establishes a theocracy unpleasing to God according to Ahasver and Leuchtentrager's later explanations (pp. 308-309). Nevertheless, Ahasver applauds Luther's rebellion against the Pope, because it has forever destroyed the unity of Christendom, thus contributing to Ahasver's own work of ending injustice and oppression (pp. 49-50). As the Wandering Jew in a travelling show, Ahasver "proves" his identity and undermines Eitzen's authority by correctly prophesying that the weathercock on the churchtower will crow three times before lightning strikes (pp. 120-21); thus, he implicitly casts himself as Jesus and Eitzen as Peter, the denier (p. 142). Called to the deathbed of Eitzen's father to assure him of Christ's salvation, Ahasver evades the issue, stating rather "'der Rabbi hat die Menschen geliebt'" (p. 146).

His most significant rebellion, however, occurs during Eitzen's disputation with the Jews. Engaged as an eyewitness to Christ's Passion, whose testimony should convert the Jews, Ahasver breaks the mold of the traditional Wandering Jew by refusing to identify Jesus as the Messiah, instead responding ambivalently: "'Er hätt sein können der Meschiach, so wie ein jeder, der geschaffen ist im Bilde Gottes, die Macht in sich trägt, ein Erlöser zu sein der Menschen'" (p. 206). His reason for denying Christ again is consistent with

71

his revolutionary views and represents a strong indictment of the Church's failure: the world is still
full of injustice and suffering instead of "der ewige
Friede, und . . . das Reich, das da kommen sollte mit
ihm und durch ihn" (pp. 206-207). When Eitzen later
tries to establish "das Reich Gottes in Schleswig" (p.
218) by oppressive means including an obligatory pastoral oath,[13] a corps of spies to ferret out heretics,
and a show trial, Ahasver appears as a Mennonite pastor from Holland to defend the accused against
Eitzen's unbending orthodoxy. Because of this inso-
lence and their longstanding antagonism, Eitzen has
Ahasver arrested and sentenced to run the gauntlet in
an episode which clearly parallels the legendary curse
scene and the Crucifixion. Condemned by Herzog Adolf
in the role of Pilate (p. 263), Ahasver begs Eitzen
after the first beating: "'Laßt mich ausruhen ein wenig bei Euch, denn ich bin wund und zum Sterben
matt,'" and Eitzen, recognizing the words, nevertheless refuses by referring to Ahasver's rejection
of Jesus (p. 270). Thereupon, Ahasver-Jesus curses
Eitzen-Ahasver to be taken by the devil, and the episode ends with Ahasver's "death" amidst dark clouds,
thunder, lightning, and a windstorm (pp. 270-71), reminiscent of the natural phenomena accompanying the
Crucifixion.

When Ahasver later fulfills his promise to come
with the devil for Eitzen's soul, this final revolutionary act on the sixteenth-century level pits Ahasver's conception of God's will for mankind against
Eitzen's strict administration of Lutheran theocracy.
Identifying Eitzen as a bad shepherd in the words of
Ezekiel 34: 10, Ahasver clarifies Leuchtentrager's explanation that Eitzen's efforts on behalf of "die
schönste geistliche Ordnung" (p. 308) have damned him
by proclaiming "'GOtt ist die Freiheit, . . . wer will
dann wagen, den menschlichen Geist in hohle Doktrinen
zu zwängen?'" (p. 309). In view of this comment, the
previous analogies between Ahasver and Jesus, and his
transformation into angelic form at the end of this
episode (p. 313), Ahasver's role in coming for Eitzen's soul must be interpreted as a revolutionary act
in the service of God's "true kingdom" despite this
Wandering Jew's association with the devil.

While these first three levels illuminate Ahasver's origins and motives and establish his creden-
tials as a revolutionary, our questions about Heym's
use of the Wandering Jew are finally answered on the
twentieth-century level and the level which transcends

time. In the twentieth century, Ahasver has returned to Jerusalem and reopened his old shop on the Via Dolorosa. Although we never meet this Ahasver directly, we know him through his friend Professor Leuchtentrager's copious correspondence about him. Leuchtentrager characterizes him as a symbol of the Jewish people because of "seine Unzufriedenheit mit den bestehenden Verhältnissen, seine Bemühungen, diese zu verändern" (p. 236). Ahasver's revolutionary nature is captured in the comment: "Er ist . . . die menschgewordene Unruhe; die Ordnung . . . ist für ihn dazu da, angezweifelt . . . und umgestoßen zu werden" (pp. 236-37). In short, he is "jüdische Ungeduld" incarnate (p. 237). Indeed, Ahasver was already deeply involved in revolutionary activity when he and Leuchtentrager met in the Warsaw Ghetto. There, too, Ahasver was a symbol for his people and seemingly a sign from the God who had forsaken them. Leuchtentrager reports: "wo er sich zeigte, schöpften selbst die Sterbenden neuen Mut; es war, als wüßten sie . . . , daß etwas von ihnen fortbestehen würde, . . . und daß ihr Leiden und ihr Tod eine Bedeutung hatten . . ." (pp. 154-55). Ahasver took part in the uprising because he believed in the "Veränderbarkeit der Welt" (p.155), but at the SS victory he turned himself into a human torch, having failed again to force God's hand.

In September 1980, however, Ahasver's efforts finally bear fruit when the Second Coming occurs. Heym daringly adapts this religious motif by restaging the legendary meeting of Jesus and Ahasver. This time Ahasver welcomes his exhausted guest, offers him refreshment, and cleans his wounds. Trying again to incite Jesus to action by asking whether he plans to be martyred once more (p. 278), Ahasver finds the militant Christ whom he had previously sought in vain to promote. Proclaiming that he has come to pass judgment, Jesus launches into an impassioned account of the nuclear Armageddon mankind is preparing to unleash. Clearly, Heym uses Jesus' words to condemn the policies of both West and East in the most authoritative way possible: "diese ganze höllische Macht befinde sich in den Händen einiger weniger Herrscher. . . , die bei jeder Gelegenheit lauthals proklamierten, sie bräuchten ihr Arsenal zur Verteidigung des Friedens, denn der Friede erfordere ein Gleichgewicht des Schreckens" (p. 280), although each side could already destroy God's creation many times over; "so sei Adam selbst, einst im Bilde Gottes geschaffen, zu . . . dem Alles-Zerstörer, dem Antichrist [geworden]" (p.280), thus fulfilling the chilling prophecy about man's future by which Lucifer justified his and Ahasver's revolt against God (p. 8). Returning to Golgotha, Jesus asks God the question which Ahasver has tried to make him raise throughout the novel: "war denn alles für nichts . . . ?" (p. 281). Recognizing that his sacrificial death has changed nothing, Jesus is finally ready to take drastic action with Ahasver to usher in the promised kingdom of God.

Ahasver, however, expects to die now that the terms of the curse have been fulfilled. Before his death, though, he accompanies Leuchtentrager to Berlin to take the soul of Beifuß in a modern parallel to Eitzen's fate. Heym does not specify what Beifuß has done to deserve this end, but certain clues suggest a possible reason. Given the obvious parallels to Eitzen's death, Beifuß' care to espouse and defend socialist views in his interpretation of the Wandering Jew, Heym's condemnation of the arms policies of both East and West, and numerous more or less veiled critical allusions to GDR socialism throughout the novel, it seems likely that Heym intends Beifuß to represent dogmatic communism, just as Eitzen represents dogmatic Christianity.[14] Symbolically, then, the fate of Eitzen and Beifuß indicates that both Christianity and communism have failed to achieve their goal of an ideal world of peace, justice, and brotherhood which Heym calls "das wahre Reich GOttes."

Five chapters scattered through the novel present a level which transcends time,[15] a level on which the superhuman characters meet to converse and act on a non-earthly plane at unspecified times. Technically, the Creation chapter also belongs to this level, although it is treated separately here to facilitate the discussion of Ahasver's origins and motives. Ahasver, the first-person narrator of these episodes largely uses past tense, although one chapter contains only the present, and others include some minimal present forms. In one conversation God censures Ahasver's continued revolutionary activity and doubts after the fall and reveals himself to Ahasver to prove man's "GOttgleichheit" (p. 129). Still seeing many contradictions in God's order, Ahasver provokes him with his "jüdische Frechheit" and loves him for losing his "divine calm" (pp. 130-31), as he later loves Jesus for his revolt. Later Ahasver and Lucifer debate the nature of God: Ahasver insists that "God is change" and Lucifer that the admittedly revolutionary God has become a strict "Ordnungshüter" (p. 177). Recognizing that Isaiah's vision (Isa. 11: 6) has not

been realized (p. 178) and convinced "daß diese Welt
verurteilt ist zum Untergang . . . durch just die Ordnung, welche GOtt ihr gegeben" (p. 179), Lucifer wants
Ahasver to join him in creating "ein Reich der Freiheit" without God (p. 179). Since Ahasver's aim is
not to get rid of God, but rather to make him fulfill
his promises, he demurs, accepting instead Lucifer's
suggestion to ask Jesus what his coming has accomplished (p. 178). Upon posing his question to a distant, seemingly uncaring Christ: "Ist das Reich gekommen?" (p. 210), Ahasver confronts him with a terrible
and accurate picture of conditions "in dem Reich, das
nach ihm gekommen ist": greed, debauchery, drunken-
ness, child-selling, drug abuse, enmity, spying, betrayal, starvation, torture, despoiling the earth's
resources, environmental pollution, and oppression,
all allegedly "im Namen der Liebe und zum Wohle der
Völker" (pp. 210-11). [16]

This catalog of horrors ends with Heym's main
concern in writing this novel: certainly, it is no accident that Ahasver alludes to the words of Isaiah and
Micah which have become the motto of the unofficial
GDR peace movement: "Kein Schwert . . . wurde je umge-
schmiedet zur Pflugschar . . . ; vielmehr nehmen sie
die geheimen Kräfte im All und machen daraus himmel-
hohe Pilze aus Flamme und Rauch, in denen alles Leben-
dige zu Asche wird . . ." (p. 211). Thus, Ahasver is
the impetus for Jesus' return to earth because he follows this alert to the nuclear threat with the advice
not to wait for the appointed time for the Second Coming (p. 212). After finding God to be an old man who
admits his failure and impotence to bend the world to
his will, Jesus finally acts on Ahasver's instigation
to rebel against God "statt abzuwarten, bis diese Welt
sich selber zum Teufel sprengte" (p. 288).

Thus, the level which transcends time merges with
the twentieth-century level in preparation for the
apocalyptic events of the final chapter, which brings
the novel's action full-circle. In many parallels to
the first chapter, Ahasver recalls how Jesus becomes
the military leader Ahasver has sought to make him and
leads the armies of the Apocalypse in a storm on the
seven heavens. [17] Taking God's place, Jesus promises
to fulfill Isaiah's prophecies of a new heaven and
earth (p. 317), which has been Ahasver's constant
goal. When God reasserts his power, putting down this
revolt like the first one, Ahasver and Jesus, rather
than Ahasver and Lucifer, are left falling through
space and not regretting their attempt, "[d]enn es

. . . mußte sein, damit alles . . . rückkehre zu dem, woher es ausgegangen, die Schöpfung zu ihrer Schöpfung und GOtt zu GOtt" (p. 314). Thus, though the rebellion itself fails, Ahasver succeeds, in part, because the former world order perishes and a final unio mystica (p. 319) unites him with Christ and a God restored to himself. The future, if there is to be one, remains unknown in this open-ended conclusion.[18]

It is not by accident that Heym's development of Ahasver's revolutionary activity on all five levels culminates in a rebellion designed to prevent nuclear holocaust. It seems singularly fitting that he should adapt the Wandering Jew, whose "appearances" have traditionally occurred in troubled times and symbolized Wirrsal (pp. 43, 205), to warn of the dangers and to offer hope in our current perilous time. The challenge of Ahasver's message is clear: individuals must resist the forces in both East and West which are escalating toward virtually inevitable nuclear conflict, change present attitudes before it is too late, and bring about the ideal world of peace, justice, and brotherhood which both Christianity and communism want, but which neither has yet achieved. Heym implies that this task can be accomplished, but that time is short. The seemingly religious message of Ahasver is, thus, really a political one. And, above all, Ahasver offers a humane message of hope, which is Heym's contribution to the peace movement currently sweeping both East and West.

The University of Tennessee, Knoxville

Notes

[1] Stefan Heym, Ahasver (Munich: Bertelsmann, 1981). Subsequent references will appear parenthetically in the text. All translations are my own.

[2] Jurek Becker, "Der ewige Jude gibt keine Ruhe," rev. of Ahasver, by Stefan Heym, Der Spiegel, 2 November 1981, p. 243.

[3] See Joseph Gaer, The Legend of the Wandering Jew, Mentor Book 326 (New York: New American Library, 1961), pp. 14, 16-18, 75-78. Leuchtentrager's brief references to these three men, as well as to the connection with John, represent basic, generally-accepted information about the legend's sources, and Gaer both

corroborates this information and provides further details.

[4] Gaer confirms the connection with Eitzen, but emphasizes that the oral reports attributed to Eitzen were recorded by others (pp. 34, 37-38). For further information on the Wandering Jew, see the chapter on "The Wandering Jew" in my dissertation ("The Image of the Jew in the Postwar German Novel," Diss. Wisconsin 1971, pp. 195-237).

[5] See Paul Johansen, "War der ewige Jude in Hamburg?" Zeitschrift des Vereins für Hamburgische Geschichte, 41 (Hamburg: Hans Christians Verlag, 1951), pp. 189-203.

[6] Conversation with Professor W. Lee Humphreys, Professor of Religious Studies at the University of Tennessee-Knoxville, December 1982.

[7] The last two meanings are given as quotations within quotations because they represent an explanation which Beifuß purportedly quotes directly from Prof. Walter Beltz.

[8] Becker also sees Heym's devil as a representative of order and Ahasver as a representative of change, but describes the devil's motivation differently: "er sieht, daß er niemals eine miserablere Ordnung zustande bringen könnte" (p. 242).

[9] Heym uses quotation marks for direct quotations from his characters on the third time level. I cite such passages as quotations within quotations, whereas I use only one set of quotation marks to cite portions not in quotation marks in Heym's text.

[10] Becker refers to this level as "die Gegenwartshandlung" (p. 240), but it is present only in regard to the tense used, not the century treated.

[11] See, for example, Gaer, p. 24. Leuchtentrager's identity with the devil is, of course, demonstrated by his name, a German version of "Lucifer." Indeed, Heym uses the same name for two devil figures in his novel: the sixteenth-century Leuchtentrager concerns himself with Eitzen; and his twentieth-century counterpart, Jochanaan Leuchtentrager, is an Israeli professor.

[12] Gaer, pp. 34, 37-38.

[13] According to Otto Brandt (<u>Geschichte Schleswig-Holsteins: Ein Grundriß</u>, 6th ed., revised by Wilhelm Klüver [Kiel: Walter G. Mühlau Verlag, 1966], p. 159), the historical Eitzen really did institute such an oath.

[14] See Jörg Bernhard Bilke, rev. of <u>Ahasver</u>, by Stefan Heym, <u>Neue Deutsche Hefte</u>, 28, No. 4 (1981), 829.

[15] Bilke refers to this level as "außerhalb von Raum und Zeit" (p. 830).

[16] Cf. Bilke, p. 830.

[17] Heym gives no date for this Armageddon, but it must occur after New Year's Eve 1980, the time when Ahasver and Leuchtentrager come for Beifuß' soul.

[18] As Heym states in the summary title of his last chapter, "es [erweist] sich . . . , daß die letzten Fragen unbeantwortet bleiben müssen" (p. 314).

The New Politics of Détente Starts at the Bottom:
The Unofficial Peace Movement in the GDR

Peter Wensierski

"If an atomic bomb were to detonate directly over
the Brandenburg Gate, then within a fraction of a second all auto bodies in Charlottenburg [West Berlin]
and Pankow [East Berlin] would evaporate. In more
distant city districts such as Marzahn [East Berlin]
and Märkisches Viertel [West Berlin] the cars would
melt. Even the concrete pilings of the bridge over
the Spree near the Friedrichstraße train station would
vanish. In Wannsee or Königswusterhausen on the out-
skirts of Berlin--many kilometers from groundzero--
the clothing of pedestrians would catch fire."

This vision of a possible atomic inferno was
painted by a twenty-two-year-old woman at a peace
meeting in East Berlin in July 1983. Such concrete
descriptions made it clear to all those present that
in Berlin, which lies directly on the seismic fault
between East and West, the consequences of a nuclear
war would be particularly absurd. A young woman from
Potsdam added, "Since the politicians of the past
thirty years have not succeeded in bringing us closer
to peace, we will have to introduce new concepts of
peace ourselves."

Such an opinion is no longer rare in the GDR. An
awakening which seemed impossible only a few years ago
is occurring among the younger generation. The GDR is
presently in the midst of one of the most interesting
political and cultural transitions it has ever experienced. Thanks to a sufficient degree of government
stability and continuity, on the one hand, and changes
in consciousness and perceived needs in some parts of
the population, on the other, a process has come into
being in the 1980s, the political significance of
which has not yet been fully recognized in the West.[1]

The state's unusual toleration of non-official peace activities within the church in recent years must be seen in this light. (In spite of the sporadic repression of individuals there has been no direct confrontation with the church as an institution.) That is, the system is moving in the direction of a more relaxed and more flexible domestic policy. Today one encounters the most varied attitudes in the GDR: both amazing political tolerance and traditional conservative Sicherheitspolitik. Using the example of the unofficial peace movement, I will discuss these developing tendencies and thus attempt to shed light on the situation of the GDR in the 1980s.

Terms such as "peace movement" and "peace" have been monopolized by the GDR state since its founding in 1949; the mandate to "serve the cause of peace" is anchored in the constitution. For decades, virtually on a daily basis, the mass media have appealed to the individual to make his personal contribution. One means of supporting peace is the "all-around strengthening of socialism," which implies primarily that the population work ever more productively in order to develop an economically strong state. A SED slogan reads: "The stronger socialism becomes, the more secure peace will be." Another method is much more direct: long-term military service in the National People's Army (NVA). Here the motto is "Peace must be armed."

Today several tens of thousands of primarily young people in the GDR have their own personal conception of meaningful peace initiatives. They are not seeking confrontation with the state, and do not dispute that the government's desire for peace is genuine, but they differ from the state in regard to the mode of securing peace and the concept of peace itself. Instead of relying on military strength and deterrence, they envision the joint securing of peace by means of gradual disarming and confidence-building measures. They believe that external peace depends on the internal peace of a society. Thus the concept of peace is broadened to include societal and environmental well-being.

This unofficial peace movement cannot be defined as classically dissident and isn't hiding behind some popular issue while in reality desiring something entirely different (i.e., a complete change of the system or "Sturz der Herrschenden"); it is not pro-West in its orientation. These peace activists are unorganized--precisely because everything else in the GDR is. Still, they are very much a movement; their concerns bind them together in a non-institutionalized manner, and they believe that collectively they can bring about political change. The existential threat of nuclear war has awakened in them a feeling of co-responsibility for the securing of peace.

It was not possible for the young people to form their own peace organization, to open their own offices, hold their own demonstrations, etc. They could and did however join forces with the one relatively autonomous mass organization in the GDR, the evangelical churches, to which half of the GDR population--approximately eight million people--still belongs. The new peace initiative merged with that of the church. This is a source of conflicts within church peace groups: conflicts between Christian-motivated and politically motivated peace engagement.

The GDR church has been nurturing its own peace conceptions for decades. The church's definition of peace is rooted in the Gospel; its essentials include non-violence, love of one's enemies, and trust. In spite of the common utopian vision of an unarmed and non-violent future, fundamental tensions between the Christian and socialist understanding of peace still remain.[2] The characteristic stringency of the socialist definition of peace excludes the possibility of any other position. Still, the churches in the GDR, as the only organizations which have retained their autonomy in the face of the SED's virtual monopoly in representing the populace, have a unique role in GDR society, a role which churches in the West, where there are many autonomous social institutions, do not play.

Two examples of church peace work during the past two decades seem particularly pertinent: the church's strong support of the right of conscientious objection during the 1960s[3] and its present support of a non-military alternative form of service ("Sozialer Friedensdienst"); and its struggle against the introduction of military instruction ("Wehrkundeunterricht") as a required course for ninth and tenth graders in the schools in the late 1970s.[4]

The months prior to the introduction of "Wehrkundeunterricht" in September 1978 were filled with waves of petitions ("Eingaben") from individuals and groups addressed to the state authorities. Appeals were also made to the churches in the hope that they might aid in the struggle to convince the authorities to cancel their plans to instate this new school course. The ensuing church protest failed. This relatively stormy and public dispute between church and state did result however in increased sensitivity on the part of the church and population in regard to subsequent state measures which have led to an ever greater militarization of GDR society.

Since the introduction of military instruction for ninth and tenth graders in 1978, military "fitness-making procedures" have been extended to include eleventh graders and apprentices. All students (including not only theologians, but also women) at state universities are now required to attend paramilitary sports camps during school vacations. The campaign to encourage voluntary longer enlistment in the army has been strengthened; obligating oneself to serve three years, instead of eighteen months, in the military is, for example, sometimes made a condition for boys' being allowed to go on to the Erweiterte Oberschule.

The fight against this militarization of society has played a major role in the peace work of the church as well as of the youth groups on the fringe of church activities. An example is the initiative requesting the creation of a "Sozialer Friedensdienst," an alternative form of service completely outside the military. In May 1981 three co-workers of the Evangelical Lutheran Church of Saxony composed a petition, which was circulated throughout the country and had collected 5,000 signatures by the fall. [5] Church leaders presented the case to the government, which responded with a resounding "no" on the issue. [6]

A second example is the open letter to Erich Honecker written by the East Berlin pastor Rainer Eppelmann and made public in September 1981. [7] In this appeal Eppelmann demanded an end to certain militaristic aspects of GDR society including: the distribution of war toys, the glorification of soldiers in school classes, school visits to army barracks, the presence of military hardware at carnivals, and military parades on national holidays. He also demanded the elimination of all measures against persons who express pacifist views.

Such demands are typical. They show that the GDR non-state peace movement is rooted in the specific conditions of GDR society and was not imported from the West. This peace initiative existed long before the missile dispute and the Western mass demonstrations.

The church protest against the introduction of military instruction in the schools in 1978 was not a hand-picked act of peace; it was rather a simple reflex action to measures taken by the state. This dispute evoked, however, the desire for a long-term and well-planned peace effort. Peace committees were set up in churches; one of the slogans they devised: "Education for Peace." In the following I will sketch the development of the church-supported peace movement in the 1980s, giving some of the milestones, and then go on to discuss the peace activities and concepts of the young people.

A thesis paper, written in 1979 by the Friedensreferat der Theologischen Studienabteilung beim DDR-Kirchenbund and addressed to peace groups, criticizes the tactics of the state peace movement:

> Public appeals, mass demonstrations, and propagandistic statements in the press and radio concerning disarmament and the restriction of these statements to specific stereotypical thought patterns and political options have led to massive over-saturation. The result is that the true core of these statements is frequently no longer heard. Media campaigns are in danger of producing resentment and rejection, thereby achieving the opposite of what they initially intended. [8]

The paper, pointing out the lack of concern with disarmament issues on the part of a broad spectrum of the church population, demanded that the church gain a new critical awareness of disarmament. This awareness should: 1) probe the causes of arms escalation; 2) criticize all concepts of security which are based solely on the might of weaponry; 3) support peace education; 4) demonstrate a concrete direction for the future through personal peace efforts (p. 94).

An example of this resolution was given that same year at the synod of the Evangelical Church of the Church Province Saxony in Halle, where the discrepancy between the peace ovations of the SED and its call for increasing military readiness was noted. A statement from its summary paper reads: "We approve of and support the efforts of our government to attain disarmament and peace. But we cannot reconcile this with certain developments in our society, such as the introduction of military education, the forced expansion of civil defense programs, and the fostering of hate effigies ["Feindbilder"]." [9]

The first peace week ("Friedensdekade"), initiated by the evangelical churches of the GDR, took place from November 9-19, 1980. Its motto, which was to reflect a basic idea of the GDR non-state peace movement, was "Make peace without arms" ("Frieden schaffen ohne Waffen"). Material prepared for this event urged people to articulate their "new perceptions" in conversations with both the church and the government. The suggestion was made that letters with the following message be sent to the Volkskammer: We thank you for all past efforts regarding disarmament and ask for their continuation in the form of "significant steps taken right here in this country." [10]

The "Friedensdekade" has come to be a central annual activity of the churches. It has been held four times (1980-1983) so far, without state intervention. According to statements made by representatives of the GDR Kirchenbund in conversation with the author, approximately 90% of all parishes have participated. That is to say, even in the villages and small towns, practically speaking wherever there's a church, there have been activities--attended, in my estimation, by several tens of thousands of people. The numbers have increased continuously. The participants are predominately members of the intelligentsia and people engaged in social professions; but many young workers also take part. Writing letters to state offices is only one of the many activities. The ten-day program includes such varied activities as poetry readings, fasting, peace services, discussions, exhibits, and theater performances.

The leitmotif "Frieden schaffen ohne Waffen" expresses the conviction that peace cannot be guaranteed by military strength and deterrence. This position of the church was expressed most clearly in declarations emanating from the Evangelical Church of the Church Province of Saxony, which convened in Halle in the fall of 1981. A special declaration formulated there protested against the concept of securing peace by means of military measures. The synod went so far as

to propose that the Warsaw Pact governments take uni-
lateral steps to encourage the process of disarmament,
for example, the withdrawal of SS-20 missiles and the
reduction of the Warsaw Pact's superiority in tanks.
Some church representatives at the Halle synod let it
be known that they would have liked to be even more
precise, but that it had proven impossible to attain
the necessary consensus among the various provincial
churches in the GDR and the sister churches in the
Federal Republic to formulate a clear rejection of the
system of deterrence. [11]

In January 1982 the East Berlin pastor Rainer Eppelmann issued an appeal which attracted attention
around the world, the "Berliner Appell - Frieden schaffen ohne Waffen."[12] The petition, which invited signatures from the GDR population, demanded the withdrawal
of all occupation forces from German soil and the creation of zones without atomic weapons in Europe. The
East Berlin church hierarchy could not support the appeal and expressed its reservations concerning both
the style and content of Eppelmann's petition. The
state lost no time in reacting to the "Berlin Appeal";
within hours of its publication in the Western press
and a subsequent meeting of the Politbüro, security
police arrested Eppelmann and numerous other signato-
ries. All were however released after having been in-
terrogated for two days, and the legal proceedings
were halted.

Eppelmann's role in the church is disputed, not
least of all because he has been an intermediary between the church and dissidents such as Robert Have-
mann, who was a co-signer of the "Berliner Appell."
He has also been criticized within the church for not
having properly informed the young pacifists who responded to the petition of the risks involved and the
limitations of their engagement, and for not having
encouraged them to use reason. The actions of the
young people are indeed often evoked more by emotion
than reason, a fact which is understandable given the
grounds of their discontent.

The reasons for the protest of GDR youth against
the militarization of their society are illustrated by
handmade posters circulating among young GDR citizens.
One displays the legs of marching soldiers and quotes
from the book released by the military publishing
house of the GDR: "A war for the defense of the socialist fatherland is beautiful. This is of course
not due to the destruction of material goods and the

loss of human lives, but rather to the high and lofty goal, the noble struggle, and the heroic deeds accomplished in the name of the people and the workers in the entire world. Such a war allows no vulgar sentiment to arise within the combatant, but rather evokes strong and pure passions producing beautiful and humane qualities within that person."[13] Another poster done by an East Berlin youth cites Soviet Marshall Yeremenko: "A feeling of beauty arises within me when I observe an organized attack by troops. It is not coincidental that one speaks of the art of commanding troops. An orchestra conductor, the artistic director of a theater, and a military commander do not only supervise; they also receive aesthetic satisfaction thereby."[14]

As long as official pronouncements of this kind exist, pacifists will react negatively to them. The GDR peace activists want an open discussion of these and other problems. The possibility of publicly expressing such opinions represents something new in the GDR. Today--at least at church-sponsored meetings--an unusual openness prevails. An early example of this was the 1981 "Dresdener Friedensforum."

On Februray 13, 1981, the thirty-sixth anniversary of the destruction of Dresden, 5,000 people gathered in Dresden's Kreuzkirche for a public discussion with church representatives on the subject of peace. Young people had come from all parts of the country. They had streamed out of arriving trains, clearly identifiable by the emblems they wore on their parkas and jackets. Some wore headbands with the inscription: "Make peace without arms." Here for the first time it was readily apparent that a new movement had been conceived. This meeting, which had come about thanks to the grass-roots pressure of the most sundry peace groups, received official church approval and was therefore spared from confrontation with government security forces; an independent youth meeting would have undoubtedly been brought to a halt.

This unusually candid discussion marked a milestone in the political landscape of the GDR. State fears of violent demonstrations had proven to be unfounded. After the meeting many of the participants walked to the ruins of the Frauenkirche, where they lighted candles and held vigil until midnight. In this way they commemorated the horrors of war and demonstrated their desire for peace, thereby showing the government that the means of their struggle for peace were to be peaceful also.

The growing disagreement over the question of peace was clearly visible in the wake of the second "Friedensdekade," which was held in November 1981. Young people had discovered the Old Testament saying "swords to plowshares" and supplemented it with a drawing of the statue representing this idea which was given to the United Nations by the Soviet Union. They sewed the emblem on their parkas and jeans, used it as a bookmarker, and pasted it on their mopeds.

The ever increasing distribution of this emblem, which coincided with a counter-campaign of the SED ("Peace must be defended, peace must be armed."), irritated the authorities and resulted in police over-reaction and coercion. In Rostock, Halle, Dresden, and East Berlin, teachers forced students to remove the emblem from their clothing. Young people were picked up by the police and hauled off to the police station. A group of Christians who had arrived in Halle for a church event were prevented from leaving the train station until they removed their emblems. Car windows were pasted over when the emblem was attached on the inside; emblems on the outside were meticulously scratched off. The same was true for apartment doors. One East Berlin youth was required to pay a penalty of 150 marks. The charge read:

> You broke the law on March 3, 1982 by wearing in public a symbolic likeness inscribed with a pacifistic slogan. This gravely disregarded the public's desire for protection and disturbed socialist communality ["Zusammenleben"]. . . . With this act you have infringed upon the sensitivities of a socialist state and caused undue annoyance. [15]

East Berlin's bishop, Gottfried Forck, who still today displays the celebrated emblem on one of his briefcases, complained in a message addressed to the congregations and dated April 14, 1982 that no clear information concerning the legal basis for the police action was proffered by the state. In a conversation with State Secretary Klaus Gysi on April 7, 1982, Bishop Werner Krusche and other officials of the Kirchenbund pointed out that the churches were at a loss to justify the government's position to their young people and that the methods employed by the government agencies gave reason to fear damage to the personal development of the young people involved. At the same time, the church leadership stressed that it was not interested in a further sharpening of the conflict. [16]

This position is characteristic of the evangelical churches in the GDR today. The church serves as mediator between the government and critically-minded youth groups. It attempts to foster understanding in state circles for the good intentions of the young people, and, at the grass-roots level, it strives to bring about a realistic estimation of what can be achieved under the present conditions. Despite their broad commitment to peace, the churches do not want to place themselves at the head of an independent peace movement. Bishop Hempel of Saxony, for example, spoke of the "limitations" of the church at the first peace forum in Dresden; it had become clear already then that the church's integrative capability is conditional. [17] The church carries out its own peace work, which at times overlaps with non-church initiatives, and is careful not to go beyond certain limits.

As mediator the church is mistrusted by both sides. From the one side come accusations of opportunism; from the other, accusations of being an opposition movement. Church leaders must live with this tension, for their political latitude is indeed limited. The church's eight million members form a political mélange, and the church leadership must take these differences into account.

The peace discussions and initiatives have continued since the deployment of the new missiles in the Federal Republic in the fall of 1983 and the subsequent additional deployment of Soviet missiles in the GDR. The church is concerned above all with the "renunciation of the spirit and logic of deterrence" ("Absage an Geist und Logik der Abschreckung"). [18] In the course of the year 1983 the non-state peace movement in the GDR branched out. [19] Church groups attempted--with varying degrees of success--to take part in official peace demonstrations with their own, sometimes pacifistic, slogans. Women's groups ("Frauen für den Frieden") were formed in several cities. Other groups participated in worldwide fasts.

In 1983 seven Kirchentage, attended by more than 200,000 people, were held in the GDR. At these meetings peace issues and other problems of GDR society were discussed with an openness reminiscent of Western freedom of speech. The year of the Luther celebration left deep marks in the GDR. The state will most likely continue to tolerate the church's peace activities--even though there will be occasional conflicts. The non-church groups will have a more difficult time of it. Some disappointed peace workers have chosen to leave the GDR; others turned to more radical acts and were arrested. But on February 13, 1984 several thousand young people gathered once again in Dresden for a peace service. Their quiet demonstration with candles and peace songs near the ruins of the Frauenkirche was not disturbed by the state security forces.

A closer look at the unofficial GDR peace movement shows that those involved are not only concerned with peace. The issue of an alternative lifestyle was raised already at the original peace forum in Dresden. It was pointed out that there is a logical connection between the peace movement and the movement to save the environment. [20] After all, what would be gained if external peace were secured and the countryside nevertheless destroyed. Ecological awareness and interest in alternative lifestyles go hand-in-hand with the struggle for peace, the same being true vice versa.

Many who were present at the Dresden peace sessions in February 1982 also participated in church-sponsored ecological campaigns during the following months. Such small-scale campaigns have become tradition in cities such as Leipzig, Dresden, Schwerin, Rostock, Neustrelitz, and East Berlin. They usually entail young people meeting for a weekend to discuss ecological issues such as alternative agriculture and nuclear power, and to plant trees, occasionally with the support of the state-owned landscaping firm, VEB Stadtgrün. The GDR media rarely deal with environmental questions; the ecological campaigns attempt to compensate for this information deficit.

The third annual campaign "Mobile without Cars" took place June 4-5, 1983, and involved dozens of GDR cities. Independent bicycle demonstrations have occurred in East Berlin and Leipzig, among other places. Even though--as is the case in the West also--these forms of criticism of present-day civilization are limited to small groups of people, their effect upon GDR society should not be underestimated.

In 1980 an ecology group in Wittenberg formulated the view that human labor should no longer be primarily directed toward the additional accumulation and accelerated consumption of material goods but rather increasingly toward intellectual or cultural activities, social concern, and a responsible lifestyle instead.[21] The group maintained that societal wealth includes not only material wealth but intellectual-cultural wealth as well, i.e., is the sum of all things that lead to the enrichment of human existence. The paper goes on to state that this interpretation of societal wealth requires a modification of both societal and individual goals; and that these changes would require sacrifice.

Sacrifice and renunciation are common topics at youth meetings. The young people express their willingness to forego the achievements of their parents' generation in favor of human relationships and character traits such as openness, tolerance, and honesty. People are viewed as the greatest wealth.

A kind of youth counterculture exists in the GDR, too. Numerous thousands of young people in East Berlin, Dresden, Leipzig, and other large cities subsist in a sort of internal emigration. Their outlook on life conforms in many ways to that of the West Berlin youth scene. Characteristic of both is the gap between generations. For many of these young people in the GDR the traditional Western and Prussian-German values no longer have appeal. Material prosperity and the collecting of consumer items--be it living-room furniture or a weekend cottage with garden patch--have lost priority. A glance at recent GDR literature, the latest GDR films, or youth culture in the large metropolitan centers--this includes "punks" as well as other disenchanted young people--readily shows that this phenomenon is already a major social movement. Yet a state dialogue with this segment of GDR youth has not yet taken place.

In my opinion, the unofficial peace movement and the ecological movement, as well as the dissatisfaction of young people with the accomplishments and life style of their parents, are here to stay. They have become a political factor with which the SED will have to learn to deal. In earlier years repressive measures could be counted on to silence individual dissidents; this is however no longer the case. Young people are insisting on the right to express independent opinions, opinions that originate at the bottom, i.e., at the grass-roots level, and not with the state.

Government peace policies could, I believe, profit from supplementation by independent disarmament and peace initiatives. In my view, the politics of détente in the 1980s will have to develop from the bottom to the top. The peace movement in the West and the independent peace movement in the GDR have much in common: both renounce the system of deterrence, the official position of both the FRG and GDR governments; in both countries, a reduction of values involving national, collective, and personal identity is noticeable among young people. Identification with their respective political and economic systems has subsided--without having been replaced by a shift to the other system as an alternative. The movements in East and West can no longer be--nor do they desire to be--classified using the traditional schematics of East versus West, capitalism versus socialism. The trauma of a basic dichotomy between the systems appears increasingly anachronistic. The hate effigies of the past are being reduced as people on both sides of the Wall discover a common point of reference, their interest in lasting peace.

Today there are many various groups in East and West desirous of the opportunity to engage in dialogue with one another. A new peace effort on this level--in contrast to the stalled official negotiations--is conceivable. This is a truly new dimenstion of détente.

The GDR peace movement can make a contribution here. As one churchman in Potsdam stated:

> If the participants in the new GDR peace movement could make the transition from letting off steam to a serious discussion of the actual issues, from the plowshare utopia to constructive imagination regarding possible new steps, then one could achieve genuine political relevance instead of expending oneself in fruitless skirmishes with the government.[22]

Berliner Arbeitsgemeinschaft für
Kirchliche Publizistik

Notes

[1] This transformation is neither particularly spectacular nor rapid. It takes a sensitive eye even to spot it, and of course such changes need to be seen in their larger context. Attempts to alter the interpretation of history (for example, the re-evaluation of the Prussian and Lutheran heritage), discussions within the educational system, changes in administrative and economic structures, developments in the cultural realm, and experiments involving the church are all part of the larger context. The attempts of the Party to lessen the economic pressures by decelerating the modernization process are insufficiently recognized. It is obvious that these factors affect the political realm.

[2] See Theo Mechtenberg, "Die Friedensverantwortung der Evangelischen Kirchen in der DDR," in Reinhard Henkys, ed., Die evangelischen Kirchen in der DDR (Munich: Christian Kaiser, 1982), pp. 355-99.

[3] See Wolfgang Büscher, Peter Wensierski, and Klaus Wolschner, eds., Friedensbewegung in der DDR. Texte 1978-1982 (Hattingen: Scandica, 1982), pp. 45-63.

[4] See Büscher, Wensierski, and Wolschner, eds., Friedensbewegung in der DDR. Texte 1978-1982, pp. 64-80.

[5] "Aufruf der Initiative 'Sozialer Friedensdienst' (9.5.1981)," in Friedensbewegung in der DDR. Texte 1978-1982, pp. 169-171.

[6] "After a lecture for theology students at the Humboldt University in East Berlin in 1981, the state secretary for church affairs in the GDR, Klaus Gysi, responded to student queries concerning the "Sozialer Friedensdienst." Reasons he gave for the state refusal included: 1) the constitutionally required readiness to defend the country; 2) the expectations of the Warsaw Pact that the GDR provide a fixed number of soldiers; 3) the view that the GDR's military strength is the greatest factor of all in securing peace. He maintained moreover that the term "Sozialer Friedensdienst" relegates armed service in the NVA to "antisocial war service." He pointed out that the vast majority of young Christians do active military service and that these people "should not be defamed" ("DDR-

Staatssekretär Klaus Gysi zum 'Sozialen Friedensdienst [12.9.1981]," in Friedensbewegung in der DDR, pp. 174-75).

7 "Brief von Rainer Eppelmann an Erich Honecker (24.9.1981)," in Friedensbewegung in der DDR, pp. 178-180.

8 "Erziehung zum Frieden - Möglichkeiten der Kirchen in der DDR im Bereich des Eintretens für Abrüstung," in Friedensbewegung in der DDR, pp. 83-84. Here and throughout the paper, translations into English from the German are my own.

9 "Beschluß der Synode der Ev. Kirche der Kirchenprovinz Sachsen in Halle (18.11.1979)," in Friedensbewegung in der DDR, p. 108.

10 Friedensbewegung in der DDR, p. 122.

11 See epd-dokumentation, No. 31/1981.

12 "Der 'Berliner Appell - Frieden schaffen ohne Waffen,'" in Friedensbewegung in der DDR, pp. 242-44.

13 This poster can be found in the archives of the Berliner Arbeitsgemeinschaft für Kirchliche Publizistik in West Berlin. The quotation is taken from Die marxistisch-leninistische Ästhetik und die Erziehung der Soldaten, which appeared in Dietz Verlag in 1979.

14 The Yeremenko quote is from Die marxistisch-leninistische Ästhetik und die Erziehung der Soldaten, p. 69.

15 The charge can be found in the archives of the Berliner Arbeitsgemeinschaft für Kirchliche Publizistik in West Berlin.

16 No official report of this discussion was published. The information stems from private sources.

17 "Fragen und Anworten beim Dresdener Friedensforum (13.2.1982)," Friedensbewegung in der DDR, p. 277.

18 See Joachim Garstecki, "Zukunft kirchlicher Friedensarbeit," Kirche im Sozialismus, 9, No. 3 (1983).

[19] See Wolfgang Büscher and Peter Wensierski, "'Der Atompazifismus ist hoffähig geworden.' Die Kirche und die Friedensbewegung," in their Null Bock auf DDR. Aussteigerjugend im anderen Deutschland (Reinbeck bei Hamburg: Rowohlt, 1984), pp. 133-64.

[20] See Peter Wensierski and Wolfgang Büscher, Beton ist Beton. Zivilisationskritik aus der DDR (Hattingen: Scandica, 1981).

[21] Beton ist Beton, p. 72.

[22] The statement was made in private conversation with the author.

Volker Braun's "Geschichten von Hinze und Kunze": A New Look at an Old Problem

Christine Cosentino

Throughout the years, Volker Braun has been preoccupied with the troublesome relationship between the Party and the people, between the leaders and those being led--a conflict which the author defined in the following way as early as 1966:

> Der aufwühlendste Widerspruch zwischen den Leuten, die in die sozialistischen Revolutionen verwickelt sind, ist der neuartige zwischen den politisch Führenden (die bewußt die Umgestaltung der Gesellschaft organisieren oder bewußt oder unbewußt hemmen) und den Geführten (die bewußt oder unbewußt die Pläne realisieren oder kritisieren).[1]

Yet while in the 1960s Braun largely focused on the masses with the intent to provoke them into assuming a more critical and responsible attitude, in the 1970s he shifted his attention to the leaders, whom he holds responsible for the emergence of a highly stratified hierarchical structure which he repeatedly calls the "pyramid."[2] This growing polarization can be observed in a comparison of an earlier (published in the FRG in 1975) and a later (published in the FRG in 1981) version of the play Hinze und Kunze.[3] The earlier version shows a somewhat disgruntled worker, Hinze, who in spite of disagreements with the Party functionary Kunze, nevertheless shakes hands with him in conciliation at the end of the play. The later version, however, presents the "Hinze-Kunze" relationship as noticeably marred by tension, since Hinze--although still collaborating with Kunze--refuses to grasp his outstretched hand. The question of how to turn this tension into a constructive stimulus in the development toward socialism continues to intrigue the author with undiminished intensity.

At the end of the 1970s Braun explored new literary means of presenting this conflict, introducing the "Hinze-Kunze"-motif into a new genre, the novel. Finished in 1981, the "Hinze und Kunze" novel is still unpublished. The ever-fighting pair also meets again in a number of short, didactic narratives called the "Geschichten von Hinze und Kunze." In the summer of 1980, thirteen of the "Geschichten von Hinze und Kunze" were published for the first time in the Scottish GDR Monitor;[4] one year later, twelve of these reappeared together with nine new stories in the West German journal Das Argument.[5] The GDR journal Sinn und Form followed suit in 1982, republishing twenty of the "Hinze und Kunze" pieces from Das Argument, plus a new one, "Bevor der Ofen aus ist."[6] According to GDR author Manfred Jendryschik, who is also a Lektor at the Mitteldeutscher Verlag, a copious collection of over eighty "Geschichten von Hinze und Kunze" will appear soon in book form in the GDR.[7]

Braun's "Geschichten" are parable-like, illustrative narratives which end with an aphoristic climax, a statement of some evident political truth or desired truth. The razor-sharp wit of these little gems stems from a seemingly playful investigation of language and hackneyed jargon that aims to lay bare a clash of dialectically opposing forces, the "Führende" and "Geführte." The reader will inevitably be reminded of Brecht's didactically provocative Herr Keuner, whose name connotes the anonymous pronoun adjective "keiner" but also suggests that everybody has a bit of "Keuner" in him. Similarly, Hinze und Kunze--by the very nature of the German idiom--characterize "everybody," i.e., the people, or "Führende" and "Geführte." The structure of the individual parables is twofold: some are dialogues between Hinze and Kunze, and others are the author's reflections about some striking revelations concerning Hinze or Kunze, or about Hinze and Kunze's relationship to each other.

Braun calls his parables "Geschichten"--a suggestive and symbolically multifaceted term. It means "story," but it is also reminiscent of the German idiom "Geschichten machen" ("to get into trouble"), or of the phrase "Geschichte machen" ("to make history"). In addition, these "Geschichten" are "Gleichnisse," the original meaning of which is "Abbild," i.e., "im-

96

age" or "concept": an "Abbild," thus, of the politically maturing worker, Hinze, and of Kunze, the Party.
It should be mentioned here that in several of his essays Braun repeatedly uses the keyword "Abbild," "Gebilde," and "Vorbild" to delineate his concept of political development and progress. By deconceptualiz-
ing the figures of Hinze and Kunze and by stripping
them of clichés, Braun proceeds from "Abbild" to "Gebilde," which means flexibility and dialectical movement toward the synthesis of the "Vorbild." All twenty-one parables reflect this "Gebilde" as a process of
sometimes strained, sometimes congenial, and often
sarcastic interaction.

In "Die großen Worte," Braun sets the tone and
target of his "Geschichten" by aiming caustic polemics
at the GDR government's custom of coming up with pret-
tified versions of reality, its obsessive practice of
"große Worte machen" when honest words would be in order. Years before, the probing Herr Keuner had voiced
similar criticism which was somewhat mitigated, however, by Brecht's choice of the neutralizing and dif-
fusing personal pronoun "we":

> "Ich habe bemerkt," sagte Herr K.,
> "daß wir viele abschrecken von unse-
> rer Lehre dadurch, daß wir auf alles
> eine Antwort wissen. Könnten wir
> nicht im Interesse der Propaganda ei-
> ne Liste der Fragen aufstellen, die
> uns ganz ungelöst erscheinen?" [8]

Braun, in contrast to Brecht, splits the "we" into
"I," i.e., Hinze, and "you," i.e., Kunze, and only in
the aphoristic punch line does the "we" appear as an
envisioned goal and the ultimate premise for true interaction:

> Kinze fragte Hinze, warum er mit so
> kalter Miene einhergehe und die Tä-
> tigkeiten im Lande herabwürdige, die
> er doch selber unablässig tue. Siehst
> du, sagte Hinze, ich bin vielleicht
> nicht gegen diese Unternehmungen, die
> vermutlich nötig sind, ich ertrage
> aber nicht, daß ihr sie mit so groß-
> artigen Namen nennt. Laß uns sagen,
> was wir machen, und du wirst mich
> womöglich lächeln sehn. (p. 588) [9]

Braun's specific mention of "lächeln" in his polemics against bombastic verbiage brings into focus another crippling disease which inhibits healthy communication: Kunze's dogged seriousness and lack of humor. The reader will be reminded of Kipper Paul Bauch's inflammatory description of the GDR: "Das ist das langweiligste Land der Erde,"[10] and of Braun's numerous pleas in his poetry for giving cathartic laughter its due place in the solution of serious problems. The absence of humor and its manifold manifestations of generosity, openness, and flexibility are seen as a stifling obstacle in the process of communication, and tantamount to stagnation. In "Ernste Regierung," Hinze raises this issue by playfully advising Kunze how to prevent political dissent: the government should simply relocate dissenting political factions to isolated areas, factions like:

> die realen und unrealen Sozialisten,
> Anarchisten, Maoisten, unsicheren
> Kantonisten usw. Kunze hielt aber das
> Pamphlet zurück und beteuerte, die
> Regierung habe keinen Humor.--Das
> macht nichts, erwiderte Hinze eitel.
> --Aber sie versteht keinen Spaß, ver-
> sicherte Kunze.--Das ist etwas ande-
> res, sagte Hinze, dann kann man nicht
> ernst machen. (p. 591)

By toying with official slogans, Braun exposes the stilted locutions of the bureaucrats as a deliberate device to camouflage a vacuum: the blatant disparity between "Führende" and "Geführte." A few years earlier, in the poem "Material II: Brennende Fragen," he had drawn attention to this very vacuum by calling it by its true name, "[das], was fehlt":

> Die . . . Worte (Reizwörter, Sprach-
> Regelungen, Memoranden zwischen den Zeilen
> Zu entziffern) haben mehr Wirkung
> Als die Dinge
> warum? weil sie verdecken
> Verallgemeinern, vervielfältigen
> weil sie verdecken was fehlt.[11]

In the "Hinze und Kunze" story "Der Unterschied," Braun sheds light again on this disparity. He sets out by demonstrating that lexical concepts like "wenig" or "viel"--when steeped in the ideology of Real-sozialismus--change in the eyes of the political beholders:

> Hinze und Kunze unterschied wenig.
> Das Gehalt, die Verantwortung, die
> Befugnisse - und daß Kunze den Unter-
> schied für nicht aufregend hielt.
> (p. 590)

The next story is a follow-up on the previous one. Braun calls for a new investigation of the political premise "Gemeinsamkeit." Hinze and Kunze's so-called mutual interests appear satirized from the start, in the very title of the anecdote, which is bluntly worded "Falscher Ausgangspunkt":

> Hinze und Kunze arbeiteten für <u>die
> gemeinsame Sache</u>! Was die gemeinsame
> Sache war, ließ sich nur sehr allge-
> mein sagen. Der gemeinsamen Sache
> war besonders hinderlich, daß sie im-
> mer die Gemeinsamkeiten betonte.
> (p. 590)

The political dichotomy now clearly established, Braun probes deeper into the problem by listing its manifestations. In a story with the ironic title "Sozusagen," he projects Hinze and Kunze as going through identical daily routines. But by rendering these activites in a contrasting juxtaposition of simple modes of expression with the embellishing rhetoric of the GDR's official press, Braun reveals the idea of "sameness" as being strikingly erroneous, or--according to his "Gebilde"-concept--as in dire need of open debate:

> Wenn Hinze redete, redete er. Wenn
> Kunze redete, führte er aus oder er-
> klärte unter großem Beifall.
> Wenn Hinze in Freital war, war er in
> Freital, während Kunze weilte und es
> zu freundschaftlicher Begegnung kam.
> Wenn Hinze in der Kantine aß, aß er,
> aber wenn Kunze in der Kantine aß,
> war das Fernsehen da.
> Wenn Hinze gestorben ist, ist er ge-
> storben. Wenn es Kunze trifft, ist
> er von uns gegangen und sein Ableben
> ein großer Verlust, denn er ist ein
> teurer Toter. (p. 590)

The nature of sharing has thus evolved as disturbingly complex. It can no longer exclusively be defined as Hinze and Kunze's common ownership of the means of production, a concept so unquestioned by

99

both and so basic to their most primitive human needs that its very existence is only mentioned in conjunction with the economic structure of the capitalist West. When asked during a visit in the other part of Germany why he, who after all has had his share of problems in the GDR, does not want to stay in the West, Hinze states one vital condition, the abolition of private property:

> Nur diese Bedingung; es gehört zu meinen primitivsten Lebensvoraussetzungen, nicht auf privates Eigentum zu sehn . . . Sehen Sie, sagte er, es ist mir schon physisch zuwider. Es bereitet mir körperliches Unbehagen . . . . Ich habe keine Lust, mich so alten Problemen gegenüberzusehen . . .
> ("Hinzes Bedingung," pp. 590-91)

But if sharing economic property is--according to Hinze--"old hat" ("ein alter Hut"), the idea of Hinze and Kunze's sharing in the very private and emotional sphere poses a delicate problem that has to be solved sometime in the future on the road to communism. In the anecdote "Ideologische Schwäche," Hinze jokingly raises the question of how to apply the ideological principles of communism to Kunze's own private affairs: desire, love, possessiveness, and marriage. Is it not egotistic of Kunze to desire a beloved woman just for himself and to earmark her through a marriage contract as "his" woman?

> Hinze sagte seinem Freund, daß er es egoistisch finde, diese liebliche Frau zu heiraten. Aber wie immer, wenn Hinze persönlich wurde, nahm es Kunze für einen Scherz. (p. 588)

But Hinze, too, gets emotionally involved with another woman. Looking at his own wife and the other suitors of the woman, he weighs the emotional gains and losses in the ensuing turmoil, shrugs his shoulders with comic resignation, and muses:

> Was war denn Glück, wenn es so viele trennte, um zwei zu einen? Es war noch eine sehr kostbare, sehr teure Sache, die man sich kaum leisten konnte. Man war noch eine arme Gesellschaft. ("Liebschaften," p. 590)

Judging from the parables discussed above, the reader might easily assume that Braun's sympathies rest with Hinze, who appears to be deprived and cheated of privileges promised to him. Yet if Braun's patience with the Party is worn, it certainly is not torn. When least expected, Kunze emerges as a low-key, unassumingly honest, and genuine representative of the masses. Endowed with what Braun envisions as the most noble political quality, i.e., uprightness ("aufrechter Gang"), he is willing to face harsh criticism even if it questions the foundations of the GDR state. By establishing freedom from political taboos, the fictionalized Kunze measures up to the highest political expectations--something that the SED has yet to do.

Turning Kunze into an active and probing agent in the "Gebilde"-process, Braun delineates his optimistic concept of "Vorbild," i.e., of what the Party ought to be. This is expressed in the parable "Bevor der Ofen aus ist," whose title suggests a pressing need for action before it is too late. In a tavern, Hinze and Kunze meet a disgruntled stoker who endlessly finds fault with the mismanaged plant where he works and who naggingly laments that his opinion is never sought in the "Arbeiter-und-Bauern-Staat":

> Statt daß man erst die Öfen besichtigt. Und sich seine Kunden ansieht. Und fragt, ob ich zurechtkomm mit dem Fortschritt. In der Bude, verstehst du, konkret, vor Ort, wo es Sache ist. Ob es mir paßt, ich meine, in den Kram hier! - Hinze beugte sich zu Kunze vor und zischte lächelnd: Aber diese Frage stellen heißt, den Staat infragestellen. Kunze, nach einer kleinen Weile, erwiderte barsch: Wenn das so ist, muß die Frage unbedingt gestellt werden. (p. 598)

But "den Staat infragestellen" ultimately does not mean that the Marxist Braun questions the goal of socialism pursued by the GDR government. The heretical point of this parable rather serves as an effective weapon against bureaucratic malpractice which threatens to stifle the revolutionary progress and bring it to a standstill; in other words, the phrase suggests the same idea which Braun conjured up a few years earlier with the metaphor of mountain climbing in the poem "Vom Besteigen hoher Berge." Not the goal of getting to the top of the mountain is in question but the choice of the right mountain: "Ist das überhaupt der Berg, den wir beehren / Oder eine ägyptische Pyramide."12

In the anecdote "Kommen und Gehen," Kunze laconically admits the extent of bureaucratic deformation. Communism will never become a reality unless the bureaucrats go:

> Hinze fragte: Wann kommt nun dein Kommunismus! Kunze erwiderte: Der kommt nie. Vielleicht, daß wir gehen. (p. 592)

Thus Kunze's bon mot points at the very distance of the utopian horizons and at the seemingly insurmountable obstacles which block the way toward the GDR's political goal. But Braun surrounds his "Geschichten von Hinze und Kunze" with an optimistic glow when he presents the strained relationship between "Führende" and "Geführte" as a temporary phase. In a manner reminiscent of the didacticism of biblical parables, Kunze uses the image of larval metamorphosis to voice his firm belief in the eventual coming of redeeming transformation: the emergence of the butterfly from the strictures of the cocoon. It should be mentioned that in his last volume of poetry, Training des aufrechten Gangs (1979), Braun published a poem, called "Larvenzustand,"13 with a very similar topic. But while in the poem, in an imagined dialogue with an alter ego, the author is preoccupied primarily with the state of larval confinement and his own feelings of political claustrophobia, in the parable "Larvenstadium," he transcends this restrictive phase for the sake of the greater whole: the entire developmental cycle, with the envisioned butterfly breaking out of the cocoon.

It is also noteworthy and indicative of Braun's lingering optimism that he puts suggestively provocative code words into Kunze's mouth--code words which he has earmarked throughout the years as an effective tool to stir up debate or "restlessness": "kriechen," "sich einpuppen," "werden," "Unbehagen," "eng," "dunkel," "Hülse," "Druck,"--and of paramount importance-- "sprengen." By allowing Kunze to speak the final words and by letting him assume several seemingly contradictory roles at the same time--the role of teacher and antagonist, leader and provocateur, friend and critic--Braun uses his faith in the Party's leadership

102

as a provocative means of criticizing the Party:

> Hinze beklagte sich intern, daß die
> freie Gesellschaft der unterdrückten
> gleiche: daß sie, als die Herren, wie
> Knechte lebten. Kunze mochte ihn
> nicht beruhigen und deutete ungefähr
> in die Luft: Siehst du den Schmetter-
> ling? Bevor er sich in den Wind
> hebt, ist er die Raupe, die nur
> kriecht und frißt, und sich einpuppt,
> bis man sie nur für eine Mumie an-
> sehen kann: dies werdende Flügelwe-
> sen. So schrieb Lenin, der politi-
> sche Unterschied des Sozialismus zum
> Kommunismus werde möglicherweise
> größer sein als der des Kapitalismus
> zum Sozialismus. Wie wahr. Aber
> ebenso wahr und wichtig, sagte Kunze,
> ist unser Unbehagen, dem die neue
> Welt eng und dunkel dünkt wie eine
> Hülse, und unser Druck, der sie
> sprengen wird.
> ("Larvenzustand," p. 529)

Probably due to its "Vorbild"-character and optimistic outlook, Braun placed the parable "Larvenstadium" at the very end of the "Geschichten von Hinze
und Kunze." This parable, which emphasizes Braun's
critical loyalty to the GDR, would have lent itself
well as a conclusion of my paper. Instead, I have
chosen another anecdote, "Ein Hinundher,"--an anecdote
deeply rooted in the "Gebilde"-process and aimed at
answering a topical question, namely why Hinze consciously decided to stay in the GDR.

After the Biermann affair in 1976 and the subsequent exodus of writers to the West, Braun--one of
the twelve co-signers of the petition written on Biermann's behalf--expressed in his poetry strong feelings
of frustration and sadness. In the poem "Der Müggelsee,"[14] hitherto unpublished in the GDR, he bitterly
laments the sudden loss of friends and fellow artists
like Sarah Kirsch, Bernd Jentzsch, Wolf Biermann, and
Reiner Kunze, whose names are explicitly mentioned.
There are other poems in which he vaguely hints that
he himself has pondered the idea of exile. The poem
"Material IV: Guevara" with its interlinked narrative
perspectives of the first and third person singular
seems to point in this direction: "Soll ich aufbre-
chen, soll ich bleiben / bei meinen Worten."[15] A sim-

ilar notion is reflected in the poem "Spiegelgasse," which--after a short contemplation on the two exiled refugees Büchner and Lenin--abruptly ends with a question addressed to himself: "Dein Zimmer leer: wer wird es brauchen." [16]

In the anecdote "Ein Hinundher," Hinze all of a sudden decides he has had enough and leaves the GDR, but he returns and continues being Kunze's "restless" partner. Against the backdrop of a skillful blending of the phrases "er macht Geschichten" and "Geschichte machen," Braun depicts Hinze's change of mind as just that:

> Hinze antwortete plötzlich so: Hier
> bleibe ich, solange ich mitreden
> kann. Wenn es darum geht zu schwei-
> gen, dann ziehe ich die Bahamas vor.
> Bald darauf reiste er auf die Baha-
> mas. Aber er kam zurück, und Kunze
> verbreitete zynisch: Er schweigt doch
> lieber hier. Aber da war das Gerede
> schon da. (p. 591) [17]

Not surprisingly, it is again Kunze, who instigates and spreads the momentous rumor about Hinze's politi- cal failure. By alluding to a confluence of meanings stemming from the political keyword "reden," Braun in- timates that it is ultimately up to the individual to decide that "reden" means "mitreden," i.e., political participation, not simply "Gerede," i.e., settling for empty words, talk, or gossip.

Since most of the anecdotes show Hinze and Kunze in dialogue, Braun seems to suggest that socialism in the GDR has indeed the potential for a meaningful ex- change of power between the Party and the people. But by couching the concept of "mitreden" in the deroga- tory term of "Gerede," he also warns that this realis- tic goal has yet to be achieved.

Rutgers University

Notes

[1] Volker Braun, "Es genügt nicht die einfache Wahrheit," in Notate (Frankfurt/M: Suhrkamp, 1976), pp. 19-20.

[2] See Ian Wallace, "The Pyramid and the Moun-

tains: Volker Braun in the 1970s," The GDR under Honecker 1971-1981, GDR Monitor Special Series, No. 1 (Dundee, Scotland, 1981), pp. 44-45.

3 Volker Braun, "Hinze und Kunze," in Stücke I (Frankfurt/M: Suhrkamp, 1975). The second edition of Stücke I (1981) contains the later revision of the play.

4 Braun, "Geschichten von Hinze und Kunze," GDR Monitor, No. 3 (Summer 1980), pp. 1-4.

5 Das Argument, 23, No. 128 (July/August 1981), 487-90.

6 Sinn und Form, 34, No. 3 (1982), 588-92. The individual "Geschichten" are quoted from this source. Page references are given parenthetically in the body of the paper.

7 Mentioned during a conversation with the author in Philadelphia/USA, March 14, 1983. A Suhrkamp edition of the "Geschichten": Berichte von Hinze und Kunze (es 1169) appeared in December 1983, too late to be treated here.

8 Bertolt Brecht, "Überzeugende Fragen," Gesammelte Werke, Werkausgabe Edition Suhrkamp (Frankfurt/M: Suhrkamp, 1967), XII, 382.

9 The underlining is my own.

10 Braun, "Die Kipper," in Stücke I, p. 22.

11 Braun, "Material II: Brennende Fragen," in his Training des aufrechten Gangs (Halle: Mitteldeutscher Verlag, 1979), p. 48.

12 "Vom Besteigen hoher Berge," in Training des aufrechten Gangs, p. 34.

13 "Larvenzustand," in Training, pp. 62-65.

14 "Der Müggelsee," in Gedichte (Frankfurt/M: Suhrkamp, 1979), pp. 120-21.

15 "Material IV: Guevara," in Training, p. 55.

16 "Spiegelgasse," in Training, p. 20.

17 It is an open question whether Braun thought

of GDR writer Jurek Becker when he wrote "Ein Hinundher." In a 1977 interview in East Berlin, Becker said
he would stay in the GDR as long as he was allowed to
publish: "Wenn es allerdings darum geht, den Mund zu
halten, dann halte ich den Mund lieber auf den Baha-
mas" ("Ich glaube, ich war ein guter Genosse," Der
Spiegel, 18 July 1977, p. 133). Becker is now living
in West Berlin.

Toward Socialist Modernism:
Ulrich Plenzdorf's "kein runter kein fern" [1]

Ute Brandes

In the mid-sixties GDR writers began to show a
new interest in experimenting with literary topics and
forms. After an initial phase of uneasiness, the Party
welcomed these innovative tendencies which would soon
win considerable acclaim beyond the borders of the
GDR. In 1971 Erich Honecker announced that there were
to be no restrictions in matters of literary technique
as long as the works reflected a basic socialist outlook. [2] This programmatic statement, to be sure, had
not evolved from a linear development of cultural policy. Ever since the GDR was founded there had been
debates within the Party and the Writers' Union about
form and content of the desired socialist literature.
Periods of "thawing" were frequently followed by restrictions, especially on the publication of innovative texts. That even after Honecker's statement the
Party still has problems in accepting experimental
works is suggested by the fact that Ulrich Plenzdorf's
short story "kein runter kein fern" has not thus far
appeared in the GDR.

Plenzdorf's narrative, which distinguishes itself
by means of its extraordinary aesthetic experimentation and modernist techniques, was published in the
West in 1978. [3] This short story combines interior
monologue with montage, the two literary techniques
which were most sharply criticized by Marxist theo-
rists, first in the 1930s when the concept of socialist realism was initially formulated, and again in
1951 when the newly founded GDR proclaimed its campaign against formalism in art and literature in the
name of a progressive German culture. [4]

Plenzdorf's short story disproves the old notions
that interior monologue and montage must necessarily
lead to antirealist tendencies or reflect a lack of

107

interest in the important political issues.[5] The central point of this text is the very precise rendering of reality as it specifically exists in the GDR:
first, as a quasi-utopian product of public projections and, second, as a complex of the everyday pressures of private reality experienced by an individual. The short story takes place in the consciousness
of a distracted and bewildered ten-year-old boy whose
first name we are never told. Roaming Berlin in search
of a strategic spot close to the Wall, he hopes to
listen in on a West Berlin rock concert to be given by
the Rolling Stones. As he wanders through the city,
troubled and driven on by the inner voices rushing
through his mind, external voices pitched high with
emotion cut into his inner thoughts. On this day the
GDR is celebrating its twentieth anniversary with a
military parade. Public loudspeakers blare out music
and speeches, and an enthusiastic voice praises the
splendid world of socialism:

> Und da beginnt mit hellem Marschrhyth-
> mus unter strahlend blauem Himmel der
> Marsch auf unserer Straße durch die
> zwanzig guten und kräftigen Jahre un-
> serer Republik, unseres Arbeiter- und
> Bauernstaates, die großartige Gratu-
> lationscour unserer Hauptstadt zum
> zwanzigsten Geburtstag der DDR auf
> dem traditionellen Marx-Engels-Platz
> in Berlin. Auf der Ehrentribüne die,
> die uns diese Straße immer gut und
> klug vorangegangen sind, die Reprä-
> sentanten der Partei und Regierung
> unseres Staates, an ihrer Spitze Wal-
> ter Ul . . . . (p. 14)

At this point the boy suddenly "tunes out" the
official speech. It is clear that his mind is preoccupied with the words and rhythms of a different drum-
mer:

> sie sagn, daß es nicht stimmt, daß
> MICK kommt und die Schdons rocho aber
> ICH weiß, daß es stimmt rochorepocho
> ICH hab MICK geschriebn und er kommt
> rochorepochopipoar. . . ICH geh hin
> ICH kenn die stelle man kommt ganz
> dicht ran an die mauer und DRÜBEN ist
> das SPRINGERHAUS wenn man nah ran-
> geht, springt es über die mauer SPRIN-
> GERHAUS RINGERHAUS FINGERHAUS SIN-

GERHAUS MICK hat sich die stelle gut
ausgesucht wenn er da aufm dach steht,
kann ihn ganz berlin sehn und die andern Jonn und Bill und die und hörn
mit ihre ANLAGE. . . .(p. 13)

The montage of the radio broadcast into an interior monologue permits a side-by-side comparison of
a two-track reality, a phenomenon that often exists in
everyday life in the GDR. The loudspeaker voice represents the official level of reality with its highly
rhetorical claims regarding socialist values and virtues. The language "from above" clashes with the boy's
own voice "from below." His inner thoughts document
the dismal effects of the officially proclaimed ideological principles when they are too stringently applied to the life of an individual. This clash of
ideology with reality is clearly reflected in the linguistic contrast among three levels of speech within
the story:

The public voices, which stand out in the text in
italicized print, inundate the city as a constant
stream of sound, and together with traffic noise evoke
an impersonal, ever present backdrop of noise.

The second level of speech is a mixture of repeated snatches of earlier conversations, parental admonitions, and half comprehended political material
learned at school. This linguistic material has been
conveniently cut into shorter phrases, ready to be recalled and repeated. Such syntactical fragments still
appear in their correct grammatical notation. They
are set off in the text by dashes.

The third level is the truly subjective, inner
world of the boy. Here we find his own reflections:
snatches of repeated, thoroughly assimilated messages;
private expressions; rhythmically accented slang; and
prefabricated clichés which are part of his personal
consciousness. As soon as the linguistic material
from the first two levels sinks down into this private
environment, it becomes an integrated part of the
boy's own voice.

Plenzdorf confronts us with sharp differences in
point of view among these three levels of speech. The
more familiar the boy feels with a voice from the outside, the more quickly he makes it part of his private
idiom by deleting syllables, mixing up consonants or
vowels, and, in general, disregarding conventional

grammar. The newly created, reduced language, for
which he is reproached at home ("Er soll nicht immer
die Endungen verschlucken, deswegen schreibt er auch
falsch," p. 18) is clearly evidence of a socio-lin-
guistic disorder. With the help of this stylistic device Plenzdorf can very effectively and precisely
point to the boy's awareness of the world around him
and demonstrate how thoroughly he has absorbed and
mixed public and private voices. Graphic, syntactic,
and stylistic characteristics help the reader to distinguish the different levels of assimilation.

The following excerpt will illustrate the turbulent interplay of the three levels (1 = public voices,
2 = repeated material, 3 = subjective level) in the
interior monologue:

1 - banner	DDR 20 DDR 20 DDR 20 DDR 20
3 - perception	DDR 20 masse licht masse leute masse fahn -
2 - poem, school	Eins, zwei, drei, wenn die Partei uns ruft sind wir -
3 - perception	hier kommich nicht durch doch fahrn
2 - poem, school	- haben früh erfahren der Arbeit Frohngewalt in düstern Kinderjah-ren und wurden früh schon alt -
3 - self-address	masse ausländer
3 - nonsense-verse	hau du ju du im gummischuh slihp ju werri well in jur bettgestell? o werri matsch wat ju sei ist kwatsch
3 - address to fantasy partner	MAMA ICH kann englisch
1 - banner	Wir sind auf dem richtigen Weg! Folgt dem Beispiel unserer Be-sten! Stärkt die Republik mit Höchstleistungen in Wissen
3 - self-address	rathaus bitte melden ICH kann sie nicht sehn hallo
1 - loudspeaker or banner	Druschba - Freundschaft Druschba - Freundschaft - Drusch
3 - self-address	masse leute wenn die alle zu MICK masse licht rathaus ICH kann sie nicht sehn ICH bin geblen esbahn esbahn ist gut esbahn mussich
3 - nonsense-verse	durch esbahn fressbahn
1 - song	auch der Rhein wieder frei. Bre-chen den Feinden die Klauen, Thälmann ist immer dabei. . . . (pp. 28-29)

In the remainder of this article, I will elaborate on these three levels, pointing first to their content and form, then to the function of their interplay. I will then compare Plenzdorf's montage technique with that in Döblin's Berlin Alexanderplatz in order to ascertain the specific innovations of the more recent text and their meaning in the context of GDR literature.

1. Public voices (in italics)

With its loudspeaker messages the socialist state conveys its official image of a just and splendid society. It professes the immediate concern for its people as one of the guiding principles of its policies. The radio voice speaks of the public's spontaneous and grateful response to the state, evidenced by the crowds marching on the occasion of its twentieth birthday. Representatives of the National People's Army are singled out as they proudly display their shining military hardware. Youth are praised for their achievements in schools and factories. The "machtvolle Marschformation der FDJ" is advancing "auf der sonnenhellen Straße hinaus - hinaus ins dritte Jahrzehnt . . . (p. 25)

The public messages in Plenzdorf's text reproduce the highly controlled rhetorical language of the official GDR. In analyzing such speeches, one can identify three techniques of political persuasion. First, they elevate the Party and the government into a heroic stance of infallibility: "Auf der Ehrentribüne die, die uns . . . immer gut und klug vorangegangen sind, die Repräsentanten der Partei und Regierung unseres Staates" (p. 14). Secondly, one finds thinly veiled borrowings from religious concepts in a new socialist context: "Seidene Banner der Arbeiterklasse und unserer Republik schweben durch die Sonnenstrahlen herab" (p. 19). The population is appreciative and responds with the national anthem: "Die Hymne der Republik steigt, von den vielen Tausend gesungen, in den Himmel" (p. 25). Thirdly, the military aspects of the parade are transposed to the realm of aesthetic heroism. Even the sun competes with and reflects the magnificence of the war machinery: "Silberglänzende Panzerabwehrraketen . . . , die schlanken Rohre schützend zum Himmel gerichtet" (p. 15). Yet, in order not to frighten anyone, the speaker seeks to minimize the martial effect by suggesting order and beauty: "Die Fußtruppen der Land- und Luftstreitkräfte sowie der Volksmarine . . . ausgerichtet wie straffe Perlenschnüre, paradieren mit hellem Marschtritt unter winkenden Blumengrüßen . . . vorbei" (p. 14). The power of nature is also evoked: "Dann zittert die Luft. Schwere modernste Kettenfahrzeuge rasseln heran und dröhnen" (p. 15). Finally, the loudspeaker voice is drowned out by the prescribed "hurrahs."

There is no better illustration of the relative ineffectiveness of these public voices than the boy's reaction to them. Instead of guiding or inspiring him, they simply remain outside of his active train of thought as an ever-present background noise. But they continue to provoke the reader's sensitivity. The contrast between the highly organized mannerisms of propaganda and the boy's confused attempts at self-articulation make one aware that this public level of speech is not a natural means of expression anymore. It has been artificially harmonized and is boastingly exaggerated, so much so, in fact, that the claims of the loudspeaker voice have lost their basis in reality.

2. Repeated material (conventional language, but fragmented)

Interspersed with the public voices are parts of former conversations, admonitions, quotes from school texts, and songs which the boy repeats to himself. These fragmented phrases typify their original speakers in their demands upon the boy. One perceives the world of his family, his life at school, and his immediate everyday reality in general as a severely restrictive environment. The boy feels helpless when confronted by his doctrinaire father, who flatly forbids his hobby of woodworking. With strict rules and intimidation the father tries to combat his son's alleged laziness and thus improve his bad grades. He demands that the boy, a worker's son, become a doctor, while doctors' children should now be workers. The boy is not permitted to play outside or watch TV ("kein runter kein fern"). The father unquestioningly adopts the public principles of an achievement-oriented society as the guidelines for his son's intellectual growth. Such regimentation, however, serves only to cripple the boy on an emotional as well as intellectual level. The father refuses to accept the fact that his son is a slow learner. He believes that all learning disabilities and deviations from the norm have been cured by the new socialist order. This view is contradicted for the reader, however, when it is filtered through the boy's consciousness: "Schwachsinn ist doch nur eine Folge kapita warte mal also kapita wo soll im Sozialismus der Nährboden für Schwachsinn!" (p. 17). The father further demonstrates his tendency to see all matters in an orthodox ideological context when he equates his wife's hasty escape from their marriage with political wrongdoing: "Eure Mutter hat die Republik verraten . . . . Ich will das Wort Mama oder Mutter für diese Frau nicht mehr!" (p. 16).

Other voices running through the boy's mind are non-threatening. His principal and special education teachers encourage his particular skills. They try to help by speaking with the father. Although they take the boy's side, their stance does little more than make the father even angrier. In order to feel at least some emotional security, the boy "drops out" into his dream world with "MICK" and "MAMA" "in WESTN." He does not seriously reflect about the political differences of the two societies. As a matter of fact, he feels quite at ease with the past of the GDR (Thälmann, anti-fascism), which he has learned about in school. His projections about his own future (as "der GRÖSSTE GITARRNMACHER in WESTN," p. 24) do not indicate any political critique or preference, but rather reflect his own skill level and real job interest in a place far removed from the reach of his father.

3. Subjective level (lower case)

Among all the turbulent and disparate voices in the interior monologue, only the passages printed entirely in lower case letters render the speaker's own, private opinions. This personal level of language, however, is also the catchall for political and teenage jargon, which has been cut down into small, handy units, stored in his mind as ready-made phrases. For instance, when the boy thinks about techniques for working with wood, entire sentences from technical books automatically come to his mind. Although he strings together fragments, which are further reduced by his own speech disorder, his thoughts are still intelligible to the reader despite his mispronunciation and dyslexic anomalies:

> vorgelege . . . sind eine zusatzein-
> richtung zur erhöhung der drehzahl
> der welle zum ballspiel bei drechsel-
> bänkn bei der verarbeitung sehr sprö-
> der holzartn zum ballspiel kiefer die
> würde ja splittern es empfiehlt sich,
> bei kiefer kernholz zu nehm, wenn über-

                haupt zum drechseln eher von den ein-
                heimichen hölzern buche esche also
                kurzfasrige hölzer . . . (p. 20)

     The span of his inner world extends from such
rational concerns to intense internal dialogues with
his mother and to various irrational dreams of gran-
deur: "ICH hab jetzt ein zimmer und holz und eine
hoblbank und ICH bin der GRÖSSTE GITARRNMACHER in
WESTN" (pp. 24-25). By capitalizing the names of certain recurring persons, facts, and places Plenzdorf
points to a hierarchy of important subjects in the
boy's fantasy realm. ICH occurs most often (50 times
in 17 pages), then MICK (32), MAMA (20), ER (father,
17); DER (his brother Manfred, 15), VERRÄTER (Manfred,
5), ER (God, 13), WESTN (11), EIKENNGETNOSETTISFEK-
SCHIN (5). In this highly subjective realm of instant
gratification, Mick Jagger's lament "I can't get no
satisfaction" has thus become one of the more important private symbols. It is further interesting that
he calls both his father and God ER, his brother DER.
He often fuses his favorite figures MICK and MAMA into
the androgynous figure MICKMAMA, who will jump across
the wall and take him along.

     The boy is at the same time plagued by fears. In
the biblical story of Cain and Abel he discovers a
parallel to his own life.[6] The Old Testament myth
serves as a leitmotif on the subjective level of the
interior monologue; it also projects the outcome of
the action of the short story beyond the open end.
From his own experiences the boy understands that God
is secretly plotting against Abel, the younger brother, although he appears to favor him over Cain. When
Cain kills his brother, God curses the murderer, but
nevertheless permits him to lead a normal life:

                aber Er wußte es schon, daß abl tot
                war von kain und verfluchte kain und
                schickte ihn in die wüste und kein
                geld und nichts und da sagte kain,
                die schlagn mich tot und da sagte ER,
                das stimmt und ER machte ein zeichn
                an kain wahrcheinlich tinte und da
                durfte keiner kain totmachn, weil ER
                nämlich gar nichts gegen kain hatte
                die steckten unter einer decke son-
                dern gegen abl und kain konnte weg-
                ziehn und heiratn und alles und abl
                war tot . . . (p. 28)

                              114

For the boy, the figures of God and father, state and Party have fused together into one large concept of authority. God's injustice is absolute. He intrigues against the weak with secret, impenetrable plans. Cain and God are working together, just as the boy's brother, Manfred (a policeman) acts according to the wishes of his father (Party): "die steckten unter einer decke" (p. 28). This authoritarian force is out to punish, not to heal or make peace. But what is the boy to be penalized for? -- He does not pursue this. Instead he escapes into his dream world with MICKMAMA because there are no other avenues of communication open to him.

When one reflects on the interplay of the three levels of voices, more general patterns become apparent. Although the hard clash of the powerful forces of the state and the helplessness of the ten-year-old are always in the forefront of the reader's attention, one can also perceive other effects brought about by the montage of voices. When his thoughts hurriedly skip along their own paths, the boy only rarely pays attention to the loudspeakers. When they do catch his fancy, some slogans simply seem to swim along with the stream of consciousness without affecting his other thoughts. But sometimes, only seconds or minutes later, a key phrase is taken up. In the boy's own usage, however, it undergoes a change. A propaganda word suddenly gets stripped of its euphemistic veils and appears in its true sense. For instance, "die schlanken Rohre" in the phrase "Panzerabwehrkanonen, die schlanken Rohre schützend zum Himmel gerichtet" (p. 15), soon finds its way into the private vocabulary of the boy. He imagines that he is a tank and, in an act of fantasizing, takes terrible revenge on his father:

> und dann würdich mit meine schlankn
> rohre auf IHN losfahrn und dann würde
> ER wegrenn aber ICH würde IHM nach-
> fahrn und wenn er in ein haus rennt
> oder in seine DIENSTSTELLE, würdich
> davor in stellung gehn und sagn, gebt
> IHN raus oder ICH schieße das ganze
> haus in klump . . . . (p. 21)

The propagandistic tone which earlier covered up the belligerent hostility of the war machine has thus been stripped off, and the phrase has returned to its true meaning.

On this linguistic level of truth there is also a playful-ironic effect. When the boy repeats to himself the often-heard admonitions of his father, he shortens them into "bite-size" pieces. Fragmented and strung together in this way, they are revealed as truisms and clichés to the reader, who easily completes them:

> ausgerechnet er nicht, das kann doch
> bloß daran, daß er zu faul. Einfach
> zu! Nie hat es das! Sieh dir meinen
> Vater an. Unter dem Kapitalismus
> nicht mal als Arbeiterjunge. Die Fa-
> milie ernährn und wie hat er sich
> hoch. In den Nächten mit eisernem
> und morgens um vier. Von mir will
> ich ganz. Aber nimm seinen Bruder.
> Leistungen sehr, wenn auch noch. Kei-
> ne Klagen, weil vom ersten Tag an.
> (p. 18)

Another humorous aspect develops in the stark contrast between the carefully constructed official speeches--which are supposed to report reality first-hand--and the hasty and almost accidental sequence of the boy's own thoughts. As he wanders through the city, his attention shifts constantly from one topic to the next. His schoolboy idiom with its private idiosyncrasies, prefabricated snatches from TV and political banners, and curses accented by beat rhythms and slang, mirrors the everyday reality of his particular age and society--a level of truth which the cumbersome and ostentatious public language cannot express.

In all these examples one finds a dichotomy between the internal and external reality of the boy. Yet the story mirrors much more than just the psychological make-up of one individual. Plenzdorf's realistic depiction of this young mind easily captures the mentality of an entire generation; moreover, the consciousness of this ten-year-old reflects the tempo and the ideological character of Berlin/GDR.

When comparing "kein runter kein fern" to Döblin's Berlin Alexanderplatz, one finds many similarities. Just like his literary predecessor Franz Biberkopf, who wanders about the same streets some forty years earlier, Plenzdorf's figure is oversaturated and overtaxed by the signals around him. Döblin's protagonist also does not perceive the multi-faceted, fast-paced city as an organic whole. [7] In Berlin Alexanderplatz montage technique is used mainly to portray two different aspects of Biberkopf's life in the metropolis: first, montage reveals how his mind works by way of the signals which Franz registers, but does not reflect upon. For instance, when he first leaves the jail, his eye catches on a large number of unrelated public documents, but he does not process them mentally. Since he picks up few other signals from his surroundings, we can hypothesize that in this scene his mind is primarily fixed on authority. [8] Second, montage particles let the city itself move into the foreground. The authorial narrator in Berlin Alexanderplatz often steps back and such material as weather reports, ticker tape, song ditties, city slang, advertisements, and the names of streets literally pile up in the text; even the heraldic symbol of Berlin is graphically printed. [9] Thus Döblin characterizes first Franz in his idiosyncrasies and, secondly, the metropolis Berlin--both are of equal stature; man and city face and confront each other.

The differences between Plenzdorf's and Döblin's usage of montage become more apparent as soon as one imagines both works without these heterogeneous particles. Although the scope of Döblin's novel would be incredibly reduced, Biberkopf's story could still run its course. [10] It is impossible, however, to strip "kein runter" of its montage parts without dissolving the figure of the protagonist. In Plenzdorf's text, compact linguistic units and jargon have shifted to the psyche of the boy and are part of his mental constitution.

Here the creative process with which every human being makes the world his own by expressing it in individually felt and chosen words has deteriorated into passing on secondhand and thirdhand material. How passively the boy reacts to all voices from the outside is apparent in the way he acquires new particles of ready-made language. Any randomly picked-up expression can give a new direction to his train of thought. Even acoustical similarities can trigger a new chain of associations ("fahn," "fahrn," "erfahren," p. 28), and sometimes the sound and rhythm of words, not their lexical meaning, make them function as a collage of concrete signals ("Kirche . . . . kirschners kleener karle," p. 30).

When this outside material is assimilated into the boy's repertoire, he cuts it up in small segments, ready to be recalled as a fragmented syntactical block of words which now is substituted for the first-hand expression of his feelings:

> schon dunkl ist ja schon dunkl scheiß
> masse licht schon dunkl wars der mond
> schien helle als ein auto blitze-
> schnelle langsam um die ecke drinnen
> saßn B was machn die hier fahrn auto
> laß sie ICH muß renn schon dunkl MICK
> ICH komm! drinnen saßn drinnen saßn
> warte mal stehend leute schweigend
> ins gespräch MAMA als ein totge-
> schossner hase überm über also er
> lief geradeaus springerhaus B masse
> B . . . (p. 30)

The boy can see that it is dark and that a police car is coming around the corner. But he does not express this in his own words; rather, a nonsense rhyme ("dunkl wars der mond schien helle") automatically pops into his mind. And even before he admits to himself that he is in danger, the ready-made verse expresses his fears ("als ein totgeschossner hase"). The boy's language is a repertoire of disparate ready-made parts. Although it is a highly original mélange of separate entities, the speaker is clearly unable to process reality into his very own version of the world.

The comparison with Döblin shows that Plenzdorf has modernized and radicalized the techniques of literary montage. While Döblin's protagonist is still able to convert outside reality into his own vocabulary, Plenzdorf demonstrates the helplessness of a mind which is oversaturated with the voices of the media, with mechanical, pre-fabricated forms of public reality, with a steady barrage of information that is not related to the inner core of his personal needs and abilities. Public reality enters the individual consciousness in a steady stream but is so contradictory to personal experience that it is not recorded in its content, but in its form, as linguistic fragments.

It is obvious that Plenzdorf has documented a contrast between public and private language which is typical for both East and West. The oversaturation of language with political jargon in the East is more than matched in the West by verbal snatches from sports, pop music, and advertisements. Helmut Arntzen has called this mixing of pre-formulated jargon and personal expression a fast-spreading "Zeitkrankheit." 11 As a new trend in our language, it has been amply documented in the "konkrete Literatur" of West German and Austrian writers. Until now, however, there has been little experimentation with such structures in the GDR. 12

While Döblin uses montage to show the general multi-faceted and unholy reality of the big city, Plenzdorf documents the specifically ideological character of the socialist metropolis. His protagonist is a child of his times and his society. And although this one boy stands for many GDR citizens who cannot meaningfully integrate the private and public sectors of their lives, the work does not present an antagonistic outlook on socialist values. On the contrary. There are voices of reason in this story which represent public institutions. The boy's principal and his teachers, in particular, are moderating forces who could lead him out of his inner isolation and confusion.

The story bitterly criticizes any doctrinaire, one-sided position on the institutional as well as on the personal level. It is significant that the boy's father is a Party functionary and that he blindly implements the public goals of an achievement-oriented society on a personal level. The individual is sacrificed for larger theoretical principles. But even when the boy himself makes an attempt to break out of his isolation in order to try to establish a feeling of community with his brother, he is misunderstood and rejected. The cry for help at the end of the story is at once the climax and the tragic end of an attempt to bridge the gap. It is obvious that such a motif--the alienated individual trying to reach out for help--has added significance for a socialist literature.

Despite all paternal admonitions the boy clings to his private fantasy world almost till the end. This spiteful attitude goes hand-in-hand with barely concealed triumphs over his brother, the "Vopo-Bulle" Manfred, whom he drives into fits of anger by calling him "Mfred der B." Yet there is a distinct change in the boy's behavior, brought about by the great danger in which he finds himself at the end of the story. He turns away from his fantasy preoccupation with his hero MICK. Instead of continuing his silent musings, his voice breaks out for the first time as he shouts an urgent cry for help to his brother, hoping that authority will for once be human and helpful. Now the boy is able and willing to address his brother by his full name, "Manfred," not the mutilated "Mfred":

> Mfred! da ist Mfred der B! er haut
> inner kirche darf keiner kein Mfred!
> manfred! MANFRED! HIER! ICH! ICH BIN
> HIER DEIN BRUDER! nicht haun mehr ICH
> BIN HIER! MANFRED! HERKOMM! Hier
> nicht haun MAN du sau   (p. 31)

With these desperate words the boy has departed from the narrow subjective perspective of his inner realm into outside reality in order to seek help from another. Seen in a more abstract, but possibly clearer context, he has (probably unknown to himself) moved towards the greater socialist goal of his society: the departure from the "I" to a community with a "You," thus reaffirming the utopian vision of brotherhood which the loudspeaker voices again and again celebrate as the achievement of the GDR. The boy's hopes for help only exist for a second, however; then they are clubbed down. The outcome predicted by the Cain and Abel story turns into reality.

The three linguistic levels, which, as shown, also typify different levels of reality, therefore have a deeper significance. The montage level of publicly propagated reality still transmits the shimmer of an utopian hope for the cooperation of all people in socialism. However, these humanitarian ideals then are drowned in the noise of tanks, in the rhetoric which seeks to smooth over and falsely harmonize all controversy. The two subjective levels of reality then demonstrate how overzealous individuals can undermine their socialist principles by blindly applying them too rigidly, contrary to individual needs. Plenzdorf thus warns that the path from subjectivity to community must be carefully nurtured for the evolution of a truly socialist society.

This short story does not attempt to harmonize existing reality. By documenting the specifically ideological character of GDR society and showing concretely present-day media manipulation and the increasingly stereotyped characteristics of individual language, it seeks instead to demonstrate the very stark truth about socialist reality.

Plenzdorf shows his commitment to a broader concept of realism by renewing modernist techniques of the 1920s. This does not contradict Honecker's call for a socialist literature, although it demonstrates a critical socialist attitude. The new attempt to document as well as narrate, evaluate, or describe involves the readers themselves in the active search for truth. A narrative with different montage levels demands the public's participation and critical involvement--the first step in a meaningful dialogue within society. Reality in "kein runter" is not fixed but ready to be shaped and participated in. One can only hope that this daring short story, which received the Ingeborg-Bachmann-Preis in 1978, will soon be made available to GDR readers also.

Amherst College

Notes

[1] This essay is a shortened and revised version of the chapter entitled "Montage im inneren Monolog" in my book, Zitat und Montage in der neueren DDR-Prosa, Forschungen zur Kultur- und Literaturgeschichte, 3, ed. Helmut Kreuzer and Karl Riha (Frankfurt: Lang, 1984), pp. 175-209.

[2] See Dokumente zur Kunst-, Literatur- und Kulturpolitik der SED 1971-1974, ed. Gisela Rüß (Stuttgart: Seewald, 1976), p. 287.

[3] Ulrich Plenzdorf, "kein runter, kein fern," in Klagenfurter Texte zum Ingeborg-Bachmann-Preis 1978, ed. Humbert Fink (Munich: List, 1978), pp. 13-31. Citations from this edition are given parenthetically in the text. Italicized words are underlined here.

[4] Kritik in der Zeit: Literaturkritik der DDR 1945-1975, ed. Klaus Jarmatz (Halle/Leipzig: Mitteldeutscher Verlag, 1978), I, 152-57. For more information about ideological aspects of aesthetic methods, see Jost Hermand, "Das Gute-Neue und das Schlechte-Neue: Wandlungen in der Modernismus-Debatte in der DDR seit 1956," in Literatur und Literaturtheorie in der DDR, ed. Peter Uwe Hohendahl and Patricia Herminghouse (Frankfurt/M: Suhrkamp, 1976), pp. 73-99; and Peter Uwe Hohendahl, "Ästhetik und Sozialismus: Zur neueren Literaturtheorie der DDR," in Literatur und Literaturtheorie in der DDR, pp. 100-62.

[5] The discussions of the Moscow Writers' Congress (1934) which formulated the dissociation of so-

cialist realism from Western modernist techniques had specifically evolved around the allegedly negative examples of such writers as James Joyce and John Dos Passos. For example, Karl Radek explained Joyce's methods as requiring the artist to "photograph a dunghill through the lens of a microscope." He further charged that interior monologue only captured non-representative, minute sections of the protagonist's inner life and therefore failed to analyze the larger cultural crisis of the times. See Karl Radek, "James Joyce oder sozialistischer Realismus," in Romantheorie: Dokumentation ihrer Geschichte in Deutschland seit 1880, ed. Eberhard Lämmert (Cologne: Kiepenheuer & Witsch, 1975), p. 270.

[6] Hans-Jürgen Schmitt focuses on the concept of "heilich" in its relation to the Cain and Abel motif in his discussion of this Plenzdorf story: "Umdeutung des Mythos: Plenzdorfs Text 'kein runter kein fern,'" in Hansers Sozialgeschichte der deutschen Literatur. Bd. 11: Die Literatur der DDR, ed. Hans-Jürgen Schmitt (Munich: dtv, 1983), pp. 317-20.

[7] Montage as an aesthetic principle is often considered to be an empirical reaction to the increasingly dissociative appearance of reality in the 20th century. See Silvio Vietta, "Großstadtwahrnehmung und ihre literarische Darstellung. Expressionistischer Reihungsstil und Collage," DVjs, 48, No. 2 (1974), 354-73; Volker Klotz, "Zitat und Montage in neuerer Literatur und Kunst," Sprache im technischen Zeitalter, 60, No. 4 (1976), 259-77; Volker Hage, ed. Literarische Collagen: Texte, Quellen, Theorie (Stuttgart: Reclam, 1981); and Helmut Kreuzer, "Zur Avantgarde- und Montage-Diskussion - und zu diesem Heft," Zeitschrift für Literaturwissenschaft und Linguistik: Montage, 12, No. 46 (1982), 7-18.

[8] Alfred Döblin, Berlin Alexanderplatz (Olten: Walter, 1977), pp. 49-51.

[9] See especially Book Two, "Der Rosenthaler Platz unterhält sich," and Volker Klotz' chapter on Döblin in Volker Klotz, Die erzählte Stadt (Munich: Carl Hanser, 1969), pp. 372-418.

[10] Jürgen Stenzel has compared the handwritten first version of the manuscript with the printed edition and shown that many montage particles were added later without altering the scope of the novel. See Jürgen Stenzel, "Mit Kleister und Schere. Zur Hand-

schrift von Berlin Alexanderplatz," Text und Kritik: Alfred Döblin, ed. Heinz-Ludwig Arnold, Heft 13/14 (1966), pp. 41-44.

[11] Helmut Arntzen, "Sätze über Sätze, Zur Sprache der Zeitgenossen," in his Literatur im Zeitalter der Information (Frankfurt/M: Athenäum, 1971), p. 346.

[12] Wolfgang Emmerich confirms this finding: "Die DDR-Literatur ist in ihr experimentelles Zeitalter eingetreten, freilich kaum im Sinne formalistischer, sprachspielerischer Experimente westlicher Kollegen." Wolfgang Emmerich, Kleine Literaturgeschichte der DDR (Darmstadt/Neuwied: Luchterhand, 1981), p. 219. See also Hans-Jürgen Schmitt, "Die journalistische Bedeutung neuerer Erzählformen," in Hansers Sozialgeschichte, pp. 304-33.

Einladung zum Lever Bourgeois:
Christoph Hein's First Prose Collection

Bernd Fischer

In his overview of the development of GDR drama
since 1980, Peter Reidel laments the long list of
young GDR playwrights who have turned away from the
drama and taken up prose instead.[1] Similar to its West
German counterpart, the GDR stage has failed to provide young authors with either suitable literary recognition or the means of reaching a broader audience.
Although he did not do so, Reidel could have included
Christoph Hein among the names on his list.

Born in Heinzendorf (today Poland) in 1944, Hein
grew up in Thuringia and, after a few years in West
Berlin attending the Gymnasium, studied philosophy in
Leipzig and Berlin. In the early 1970s he began his
career at the Volksbühne in Berlin, first as a Drama-
turg and later as a writer of historical plays. Although his plays, among them "Schlötel oder Was solls"
(1974), "Cromwell" (1975), and "Lassalle fragt Herrn
Herbert nach Sonja" (1978),[2] received critical acclaim, they have, to my knowledge, not been performed
on the major GDR stages. Among critics Hein gained
the reputation of being a playwright of unusual talent
interested in developing new forms for the historical
play. With this image in mind, the critics were not
overly concerned by the fact that the mixture of history and everyday life which Hein uses in his plays
tends to deconstruct the historical models favored in
the GDR.

Only after Hein, in the 1980s, began to publish
prose works and, as a consequence, to be recognized by
a broader audience, does one detect a certain uneasiness among his critics. While they could applaud
Hein's dramatic experiments with the bourgeois hero
Cromwell,[3] they felt compelled to guard history against

the "excesses" of literary treatment in the case of the socialist revolutionary Lassalle. Christoph Funke, for example, deems Hein's use of an historic <u>Verfremdungseffekt</u> to be too politically disruptive and accuses Hein of creating an arbitrary picture of Lassalle as a decadent bohemian purely for the sake of sensation.[4] Peter Hacks summed up the increasing shifts between admiration and unease in the critics' views of Hein's plays: "Er gehört zu jenen wenigen, die mit der Sprache keine Sorgen haben. Christoph Hein hat Gewalt über die Worte. Sein Problem war der Inhalt, der ja jedenfalls das leichtere Problem ist."[5] In his econium on the occasion of Hein's being awarded the Heinrich Mann Prize in 1982, Hacks optimistically described Hein's search for a new realism as "Hochachtung vor dem Wirklichen"; at the same time he warned, however, that it should not be confused with "Objektivismus," that at best it could be called "aufgeklärter oder abgefeimter Naturalismus."[6]

In 1980, Aufbau Verlag published Hein's first prose collection, <u>Einladung zum Lever Bourgeois</u>, in its series Edition Neue Texte.[7] In the fall of 1982 Hoffmann und Campe published a <u>Lizenzausgabe</u> of the work entitled <u>Nachtfahrt und früher Morgen</u>.[8] Contained in both editions are five short prose works, two of which, like Hein's plays, treat historical subjects: "Einladung zum Lever Bourgeois" and "Die russischen Briefe des Jägers Johann Seifert." The other three, "Aus: Ein Album Berliner Stadtansichten," a loosely connected series of short texts, "Leb wohl, mein Freund, es ist schwer zu sterben," and a Kleist adaptation, "Der neue (glücklichere) Kohlhaas," deal with prewar and postwar German and GDR reality.

The title story of the GDR edition, "Einladung zum Lever Bourgeois," invites us to observe the poet and court historian Racine at his morning ritual of preparing body and mind for the day ahead, much as Racine is occasionally allowed to experience the "lever du roi" of Louis XIV. We see in Racine a courtier in the process of moving towards political sympathy with the bourgeoisie; he has written a list of grievances concerning the conditions of the state and distributed it at court. The dilemma of the court poet as servant and critic of power--a theme which has almost become a new genre in GDR literature[9]--is presented by means of a concrete historical example.

Racine, at age fifty-nine, is already a sick man when the reader witnesses his thoughts during the tortuous morning effort to complete his toilet. His illness has left him weak, moody, and withdrawn; he is alienated from the younger members of the court society. His bowels, in which the sickness rages, appear to have become his image of the world: "Der Darm als Weltsicht" (p. 8).

Suffering physical torment while sitting on his "Golgathathron" (p. 18) each morning, Racine is at the same time spiritually tormented by painful memories of his life spent as a playwright and courtier: for example, his weakness and failure to act when confronted with incidents of tangible societal misery. As royal war historian, he had witnessed an act of soldierly brutality, which Hein describes in a few short sentences:

> Eine holländische Bäuerin war vergewaltigt worden, man fand sie dann zusammen mit ihrem Kind in der Stallung tot auf. Die Untersuchung wurde eingestellt, um höhere Interessen nicht zu inkommodieren. Alltag der Armee. Der Bauer, der die drei Offiziere angezeigt hatte, . . . verübte später-- wie der französische Kommandant im Dorf bekanntgeben ließ--Selbstmord. Schuldig des Diebstahls von Militäreigentum. Bemerkenswert daran, daß er sich in seiner Scheune mehr als zwanzigmal eine Forke in den Körper gestoßen haben mußte, so daß sein Leib in zwei Teile zerriß. (pp. 10-11)

Racine had looked away, unable to cope with this injustice. And he still assures himself that he bears no guilt:

> was hätte er ausrichten können. Er, ein kleiner Geschichtsschreiber, gegen die allmächtige, allgegenwärtige Armee. . . . Sollte er in die Scheune gehen, um dann Mord, Mord zu schreien? Die reinen Helden in der Literatur. Auf der Bühne ist es angebracht. (pp. 11-12)

He tries to reduce his feeling of guilt with other rationalizations such as: "Vielleicht ist die Fähigkeit, ein Verbrechen verschweigen zu können, die Bedingung der menschlichen Rasse, in Gesellschaft zu leben" (p. 13).

Racine is faced with the question of accepting or rejecting the power of the state, of tolerating or combating the concept of its "higher interest." He hesitatingly recognizes the opportunism and cowardice involved in the first of the two alternatives: "Das 'höhere Interesse' eines Staates anzuerkennen, ist bestialisch, möglicherweise, aber die Voraussetzung seiner weiteren Existenz. Der des Staates, des Individuums ohnehin" (p. 13). One hand washes the other: "Und der verdiente Staatsbürger ist zu ehren um seiner schweigenden Mitwisserschaft willen" (p. 13).

It is this spiritually and physically ailing Racine who has written the critical pamphlet on the condition of the state and secretly distributed it at the court: "Auf diese wenigen Druckseiten 'Das Elend des Volkes' ist er stolz" (p. 24). The transformation of the courtier to hero of the bourgeoisie is not based on political or philosophical motivations in Hein's portrayal. Hein reveals instead the very personal motivation for his decision. Racine's revolutionary act is that of a sick and bitter old man who at the end of his life is seeking to find some value in it after the many political and personal sacrifices he has made--in addition to those described, he renounced the woman he loved for a career-oriented marriage and betrayed the spiritual home of his youth, the Jansenist cloister Port Royal. His boldness is not a result of heroism but rather of his age and illness, which make any consideration of his career at court superfluous.

The most positive comment one can make about an historical narrative is, in my opinion, that the figures are thoroughly plausible. This is certainly the case with Racine. The humanness of his memories makes the personality of Racine accessible despite the historical distance. The obvious implications for the writer of today make his dilemma relevant. Hein repeatedly makes the transition from detailed description of outward reality to the depiction of Racine's inner thoughts without undue stylistic maneuvering; indeed, the transitions are barely noticeable. Hein manifests, furthermore, a rare feeling for the limitations of the Handlung, which is condensed to a time span of a few hours; he has the intellectual self-discipline to keep the psychological, historical, and philosophical aspects of the narrative within reasonable limits--something which is not always the case in the foremost works of contemporary GDR literature.

In "Die russischen Briefe des Jägers Johann Seifert" Hein deals with an intellectual from the first half of the nineteenth century who doesn't fit easily into the view of history held either in the East or the West: Alexander von Humboldt. The letters of this epistolary narrative, written by Humboldt's butler, Seifert, to his wife in Berlin during Humboldt's trip to Russia in 1829, are of course fictitious, but in his foreword Hein presents them as authentic documents which he is publishing in the interest of history. Hein reaches a new level of thoroughness in this narrative, which is characterized by an accurate knowledge of the sources and his reconstruction of the language appropriate to Seifert's time and social standing. The result is so skillful that Hein's editor, Günther Drommer, admits in the appendix to the GDR edition that he at first took the letters to be historical documents.[10] History from the point of view of the lower class. As we shall see, however, Hein's proletarian author does not play the role of the promoter of progress, but rather appears as Humboldt's conservative counterpart--a fact which was noted in GDR criticism of the work.[11]

The themes of this story develop out of the somewhat unusual friendship between the enlightened, liberal, aristocratic man-of-the-world and scientist Humboldt and his poorly educated, pious, and patriotic butler. A certain degree of so-called natural (classless) propriety binds the two together in the reactionary, antagonistic world of the Holy Alliance--in spite of the fact that they have completely different problems and that neither really understands the restraints experienced by the other.

The sixty-year-old Humboldt, like Racine, is confronted with the problems of the courtier, a theme which is apparently of special interest to Hein. Seifert reports, for example, Humboldt's reflection: "Ein Göthe, ein Schelling, sie alle seien begehrlich, im Schatten der Macht zu sizzen, und es mag darin ihrem Thun Förderliches stekken" (p. 136). Humboldt is far more pessimistic about his own role in Restoration Europe; he draws clear parallels between himself and the notorious Gundling, the intellectual court fool of the Prussian soldier king, Friedrich Wilhelm:[12]

> Ieder, ist er nur adelig gebohren,
> kaum dass er das Sprechen erlernte,
> erlaube sich Unverschämtheiten mit
> ihm und unwürdige Scherze. Einer ge-
> langweilten HofKamarilla habe er zur
> AbendUnterhaltung Zeitschriften vor-
> zulesen, wobei man seiner nicht ach-
> tet und parlirt, gähnt oder schläft.
> (pp. 133-34)

Humboldt is both a confirmed devotee of the Enlightenment and a worldly pessimist. He judges the French
Revolution, in Seifert's words, as follows: "Da sei
keine Regierung, die dem Volke Worth gehalten; keine,
die ihre SelbstSucht der Gesellschaft untergeordnet
habe" (p. 172). But Humboldt at the same time knows
"dass ein Humanist notwendig ein Häretiker sein müsse"
(p. 115). In striving toward Enlightenment ideals he
must thus content himself with the realm of natural
science (although even it too is subject to numerous
restrictions); almost defiantly convinced of the importance of science, Humboldt attempts to shut out all
political and social events. This worldly intellectual is faced with problems which simultaneously con-
cretize the historical situation and make allusion to
the present: for example, the paralyzing, allpervasive
patriotic propaganda, the surveillance of citizens
(Seifert is compelled to spy on Humboldt), burocratic
red tape, and restrictive sexual mores.

Inspired by the simplistic dogmas of Christianity
and patriotism, Seifert's world view has hardly anything in common with Humboldt's liberalism. Although
he suffers from the same strictures as Humboldt, albeit on different levels, he is not willing or able to
see the connections that Humboldt makes. When confronted with these problems, he takes the side of the
state. Humboldt, on the other hand, lacks Seifert's
carefree and lighthearted sense of honor, a quality
which has no place in the former's complicated strategies of intellectual survival.

In spite of their differences the two men share a
personal friendship. The friendship is possible because both are able to put aside their beliefs and
prejudices when human virtues, such as trust and concern for others, or at least respect, are at stake in
an environment hostile to both of them. Admittedly
this is a rosy picture of an apolitical friendship between members of two different classes--the sort often
found in trivial literature. However, Hein's strength

lies precisely in his ability to give credibility to trivial historical situations by skillfully shifting between history and fiction, which allows him to represent history without overburdening his heroes with undue, schematic claims of historical class-consciousness, revolutionary perspectives, etc. This is particularly true in this story, since many of the details of Prussian and Russian history can be read as historical reflections on the present as well.

A frequently noted trend in recent GDR literature is the reworking of literary texts by nineteenth-century German authors; numerous biographical studies also attest to a new confrontation of GDR literature with the German literary heritage that has little in common with the search for socialist models in the 1950s and 1960s. Special interest is being taken in writers such as Karoline von Günderrode, Bettina von Arnim, E.T.A. Hoffmann, Hölderlin, and Kleist. Hein has followed suit with an adaptation of Kleist, "Der neue (glücklichere) Kohlhaas." This story, however, can be considered historical only in terms of style. Hein's consistent attempt to imitate Kleist's language seems at times too playful; on the other hand, the stylized language provides a sort of Verfremdungseffekt in his story about GDR daily life.

Hubert K., a bookkeeper in a state-owned chair factory in Thuringia, files suit against the management and union leadership of the factory for illegally withholding forty marks from his annual incentive premium. This touches a sensitive nerve in the East German understanding of the state and its judicial system, just as the illegally required tolls and confiscation of Kohlhaas' horses in Kleist's story hit a sore spot in the absolutistic concept of justice. As in Kleist's novella, individual rebellion against the power mechanisms of the state ends in the social destruction of the individual.[13] The people around Hubert K.--from his colleagues to his wife--react to his rebellion with mockery, behind which thoughtless conformity and wavering fear are hidden. The deus ex machina ending--two supreme court judges rush to Hubert K.'s town in black government limousines with a reversal of the management decision--is in reality not an ending at all. It does as little to resolve the conflict as does the Brandenburg judgement in Kleist's story. K.'s family is broken apart; he is labelled a "verfluchter Gottesnarr" (p. 103) by his mother-in-law. The parentheses around the adjective "glücklichere" in the title serve as an early indication of the political tension within the text.

It seems that no subject can be too small or commonplace for Hein. The six texts which appear under the title "Aus: Ein Album Berliner Stadtansichten" are further evidence of Hein's talent for the exact but modest literary study, the genre picture, or the skeleton-like framework of a novel. The text "Friederike, Martha, Hilde" consists, for example, simply of biographical data on three women from consecutive generations of German history. Hein's radical sacrifice of all adornment makes the inhuman deformations of the lives of these women starkly apparent, for it is the very normalcy of their lives ("ihr Leben sei durchschnittlich und zufriedenstellend verlaufen," Hilda remarks, p. 40) that is scandalous.

Other short texts in this series describe peculiarities of everyday life, for which Hein has an eye. They are reminiscent of nineteenth-century anecdotes, for instance, the anecdotes that Kleist published in his Berliner Abendblätter. Like Kleist, Hein appears to be fascinated with the effect of contradicting the reader's presuppositions in these seemingly simple and modest anecdotes. Hein's story "Die Witwe eines Maurers" can serve as an example. After her husband was killed in the street fighting of the 1918 revolution in Berlin, the unpolitical young widow received, almost against her will, a pension from the government--first from the government of the Weimar Republic, then of the Third Reich, and finally of the GDR. Under each government her husband is declared a hero of the state on the basis of newly defined and contradictory premises. Regarded by her neighbors as a greedy conformist, the woman finds her social existence destroyed.

Finally, I will consider the text with the pathetic title "Leb wohl, mein Freund, es ist schwer zu sterben." Concealed behind the sentimental "hit-song" title is the simple tragedy of an overweight woman who goes to visit a former boyfriend, who has long since married. Hein manages to capture the depression of the young woman by concentrating on the external circumstances of her trip--and not delving into her psyche. His description of her nervous loneliness almost achieves the intense visibility of a film:

> Ein junger Mann, der ihr gegenüber
> saß, beobachtete gleichfalls interes-
> siert, wie sie verlegen nach der Fahr

> karte suchte, wobei sie mit ihren
> breiten Lippen etwas Unhörbares vor
> sich hin murmelte. Belustigt von der
> aufgeregten Frau sahen sich die Män-
> ner für einen Moment an. (p. 71)

As a result of his search for a new realism, the
study, the genre picture, and the historical narrative
are the main forms in the highly structured writing of
Hein's first prose volume--much as they were at the
beginning of the age of realism in the first third of
the nineteenth century. In all of the texts in this
volume, both historical and contemporary, Hein's specific version of realism revolves around particular
traits which might best be labeled halfheartedness,
personal shortcomings (without personal fault), weakness under the pressures of forces determining one's
life, etc. For example, the only brief moment of love
that Hein allows in this collection (in "Nachtfahrt
und früher Morgen") involves a married woman's passion
for a man who is young and self-righteous enough to
allow himself to despise the halfheartedness of her
husband, who plans (unsuccessfully) to flee the GDR,
not out of anger or conviction, but out of weakness.
While Hein's intellectual heroes of past centuries
could still reconcile themselves to the absurdity and
brutality of their times for the sake of higher scien-
tific, artistic, or political goals, as illusory as
these might have been, his contemporary figures lack
even these motivations. Spiritlessness reigns as a
law of everyday life, even in its smallest details.

GDR criticism has special difficulties with this
attitude, as can be seen in the discussion of Hein's
latest prose work, Der fremde Freund or Drachenblut,
as the West German edition is titled,[14] in the Weimarer Beiträge. It is the story of a forty-year-old
woman physician who has hardened herself against all
emotion, both in her professional and in her private
life. Klaus Kändler regrets, for example, the absence
of a positive resistance in the heroine against the
negative quality of her life.[15] Ursula Wilke writes:
"Das Ganze stimmt nicht. Die Novelle ist unwahr. . .
Der Fatalismus. Das Fatale, nahezu als das Normale
ausgewiesen, das stimmt nicht."[16]

Hein's writing is characterized by his disillu-
sioned realism, his obsession with negative aspects of
history and society, and his attempt to break with
stagnant historical and political-ideological patterns
by presenting the private details of intellectual and

proletarian life and suffering throughout history. One of the formal means he uses to present this view of reality is the sacrifice of all authorial interpretations. As a result of this authorial distance, the texts are punctuated with gaps in meaning which challenge the reader's patterns of understanding. Neither political nor philosophical thoughts are allowed to detract from the concrete realism. In the historical texts one occasionally finds ideological discourses, for example, statements made by Humboldt or Racine, but even there the author remains in the background and allows all emerging viewpoints equal treatment. This formal objectivity is visible also in Hein's use of narrative perspectives which view the characters from the outside or, as in the example of Der fremde Freund, with the limited perspective of the Ich-Form. In both cases, the reader is obliged to read between the lines, to think for himself. 17

Style and content are bound together in this essential aspect of Hein's prose, in this "deep respect for reality" (to place Hacks' phrase in a new context). His avoidance of ideological judgement, his iconoclasm, and the consequences for his writing style make the concern of GDR critics such as Hacks, when he speaks of Hein's "Naturalismus" and avoids the term "Objektivismus," understandable.

Ohio State University

Notes

1 Peter Reichel, "Anmerkungen zur DDR-Dramatik seit 1980. Teil I," Weimarer Beiträge, 29, No. 8 (1983), 1403-26; "Anmerkungen zur DDR-Dramatik seit 1980. Teil II," Weimarer Beiträge, 29, No. 10 (1983), 1709-28.

2 Christoph Hein, Cromwell und andere Stücke (Berlin/Weimar: Aufbau, 1981). See also Rudolf Münz's interesting afterword, pp. 299-320.

3 Cf. Frank Hörnigk, "Christoph Hein: Cromwell," Weimarer Beiträge, 29, No. 1 (1983), 33-39.

4 Christoph Funke, "Spiel mit Geschichte," in Rezensionen zur DDR-Literatur. Kritik 81 (Halle/Leipzig: Mitteldeutscher Verlag, 1982), pp. 30-34.

[5] Peter Hacks, "Heinrich-Mann-Preis 1982," Neue Deutsche Literatur, 30, No. 6 (1982), 162.

[6] Hacks, p. 161.

[7] Christoph Hein, Einladung zum Lever Bourgeois (Berlin/Weimar: Aufbau, 1980). Subsequent page citations given parenthetically in the text refer to this edition.

[8] Christoph Hein, Nachtfahrt und früher Morgen (Hamburg: Hoffmann und Campe, 1982). One story, "Der Sohn," was not published in the West German edition. It traces the mechanisms of socialization in school and family or, more accurately stated, the failure of these institutions to meet the needs of a child and adolescent. The story is one of the weaker ones in the collection, which is perhaps the reason for its exclusion.

[9] See, for example, Klaus Poche's Atemnot, Günter de Bruyn's Preisverleihung, Werner Heiduczek's Der Tod am Meer, and Martin Stade's Der König und sein Narr.

[10] Günther Drommer, "Typische Bemerkungen zu untypischen Texten," in Christoph Hein, Einladung zum Lever Bourgeois, pp. 187-88.

[11] Ursula Heukenkamp deems a proletarian such as Seifert to be simply unhistorical ("Die fremde Form," Sinn und Form, 35, No. 3 [1983], 630).

[12] Gundling enjoys surprising popularity in contemporary GDR literature. He has been treated in Heiner Müller's Leben Gundlings Friedrich von Preußen Lessings Schlaf Traum Schrei and in Martin Stade's Der König und sein Narr as well.

[13] Hein deals with comparable themes of socialist life in the comedy "Schlötel oder Was solls."

[14] Christoph Hein, Der fremde Freund (Berlin/Weimar: Aufbau, 1982). West German edition: Drachenblut (Darmstadt/Neuwied: Luchterhand, 1982).

[15] "Für und Wider: Der fremde Freund von Christoph Hein," Weimarer Beiträge, 29, No. 9 (1983), 1641.

[16] "Für und Wider," p. 1653.

[17] As Bernd Leistner points out, for example, the reader must pay special attention to Hein's use of language in the characterization of the heroine: "Und der Autor weiß mit der Maske dieses Sprechens denn auch so umzugehen, daß Schutz- und Täuschungsfunktion (in bezug auf die sich mitteilende Figur) kenntlich wird" ("Für und Wider," p. 1644).

From Grey East to Golden West: Fritz Rudolf Fries
and GDR Travel Literature

Cecile Cazort Zorach

Travel literature, because its themes and conventions are so directly determined by the culture in
which it arises and for which it is written, often
does not itself travel well. The expectations of one
society's readers at a given time may differ radically
from those of another society's readers or from those
of the same society in a different time. Thus few
travel books endure and few are translated. Fritz
Rodolf Fries, a writer whose fiction enjoys a mixed
reputation in both East and West,[1] has produced a
particularly large volume of travel writing. Though
not much heeded abroad, Fries' travel works, compris-
ing four volumes to date, have made a noteworthy contribution to this form of literature in their own
country, and many of them can be read with interest
and pleasure by serious readers outside the GDR.[2]

Although Fries' fiction frequently uses motifs of
travel or geographical displacement and although obvious thematic and stylistic parallels exist between
the fictional works and his non-fictional travel writing, the discussion here will focus exclusively on the
latter. Travel literature in this context is to be
understood as an area of non-fiction bordering on but
distinct from autobiography. Unlike autobiography or
travel fiction, non-fictional travel essays and narrative derive much of their weight and substance from
their presentation of a geographical reality as, at
least ostensibly, an end in itself, as inherently
valuable and interesting.

Fries' own mixed cultural heritage--as son of a
Spanish mother and a German father, with a bilingual
childhood spent partly in Spain, an education in Romanistik and Anglistik, a passionate love of Hispanic

137

culture, and dedicated work as a translator and mediator of both classical and contemporary Hispanic literature in the GDR--has left its mark on his travel
writing in the form of a rare sensitivity to other
cultures and an acute awareness of both the clichés
and the conventions which writing about other lands
entails. His travel writings cover an unusually wide
range of geographical areas: Spain, where he has numerous relatives; Cuba, which he visited with his
Leipzig mentor, the Romanist Werner Krauß, in 1963;
Poland; Albania; France; Belgium; the United States;
and areas of his own country, among others. The discussion below of three widely differing works--an
early sketch about Poland, a later essay on Cuba, both
from the collection Alle meine Hotel Leben, and his
1979 book on Spain, Mein spanisches Brevier--will
seek to highlight the main features of Fries' travel
writing against the background of GDR travel writing
as a whole.

What makes a good travel book? The quality of
travel writing depends to a large extent on the sensitivity with which the traveler perceives and tries to
interpret a foreign world and on the skill with which
he presents his perception and interpretation to members of his own culture. This kind of literature thus
requires that the traveler learn to perceive and identify the "otherness" of the other culture rather than
simply to project upon it his own often unquestioned
national or cultural preconceptions. Some travelers
manage to note various differences between home and
abroad without interpreting them coherently or convey-
ing them convincingly to readers. Others, seeking to
interpret such differences in terms which will be com-
prehensible to the folks back home, may consciously or
unconsciously give their experiences an apparent unity
of vision by resorting to clichés, stereotypes, or
journalistic conventions established by earlier writers or by their society's current standards of journalism. Travel writers who avoid this pitfall may
succeed in painting isolated vignettes or capturing
fragments of the foreign world to pique readers' curiosity and entertain them with novelty and originality
without however yielding a satisfying image of this
world as a whole.

Although it is difficult to generalize about a
particular society's travel literature and although
travel writing covers a broad spectrum from everyday
journalism to self-sufficient literary art, GDR travel
writing as a whole displays certain characteristics

which distinguish it from similar writing in the non-socialist West. Chief among these is its strongly, sometimes explicitly articulated, didactic impulse.[3] In the hands of unskilled writers this didactic tendency appears in its crassest form as tedious denunciations of the fascist past, bathetic declarations of solidarity with the comrades in other socialist lands, or as predictable jibes at the vulgarity of tourists from capitalist countries.[4] Even in works standing above this level of name-calling, the sometimes mechanistic imposition of the society's own ideological categories onto the interpretation of other societies may appear to a non-GDR reader as an artificial schematization of complex empirical realities.[5]

At his best, Fritz Rudolf Fries succeeds in circumventing the various perils associated with travel writing in general and GDR travel writing in particular. Though eschewing the brutally witty demolition of clichés and jargon through which his first novel, Der Weg nach Oobliadooh, attracted such attention, Fries in his travel writing finds inventive ways of avoiding stereotypical thinking, often using parody, fantasy, myth, literary allusion, or experimentation with other modes (fiction and dialogue, for example) to cast light on the different aspects of the foreign reality. Fries, as a highly literate writer sensitive to the many traditions which have influenced German travel literature, has, in his best pieces, adopted literary conventions from many of these traditions, thus overcoming provincial didacticism and diffuse trivialization in relating his encounter with foreign realms. His experimentation with various conventions and traditions has permitted him to communicate his own particular perspective on both East and West in a spectrum of nuances which cannot be captured by the silly rubrics of "gold" and "grey" in the rather facetious title of this paper. Indeed, two of his most brightly glittering pieces, in the sense of their ebullient wit, are the early ones on Poland and Albania, while his 1979 work on Spain skillfully captures the many somber shadows on the sunny landscape of that nation.

In his 1961 sketch on Poland, "Die polnische Reise. Ein Fragment," Fries showed his broad critical perspective in his choice of literary models.[6] His unconcealed indifference to socialist realism, indeed, his unregenerate skepticism toward realism as an absolute aesthetic criterion, and his debt to the romantics emerge strongly in this and his other early writings. [7] The six-page Polish sketch announces in its title a fragmentary quality hearkening back to Sterne and Heine, whose <u>Sentimental Journey</u> and <u>Reisebilder</u> have left a clear imprint on the text. The abruptness of the opening sentences--"In Polen, sagt Kazimierz Brandys, haben wir das alles längst hinter uns gelassen. So fuhr ich nach Warschau" (p. 53)--recalls the opening of Sterne's book, "They order, said I, this matter better in France," with its following announcement of Yorick's decision to travel there. Like the works of Sterne and Heine, Fries' modern sentimental journey represents a deliberate refusal to present a recognizable and verifiable description of reality. The narrator, who never leaves his train compartment, gives no specific information about Poland, contenting himself instead with tongue-in-cheek portraits of fellow travelers and an account of a stop in the station in Lodz. The traveler's relentless irony toward his compatriots, in which his disdain for their philistinism plays a major role, shows Fries' debt to both Heine and Jean Paul.

The adherence of this text to romantic literary tradition and its deviation from conventions of GDR travel journalism has baffled at least one reviewer in the GDR, who seeks to attribute the paucity of empirical detail to the trip's nocturnal setting and who then finds value in the understanding which the text shows of "unser Verhältnis zum Nachbarland als geschichtlicher Auftrag." [8] Since the eleven-hour journey does not occur all at night (the train arrives in Lodz in the late afternoon), the sparseness of detail cannot be explained in this way. Moreover, the question of the GDR's relationship to Poland occupies a problematic position in the text. For example, recounting the crossing of the Oder and Neiße, Fries forgoes any political or historical reflections on the boundary, using the occasion, instead, to comment on the other passengers:

> Nach Überquerung der Oder und Neiße
> sprachen der Gebrauchsgrafiker und
> ich über den durch die Abteile schla-
> genden Lärm der skatspielenden Fuß-
> baller, denen nun nicht mehr in die
> Mitropa zu entkommen war, weil von
> jetzt an die polnische Währung galt,
> über die wir vor unserer Ankunft
> nicht verfügten. (pp. 53-54)

The traveler shortly thereafter arouses the reader's

expectations with the comment, "Lange sah man nichts von den polnischen Zuständen" (p. 54), but a later discussion of these "Zustände" fails to occur. Upon sampling his first Polish bread, the German observes, "Doch konnte es auch in Berlin gebacken worden sein; wir waren nicht ganz sicher. Der Gebrauchsgrafiker wollte die Reiseleiterin fragen" (p. 54). The travelers' first glimpses of a Polish city likewise failed to yield any dramatic interpretation of Polish reality, or, indeed, of any reality outside the narrator's subjectivity: "Nun sieht Łódź vom Zug so aus, als sei man hier zur Schule gegangen. Auch Thomas hatte wohl dieses Gefühl, weil er wenig später damit anfing, mir Schulgeschichten zu erzählen" (p. 55).

The account of the stop in Lodz, however, circuitously leads to a reference to the German occupation of Poland mentioned above by the reviewer. As the train sits in the station, a freight train pulls up on an adjacent track. Railway workers roll large wagons up to the doors and unload onto them the carcasses of wild boars, eliciting a conversation between the narrator and a woman in his tour group. Their discussion makes the elusively ironic posture of the narrator clear:

> Man sieht gar kein Blut, sagte sie.
> Das ist längst verkrustet, sagte ich. In all den Jahren. Es sind ausgestopfte Bestien für das Heimatmuseum in Łódź.
> Sie sah mich von der Seite an. Jetzt fiel mir auf, daß sie ja die Frau des Ökonomieprofessors war, und ich sagte deshalb: Das Blut ist an Ort und Stelle schon verarbeitet worden, man nimmt es zum Einfärben der Blutwürste und gelegentlich als Anstrich, eine Neuerung.
> Ach so, sagte sie und fand nun die Schweine ganz lustig. (p. 56)

The narrator's facetious fabrication warns his reader not to take his interpretation of foreign reality too seriously. Now the conversation turns to art, the philosophy professor addressing the question of the situation of the arts in Poland:

> Na ja, was die hier für Kunstauffassungen haben, bedenklich. Ich sah doch tatsächlich in einer Ausstel-

lung, das letzte Mal, als ich in Warschau am Hegel-Kongreß teilnahm (ich
konnte mich nicht erinnern, daß ein
solcher in Warschau stattgefunden
hatte), ein Stilleben, das, wie ich
mir übersetzen ließ, den Titel trug:
Wildschweinjagd in Lublin. Was glauben Sie, was man auf dem Bild zu
sehen bekam.
Die sinnbildliche Darstellung vom
Ende der Okkupation? sagte ich.
Ja, wenn es das gewesen wäre, er-
widerte der Professor. Aber es war
viel schlimmer. . . . die Verfrem-
dung wird hier so weit getrieben,
daß auf dem Bild nur noch schwarze
Kleckse zu sehen waren, um die etwas
Grün gruppiert war.
Ach, sagte Thomas.
Ich schaute wieder aus dem Fenster.
                                    (p. 57)

The professor's dogmatic realism cannot countenance
any kind of abstraction. It is presumably this kind
of philistine insistence on realism in art which the
traveler is seeking to escape in Poland. Only after
the conversation with the professor does the opening
sentence of the "Polnische Reise" become intelligible:
"In Polen, sagt Kazimierz Brandys [a prominent Polish
writer who has since emigrated to the U.S.], haben wir
das alles längst hinter uns gelassen," as though
Poland had long since resolved questions of aesthetics
still hotly argued about in the GDR. The travelers'
conversation underlines the discrepancy between the
two cultures, the deficiencies of mutual understanding, rather than elucidating the relationship as "geschichtlicher Auftrag."

The piece's final paragraph once again reveals an
aggressive irony whereby a traveler's shallow analysis
of the historico-political relationship between Poland
and Germany is rejected. Here the clichés, bathos,
and inflated rhetoric of the passage show the narrator's dutiful attempt to imitate the style of popular
travel writers.

Und wie hat Ihnen die polnische
Landschaft gefallen? würden mich zu
Hause die Remans fragen, unsere Nach-
barn, die ihre Vorstellung von Aus-
land nach den Berichten großer Reise-

schriftsteller gestalteten.

Die polnische Landschaft, würde ich sagen, glauben Sie mir, beginnt schon hinter Strausberg. Eine gleichmäßig sandige, von vereinzelten Kiefern bestandene Landschaft, auf der Kohl und Zuckerrüben gedeihen. Ja, doch, es gibt einen Unterschied. Die Nebelfelder hinter der Oder verwischen nicht die Hochspannungsleitungen um die KZs. Die Seen zwischen Baumstämmen blenden wie geschliffene Bajonette. Würde ich sagen, im behaglich geheizten Zimmer am Rande der S-Bahn. Die Äcker sind mit Asche gedüngt, würde ich sagen, das polnische Brot schmeckt nach Asche. Es ist die Auferstehung . . . ich begann das Land zu lieben, noch ehe uns Marek die Revolutionsetüde . . . (p. 58)

Readers unfamiliar with Der Weg nach Oobliadooh, which to date has not appeared in the GDR, may miss some of the parody of jingoism and clichés in which Fries here is indulging as he did in the novel. The text itself provides clues, however, especially the mention of the bread, which previously has been described as tasting just like German bread, and in the concluding ellipsis, which brings the piece to an end in the middle of a sentence, a convention established by Sterne and continued in other sentimental journeys.

Fries' later travel writing adopts a more sober tone, gaining in empirical substance and coherence what it loses in exuberant wit. In his "Kubanische Kalenderblätter," based on his trip to Cuba with Krauß in 1963 but not written until 1976, Fries moves from the grey East of Lodz ("auf dem grauen Bahnsteig, im grauen Spätnachmittag," p. 55) to the golden West of the Caribbean. The incarnation of the new socialist revolutionary state, the outpost of Marxism in the imperialist western hemisphere, Cuba, as a subject of GDR travel writing, lends itself to clichés. Although Fries' political sympathies clearly lie with revolutionary Cuba, he skillfully avoids a schematic or facile interpretation of Cuba.[9] He does this largely by emphasizing the tension between the rich heritage of Cuban tradition--the myths, the fantasies, the superstitions--and the contemporary everyday business of building a new society. In a short introduction Fries disclaims any validity of the piece as a document of contemporary Cuba and declares: "Womöglich bin ich nie in Kuba gewesen" (p. 7).

The historical time of the journey is of crucial importance for this tension between tradition and revolution. Taking place a brief five years after the revolution, Fries' visit reveals to him some of the excitement and expectation arising at a new beginning, a theme which occurs elsewhere in Fries' writing, particularly in Der Weg nach Oobliadooh and in his book on Spain. The title "Kubanische Kalenderblätter" points to the passage of time, and implies both the historical change evident in Cuba during Fries' visit and that which occurs there between his visit and his much later writing of the piece. Here, as in his other works, Fries leaves it to others to enumerate and applaud the achievements of progress. The narrator casts himself as a modern Columbus, the explorer who "hatte zu den geographischen Fantasien der Renaissance die dazupassenden Länder finden wollen" (p. 11). Just as Columbus stumbled onto Cuba in his search for mysterious, miraculous places like Cathay and Cipango with their innumerable riches, Fries, too, in search of the golden, though not of gold, approaches Cuba as a legendary land and concludes his "Kubanische Kalenderblätter" with the exclamation: "So, auf denn nach Cathay!" (p. 27).

In his writing about Cuba Fries often elucidates reality through images of changing myths and an examination of their particular iconography. Against this background Castro appears in mythic dimensions as the folk hero par excellence, one of the race of "jene sagenhaften Bärtigen aus der Sierra" (p. 15). Another mythic figure in the text is the American folk hero John F. Kennedy, whose role in the Bay of Pigs invasion makes him the "bad guy" antagonist to "good guy" Castro. The assassination of Kennedy, which occurs at the end of the trip, punctuates the dramatic conflict between the two and reinforces the question of how myth and folk tale evolve as the traveler and his hosts speculate about interpretations of the historical event: "Jede Art Spekulation ist im Augenblick möglich. Wer war der Mörder? Was geschieht, wenn es ein Kubaner ist, von der CIA, vom FBI zum Kubaner gemacht wird?" (p. 26).

The narrator decides to test this land's possibilities by seeking out areas beyond those in the officially approved picture of Cuba. On an adventurous excursion into Havanna's old quarter, he finds a lost

144

paradise which offers, in addition to pleasures like rum and cigars, a few forbidden fruits in a black bordello. He delights in finding here an ancient and exotic institution which boldly defies the glib official assertions about the complete eradication of prostitution.

The resolute refusal to pigeonhole experience into rigid schemes finds an ironic reversal in Cuba itself when the two travelers from the GDR are labelled, despite careful clarification, as "soviéticos." Fries' laconic comment, "Zwischen Playa Girón und Guantánamo ist die Welt durchaus einfach zu überblicken und in zwei Lager geteilt" (p. 22), implies his own dissatisfaction with such a simplistic interpretation of international relations, or of reality in general.

The value of Fries' "Kubanische Kalenderblätter" lies in their convincing presentation of a reality in dynamic transition. The vitality and expectancy which Fries sensed in Cuba in 1963 are also present in his description of Spain, which he visited in 1976-77. Mein spanisches Brevier (1979) is a substantial work, both quantitatively and qualitatively.[10] Its twenty-five chapters address different aspects and regions of contemporary Spain and testify to Fries' knowledge of the country's history and culture. The pieces form a loosely unified narrative, linked by thematic strands and punctuated by a clear opening and conclusion.

The book as a whole, like most of the individual chapters, opens with an epigraph. The epigraphs, most of which come from Spanish writers, reinforce Fries' attempt to present the country from various perspectives as a complement to his own. The opening epigraph, taken from a seventeenth-century Spanish work, Baltasar Gracián's El Criticón (1658), sets the tone of the work in several ways. It presents a dialogue between two characters, part of which runs as follows:

Andrenio: Sage mir also, was hast du dir für
          einen Begriff von Spanien gebildet?
Critilo : Keinen üblen.
Andrenio: Also einen guten?
Critilo : Auch nicht.
Andrenio: Demnach, weder gut noch übel?
Critilo : Das sage ich auch.
Andrenio: Wie denn?
Critilo : Einen bitter-süßen Eindruck. (p. 5)

The dialogue form is important for the book as a

whole, in which it often manifests itself as debate. Fries shows himself in discussions with various Spaniards, often members of his own family. Numbering among its members a few Franco-sympathizers and some Basque nationalists, the family is a microcosm of the political diversity emerging after the end of Spanish fascism. A cousin, Carmen, in particular, is cast as an astute political observer and trenchant social critic, against whom the narrator himself sometimes appears as a backward-looking romantic. The reappearance of fruitful dialogue and debate is the most striking feature of Spain emphasized in the book. Fries observes, for example: "Der Caudillo ist noch kein Jahr unter Marmor und Fels auf ewig ins Nichts versenkt worden, da kommt alles zur Sprache, worüber ein Menschenalter geschwiegen wurde" (p. 18). Toward the end of the book, he asks a young filmmaker, "Was bedeutet für dich das Ende des paternalistischen Franco-Staates?" The answer is, "Daß alle Fragen gestellt werden können und manche keine Antwort finden" (p. 147).[11]

The use of dialogue and debate to emphasize diversity underlines Fries' desire, important to his other books but here a central theme, to avoid both simplistic name-calling and shallow idealization. On the very first page of the book Fries addresses the question of clichés, using the arch-cliché of tourism in Spain, the bullfight, to examine clichés in general. In this opening chapter, entitled "Tod am Nachmittag" and prefaced by a quotation from Hemingway's novel, Fries tries, not altogether successfully, to interpret the bullfight as a metaphoric ritual, much as he did at the end of the novel Das Luftschiff. Here "der ständige Rollentausch" (p. 10) of man and animal conveys the difficulty and artificiality of attributing qualities and motives to particular individuals or groups: "Wie jedes Spiel läßt auch der Stierkampf Möglichkeiten der Identifikation offen" (p. 11).[12] The bullfight sets the tone for an openness to a multivalent reality which must be perceived without prejudice: "[wir] stülpen . . . die Taschen samt Futter um und um und lassen alle Vorurteile fallen . . . und drücken die Redensart, das kommt mir spanisch vor, in den nächsten Papierkorb, wo sie seit dem dreißigjährigen Krieg, der das Wort nach Deutschland brachte, hingehört" (p. 28); he discovers "wie immer in Spanien ist die Wirklichkeit anders als das Vorurteil" (p. 64).

The refusal to seize upon predictable rubrics informs the style of the text. One technique whereby the author conveys the unpredictable nature of Spanish reality is the use of unannounced forays into fantasy, recounting, for example, an event or scene for a few sentences and then abruptly stating, "Später entdeckten wir die Kameras hinter den Bäumen, alles eine Filmszene . . ." (p. 30), or, after reproducing a dialogue, "Während ich mir diesen Dialog vorstelle . . ." (p. 80). The implication here, which extends to the empirical reality of Spain, is that everything is possible, that one does not know what course events will take.

Fries' encounter with Spain combines intimate personal associations of the past with an inquiring and open look into the country's future. At the same time the book, more than Fries' other travel writings, gives the author occasion for indirect self-scrutiny. The most personal chapter is not any of those dealing with the writer's private connections to Spain. It is, instead, the odd concluding chapter, "Nachsatz, Lebenslehre oder die Passionen der aufklärerischen Seele," a eulogy for Werner Krauß. At first glance it appears to be an awkward and deviant appendage to the book, with no integral connection to the journey; its frank emotions and occasionally unrestrained rhetoric seem at odds with the rest of the text. Here Fries writes not as the ironically detached or at least courteously distant travel writer but as the bereaved son. His remarks cast light on himself as a writer and, within the context of the book itself, appear as a kind of apologia, though not an apology, for what he has tried to do in his text. Through his selection of quotations from Krauß' writings, Fries says much about himself as a writer.

The chapter on Krauß reveals a tension between Fries' own perspective and what he sees as the official stance toward art in the GDR. He notes, for example, that the official funeral oration omits mention of Krauß' novel, PLN (Postleitnummer), so important for Fries himself (p. 198). What he presents of the oration sounds drearily like bureaucratic labels which could apply to numerous other scholars:

> Die Rede geht an diesem Vormittag über den bekränzten Sarg: Der international hochangesehene Gelehrte, der hervorragende Wissenschaftler und Hochschullehrer, der drei Jahrzehnte maßgeblich zur Entwicklung der marx-

istisch-leninistischen Literaturwissenschaft und Romanistik in der DDR
beigetragen hat. (p. 189)

Fries, moreover, suggests qualities of his society
which created a certain distance between it and the
writer Krauß, and, implicitly, himself. Writing of
Krauß' indifference toward a reprinting of his novel,
Fries asks, "Wollte er in einem Land, das sich nicht
einmal in seinen Sprichwörtern lachend von sich selber
distanzieren kann, in der Zeit des Wiederaufbaus nicht
die Säure seiner Aphorismen ins notwendig menschen-
freundliche Bild geben?" (p. 194).

The most important manifestation of the Krauß-
Fries relationship appears in a quotation from the
former's book on Gracián, which can be read as Fries'
own credo, a credo which has not always endeared him
to critics:

Die Sprache soll mehr andeuten als
aussagen--die Wahrheit darf niemals
ganz in Worten verausgabt werden.
Man darf dem Verständnis keine beque-
men Brücken bauen, sondern muß immer
am anderen Ufer stehen. Die Rätsel-
rede bedient sich des Lakonismus . .
. Die Sprache spiegelt nicht einfach
den Gedanken, sondern ist seine Erzeugung . . ." (p. 195)

Fries admits to having used this last sentence in a
more extreme form, "Die Sprache spiegelt nicht einfach
das Leben, sondern ist seine Erzeugung," to defend his
first novel, Der Weg nach Oobliadooh, against criticism which Krauß voiced after reading the manuscript.
It is doubtful whether Fries would wish to apply the
quotation, especially in its latter form, to his travel writing. But Krauß' emphasis on creating a reality
which suggests rather than reproduces the empirical
world and which leaves much room for the free play of
fantasy and imagination in interpretation clearly provides Fries with a model for all his writing. As a
valuable antidote to a pedestrian realism which so
often mars travel accounts and to the facile, comfortable assertions about a foreign reality which this
form of writing invites, the comments of Krauß in this
chapter are appropriate to Fries' endeavour in Mein
spanisches Brevier.

Each of these three works represents an imaginative and sincere attempt to create a coherent, compelling image, though not a mirror reflection, of a world unknown to most of its readers. In this age of mass communications Fries' travel pieces function not as the transmission of factual data but as a document of the ways in which different cultures partially determine how their members interpret worlds beyond their boundaries, how individual travelers struggle to achieve their own independent interpretation of other cultures apart from their own cultural preconceptions, and how an artist tries to put this endeavor into a coherent expression without recourse to pre-established rubrics and clichés. All of these works travel well from East to West and confirm for the American reader an observation of Elias Canetti, a writer with whom Fries feels an affinity,[13] "Es ist ein besonderes und viel zu wenig genütztes Glück, daß es Reisetagebücher aus fremden Kulturen gibt. . . ."[14]

University of Michigan

Notes

[1] Fries is known in the West mainly for his exuberantly funny lyrical novel Der Weg nach Oobliadooh, published by Suhrkamp in 1966 and misunderstood in both East and West as a dissident work. Only in recent years has it come to be mentioned in critical discussions of Fries in the East, where it has yet to appear. His second fictional work, a collection of stories, Der Fernsehkrieg (1969), gave Fries legitimacy in the GDR but was viewed as politically conformist in the West. A second novel, Das Luftschiff (1975), evoked lukewarm response in both East and West. A third novel, Alexanders neue Welten, appeared in 1983. Fries appears to enjoy a solid reputation in the GDR as a translator of Spanish literature. He has translated works of Borges, Cortázar, García Marquez, among others, and has published a full-length biography of Lope de Vega. For varying appraisals of Fries, see Werner Liersch, "Spaziergänge in das Reich der Luft," Neue Deutsche Literatur, 23, No. 7 (1975), 127-131; Karl Mickel, "In zwei Kulturen leben: Laudatio zur Verleihung des Heinrich Mann Preises 1979," NDL, 27, No. 8 (1979), 160-64; Friedrich Albrecht, "Zur Schaffensentwicklung von Fritz Rudolf Fries," Weimarer Beiträge, 25, No. 3 (1979), 64-92; Werner Brettschneider, Zwischen literarischer Autonomie und Staats-

dienst: <u>Die Literatur in der DDR</u> (Berlin: E. Schmidt, 1972), p. 136.

[2] Fritz Rudolf Fries, <u>Seestücke</u> (Rostock: Hinstorff, 1973); <u>Mein spanisches Brevier</u> (Rostock: Hinstorff, 1979); <u>Alle meine Hotel Leben: Reisen 1957-1979</u> (Berlin: Aufbau, 1980); Fritz Rudolf Fries and Lothar Reher, <u>Erlebte Landschaft: Bilder aus Mecklenburg</u> (Husum: Druck und V.-G., 1982).

[3] Manfred Jendryschik, for example, begins the postscript to his anthology of travel writing about other socialist countries by quoting remarks of Volker Braun about the international nature of socialist revolutions and about the historical significance of the integration of socialist societies (Jendryschik, <u>Auf der Straße nach Klodawa: Reiseerzählungen und Impressionen</u> [Halle: Mitteldeutscher Verlag, 1976], p. 496). Similarly, a review in <u>Weimarer Beiträge</u> of a book on the Soviet Union by Richard Christ, one of the GDR's best travel journalists, notes the work's attention to "die Frage nach dem politischen Handeln, der geistig-moralischen Verantwortung des einzelnen gegenüber der Sowjetunion" and "die Frage nach der deutsch-sowjetischen Freundschaft," questions which--of course with respect to other political configurations--do not play an important role in West European or American travel writing (Edelgard Schmidt, "Richard Christ: <u>Um die halbe Erde in hundert Tagen: Reisegeschichten</u>," in <u>Weimarer Beiträge</u>, 23, No. 11 [1977], 153). In this context a definitive emphasis falls on a perspective turned toward the future, an orientation implicit in much GDR travel writing with its attention to social change, its view into "das Dritte Jahrtausend," the latter phrase again Jendryschik's borrowing from Braun (p. 497). GDR travel writing in general appears to owe more to the conventions of the politically oriented travel essay established in Germany by Forster's <u>Ansichten vom Niederrhein</u> and developed further by the journalism of Junges Deutschland than it owes to other traditions of German travel writing (such as the sentimental journey, the autobiographical narrative of personal development in travel, the speculative semi-philosophical travel essay or the impressionistic feuilleton).

[4] For example, see Jendryschik, pp. 58, 167, 180, 43-44, 136.

[5] An otherwise good travel book which is limited by such schemes is Rolf Schneider's <u>Von Paris bis</u>

150

Frankreich (Rostock: Hinstorff, 1977), in which the author's preconceptions determine his response to France. In some ways more successful as a travel book is Inge von Wangenheim's journalistic Reise ins Gestern, much maligned in the West for its doctrinaire analysis of the Federal Republic. Rather than simply dishing up clichés and stereotypes and presenting them as her experience, von Wangenheim at least attempts to depict her GDR traveler during her four weeks in Munich as developing and formulating a sincere interpretation of the other Germany.

[6] Fritz Rudolf Fries, "Die polnische Reise. Ein Fragment," in his Alle meine Hotel Leben: Reisen 1957-1979, pp. 53-58. All subsequent page citations will appear in parentheses in the text.

[7] For a thoughtful analysis of the relationship between Fries and Jean Paul with regard to Der Weg nach Oobliadooh, which also casts light on the early travel pieces, see Bernhard Greiner, "Sentimentaler Stoff und fantastische Form: Zur Erneuerung frühromantischer Tradition im Roman der DDR (Christa Wolf, Fritz Rudolf Fries, Johannes Bobrowski)," in DDR-Roman und Literaturgesellschaft, ed. Jos Hoogeveen and Gerd Labroisse. Amsterdamer Beiträge zur neueren Germanistik, Vols. 11-12 (Amsterdam: Rodopi, 1981), pp. 249-381. For Fries' own comments about his literary models, see his eulogy for Werner Krauß at the end of Mein spanisches Brevier and his comments in interviews, especially in Friedrich Albrecht, "Interview mit Fritz Rudolf Fries," Weimarer Beiträge, 25, No. 3 (1979), 38-63.

[8] Wolfgang Predel, "Reisen als geistige Lebensform: Fritz Rudolf Fries, Alle meine Hotel Leben," Neue Deutsche Literatur, 29, No. 6 (1981), 127.

[9] For much more schematic descriptions of Cuba by visitors from the GDR, see Jean Villain, "Nächtliches Tribunal in der Schalterhalle," in Jendryschik, pp. 460-70; and Hilde Rubinstein, "Meine kubanische Reise," Sinn und Form, 33, No. 4 (1981), 941-57.

[10] Fritz Rudolf Fries, Mein spanisches Brevier (Rostock: Hinstorff, 1979). All citations of this work will refer to this edition, and page numbers will be given in parentheses in the text.

[11] At the same time the visitor from the GDR recognizes the pitfalls of unchannelled pluralism; the

filmmaker's remark occurs, after all, in a transvestite bar, where the exquisitely disguised personnel would not greatly impress Fries' readers back home. Predel, in his review of Alle meine Hotel Leben, which includes a variation of the Barcelona chapter from Mein spanisches Brevier, sees the transvestites as a comment on the shallow quality of freedom after Franco: "Miró, Dali, Picasso eröffnen den Blick auf Barcelona und seine Transvestiten, die - so sehe ich es jedenfalls - einen ziemlich müden Gruß der 'neuen Freiheit' aus der Metropole Kataloniens herüberschicken", p. 129).

[12] Other examples include the countess, "schön und heiter wie eine baskische Bäuerin" (pp. 64-65), who does all the housework herself, or the pair whom the traveler interprets as a businessman and an intellectual, only to discover that the businessman is discussing the latest poetry of the Spanish leftist poet Alberti and the intellectual the trading of Spanish oranges on the world market (p. 28).

[13] See, for example, Friedrich Albrecht, "Interview mit Fritz Rudolf Fries," p. 40.

[14] Elias Canetti, Das Gewissen der Worte (Frankfurt/M: Fischer, 1975), p. 66. As examples Canetti mentions the book of a seventeenth-century Chinese traveler in India and that of a fourteenth-century Arabic journeyer in various parts of the Muslim world, India and China.

Peter Gosses lyrische Navigationsversuche

Fritz H. König

Wie Günter de Bruyn, Axel Schulze, Joochen Laabs und Manfred Jendryschik ist auch Peter Gosse ein DDR-Autor, der über den Umweg eines praktischen Berufes verspätet zum Schreiben kam. 1938 in Leipzig geboren, studierte er von 1956-62 Hochfrequenztechnik in Moskau und war bis 1968 in der Radarindustrie tätig. Nach einem ersten Startversuch als freischaffender Künstler ist er seit 1971 als Dozent am Literaturinstitut "Johannes R. Becher" in Leipzig tätig. 1969 erhielt er den Kunstpreis von Halle-Neustadt und den Kunstpreis der Stadt Leipzig. Ähnlich wie Laabs und Jendryschik produziert auch Gosse sowohl Prosa als auch Lyrik, wobei die eigene Lebenserfahrung, die Zeit in Moskau, die Berufstätigkeit in seinen Werken ihren Niederschlag finden. Titel seiner Sammlungen wie Antennendiagramme, Ortungen sind nicht von ungefähr, auch nicht ein guter Teil der Metaphorik, die auf Technisch-Naturwissenschaftliches zurückgeht.

Von Peter Gosse liegen bislang die folgenden Werke vor: Antennendiagramme (1967), Eindrücke und Reportagen seines Moskauaufenthaltes in Prosa; Antiherbstzeitloses, eine erste Gedichtsammlung aus dem Jahre 1968; weitere Reportagen in Zusammenarbeit mit anderen Schriftstellern unter dem Titel Städte machen Leute (1967). Danach folgt ein längerer Hiatus. Im Jahre 1975 erscheint eine Sammlung weiterer Gedichte und Prosanotate, Ortungen, und schließlich im Jahre 1982 ein Essayband literarisch-kunsthistorischer Natur mit dem Titel Mundwerk und der letzte Gedichtband, Ausfahrt aus Byzanz.¹ Ferner hat er dramatische Texte geschrieben. Für sein Hörspiel Leben lassen erhielt er 1981 den Hörspielpreis. Gosse ist auch als Herausgeber tätig gewesen. Beispielsweise liegen eine Ausgabe von Adolf Endlers Gedichten im Reclam Verlag und eine Ausgabe von Petrarca-Übersetzungen in der Reihe

Es wird in diesem Rahmen nicht möglich sein, auf Gosses Gesamtwerk einzugehen, und ich werde meine Ausführungen auf seine drei Lyriksammlungen beschränken. Es ist interessant, seinen Weg als Lyriker zu verfolgen, denn er macht von Sammlung zu Sammlung jeweils eine größere Metamorphose durch. Der begeisterte Positivist beginnt Fragen zu stellen, die sich mehr und mehr von außen, von der Umwelt, nach innen kehren. Zweifel schleichen sich ein: Was ist wirklich Wirklichkeit?

Zu seinem lyrischen Erstlingswerk, <u>Antiherbstzeitloses</u>, hat Gosse folgendes zu bemerken:

Das Titelwort spricht sich gegen Herbstiges
und Zeitloses und Blümeliges bereits aus,
hinzuzufügen wäre vielleicht: Hat die Blume
                              Herbstzeitlose
        kühle Farben
(bestenfalls das indifferente Farbensammel-
                              surium Weiß)
        und Kolchizin,
ein Entwicklung hemmendes Gift.
Zwar ist vielen Arbeiten (s.u.) anzumerken:
geschrieben nicht in einem Jahr der unruhigen
                              Sonne.
Aha, sagt mein Bruder, der mein Freund ist,
                              erläuterst,
da sieht's bös aus.   (S. 5)

Der Titel ist ein cleverer Gag, und die eben zitierte Vorbemerkung wäre--und da ist dem Bruder zuzustimmen--gar nicht nötig. Sie benötigt auch kaum der Interpretation. Sie wendet sich gegen Herbstiges; nun ist der Herbst eben als Erfüllungs- und farbenprächtige Todesmetapher ein Tummelplatz für Lyriker der Bourgeoisie, von den Erntebacchanalien eines Keats bis zu den blauen Astern, die sich fröstelnd am Traklschen Brunnen neigen. Ganz klar, dies paßt nicht zum sozialistischen Aufbruchs- und Pioniergeist; ebensowenig das "Blümelige," d.h. stilistisch und inhaltlich Artifizielles, <u>ars artis gratia</u>-Denken, das auch einen Fremdkörper in der sozialistischen Literatur darstellt. "Zeitloses" ist ebenfalls nicht gefragt, da es oft an der gegenwärtigen Realität vorbeigeht. Die losgelöste Kühle der Farben, die auf egozentrische Nabelschau hinausläuft, ist nicht erstrebenswert, eher warme, leuchtende Farben, beispielsweise das Rot des persönlichen Engagements für die gemeinsame Sache.

Und natürlich soll keine Entwicklung gehemmt werden, besonders nicht die der Revolution.

Von den 34 Gedichten in dieser ersten Sammlung sind gut die Hälfte politisches Manifest, politisches Glaubensbekenntnis, das sich aber nicht in leblose ideologische Höhen versteigt, sondern stets den Alltag im Auge behält, persönliches Engagement demonstriert. Dabei muß hinzugefügt werden, daß hier der Begriff Realität absichtlich vermieden wird, da dieses Konzept bei Gosse, von seinen theoretischen Anmerkungen aus gesehen, nicht eindeutig ist, wie ich weiter unten noch zeigen werde.

Im Gedicht "Inventur Silvester 64" heißt es u.a.:

> Drei Jahre, zwei Pfund Lyrik,
> während mein Staat schuftet und schwitzt.
> Schluß mit der Kindheit.
> Ich werde exportreife Radars mitbauen,
> werde Mehrprodukt machen,
> werde mitmischen. (S. 34)

Dem Rat der Stadt Leipzig wird vorgeschlagen, sich an Bauprojekte heranzumachen, die zwecknah und inspirierend sind:

> Ich beispielsweise will mitmischen fünf,
>   sechs Abende wöchentlich.
> Ich bring noch ein Dutzend mit,
> Hemdsärmelige, denen's nicht ist um ein
>   bißchen unbezahlten Schweiß.
> ("An den Rat der Stadt Leipzig", S. 36)

Die Vorbilder für dieses individuelle Steineschleppen zum Prachtbau des Sozialismus kommen, und wie könnte es anders sein, vom großen Bruder im Osten. Denn dort läßt z.B. der Schachweltmeister Botwinnik die müßigen Tüfteleien sein und benutzt sein spezielles Talent der Gedankenakrobatik dazu, Computer zu programmieren: "Doch meinen Gin heut, den trink ich / . . . um den' still geworden ist, zu: / Botwinnik, der nun Rechner programmiert" (S. 42).

Keine Vorbilder, sondern deren Gegenteil kommen aus der entgegengesetzten Himmelsrichtung, und der "Messeonkel A." bei der Leipziger Messe muß aufgeklärt werden über die Vorzüge der Menschen, die im Sozialismus verankert sind: "Leute, von zehn Loreleis nicht geschweige für fahrbaren Untersatz / wegzuholen aus diesem Staat . . ." (S. 29).

Von (ost)deutscher Warte aus bleibt, was die weltpolitische Lage betrifft, nur der Traum vom Weltfrieden, der in dem "Vorschlag" gipfelt:

sofern der Große Vorschlag ABSOLUTE ABRÜSTUNG
                UNTER INTERNATIONALER KONTROLLE
der bekanntermaßen sowjetische . . .
von den gestrigen Regierungen akzeptiert würde

Da könnten die Waffen ins Philippinentief
geschüttet werden. . . .

Die Beringstraße ließe sich mit nichtrostendem
                Schrott
zuwerfen, der Sellerie wüchse hoch
hinauf bis Baffinland, hört man, bis
                Tschuktschens.
                                ("Vorschlag," S. 49)

Die angeführten Gedicht-Beispiele sind thematisch eher eindimensional und etliche davon auch in ihrer Bildlichkeit nicht eben originell. Andererseits enthält Antiherbstzeitloses aber auch Besseres. Zwar nichts "Herbstiges," aber immerhin "Sommerliches" und "Wintriges" und somit vielleicht doch "Zeitloses." Es ist der Mühe wert, sich ein Gedicht dieses Typs, der sich vornehmlich mit Reise- und Natureindrücken befaßt, näher anzuschauen:

                Tatra (natürlich die Hohe)

Unten wuchsen uns saftarme Bäume nach,
rauhbereift, wie überzüchtete Elchgeweihe--
nun stehen wir, Tieflandsbuchtler
und satt momentan der Mählichkeit der
                Ebenemühen,
stehn Graten obenauf: ein Problem für
                Somnambulisten.

Dies zur Einleitung, und den Schluß setzt das
                Wadenbein,
das knapp überm Schi diesen Bergen nicht
                standhielt, was tut's:

Hier stülpen sich Wasserfälle brisant
in, die konturlosen Himmel hochhalten: die
                Schluchten,
und: Kompromißlos aufwärts! heißt dem Horizont
                die Losung,
die nichtwaidmännische (in dieser rennsteig-
                losen Berauschnis).

In die kommt, Leute, per selbstgeschriebne
                    Einladung etwa
(auch DER-Preis-wert ist dieses ungeblümte
                    Terrain):
Hier hast du fast Jodellust, hier heitert's an
                    ohne Ginkonsum,
hier bergpredige ich anstandslos und übers
                    Zeilenmaß hinaus:
Nicht in Sesseln zum Beispiel legt euer Geld an,
                    Ohrringe
nötigenfalls schenkt, daß morgens Augringe seien.
                    (Das nebenbei.)

Obwohl hier nicht Elbrus, der Traumhafte,
der Stirb-und-werde-Berg, seine nahbaren Brüste
                    herzeigt--
hier steh ich nicht weniger gern als, wo das
                    Hemd zwar um den Bauch bleiben mußte:
auf Dubnas Beschleunigermagneten von der Größe
                    reichlicher Mammuts.
Für blaue Vakuumpumpen stellt hier Wind ohr-
                    befriedende Phonzahl,
treibt Schneekristalle zu Aureolen, blühenden--
                    und hoch ins kristalline Gestein,
er wird um die 4 sein nach der Skala des Manns
mit dem Namen Beaufort, der ist schön:
                    schönstark.
                                   (S. 8-9)

    Was an diesem Gedicht besticht, ist die Aneignung
der Natur. Auf dem Berg stehend ist die gesamte Natur
unter einem, d.h. einem untertan, sie steht, auch von
der Ästhetik her gesehen, im Dienst des Menschen und
ist somit in ihrer Majestät mit der Erhabenheit des
vom Menschen Geschaffenen vergleichbar. Die "renn-
steiglose Berauschnis," entfacht von der Natur, ist
direkt übertragbar auf die "Beschleunigermagneten von
der Größe reichlicher Mammuts": Im Wind am Ende verei-
nigen sich Natürliches und Technisches, er wird mit
Beauforts Skala gemessen. "Schönstark" ist die deutsche Übersetzung des Namens Beaufort, schön stark ist
dann auch der Wind. Wie die industrielle und die gesellschaftliche Entwicklung wird die Natur nicht sta-
tisch gesehen, sondern in Bewegung ("Unten wuchsen uns
saftarme Bäume nach," "Hier stülpen sich Wasserfälle
brisant," "Schneekristalle" werden "zu Aureolen" getrieben). Bewegung entspricht, auf menschlich-gesell-
schaftliche Ebene übertragen, Entwicklung. Die Winterlandschaft auf dem Berggipfel ist auch deshalb so
berauschend oder inspirierend, weil alles vertikal an-
geordnet ist, alles nach oben strebt: "Kompromißlos

aufwärts! heißt dem Horizont die Losung . . ." Das
könnte beinah auf einem Spruchband stehen.

Genießbar wird diese Gipfel- und Entwicklungs-
ekstase durch regelmäßiges Abgleiten ins arg Mensch-
liche. Das Wort "Tieflandsbuchtler" ist leicht ab-
schätzig. "Tieflandsbuchtler" haben dann auch, wie zu
erwarten, Schwierigkeit in der Berglandschaft, brechen
sich beispielsweise das Bein. Man gibt für gewöhnlich
"Ginkonsum" zu, der nur in dieser Situation nicht nötig ist, und denkt auch, beim Anschauen der Kuppen und
Schluchten, ans andere Geschlecht. Der Kernspruch
"Kompromißlos aufwärts!" wird gemildert durch das folgende Wort "Losung." Normalerweise käme man in diesem
Kontext nicht auf die Idee, daß das Wort in der Jäger-
sprache so viel wie "Mist" bedeutet, also muß dazu ge-
sagt werden "nichtwaidmännische" Losung, damit wir auf
die Idee kommen, die betontermaßen fehl am Platz ist.
Die beschriebene und in Besitz genommene Berg- und
Winterlandschaft, "das ungeblümte Terrain" ist auch
für Westtouristen "preiswert," in der Doppelbedeutung
des Wortes (vom bundesrepublikanischen Reisebüro DER
ist die Rede, und zwar nebenbei, in Klammern). Aber
die Einladung "kommt, Leute" ergeht an alle, an alle
Welt, was im Einklang steht mit den kosmischen Dimen-
sionen des Gedichts.

Bemerkenswert ist die Sprache. Wie von der Landschaft Besitz ergriffen wurde, so wird auch von der
Sprache hier Besitz ergriffen. Gosse bemüht sich eindeutig, seine eigene Sprache zu sprechen. Bezeichnend
ist, daß viele Worte in ihrer Doppelbedeutung verwen-
det werden ("Losung," "Beaufort"), daß neue Adjektive
("saftarm," "nichtwaidmännisch," "rennsteiglos," "ohr-
befriedend"), auch neue Verben ("bergpredigen") gebil-
det werden. Vergleiche sind innovativ: "Bäume . . .
rauhbereift wie überzüchtete Elchgeweihe," "Ohrringe"
--"Augenringe". Aber Gosse ist hier noch im Anfangs-
stadium, seine lyrische Ausdrucksweise ist noch in
statu nascendi, daher ist die Sprache in den einzelnen
Gedichten noch sehr unterschiedlich. Auf der negativen Seite ist zu verbuchen, daß Verschiedenes sehr gesucht und konstruiert wirkt, daß bisweilen die Wortak-
robatik befremdet.

Antiherbstzeitloses schließt mit einem Versprechen, in der Zukunft Gedichte zu machen über "die
handliche Einfachheit der Welt," über "die Sicherheit
der Zukunft," "die Arbeitslust in jedem," "die neue
sozialistische Ökonomiepolitik" (S. 57). Es wird zu
untersuchen sein, ob dieses Versprechen eingelöst wird,

ebenso, ob diese Gedichte "in der leger steigenden Art eines Luftballons" (S. 57) erzählt werden. Letzteres war in der ersten Sammlung wenigstens nur teilweise der Fall.

Der zweite Band, Ortungen, sieben Jahre später erschienen, gibt außer Lyrik auch einige theoretische Anmerkungen, z.B. ein Kapitel über das sozialistische Gedicht. Es wird folgendermaßen definiert:

> Erstens: Es ist ein Gedicht, das Sozialismus befördern will, d.h. beitragen will zur Entwicklung der im Sinne der Aneignung der Natur durch das Individuum günstigsten Gesellschaftsstruktur, der der prinzipiellen (Macht-) Gleichheit der Leute.
> (S. 117)

Gute Ansätze zu dieser Art von Gedicht gab es bereits in der ersten Sammlung. Ferner erfahren wir zu diesem Thema:

> Da werden uns . . . nicht die Gefühle von den Dingen gegeben, sondern die Dinge so, daß wir sie fühlen können und . . . sie ihr Wesen bloßlegen. . . . [Das] Gedicht ist also nicht sublimiert zum Symptom des derzeitigen Gesellschafts- (Unter-) Bewußtseins, sondern versteht sich als Modell der Wirklichkeit. Es kann und soll an dieser überprüft werden von uns Rezipienten, wir treten damit--produzierend--neben den Produzenten . . . . Politisches und Intimes werden sich besagtem Gedicht nicht als gegensätzlich, ja einander ausschließend auftun, sondern als einander bedingend, nahe und sich nähernd. (S. 117-18)

Es folgen noch zwei wichtige Merkmale des poetischen Modells:

> Das poetische Modell sollte sich an großen zeitlichen und räumlichen Räumen konstituieren. . . . Ein weitgreifendes poetisches Modell muß alle Möglichkeiten, die Realität zu erkennen . . . nutzen. (S. 121)

159

In diesem Sinne sind Gosses Gedichte zweifellos sozialistisch. Definitionsschwäche: man ist nach wie vor nicht ganz sicher, was es mit dem Realitätsbegriff auf sich hat. Dreht es sich um soziale, politische oder einfach gegenständliche Realität, oder um Wirklichkeit schlechthin?

In Ortungen ist die Sprache homogener geworden. Zu den bereits angeführten individuellen Gosseschen Sprachmerkmalen treten hier eine zunehmende Apokopierung und Synkopierung und damit eine gewollte Annäherung ans Volks- oder Umgangssprachliche einerseits und an stilistische Traditionen, die in die Zeit des Barock zurückgehen, andererseits; außerdem findet eine zunehmende Fragmentation der Syntax statt, ein Vorgang, der ein Spannungsfeld herstellt zwischen Handlung, Bild und Reflektion.

Jürgen Engler, in seinem 1983 in den Weimarer Beiträgen erschienenen Aufsatz über Gosses Lyrik meint zu diesem zweiten Gedichtband, er wende sich "den ökonomischen, sozialen und politischen Verhältnissen zu, den Zwängen und Notwendigkeiten, den konkreten Widersprüchen und Konflikten, die die beschworenen und erwünschten Aktivitäten befördern oder auch hemmen." [2] Man kann das auch auf einen anderen Nenner bringen und schlichtweg sagen, daß sich der Überschwang der anfänglichen Begeisterung etwas gelegt hat. Einiges läßt sich nicht vereinfachen, ist komplex, duldet keine Schwarz-Weißzeichnung, erfordert vielmehr eine differenzierte Ausdrucksweise und ab und zu ein gerüttelt Maß Pragmatismus.

Als Beispiel dafür mag gleich das einleitende Gedicht "Dreiländereck" in Ortungen dienen. Es wendet sich wiederum gegen das Nationale, dessen Gefahren bekannt sind und das im Gegensatz zu einem sozialistischen Weltbürgertum steht. Während sich Gosse in dem Gedicht "Unzufälliges" in Antiherbstzeitloses noch damit begnügt, einfach, wenn auch ironisch, zu fragen:

> Wie weit übrigens hätte deutsche Liebe zu
> reichen, bis Schaffhausen,
> fällt ab hinterm Rheinfall? Oder bis Bern,
> gelegen ebenfalls in Landschaft hiesiger
> Zunge?   (S. 52)

häuft er in "Dreiländereck" Bild auf Bild und endet im Grotesken. Auf diese Weise gelingt es ihm, die Fragwürdigkeit des Nationalen, des kleinkarierten--und natürlich vor allem westlichen--Nationaldenkens viel wirkungsvoller zu betonen:

> Laufen rauf penibel gebuntete Pfähle,
> schillernde
> Warzengrate des Kraken, des Mercedesstern
> regenbogener Schatten läuft auf
> den, der da sitzt, der drei ist, ja aber
> mit so schmalem Arsche bewaffnet. Das
> harakiriet.
>
> Da fall ich um auf das Rückgrat, auf die
> Lider
> geraten mir Münzen: welchen Landstrichs?
> Vielleicht, wenn haarscharf überm Strich
> liegt die verschiedne Nase: verschiedene?
> Jene Eins links und rechts jene andre, das
> ist zum Umfalln. (Ortungen, S. 7-8)

Hier ist der imperialistische Krake, der mit unzähligen Armen um sich greift und vom Nationaldenken lebt--der Mercedesstern--geradezu zum Symbol für den Grenzverlauf in einem Dreiländereck prädestiniert und ebenso der im wahrsten Sinn des Wortes gepfählte Wohlstandsgnom, der nicht der Komik entbehrt und auch dann in der letzten Strophe gebührend belächelt wird. Und hier kommen wir, wenn wir die zitierte Definition des sozialistischen Gedichts anwenden, etwas ins Schleudern: "Modell" ist vielleicht auch das "Dreiländereck," aber wofür, für welche Realität? Der Widerspruch zwischen bestehenden Tatsachen und Erstrebenswertem ist nicht zwangsläufig ein dialektischer. Für mich jedenfalls ist die Definition des sozialistischen Gedichts inkomplett, solange nicht Definitionsvokabeln wie "Realität" geklärt werden.

Grenzthematik und auch über Grenzen Greifendes ("Olympische Spiele") charakterisieren die sechs Gedichte, die Teil I von Ortungen ausmachen. Beiläufig sei erwähnt, daß die Gedichte dieser Sammlung in fünf Teile untergliedert sind, von denen jeder einen lockeren thematischen Zusammenhang hat; die Einteilung könnte auch chronologisch bedingt sein, d.h. von der Entstehungszeit der Gedichte abhängen.

Teil 2 wendet sich dann in insgesamt drei Gedichten den ökonomischen Gegebenheiten zu. In den zwei ersten wird der westliche Klassenfeind schlicht überlistet, im letzten wird DDR-Gegenwart bewältigt: man muß sich mit dem Ruß abfinden, denn Briketts müssen zwecks harter Währung in den Westen gehen, damit bei-

spielsweise Kaffee gekauft werden kann. Hier liegt
ein Zwang der Umstände vor:

> da klettert nachts (weils da keiner, weil schla-
>   fend plus nachts so ganz direkt sieht)
> der Ruß auf Fenster-Brettblech und -Scheibe
>   oder die Betten drauf:
> Du säufst ihn, wenn der Kaffee, hart berappt,
>   morgens wie wild ins Speiserohr kommt
> und lacht: "Friß oder sauf!"   (S. 20)

Wiederum bleibt dieses Gedicht, wie viele andere
in dieser Sammlung, auch im Pragmatismus verhaftet,
der in dem Gedicht "Munterung an Dädalus" aus Teil 3,
dem Kerngedicht dieser Sammlung und einem der wichtigsten und auch geglücktesten Gosse-Gedichte überhaupt,
zum Programm erhoben wird. Es fängt mit den Worten
an:

> Solang Du ein Kerl bist, folge dem Sohne nicht!
> In den Horizont ziel, dort muß das Land sein,
>   Dädalus,
> Zieh in die Stoßstelle zwischen Bläulichem
>   und vagerem Blau, hinterlaß
> Hinterm Bauch die Lockung des Azur!
> Fokussier aufs Mähliche! . . .
> . . . . . Fokussier auf die Mitte . . . (S. 23)

Von ikarischen, idealistischen Höhenflügen sind
wir hier beim Weg der Mitte, beim Machbaren, beim rea-
listisch Möglichen gelandet. Gosse selbst sieht das
auch so: "Dann mäßigte sich der Eifer in ein erwachse-
neres Denkangebot: Dädalus."[3] In einem gut durchdach-
ten und einfühlsamen Aufsatz, "Die Mitte oder Munterung an G.," setzt Manfred Jendryschik das Gedicht in
einen literarischen Zusammenhang und zieht folgenden
Schluß:

> Literatur braucht den Mittelweg, das
> bedeutet ihre Macht; sie braucht die
> entstandenen Übereinkünfte, und alle
> einst so provokativen wie produktiven
> Neuerungen innerhalb der Künste stel-
> len sich im Rückblick als ziemlich
> leicht integrierbar heraus.[4]

Nun ist dieses Gedicht aber nur in seinem äußeren
make-up zurückblickend, im Wesen eher vorausblickend.
Worum es geht, ist ein fortlaufendes Abtasten der un-
teren und oberen Grenzen, der Grenzen der Möglichkeiten. (Jendryschik bezeichnet es als "beschwörende Os-

162

zillation von Augenblick und nächstem Schritt.")[5] In
diesem zukunftsgerichteten Tasten und der resultieren-
den Oszillation liegt elementare Produktivität, Entwicklung, ohne die die Kunst, die Gesellschaft und jeder einzelne Lebensbereich nicht auskommen. Somit
charakterisiert das Wort "Pragmatismus" diesen Vorgang
sehr unvollkommen, denn Praktisches und Theoretisches
verschmelzen hier widerspruchslos zu einer Einheit.
Das Gedicht ist auch im Einklang mit der Gosseschen
Hauptforderung ans sozialistische Gedicht: "Nicht ein
Ergebnis ist uns vorgesetzt, sondern wir 'erfahren'
den dialektisch sich vorantreibenden Vorgang, der zu
jenem Ergebnis führt" (Ortungen, S. 118). Das Modell
besteht somit weitgehend aus gedanklichem Prozeß.

Im 4. Teil der Sammlung wenden wir uns wiederum
ökonomischen Aspekten zu. Da gibt es Gedichttitel wie
"Aussage des Chemikers G. zur Havarie in der Waschmit-
telfabrik"--die Worte des Chemikers spiegeln das Für
und Wider bei der Einführung eines neuen Produkts,
auch hier ein Ringen mit dem Möglichen. In "Der Technische Leiter B. begründet" ist ein Fabriksleiter in
die Forschung versetzt worden, was ihn dazu beflügelt,
in der ihm verbleibenden Zeit "dieses lächerliche Fa-
brikelchen / rasch aus den Miesen zu zerren" (S. 47).
Bei dieser Arbeit im Kollektiv findet er zu seiner ei-
gentlichen Lebensaufgabe, zum Wesentlichen. Hier zwin-
gen die Umstände zum Erkunden der Möglichkeiten. Der
letzte und 5. Teil der Sammlung besteht aus einem ein-
zigen, sieben-teiligen Gedicht, das Betrachtungen zum
Fall Chile bringt, die auch auf andere Länder zu übertragen wären, in denen gewonnene Freiheit rückläufig
wird und die Mittel fehlen, sie zurückzugewinnen.

Nach sieben-jähriger Sendepause erschien 1982
Gosses dritter Gedichtband, Ausfahrt aus Byzanz.
(Auch zwischen den ersten beiden Gedichtsammlungen la-
gen sieben Jahre.) Es müssen für Gosse nur sieben
fette, sprich produktive Jahre gewesen sein, denn dieser neue Band ist breiter, variierter als die vorher-
gehenden, von sprachlicher Konsistenz und großer Aus-
druckskraft. Der Lyriker von Antiherbstzeitloses und
Ortungen ist kaum wiederzuerkennen, höchstens noch an
stilistischen Eigenarten; er hat eine Metamorphose
größeren Ausmaßes durchgemacht.

Zunächst mal der etwas mysteriöse Titel: Engler
sieht die Formel "Byzanz" als das Hineintragen der
Vorgeschichte in die eigentliche, sprich sozialistische Geschichte und führt weiter aus:

163

> Sie steht für Cäsarismus, Bonapartis-
> mus, für einen Zentralismus ohne ent-
> faltete demokratische Strukturen, für
> die Vergötterung des Oben, das der
> Kritik und Rechenschaftslegung entzo-
> gen ist, für Personenkult und er-
> starrtes Protokoll, für die Entmach-
> tung der Theorie und ihre Unterord-
> nung unter die jeweilige Staatsräson:
> Die Fahrt aber geht zum Gegenteil von
> alledem: zu wachsender Demokratie und
> zunehmender sozialer Gleichheit. [6]

Ich habe an dieser Titelinterpretation nichts
auszusetzen, sofern sie DDR-Realitäten einbezieht,
d.h. sich nach innen und nicht nur nach außen richtet.
Ebensowenig auszusetzen war am Lob des Pragmatismus,
wie er im Gedicht "Munterung an Dädalus" gefordert
wurde, falls man nicht vergißt, daß das Beispiel Dädalus im Sinne der Mythe den illegalen Grenzübertritt
einschließt, der, obwohl nicht im Zentrum des Interesses, trotz allem mitschwingt und sozusagen mit-
fliegt. Auch beim Titel "Ausfahrt aus Byzanz"
schwingt einiges mit. Denn Byzanz ist auch als "Ost-
rom" bekannt, und Ausfahrt ist quasi einem Ausflug
gleichzusetzen, bezieht, unter anderem, eine Rückkehr
ein, ist also zeitlich begrenzt. Über die Absichten
des Titels kann man natürlich getrennter Ansicht sein;
was bleibt, sind die semantischen Tatsachen.

In der fünf-teiligen Sammlung liegen insgesamt
siebzig Gedichte vor, es kann hier natürlich nicht auf
jedes einzelne eingegangen werden, was ja auch bei den
beiden bereits beschriebenen Bänden nicht möglich war.
Ich kann nur ein paar Beispiele herausgreifen, die ich
für wichtig und bezeichnend halte.

Das erste Gedicht heißt "Hymne in Rainers Garten"
(damit ist wohl Rainer Kirsch gemeint):

> Da schlängelteduckte ich, und mit Lust, durch
>   untern verhießenen Obstbäumen, durchströmt
>   wie Euter,
>   unter schwer taumelnden prangenden Fruchtgehän-
>   gen, kirschgrün
>   und nußgrün und pflaumengrün ununterscheidbar
> in den zart durchschatteten glimmenden Tönungen
>   Grüns,
>   und das Licht unaufhörlich sickerte, schlüpf-
>   te, lustwandelte

in den schäumenden Laubwerken, durststrotzend,
die Bottl
im Hemd seufzte bei jeder Verbeugung. (S. 7)

Ich erwähnne dieses Gedicht, weil es eines der relativ
wenigen ist, das sich mit Natur befaßt, und zwar be-
zweckt die sprachliche Berauschung nicht Feier der Natur, wie wir sie bei einem Axel Schulze finden, sondern gefeiert wird hier die Lebenslust, Freundschaft,
die Vorfreude auf einen Besuch. Wie auch im Gedicht
von der Tatra ist Natur nicht Selbstzweck, sondern
Gefühlskatalysator, Vergleichsfaktor, menschlichen Belangen untergeordnet.

Die Gedichte des ersten Teils tragen den Titel
"Ortschaften," sind also alle ortsbezogen. Die Thema-
tik wechselt von der überschäumenden Lebensfreude in
"Rainers Garten" hin zur Beschreibung des Todes als
Eingang ins Nichts, bzw. als Eingang in Alles, ins
All. Mikrokosmos und Makrokosmos sind präsent. In
"Das Grabfeld von Schladitz" wird Landschaft, Natur,
wie durch ein Teleskop nahegerückt, um nach der statt-
gefundenen Verschmelzung, Auflösung sich wieder zu
entfernen.

Noch an Erde schon in Erde die Schuh,
im sachten Wurzelzweigen, zwischen
den Stämmen verliern sich die unauf-
hörlichen Felder in verjüngenden Zei-
len, wiegendes, fern rieselndes, dann
stehendes Grün. (S. 16)

Ebenso wie Thematik und Bilder wechselt auch ka-
leidoskopartig die Form. Während ausgeglichene Prosa
im "Grabfeld von Schladitz" die Sanftheit und Natür-
lichkeit des Todes unterstreicht, setzt sich die
"Drispether Elegie" mit dem Tod durch die syntaktisch
fragmentierte Schilderung von Gegensätzlichem auseinander: Vergangenheit und Gegenwart stehen sich anti-
thetisch gegenüber, aber Gegenwart ist auch sich wie-
derholende Vergangenheit; Kosmisches (die Milchstraße)
steht einem menschlichen Lungenflügel gegenüber. Aber:

Die Lungenflügel, ich spür sie, kommen.
Jetzt gehen sie, wie die Galaxien jetzt, deine
meine,
Zu unsern fernen Zeiten, wieder und wieder
Das Fleisch flügelt: Ists denn kein Trost . . .
(S. 13)

Eben dieser Trost mischt sich mit Trauer. Das Resul-

165

tat ist mäßiger oder besser: gemäßigte Hoffnung für
die Menschheit, beziehungsweise deren Chance für die
Zukunft.

Von zentraler Bedeutung scheinen mir in der Ausfahrt aus Byzanz diejenigen Gedichte zu sein, die mit
dem Titel auch thematisch in Verbindung stehen, d.h.
geschichtliche Perspektive einbeziehen. Besonders
hervorheben möchte ich in diesem Zusammenhang ein Gedicht: "Ugarit" (alte Hafenstadt in Syrien, bekannt
als archäologische Fundstätte).

> Die Stadt ihr Grabhügel.
> In Gras, Anis, Schafgarbe stehend,
> stehst du auf einem Dach, unter dem du
> durch zackige Durchbrüche der Schatzsucher,
>   säuberliche der Archäologen
> den Fußboden siehst: das Dach
> des vormaligen Hauses undsoweiter.
> In die Steigerungen des Schwarz
> verliern sich des weißlichen Steins Fügungen.
>
> Viermal wieder stand, viermal vom Beben verheert,
> Ugarit--Phönix könnte es heißen. Menschen
> mußten herbei (Pelasger, was weiß ich),
> der 5. Stoß saß, und Natur
> wächst über die Sache.   (S. 9)

Das Gedicht ist auf Gegensatzpaaren aufgebaut:
Stadt--Grabhügel, Dach--Fußboden, Archäologen--Räuber.
Zwischen diesen Gegensätzen werden, wiederum wie im
Dädalus-Gedicht, Möglichkeiten abgetastet. Die endgültig zerstörte Stadt kann Metapher sein für den
einzelnen Menschen, auch über ihn wird sich ein Grabhügel häufen, wird Natur wachsen; sie kann Metapher
sein für eine untergegangene Zivilisation und somit
durch Analogiebildung in Beziehung gesetzt werden mit
unserer Zivilisation, gleichgültig, ob ein westliches
oder östliches Vorzeichen gesetzt wird. Außerdem: ist
die endgültige Zerstörung wirklich endgültig, oder
gibt die darüberwachsende Natur Anlaß zur Hoffnung?
Grotesk auch die Vorstellung auf eigenem Grabhügel zu
stehen mit ungewisser Blickrichtung. Die Ausfahrt aus
Byzanz gestaltet sich hier zum Kreisverkehr, läßt ent-
weder viele oder gar keine Antworten auf ungestellte
oder nur andeutungsweise gestellte Fragen zu.

An diesem Punkt gibt Gosse mit einer gehörigen
Portion Ironie das Dilemma zu (die letzte Strophe des
Gedichts, oben unterschlagen, wird jetzt nachgelie-
fert):

Ein Schluß fehlt, ich spüre es,
mir fällt kein Schluß ein.
Die Stadt ein grüner Hügel.
Eine tatsächliche Ziege, mählich käuend.
Wir drei Touristen, natürlichen
Tods gewiß. Gewiß doch!
Blau blaut das Mittelmeer.

Wiederum das schon früher erwähnte Gemisch von
Trost und Trauer hier, von Hoffnung und ironischem
Achselzucken. Bevölkert wird der Grabhügel durch eine
tatsächliche, wiederkäuende Ziege, unbeeinflußbare
Realität, vor der wir als Todestouristen stehen, ewige
Vorgänge, die wir aus zeitlich begrenzter Perspektive
mit beengtem Blickfeld sehen. Was zu diesem Zeitpunkt
an Inhalt und Idee noch nicht aufgelöst ist, wird
durch das Wortspiel mit "gewiß" zunichte gemacht, und
die Zeile "Blau blaut das Mittelmeer" führt stilisier-
tes touristisches Naturgefühl--die Farbe blau als
Ewigkeitssymbol--und somit das ganze Gedicht ad absurdum. Eine allerletzte Zeile wäre hier, beispielsweise
im Ernst Jandlschen Reduktionsgedicht: bla bla bla.

Ohne Zweifel hat Gosse in diesem Gedicht einen
weiten Weg zurückgelegt vom eher gradlinigen Lob- und
Preislied auf den Sozialismus, sowohl gedanklich als
auch sprachlich. Nicht, daß diese neue Art von Lyrik
mit sozialistischen Belangen unbedingt im Konflikt
steht, denn die Methode des Schreibens, das Suchen
nach einem gangbaren Weg, nach Dädalus, das Bemühtsein
um den gedanklichen Prozeß als Vehikel zur Realisie-
rung einer menschlicheren Gesellschaft, hat sich nicht
geändert. Aber diese neue Lyrik bezieht die Ambiva-
lenz der Dinge ein, die Komplexität der Vorgänge,
schreckt vor Eindeutigem zurück, unterstreicht Viel-
deutigkeit und kommt, wenn überhaupt, zu vorsichtigen,
differenzierten Schlüssen, die vieles offen lassen.
Hauptingredienzen vieler der Gedichte in diesem neuen
Band sind Situationskomödie, stilistische und inhalt-
liche Ironie sowie Sarkasmus, ohne welchen die Lyrik
heutzutage weder in Ost noch West auskommen zu können
scheint.

In einem dem Freund Manfred Jendryschik zugeeig-
neten Gedicht "Schwebe" blickt Gosse zurück auf sein
früheres Leben und zieht das Fazit: "da kamen die uns
ziemlich skurril vor, die wir gewesen waren" (S. 53).
Man ist arriviert, hat's geschafft. Fragt sich nur,
wo man angekommen ist und was man geschafft hat, und
wehmütig denkt man an Entbehrungen früherer Jahre,
aber auch an die Begeisterung, die Dynamik, den Pio-

niergeist. Dieser individuelle Gefühlszustand läßt
sich natürlich relativ einfach auf die Gesellschaft
übertragen, wo die Entwicklung parallel gelaufen ist.
Jürgen Engler spricht in diesem Zusammenhang von einer
"gefestigten" aber auch "verfestigten" und somit in
gewissen Verkehrsformen erstarrten Gesellschaft.[7] Der
Titel "Schwebe" klingt einerseits wiederum ans Däda-
lus-Motiv an, läßt andererseits eine Vielzahl an Möglichkeiten offen, auch negativer. Gegenwärtig ist
wiederum das Gegensatzpaar Trost und Trauer.

In engem Zusammenhang mit "Schwebe" ist das Gedicht "Zwischenbilanz" zu sehen. Auch hier wird in
Gegensatzpaaren Hoffnungsvolles und Fragwürdiges in
der gesellschaftlichen Entwicklung gegenübergestellt
und abgewogen. Hie Ekel und Verzweiflung an Datschen,
Westautos und Privilegiertensystem, da Freude am ein-
fachen ehrlichen Einsatz einer alten Arbeiterin. Aber
wohin am Ende das Zünglein an der Waage ausschlägt,
wissen wir nicht, und die weit kreisenden Gedanken
kehren am Ende zur eigenen Person und Position zurück
und zur Schwierigkeit der Dädalus-Lage zwischen Sonne
und Wasser, und bezeichnenderweise endet das Gedicht
mitten in einem Satz:

zwischen diesem Zwischensein, zwischenstehend
oder -gestellt
oder wie, und war es das Sein? War das das
Dasein?

Zwischen meiner Furcht, du könntest ohne Furcht
sein um mich, und meiner Furcht, du könntest
in Furcht sein. Denn
wollte dich furchtlos, doch wär am Verzweifeln
(S. 124)

Vom Glaubensbekenntnis hat Gosse seinen Weg zur
Theodizee gefunden und weiter zu Antworten, die, wie
sich's herausstellt, nicht befriedigen und Generationen weiterer Fragen zeugen. Die Art von Gedichten,
die er in Antiherbstzeitloses versprach, produzierte
er bereits in Ortungen und überholte er in Ausfahrt
aus Byzanz. Nur Gedichte, erzählt "in der leger steigenden Art eines Luftballons," sind ihm eigentlich nie
gelungen. Sie sind meistens zu intellektuell zerklüf-
tet und fragmentiert--Gedichtlandschaften. Der Schwe-
beflug, der auch thematisch angestrebt wird, findet
stilistisch kaum statt.

Es bleibt zu hoffen, daß der nächste Gedichtband
nicht weitere sieben Jahre auf sich warten läßt und

vielleicht eine neue Metamorphose aufzeigt.

University of Northern Iowa

Anmerkungen

[1] Alle Werke sind im Mitteldeutschen Verlag Halle-Leipzig erschienen. Alle Seitenangaben erscheinen im Text in Klammern.

[2] Jürgen Engler, "Byzantinisches und Karnevalisches," Weimarer Beiträge, 29, No. 3 (1983), 491.

[3] Jürgen Engler, "Gespräch mit Peter Gosse," Weimarer Beiträge, 29, No. 3 (1983), 482.

[4] Manfred Jendryschik, "Die Mitte oder Munterung an G.," in Lesarten, Texte zu Gedichten, hrsg. von Christian Löser (Berlin/Weimar: Aufbau Verlag, 1982), S. 273.

[5] Jendryschik, S. 285.

[6] Engler, "Byzantinisches und Karnevalisches," S. 499.

[7] Engler, "Byzantinisches und Karnevalisches," S. 504.

Zum Selbstverständnis junger Lyriker in der DDR:
Kolbe, Anderson, Eckart

Günter Erbe

Die Rede ist von Autoren, die nach 1945 bzw. 1950
geboren sind und in den 70er Jahren zu schreiben be-
gonnen haben bzw. mit ersten Veröffentlichungen, zumeist mit Gedichtbänden, hervorgetreten sind. In ihren Erfahrungen unterscheiden sich die Angehörigen
dieser Generation erheblich von älteren Autoren, von
denen sie sich oftmals politisch und künstlerisch ab-
grenzen. Die jüngeren Schriftsteller haben die Jahre
des Aufbaus, der sozialen und ökonomischen Umwälzungen, nicht bewußt erlebt. Ihr Gesellschaftsbild präg-
te sich erst Ende der 60er Jahre und im Laufe der 70er
Jahre heraus, als die großen Klassenschlachten schon
geschlagen waren und die DDR sich als neues Gesell-
schaftssystem gefestigt hatte. Einschneidende soziale
Auseinandersetzungen fanden anderswo statt: die Stu-
dentenbewegung in den westeuropäischen Ländern, der
Vietnamkrieg, der Prager Frühling, die Pariser Mai-Er-
eignisse des Jahres 1968. Stützt man sich auf Selbstzeugnisse dieser Autoren, so trug auch die sozialistische Erziehung ganz andere Früchte, als von den Herrschenden erwartet. Die kurze Blütezeit, die dem Marxismus in den westlichen Ländern beschieden war, konnte
auf die DDR nicht ausstrahlen. Zu sehr war der Marxismus dort zur Ideologie erstarrt und durch die gesellschaftliche Praxis bei den jungen Intellektuellen
diskreditiert. Diese Feststellung läßt sich sicher
nicht verallgemeinern, doch trifft sie wohl auf jene
nicht geringe Anzahl künstlerisch engagierter Intel-
lektueller zu, die sich ein unabhängiges Denken zu be-
wahren gesucht haben.

Begrenzt in ihren Erfahrungen auf das kleine Land
DDR und die östlichen Nachbarländer, wird Lesen
für junge Menschen in der DDR zu einem geistigen
Abenteuer, einem Ausbruchsversuch in fremde Kontinen-

171

te. Fragt man jüngere Autoren nach literarischen Vorbildern oder Leseeindrücken, so werden Namen genannt wie Hamsun, Bobrowski, Dostojewski und Döblin. Philosophisch von Gewicht sind u.a. Schopenhauer, Nietzsche und Sartre.[1] Dies ist zu verstehen als Reaktion auf den Staatsbürgerkundeunterricht, als Korrektiv zur Schulauffassung. Von einem Überwiegen einer "proletarisch-revolutionären" oder "sowjetisch-realistischen" oder auch nur "bürgerlich-progressiven" Literaturtradition kann keine Rede sein. Die Jüngeren mucken auf gegen überlieferte Schemata und Doktrinen, nehmen provokativ die als irrationalistisch oder reaktionär verteufelten Gegenpositionen ein. Stephan Ernst, ein junger Lyriker, formuliert es so:

> Die Literatur ist eine Art Opposition
> . . . Sie ist Gegenwehr zuerst zu den
> Erwachsenen, zur Schule, später auch
> ideologisch . . . Ein bestimmtes Bewußtsein von einem Ungenügen braucht
> Literatur als Gegenwehr gegen seine
> Umwelt, auch gegen politische Konzeptionen und meinetwegen auch gegen
> marxistische Philosophie, sagen wir:
> gegen kollektive Vereinnahmung.[2]

Kunst dient nicht so sehr der Veränderung im Großen, Ganzen, sie ist Lebenshilfe, sie ist Stütze des Individuums, nicht der Gesellschaft.

Die Lyriker-Generation der Braun und Mickel war in den 60er Jahren mit einer Art "DDR-Messianismus" angetreten. Sie betrachtete sich als Teilhaber einer großen gesellschaftlichen Bewegung. Die Angehörigen dieser Generation--neben Volker Braun und Karl Mickel sind vor allem Sarah und Rainer Kirsch, Adolf Endler, Wolf Biermann, Reiner Kunze und Uwe Greßmann zu nennen--, die sich ab 1962/63 auf Lyrik-Abenden und mit ersten Einzelpublikationen zu Wort meldeten, entdeckten Unvollkommenheiten, wo die Älteren noch Fortschritt sahen.[3] Aufgewachsen in der DDR und geprägt von Idealen der Zeit des Aufbaus und der gesellschaftlichen Neugestaltung, verstanden sie sich als engagierte Sozialisten, die Anstoß nahmen an der kleinbürgerlichen Enge und der Selbstzufriedenheit der herrschenden Bürokratie. Die offiziöse Reaktion auf die damals jungen Debütanten beanstandete denn auch das Mißbehagen an der Umwelt, die Düsterkeit und Rätselhaftigkeit in den Bildern, die Klagen über nicht erreichbares Glück.

Bei den jüngeren Autoren heute ist die Bindung an die DDR weniger fest. Für sie sind die wesentlichen gesellschaftlichen Prozesse schon gelaufen. Uwe Kolbe im Gespräch mit der Literaturwissenschaftlerin Ursula Heukenkamp: "Meine Generation hat die Hände im Schoß, was engagiertes (!) Handeln betrifft. Kein früher Braun heute . . . Ich kann noch weitergehen und sagen, daß diese Generation völlig verunsichert ist, weder richtiges Heimischsein hier noch das Vorhandensein von Alternativen anderswo empfindet."[4] Die Schriftsteller der älteren Generationen konnten sich noch mit den gesellschaftlichen Vorgängen in den 60er Jahren identifizieren. Die jüngeren ziehen sich auf engere, unmittelbar überschaubare gesellschaftliche Bereiche zurück, in denen sie ihre Erfahrungen machen und mitteilen können. "Das Interesse für soziale Probleme ist schon da, aber gestaltbar sind sie für mich nur da, wo sie mich unmittelbar betreffen," meinte Gerd Adloff.[5] Den Älteren wird der Vorwurf gemacht, daß sie den öffentlichen Meinungsaustausch scheuten. Einer der wenigen, die sich der Auseinandersetzung mit der jungen Generation in dem begrenzten Rahmen, in dem das in der DDR überhaupt nur möglich ist, stellen, ist Franz Fühmann. Er sieht die Chance der jungen Schriftsteller darin, das, was seine Generation versäumt hat, zu leisten: sich umfassend im Kunstwerk auszudrücken. Die Jüngeren verfügten zwar nicht über eine Fülle von Erfahrungen wie die Älteren, doch eines hätten sie diesen voraus: ihre Homogenität. Den Älteren sei vorzuwerfen, daß sie ihre Erfahrungen bisher kaum literarisch gestaltet hätten. "Der große Stoff, das große Erlebnis, das große Thema allein macht noch gar nichts . . . ."[6]

Junge Autoren, deren Arbeiten aus politischen und ideologischen Gründen bei den kulturpolitischen Instanzen auf Skepsis oder Ablehnung stoßen, sichern sich oftmals die Unterstützung älterer, renommierter Kollegen, um eine Veröffentlichung ihrer Texte zu erreichen. So hat sich z.B. Fühmann für Uwe Kolbe, Kunert für Hans Löffler und Mickel für Bert Papenfuß eingesetzt. Doch selbst die Fürsprache eines anerkannten Autors hilft nicht in jedem Fall. Frank-Wolf Matthies konnte zwar mit Hilfe von Fühmann einzelne Gedichte in der Zeitschrift Sinn und Form publizieren; eine Einzelveröffentlichung jedoch blieb ihm ebenso wie Bert Papenfuß und Sascha Anderson in der DDR versagt. Größere Veröffentlichungen von Matthies und Anderson sind nur im Westen erschienen.

Ich habe bisher sehr allgemein vom Befinden, vom

Selbstverständnis der jüngeren Schriftstellergeneration gesprochen. Schaut man genauer hin, lassen sich bei aller Übereinstimmung in den Grundbefindlichkeiten unterschiedliche Richtungen und Bestrebungen ausmachen. Ich möchte das Gesagte deshalb durch Beispiele aus der Lyrik im einzelnen belegen.

Die nach 1945 geborenen jungen Lyriker fügen sich durch dieses Datum noch nicht zu einer homogenen Gruppe. Es fällt auf, daß die in den 40er Jahren Geborenen (z.B. Richard Pietraß, Brigitte Struzyk, Bernd Wagner) andere biographische Voraussetzungen mitbringen als die nach 1950 Geborenen. Sie verfügen zumeist über eine akademische Ausbildung und haben mehrere Jahre beruflicher Tätigkeit hinter sich, ehe sie ihre ersten Gedichte publizieren. Sie sind aufgewachsen mit einem noch ungebrochenen Leistungswillen und der Vorstellung, in der Gesellschaft Karriere machen zu können. Auffallend ist dagegen, daß viele der jüngsten, in den 50er Jahren geborenen Lyriker sich von vornherein ganz aufs Dichten, auf die künstlerische Arbeit als einzig annehmbare Lebensform konzentrieren. Sie verzichten aufs Studium, sind nicht bereit, eine dreijährige Verpflichtung zur Armee einzugehen (18 Monate sind die Regel), verweigern sich einer beruflichen Karriere und schlagen sich lieber als Hilfsarbeiter durch. Die Neigung, in irgendeiner Weise aus der Gesellschaft "auszusteigen," hat in dieser Altersgruppe zugenommen.

Als einen Repräsentanten der jüngsten Lyriker-Generation könnte man Uwe Kolbe ansehen. Kolbe, 1957 in Berlin geboren, wurde 1976 durch die Zeitschrift Sinn und Form zusammen mit Frank-Wolf Matthies einer größeren Öffentlichkeit vorgestellt.[7] Sein erster Gedichtband, Hineingeboren, erschien 1980 im Ostberliner Aufbau Verlag und wurde 1982 im Suhrkamp Verlag Frankfurt als westdeutsche Lizenzausgabe herausgebracht. In seiner Suche nach neuen Ausdrucksformen geht Kolbe auf den Expressionismus und die deutsche Frühromantik zurück. In der Diskussion im Anschluß an eine Lesung in der Westberliner Autorenbuchhandlung im Frühjahr 1982 setzte sich Kolbe von Volker Braun und Wolf Biermann ab. Brauns Gedichte fand er zu schematisch. Biermann fixiere sich zu sehr auf Parteijargon und Bürokratensprache, denen er Negativlosungen abgewinne. Als einziges Vorbild nannte er den 1941 geborenen DDR-Lyriker Wolfgang Hilbig, dessen Texte mit Ausnahme eines kleinen Bandes mit Lyrik und Prosa in Buchform bisher nur im Westen erschienen sind.[8]

Kolbe stellt seinem ersten Lyrik-Band Verse des französischen Dichters Paul Verlaine als Motto voran:

Durch ihre Adern fließt das Blut wie
Gift so fein
und rollt seltsam und brennt, wie
Lavaströme kochen,
bis trist das Ideal verschrumpft ist
und zerbrochen.

Die existentielle Grundbefindlichkeit des Autors Kolbe äußert sich besonders prägnant in dem Titelgedicht dieses Bandes:

Hineingeboren

Hohes weites grünes Land,
zaundurchsetzte Ebene.
Roter
Sonnenbaum am Horizont.
Der Wind ist mein
und mein die Vögel.

Kleines grünes Land enges,
Stacheldrahtlandschaft.
Schwarzer
Baum neben mir.
Harter Wind.
Fremde Vögel. [9]

Das Gedicht beschreibt die innere Zerrissenheit eines lyrischen Ich, einen gesellschaftlichen Ort, an dem man nur als Gespaltener existieren kann. Die Literaturwissenschaftlerin Ursula Heukenkamp kommt bei der Betrachtung der Gedichte Uwe Kolbes zu dem Urteil:

Mit den bekannten Konfliktfiguren von
Ideal und Wirklichkeit läßt sich das
Bild von der Welt, das in dieser Kon-
stellation hervortritt, nicht fassen.
Mit einem großen Weltentwurf tritt
diese Lyrik nicht an. Auch würde man
vergeblich nach dem Ich suchen, das
sich mit seinen Ansprüchen und Ent-
würfen der Gesellschaft als Maß und
moralische Instanz vorstellt und ent-
gegensetzt. Das Ich in den Erstlin-
gen der sechziger Jahre war ein anderes. [10]

Kolbe wohnt wie andere junge Lyriker in einer

175

Hinterhofwohnung im alten Ostberliner Arbeiterstadt-
teil Prenzlauer Berg. Er begann sehr früh, Gedichte
zu schreiben und hatte das Glück, in Franz Fühmann einen Mentor zu finden. Nach dem Abitur nahm er an einem Sonderlehrgang am Literaturinstitut J.R. Becher in
Leipzig teil. Nach dem Militärdienst arbeitete er als
Transportarbeiter und Lagerverwalter. Heute kann er
offenbar von Einnahmen aus literarischer Tätigkeit leben. Unter den jungen Schriftstellern der DDR--so
seine Selbsteinschätzung damals in der Autorenbuch-
handlung--sei er eine Art staatlich anerkannte Reprä-
sentationsfigur. Es gäbe andere (z.B. Sascha Anderson
und Bert Papenfuß), die die gleiche literarische Po-
tenz besäßen, aber nicht veröffentlichen könnten.
Seine Haltung, auch die in seinen Gedichten hervortre-
tende, bezeichnete er als unpolitisch. Die Zeit für
politische Literatur sei vorbei. Als Beispiel für politische Lyrik, wie sie in der DDR von offizieller
Seite gern gesehen werde, nannte er Steffen Mensching
(geb. 1958). Die wirklich potenten, schöpferischen
Talente seien eher unpolitisch.

Kolbes Äußerungen bei seiner Westberliner Lesung
waren der Anlaß für einen "Offenen Brief," den sein
früherer Freund Frank-Wolf Matthies (geb. 1951), der
seit 1981 in Westberlin lebt, an ihn richtete.[11] Matthies wirft Kolbe Bewegungsunfähigkeit, Autoritätshö-
rigkeit und Selbstentmündigung vor. Seine Feststellung, es gebe unter den jüngeren Talenten niemanden,
der politische Gedichte schreibe, wird von Matthies
mit dem Hinweis auf Sascha Anderson und Lutz Rathenow
(geb. 1952) korrigiert. Matthies sieht bei Kolbe einen Hang zum Karrierismus und Duckmäusertum und
schließt seinen Brief mit dem Appell: "Jeder hat die
Pflicht, darüber zu wachen, daß er nicht zum Lumpen
wird: ganz besonders der Künstler/Schriftsteller, der
seinen Beruf ja freiwillig öffentlich ausübt, also die
Verpflichtung angenommen hat, Moralist zu sein--und
nicht Karrierist."

Die Kontroverse Kolbe-Matthies spiegelt das ge-
spannte Verhältnis wider zwischen Autoren, die wie
Matthies in der DDR nicht veröffentlichen konnten und
wegen ihres politischen Engagements inhaftiert wurden
und jenen, die wie Kolbe trotz vieler Schwierigkeiten
gedruckt und geduldet werden. Der Vorwurf der Autori-
tätshörigkeit läßt sich angesichts der jüngsten Vorgänge um Uwe Kolbe kaum aufrechterhalten. In einem
Debütantenband war ein verschlüsselter Text mit dem
Titel "Kern meines Romans" von ihm erschienen, der,
liest man nur die Anfangsbuchstaben der aneinanderge-

reihten Wörter, folgende Schmähung der Herrschenden
ergibt:

1. Eure Maße sind Elend
2. Euren Forderungen genügen Schlei-
   mer
3. Eure ehemals blutige Fahne bläht
   sich träge zum Bauch
4. Eurem Heldentum den Opfern widme
   ich einen Orgasmus
5. Euch mächtige Greise zerfetze die
   tägliche Revolution. [12]

Das Buch wurde nach Bekanntwerden des skandalösen Tex-
tes eingezogen und der Autor Kolbe geriet unter Be-
schuß. [13] Vorher war jedoch bereits sein zweiter Lyrik-
Band, Abschiede und andere Liebesgedichte, im Aufbau
Verlag (1981) erschienen. [14]

Liest man die Gedichte des 1953 in Weimar geborenen und heute in Ostberlin lebenden Lyrikers Sascha
Anderson, erscheint Kolbes Feststellung, es finde sich
unter den jüngeren, ernstzunehmenden Talenten niemand,
der noch politische Gedichte schreibe, in der Tat un-
zutreffend. Es gibt unter den jungen Lyrikern in der
DDR wohl kaum jemanden, der mit gleicher Radikalität
und sprachlicher Virtuosität das Gefühl der Verloren-
heit und Hoffnungslosigkeit in der Welt des realen Sozialismus in poetische Bilder umzusetzen weiß wie Anderson. Die Sprache allein, wild, polemisch, experi-
mentierend, vollgestopft mit Assoziationen, stellt
schon eine politische Provokation dar. Der Gestus des
Aufschreis, der rebellische Ton erinnert an die ag-
gressiven Töne der Dichter der amerikanischen "beat
generation." Das Motto seines ersten Bandes, Jeder
Satellit hat einen Killersatelliten, lautet:

lettern schwarz auf weißem grund
solange die nationen ihre rolle spielen
(schwarz als reaktion auf weiss
weiss als reaktion auf schwarz)
vielleicht sollte man die wahrheiten
die durch die literatur verbreitet
werden grau auf grauem grund
drucken. ich weiß keine weltanschauung
keine fernfahrkarte oder
weiteres ding worauf mehr
als der preis geschrieben steht
ich habe ausser meiner sprache keine
mittel meine sprache zu verlassen [15]

Die Zerrissenheit, die in den Gedichten Kolbes an-
klingt, ist bei Anderson radikalisiert durch das Gefühl grenzenloser Ohnmacht.

>   wer ich bin werden wir
>   sehen auf der fotomontage mein herz
>   kreuzt der graue schatten
>   unserer achtundvierzig gestrigen stunden
>   das gelb meiner ohnmacht
>   ich kann mich erinnern eines tages
>
>   ich selbst wollte die formel meines sterbens
>   finden
>   und nannte meine erinnerungen
>   gelb
>   ich erwarte nichts
>   weisst du die dinge vergessen uns
>   schneller als wir denken
>   und ich weiss nicht wer es war
>   (S. 24)

Die Grundhaltung in diesem Gedicht erinnert an
den Gestus des Sprechens in den letzten Stücken des
DDR-Dramatikers Heiner Müller. Die Ohnmacht des einzelnen, die sich artikuliert, ist jedoch auch hier
nirgends Anlaß zur Wehleidigkeit, sondern äußert sich
in einer Haltung "harter Passivität und neu gerichte-
ter, gespannter Aktivität," wie sie der Literaturwissenschaftler Walter Höllerer für die junge amerikanische Beat-Lyrik der 50er Jahre nachgewiesen hat:

>   Zunächst heißt "beat" "todmüde", "wi-
>   derstandslos", ausgelaugt durch ein
>   Aufgebot von Propaganda-Argumenten
>   und widersprüchlichen Erziehungsparo-
>   len . . . Aber zugleich verbindet
>   sich mit diesem Begriff weniger das
>   deutsche "geschlagen", als vielmehr
>   "auf sich konzentriert", "nach in-
>   wärts gerichtet", und auf solche Art
>   impulsiv. [16]

Von dieser Impulsivität, Experimentierlust und Lust an
der Provokation zeugte das Gedicht "eNDe IV," dessen
Titel auf die Initialen der Parteizeitung Neues
Deutschland anspielt:

>   eNDe IV
>
>   östwestlicher die wahn
>   machs gut mit spekulatius

machs gut mit kohlenanzünder dem weissen
machs gut mit erika love again
machs gut schöne grosse blonde leere
rin machs gut ödipus oben
machs gut unten mitte spiegelverkehrt
eine nuance zu concafé machs gut
augenblick signiert machs gut eins
tv zwei
die macht sie fördert frauenliteratur
    unter dem aspekt
steigt laicht das bewusstsein ein
    frontstaat zu sein
machs gut im aquarium
sitzen immer die anderen machs gut
amnestie für die angebrochene
packung kekse marke favorit
                                        (S. 59)

Andersons respektloser Umgang mit dem klassischen Erbe
--der Band enthält eine schöne Parodie auf das Goethe-
Gedicht "Dämmrung senkte sich von oben"--, sein freier
Umgang mit tradierten lyrischen Formen, die Kompromiß-
losigkeit, mit der er gesellschaftliche Tabus auf-
greift, machen eine Veröffentlichung seiner Texte in
der DDR gegenwärtig unmöglich.[17]

    Beinahe manierlich nimmt sich neben Sascha Ander-
son die Lyrikerin Gabriele Eckart aus. Sie ist 1954
in Falkenstein/Vogtland geboren und studierte nach dem
Abitur in Berlin Philosophie. 1976 veröffentlichte
sie ihren ersten Gedichtband in der Reihe "Poesieal-
bum." 1978 folgte ein zweiter Gedichtband unter dem
Titel Tagebuch im Verlag Neues Leben. Gabriele Eckart
absolvierte ebenso wie Kolbe einen Sonderkurs am Literaturinstitut in Leipzig und leistete im Rahmen der
FDJ Kulturarbeit auf dem Lande. Sie hat 1982 im Verlag Neues Leben einen ersten Prosaband, Per Anhalter,
vorgelegt. Zahlreiche Gedichte von ihr sind in Anthologien, Literaturzeitschriften und Zeitungen veröffentlicht worden. Sie ist wohl die erfolgreichste
junge Lyrikerin in der DDR, was sicher damit zusammen-
hängt--sieht man einmal von den literarischen Qualitä-
ten ab--, daß sie lange Zeit von der FDJ besonders ge-
fördert wurde.

    Die im Band Tagebuch gesammelten Gedichte geben
Auskunft über den Lebensweg eines jungen Mädchens, das
weltabgeschieden in dörflicher Umgebung aufwächst und
schließlich in den Strudel der Großstadt Berlin gerät.
Die Gedichte umspannen einen Zeitraum von sieben Jahren. Sie ergeben eine intime Chronik dieses Lebens.

Das Eingebettetsein in eine vertraute Umwelt, die Irritationen als Folge des Ortswechsels, erste Liebe, Enttäuschung, Alleinsein, Sich-nicht-mehr-Zurechtfinden sind Wegstrecken, notiert in tagebuchähnlicher Abfolge. Vor ihrem Philosophiestudium schreibt sie:

> Nun will ich nicht mehr umhertappen länger
> mit meiner Wünschelrute Gefühl durch die
>   Welt,
> wobei ich sie ja doch nie erfuhr, ihre
>   Gründe,
> und wie ich sie, die Welt, betreiben kann,
> damit sie mich nicht betreibt, blindlings,
> ausspielt als mögliche Lusche.
> Wie kann ich selber mich schon ausspielen,
> nach welchen Gesetzen, sie mitbetreiben,
>   die Welt? [18]

Fünf Jahre später in "Tagebuchnotiz, Juni 1977" heißt es:

> Diese Hellsicht,
> ersehnte,
> da hab ich sie nun,
> wie das ist mit dem Leben - sein Grund,
> nun bin ich gebeugt über ihn,
> mit jeder Faser, starre hinein -
> und weiß plötzlich nicht mehr
> WOZU, was ich bloß damit soll
> und mit mir -
> da ich nicht mehr vertrage, wie er -
>   und brülle -
> sacht, der Wind, es streichelt, das
>   blühende Feld.   (S. 84)

Gabriele Eckart gehört nicht zu jenen jüngeren Autoren, die vorwiegend aus einem Zustand innerer Zerrissenheit heraus schreiben. Selbst wo sie sich zu ihrer Ratlosigkeit bekennt wie in dem zitierten Gedicht, trägt diese mehr episodischen Charakter, erscheint als etwas Vorübergehendes. In einem Gespräch mit der Kritikerin Ursula Heukenkamp, an dem auch Uwe Kolbe und Bernd Wagner (Lyriker und Prosaautor, geboren 1948) teilnahmen, äußerte sich Gabriele Eckart zum Vorwurf der Innerlichkeit, der öfter der jüngsten Lyrikergeneration gemacht wird:

> Die Aussagen über die Zeit und Gesellschaft werden zaghafter, unbestimmbar. Ich stelle lieber Fragen, als runde, feste Sätze auszusprechen,

oder verstecke mich hinter vagen,
nicht richtig faßbaren Metaphern, die
nur meine Ratlosigkeit andeuten.
Aber ich spüre, das ist nur vorüber-
gehend, dauert nur so lange, bis ich
mir bestimmte "große", soziale Dinge
neu und tiefer als früher durchdacht
habe, mich meiner Gedanken wieder sicher fühle. Dann werden die Arbeiten auch wieder sozial konkreter,
sprechen direkter zu anderen. [19]

Gabriele Eckart wird sich weiter an ihrem Grund-
thema, dem konflikthaften Verhältnis von Ideal und
Wirklichkeit, abarbeiten, einer Problematik, die des-
illusioniertere Autoren wie Kolbe und Anderson bereits
hinter sich gelassen haben.

Die in der Zeitschrift Weimarer Beiträge 1979
erstmals ausführlicher dokumentierten Selbstzeugnisse
der jüngeren Autorengeneration haben bei den kulturpolitischen Instanzen scharfe Zurechtweisungen ausge-
löst. Am härtesten ins Gericht mit den jungen Autoren
ging der für Kultur zuständige FDJ-Sekretär Hartmut
König--er selbst ist als Verfasser von Liedtexten her-
vorgetreten--, der sich auf der FDJ-Kulturkonferenz im
Oktober 1982 zu der Bemerkung hinreißen ließ, die in
den Weimarer Beiträgen abgedruckten Äußerungen "stamm-
te[n] aus dem Munde von Leuten, deren ignorante, wirk-
lichkeitsfremde Mitteilungen über das, was sie für das
alltägliche Leben des Volkes halten, jedem jungen Menschen, der mit beiden Beinen wirklich in unserem Leben
steht, mehr als eigentümlich erscheinen müssen."[20]
Diese scharfmacherische Reaktion findet ihr Pendant in
einem Leserbrief, den die Zeitschrift für junge Literatur Temperamente abdruckte, in dem den jungen Autoren Koketterie, Mangel an kämpferischem Mut und Feti-
schisierung der Oberfläche vorgeworfen wird.[21]

Sachlicher und differenzierter sind die Stellung-
nahmen der Literaturwissenschaftler und -kritiker.
Eine insgesamt positive, um Verständnis bemühte Würdigung versuchen Ingrid und Klaus-Dieter Hähnel. Sie
meinen, daß die Entwicklung von Selbstbewußtsein des
lyrischen Ich bei den Älteren parallel lief zur gesellschaftlichen Entwicklung: "Das Gefühl eines ganz
unmittelbaren Beteiligtseins, eines Gebrauchtwerdens
war der selbstverständliche Grundgestus jener Lyrik."[22]
Für die jungen Autoren heute sei diese grundsätzliche
Parallelität individueller und gesellschaftlicher Entwicklung nicht mehr gegeben. Die Zeit der großen

Kämpfe sei vorbei. Die Errungenschaften der neuen Gesellschaft seien gesichert, das Tempo der gesellschaftlichen Entwicklung habe sich verlangsamt. Hähnels lassen unerwähnt, daß die von ihnen für die 60er Jahre behauptete Übereinstimmung von politischen Zielsetzungen und Ansprüchen der Kunst sich im Rückblick oftmals als ein Verhältnis der Unterordnung der Kunst unter politisch-ideologische Zwecke erweist. Die Ernüchterung, die spätestens seit der Biermann-Ausweisung 1976 unter den Intellektuellen in der DDR eingekehrt ist, trug zu einer kritischen Neubewertung literarischer Arbeiten aus den 60er Jahren bei. Die jüngere Generation kann dort ansetzen, wo die Älteren schließlich aufgrund mühsamer Erfahrungen angekommen sind: in der nüchternen Einschätzung des politisch Möglichen, in der ideologischen Desillusionierung.

Fühmann hat zweifellos recht, wenn er feststellt, seine Generation habe sich darüber bisher kaum Rechenschaft abgegeben. "Keine Gelegenheit also für große Kämpfe? Wohin dann mit der eigenen Kraft?" (S. 131) fragen Hähnels. Sie stellen fest, daß für die Jüngeren die Nöte und Defizite des gelebten Lebens die wirklichen Kunstanlässe sind. Gedichte entstünden als persönliche Lebenshilfe. Ihre Untersuchung gipfelt in dem Nachweis eines grundsätzlich veränderten Funktionsverständnisses von Literatur bei den jungen Literaten. Ein Funktionsverständnis, "das der Literatur eine Aufgabe und Möglichkeit im Hinblick auf die fortschreitende Veränderung der Gesellschaft einräumt" (S. 134), stehe vorerst nicht zur Diskussion. Wenn die jungen Poeten auch Grundpositionen eines sozialistischen Literaturverständnisses preisgäben, jeder für sich bestrebt sei, einen Weg zu finden, so bleibe es doch bei dem "Versuch, innerhalb dieser Gesellschaft einen Platz zu finden" (S. 134). Die jungen Autoren seien also keine Aussteiger, Nihilisten oder Wertezertrümmerer.

Mit dieser versöhnlichen Feststellung möchten sich die Literaturwissenschaftler Mathilde und Rudolf Dau nicht zufrieden geben. Sie erheben Einspruch gegen die Behauptung, den meisten jungen Lyrikern ginge es nur um die Artikulation persönlicher Nöte. Die "wesentliche Tendenz" junger Lyrik käme darin nicht zum Ausdruck. "In Anthologien oder Einzeleditionen greifbare Texte aus dem Umkreis der Singebewegung, des Chansons, des 'politischen Theaters' oder anderer 'operativer' Wirkungsfelder werden keiner Interpretation für würdig befunden."[23] Ebenso würden Gedichte, die sich mit dem Thema Geschichte befassen, von Hähnels weitgehend ignoriert (z.B. Gedichte von Bernd Wagner, Brigitte Struzyk, Uta Mauersberger bis zu Hans Brinkmann und Thomas Böhme). Tendenzen des "Rückzugs" auf ein eingeengtes Feld der "Selbstfindung" ließen sich nicht in den Rang einer allgemeingültigen Gesetzmäßigkeit erheben.

Sicher wird man nicht behaupten können, daß Kolbe und Anderson die Repräsentanten der jungen DDR-Lyrik sind. Sie sprechen nicht für die junge Generation. Sie sind nur ihr sensibelster Teil. Sie sprengen mit ihren Gedichten die Grenzen, die der Staat setzt. So sehr sie auch durch das kleine Land DDR geprägt sind, erobern sie sich die Welt durch das Medium, das ihnen als Dichter zur Verfügung steht: die Sprache. Noch einmal Sascha Anderson: "Ich habe außer meiner sprache keine mittel meine sprache zu verlassen."

Freie Universität Berlin

Anmerkungen

[1] Vgl. Siegfried Rönisch, "Notizen über eine neue Autorengeneration," Weimarer Beiträge, 25, Heft 7, (1979), 5-10.

[2] "Vorbild--Leitbild. Joachim Nowotny im Gespräch mit Wolfgang Berger, Stephan Ernst, Ingrid Hildebrandt, Rainer Hohberg, Annerose Kirchner, Christine Lindner, Thomas Rosenlöcher," Weimarer Beiträge, 25, Heft 7 (1979), 17.

[3] Vgl. Harald Hartung, "Die ästhetische und soziale Kritik der Lyrik," in Die Literatur der DDR, Bd. 11 von Hansers Sozialgeschichte der deutschen Literatur, hrsg. von Hans-Jürgen Schmitt (München: Hanser, 1983), S. 261-303.

[4] "Ohne den Leser geht es nicht. Ursula Heukenkamp im Gespräch mit Gerd Adloff, Gabriele Eckart, Uwe Kolbe, Bernd Wagner," Weimarer Beiträge, 25, Heft 7 (1979), 46.

[5] "Ohne den Leser geht es nicht," S. 48.

[6] Franz Fühmann, Nachwort zu Uwe Kolbe, Hineingeboren (Frankfurt/Main: Suhrkamp, 1982), S. 135.

[7] Vgl. Sinn und Form, 28, Heft 6 (1976), 1265ff.

[8] Wolfgang Hilbig, Stimme Stimme. Gedichte und Prosa (Leipzig: Ph. Reclam jun., 1983).

[9] Uwe Kolbe, Hineingeboren, S. 46.

[10] Ursula Heukenkamp, "Das Ungenügen an der Idylle," Sinn und Form, 33, Heft 5 (1981), 1121.

[11] Vgl. Frankfurter Rundschau, 11. Mai 1982, S. 11.

[12] Bestandsaufnahme 2, Debütanten 1976-1980 (Halle/Leipzig: Mitteldeutscher Verlag, 1981), S. 82f.

[13] Vgl. Hartmut Königs Rede auf der FDJ-Kulturkonferenz vom Oktober 1982, Junge Welt, 22. Oktober 1982, S. 3ff.

[14] In der Bundesrepublik 1983 erschienen im Suhrkamp Verlag Frankfurt/Main.

[15] Sascha Anderson, Jeder Satellit hat einen Killersatelliten (Westberlin: Rotbuch Verlag, 1982), S. 7.

[16] Walter Höllerer, "Junge amerikanische Literatur," Akzente, 6, Heft 1 (1959), 30.

[17] Andersons zweiter Gedichtband totenreklame, eine reise, der ebenso wie der erste Band Zeichnungen des Dresdner Graphikers Ralf Kerbach enthält, ist 1983 im Rotbuch Verlag, Westberlin, erschienen.

[18] Gabriele Eckart, Tagebuch (Berlin: Verlag Neues Leben, 1978), S. 24.

[19] "Ohne den Leser geht es nicht," S. 50.

[20] Junge Welt, 22. Oktober 1982, S. 3.

[21] Vgl. Sylvia Kögler, "Zur Diskussion junger Künstler," Temperamente. Blätter für junge Literatur, o. Jg., Heft 2 (1980), 140-144.

[22] Ingrid und Klaus-Dieter Hähnel, "Junge Lyrik am Ende der siebziger Jahre," Weimarer Beiträge, 27, Heft 9 (1981), 130.

[23] Mathilde und Rudolf Dau, "Noch einmal: Junge

Lyrik am Ende der siebziger Jahre," <u>Weimarer Beiträge</u>, 28, Heft 3 (1982), 155.

Another Perspective:
Young Women Writers in the GDR

Dorothy Rosenberg

The appearance during the mid-1970s of Trobadora Beatriz, Karen W., Blitz aus heiterm Himmel, and Guten Morgen, du Schöne demonstrated the existence of a lively and critical woman-directed literature in the GDR.[1] Over the past decade this body of literature has continued to grow and, without losing sight of the question of the status of women in GDR society, has broadened its focus beyond so-called women's issues. In this paper, I would like to look at a sampling of recently published works by young women writers, both to introduce them to those who are not yet familiar with their works and to see how the issues they raise and their approaches to them differ from those of their predecessors.

In an interview conducted in the summer of 1982, a writer born in 1949 described herself as "ein Kind dieser Republik."[2] The expectations of the children of the 1940s and 1950s were shaped by their experience of socialism in the period of rapid progress and economic growth from the mid-1950s to the mid-1970s. Now, a slower pace of change and the emerging ecological and sociological contradictions of an advanced industrial society are leading to a new and more critical awareness of the complexity of the social system which is both the context and the subject matter of these young writers.

The writers discussed in this paper were all born after 1940.[3] Many of them are very conscious of belonging to a special group, the first generation to have grown up entirely within the socialist system. This, in itself, has given them a very different perspective on social issues. Their exposure to the fascist and capitalist cultures which shaped their par-

ents' lives has been only second hand; still, the past
has continued to influence their lives both directly
and indirectly. Helga Schubert writes:

> Jahrgang 1940. Die ersten Schulanfän-
> ger in Deutschland, die nicht mit
> Heil Hitler die Schulstunde begannen.
> Unschuldige damals.
> Die Erinnerung an Tieffliegerangrif-
> fe, Bombenexplosionen, Panzergrollen,
> Flüchtlingstrecks, Weihnachtsbäume am
> Himmel. Sie verdirbt uns das Feuer-
> werk und das Gewitter und den Anblick
> einer Parade.
> Meine Generation ist vierzig.
> Vor uns endete die Begeisterung.
> Und wir sehen immer noch zu. [4]

> Wir schämten uns, Deutsche zu sein.
> Auf Zehenspitzen gingen wir in die
> ehemals deutschen oder von Deutschen
> besetzten Länder, in ihre Städte.
> Nur nicht als Deutscher erkannt wer-
> den. . . .
> Wir waren stolz, wenn uns jemand sag-
> te, das habe ich nicht gedacht, daß
> du Deutscher bist. . . .
> Nur manchmal sind wir insgeheim stolz,
> zu diesem Volk zu gehören. . . . Aber
> das würden wir nie zugeben.
> Nie. (pp. 23-24)

And the burden of not having experienced the past
weighs equally heavily:

> Wir gingen durch die offenen Türen,
> immer schneller, wir liefen. Und hin-
> ter uns schlugen die Türen zu, links
> und rechts kein Ausgang, nur eine of-
> fene Tür vorn. Flucht nach vorn.
> Ich weiß gar nicht, ihr seid alle so
> nervös. Als ob euch jemand treibt.
> Freut euch doch mal an der Gegenwart.
> Sieh mal, wie schwer wir es hatten,
> Nazizeit, Krieg, Männer im Krieg ge-
> blieben. Und ihr? Könnt studieren.
> Verdient viel.
> <u>Was habt ihr eigentlich dauernd zu
> mäkeln?</u>
> Offene Türen als Vorwurf.
> Nicht unsere eigenen offenen Türen. (p. 20)

Since one of the purposes of this paper is to introduce new women writers, I began by looking for members of the postwar generation who had recently (1979 or later) published a first book. The five I have chosen, Monika Helmecke, Beate Morgenstern, Maria Seidemann, Renate Apitz, and Doris Paschiller, represent a variety of educational and professional backgrounds. One is a university professor, another a housewife, another a cultural functionary in a factory. What unifies them is not only a concern for the position of women but the logical extension of this concern to encompass the situation of all non-standard individuals in GDR society.

Monika Helmecke was born in 1943, and worked as a typist before studying data processing. She is married, has three children, and describes herself as a housewife and free-lance writer.[5] Her first book, Klopfzeichen, a collection of short stories, appeared in 1979.[6]

The stories in this volume cross and recross the divide between fantasy, reality, sanity and insanity. Helmecke is particularly fascinated with the power of fantasy to both delight and terrify. She plays with this dualism in several stories in which characters use their imagination to escape from a stiflingly oppressive reality only to find that fantasy unleashed can quickly edge beyond control. The balance suddenly shifts. The characters, if they are lucky, retreat to the solid reassurance of normality; in some stories, they lose their grasp on reality and drift off into worlds from which they cannot return at will.

The title story describes the gradual nervous breakdown of an isolated and lonely woman who becomes obsessed with communicating with the child that she has aborted. Unable to establish contact with the world around her, she finally withdraws into her own body in her search for companionship. Locked in her apartment, she develops a set of morse-code signals by which the now non-existent fetus tells her to eat, sleep, or listen to it. The story ends when it orders her to go to the hospital so that it can be born.

Another story, "Erich," begins abruptly with three pages of question-and-answer dialogue between the narrator and the title character in one of his fantasy roles. What follows is the narrator's description of weekends spent with her fiancé, a gentle, intellectual misfit who lives with his mother and

189

sidesteps responsibility and the career ladder by escaping into music and fiction. The description of their walking tours and evenings together is continually interrupted by Erich's slipping into his fantasy world and telling stories which he makes up as he goes along. The reader is shifted from one level of text to another without transition or explanation, and is left with a feeling of the fragility of reality.

When a job transfer to Erich's town offers the narrator the chance to combine her everyday life with her weekends, she is inexplicably terrified. She flees back into concrete daily life, dropping Erich and soon marrying a gregarious, ordinary colleague. For years she is haunted by a sense of loss which slowly undermines her marriage until a chance meeting with Erich reveals him to be married, successful, and slightly overweight.

This collection also includes two stories about mothers caught between children and a personal creative life. One is a fantasy and the other a starkly detailed report of a day in the life of the mother of an infant and a small child. Both women are overwhelmed by the constant demands of their small children, and try to escape, one with the aid of a bad fairy, the other through alcohol. Both stories end with the recognition that there simply is no adequate solution to the problem.

In these and other stories, Helmecke is concerned with how people respond to isolation and alienation, how they cope with a hostile environment, and how they struggle to maintain an emotional balance in a complex and indifferent society.

Beate Morgenstern's first book, Jenseits der Allee, also appeared in 1979.[7] Morgenstern was born in 1946 and grew up in a pietist family. She studied art history and Germanistik, held various jobs after leaving the university, and is now a cultural functionary in a Berlin factory.

Morgenstern's central themes are also isolation and alienation in a highly structured society. Many of her stories focus on individuals who don't or can't conform to social expectations. They are outsiders who feel rejected and stigmatized by their peers. Some struggle, sometimes to the point of self-destruction, for some form of social recognition to counterbalance their sense of inadequacy or failure. Others struggle just to make contact.

In "Ein gutes Mädchen," Ilsemarie, an unpopular, unattractive, ungifted student, sees her role as a FDJ leader as her only chance to excel. When her efforts are met with indifference, she becomes increasingly determined and finally obsessed with forcing her classmates, if not to admire her, at least to accept her authority. Her stubborn pursuit of this goal leaves her physically ill and completely alienated from her peers.

The sense of alienation is explored in several stories which center on attempts to communicate. Many of Morgenstern's characters try desperately to break through their isolation and finally talk to, rather than past, one another. While some fail, in "Jenseits der Allee," two women do manage to establish contact with one another. Carefully exploring one another's tastes and opinions, and backing away from any points of disagreement, they tentatively establish some common ground on which to begin a friendship. In other stories, characters simply move past one another, enclosed in their inability to grasp or communicate their emotions. Unable to break out of their isolation, they smother their sense of frustration in anger, alcohol, or denial.

Morgenstern's narrative style is very low-key and controlled. She uses small pieces of conversation and details of daily life to construct her stories mosaic-fashion. Very little happens in these stories; what little action does take place serves to reveal character. Several stories simply present people thinking or talking. The narrative perspective alternates between dialogue, private thoughts, and purely external description, producing a sense of emotional distance from the characters.

Morgenstern does not pass moral judgment on her characters. While "Ein gutes Mädchen" and "Bruno," another story in the volume, both involve individuals who deform themselves in an attempt to fit into a social mold and who try to use that mold to control others, the characters appear as much victims as those they try to manipulate; they are trapped within a rigid set of conventions. Morgenstern's stories do not interpret events or offer simple explanations; the author chooses and arranges her details with great sensitivity to many very different characters in a wide range of conflicts, and leaves the reader with no easy answers.

Maria Seidemann has published poetry in periodicals and anthologies for several years. Her first prose volume, Der Tag an dem Sir Henry starb, appeared in 1980.[8] Seidemann was born in 1944 and is now a free-lance writer.

The stories in this volume vary widely in style and subject. They run the gamut from standard defense-of-socialism and the struggles-of-the-past stories, such as "Champagner für die alten Damen," to thoughtful and critical explorations of the German heritage of nationalist arrogance and the passive acceptance of authority. Several stories revolve around the collective denial of reality and the power of the group to enforce conformity as the price of social integration.

Two stories, "Der hilfreiche Rabe" and "Der Brückenbauer," involve the problems of single mothers caught between children and career. While the problems are distressingly real, in both stories they are solved through the intervention of the supernatural: in the form of a talking raven in the first, and a magic hood in the second. In another sketch, "Kloster am Berge," the narrator describes a nightmare:

> Ich rief Lore zu, wie froh ich wäre,
> könnte ich das Kind auf meinen Rücken
> binden, um die Hände frei zu haben.
> Sie antwortete: Mit dem Kind schaffst
> du es nie. Ich schrie sie erschrok-
> ken an: Soll ich es etwa ins Wasser
> werfen? Da sagte sie: Vor dieser Ent-
> scheidung stehen wir früher oder spä-
> ter alle einmal. (p. 10)

While Seidemann tends to use a straightforward narrative technique, satire, magic, fantasy, dreams, and alternate realities undermine the soberness of her style and offer a means of resolving insoluble conflicts and of softening her criticism. "Der Brückenbauer" simultaneously raises and defuses the question of the role of class in GDR society. The main character, Benita, had been abandoned by her mother, a prostitute who moved to West Berlin. When Benita became pregnant, her lover, an FDJ functionary, first planned to marry her, but later decided that her class background and life history would be too great a burden on his career. In the course of time, Benita learns that the key to success is the possession of a magic hood

192

which "disguises the wearer's true nature" (p. 43).
She discovers a society of hood-wearers. The members
are not very nice people, but their qualities of individualism and opportunism are the necessary prerequi-
sites for social advancement and a successful career.
In the end, Benita decides to burn her hood to be able
to share her life with the bridge builder of the title, having decided that success, after all, isn't
everything.

The unevenness of this collection is sometimes
disconcerting. A sensitive character sketch may be
followed by a formula set piece. On the whole, however, Seidemann offers thoughtful explorations of contemporary social and political issues: the attitudes
of GDR citizens toward visiting relatives from the
West, or their own visits to the socialist countries
which were formerly occupied territories, as well as
the problems of individual integration into an achievement-oriented, highly structured, and conformist society.

Another recent volume of short stories is Renate
Apitz' Evastöchter, subtitled "Ein Dutzend Dutzendge-
schichten," and published in 1982. [9] Most of these
stories deal with the relationships between men and
women and focus on how habit, outmoded role models,
and traditional attitudes undermine real communication
and understanding between the sexes. In "Spinat mit
Ei," a couple known for their long and harmonious marriage is chosen to represent the wife's work unit in a
quiz show. In the course of the story, it becomes
clear that the marriage's harmony depends entirely on
the wife's good-natured willingness to adjust to her
husband's moods and demands.

Many of Apitz' stories offer a critical view of
the lives of mature women in the GDR. "Die harmoni-
sche Else" begins with the first-person narrator's
speculating about her professor: "wie wird so eine
Frau Doktor der Wissenschaft? Ich meine, wie sie wohl
beides unter einen Hut bringt, die Frau und die Ge-
lehrte?" (p. 92). She imagines a scenario: Else must
have married young and then studied after her marriage
failed. But then she can think of no plausible reason
for Else to remarry. In a second attempt, she imagines Else remarrying but cannot see how she could combine her duties as a housewife with the demands of her
career without neglecting one or the other. Finally,
the narrator gives up in disgust and ends with a
brief, flat, and totally unbelievable happily-ever-

after version which simply ignores the conflicts between career and family. This story can be read as a bitter comment on the standard role models offered women in fiction.

In these and other stories, Apitz displays both sensitivity to her characters and a sense of humor. Her generally realistic style is leavened by the brief appearance of a devil, authorial interruptions, and several experiments with alternate narrators.

I would like to include one longer work in this discussion, Doris Paschiller's Die Würde, which appeared in 1980.[10] Paschiller's novel is frequently cited in the GDR as the best study of contemporary working-class marriage.[11] Her characters and their lives are utterly real. Robert and Johanna work in a Berlin factory. He is a forklift driver; she works in the drafting room. They and their friends are not the idealized, upwardly mobile, politically active model workers of socialist realism. Nor are they the young professionals of most current fiction. They are ordinary workers, reliable, politically indifferent, suspicious of bureaucracy, and derisive of ambition. They have vague hopes for a better life, but cannot imagine what it would be like. They are unable to grasp or express the causes of their dissatisfaction. They feel frustrated and trapped, and escape with alcohol and popular music.

Johanna is five months pregnant when they marry:

> Natürlich hätte sich Johanna dazu entschließen können, ein Kind alleine zu erziehen, was sie bestimmt des öfteren in Erwägung gezogen hatte, um dem zu entgehen, was gemeinhin mit einer gewissen Art von Unterordnung verbunden war, über die man nicht sprach und aus der man sich mit andauerndem Bemühen herauszulavieren versuchte.
> Aber das andere hieße wohl, sich ganz und gar opfern. Nur Mutter sein, in jeder Anschauung, die man vertritt. Dein Kampf ist Mutter, in erster Linie Mutter. Nur als Mutter für dein Kind das Brot verdienen. Einen Mann kennenlernen, nur als Mutter. Nur Mütter zu Freundinnen haben und wieder Mütter zu erziehen. (p. 13)

Paschiller describes Johanna's daily round of breakfast, trip to the day-care center, work, back to the day-care center, shopping, housework, and child-care. Robert spends his evenings either in front of the television with beer or drinking in the Kneipe. Their one-room Hinterhof apartment is dark and crowded; there is no bathroom. The baby sleeps in the kitchen. The only refuge is the Kneipe, to which Robert escapes ever more frequently, leaving Johanna alone with the baby. Afraid that she is a failure as a mother and as a person, Johanna runs away. Robert finds her and brings her back, but she runs away again. Both of them feel helpless and confused by her frustration. After an absence of six weeks, Johanna returns, and they agree to try to begin again.

Paschiller's almost naive style emphasizes her characters' inability to articulate their frustration or their hopes. Paschiller doesn't provide any critical analysis or offer any solutions. She merely describes working-class life and ordinary people with breathtaking precision.

If there is a common stylistic tendency in contemporary writing in the GDR, it is the willingness to experiment. The omniscient author is no longer the rule. Flashbacks, intercutting, multiple levels of narration, inner monologue, fable, science fiction, and surreal elements, all unthinkable fifteen years ago, appear serenely cheek by jowl with straight realism in collections and anthologies.

While the center of concern continues to be the relationship between the individual and society, the emphasis has shifted toward making society fit for people to live in, instead of training people to live in society. Individuals can now have needs and make demands on society. Conflict can be open-ended. Mistakes and problems can lie within the collective or with society instead of only in individual failings. The well-rounded "socialist personality" is disappearing, along with typical or model characters, and being replaced with a far more believable variety of humans.

The generation of writers who first began publishing in the mid-1970s are the first who have been able to write critically from the very beginning of their careers. Unlike their predecessors, they have not had to first serve an anti-fascist or Bitterfeld apprenticeship in order to establish their right to comment on the social shortcomings that they see. Nor do they remember the bad old days as a mitigating counterbalance to current conditions. These writers compare what they have been taught to what they have learned, measure GDR socialism by its own standards.

Of course, anyone writing in the GDR today is aware that what they choose to write about and how they write about it is a political as well as a personal decision. This constant awareness cannot fail to result in a pervasive self-censorship, which is reinforced by the steady trickle of politically critical young writers to the West. The fact that comparatively few women writers have left may, to some degree, be explained by GDR women valuing their relatively superior social and economic position compared to the FRG, and believing that their status is more likely to improve under socialism than capitalism.

Change has been less rapid and progress less visible in the past decade, especially in regard to the status of women, and these young women writers express frustration at the slackening pace and the emergence of limits. Still, the majority of the young writers I interviewed in 1982 expressed optimism that the problems can be solved. Although the GDR has declared itself a "non-antagonistic class society," writers like Paschiller, Morgenstern, and Seidemann criticize the newly legitimized class structure and the conformism required to succeed within it. They and others interviewed describe the stifling lack of space for the young to experiment and their alienation within a highly structured Leistungsgesellschaft, and oppose the GDR's substitution of material incentives and consumerism for revolutionary idealism and social change.

Above all, they are concerned with the human side of social questions. The GDR today is faced with all of the social problems of any advanced industrial society. These writers are trying to investigate the complexity of this new stage. The naming and describing of problems is the first step toward their solution.

Colby College

Notes

[1] Irmtraud Morgner, Leben und Abenteuer der Trobadora Beatriz nach Zeugnissen ihrer Spielfrau Laura (Berlin/Weimar: Aufbau, 1974); Gerti Tetzner, Karen W. (Halle: Mitteldeutscher Verlag, 1974); Brigitte Reimann, Franziska Linkerhand (Berlin: Neues Leben, 1974); Blitz aus heiterm Himmel, ed. Edith Anderson (Rostock: Hinstorff, 1975); Maxie Wander, Guten Morgen, du Schöne (Berlin: Buchverlag der Morgen, 1977).

[2] Personal interview, Leipzig, July, 1982. The person interviewed preferred not to be identified.

[3] No birthday was available for Renate Apitz.

[4] Helga Schubert, Das verbotene Zimmer (Darmstadt/Neuwied: Luchterhand, 1982), p. 15. Subsequent page references will be given parenthetically in the text.

[5] Im Kreislauf der Windeln. Frauenprosa aus der DDR, ed. Horst Heidtmann (Basel/Weinheim: Beltz und Gelberg, 1982), p. 273.

[6] Monika Helmecke, Klopfzeichen (Berlin: Neues Leben, 1979).

[7] Beate Morgenstern, Jenseits der Allee (Berlin/Weimar: Aufbau, 1979).

[8] Maria Seidemann, Der Tag an dem Sir Henry starb (Berlin: Eulenspiegel, 1980).

[9] Renate Apitz, Evastöchter (Rostock: Hinstorff, 1982).

[10] Doris Paschiller, Die Würde (Berlin: Buchverlag der Morgen, 1980).

[11] Interviews conducted in the summer of 1982.

"Ein Schaffender am Menschen":
The Image of the Teacher in Recent GDR Fiction

Merle Krueger and Carol Poore

The importance attached to the teaching profession in the GDR was already in evidence in the Soviet Occupation Zone in the first weeks and months after the end of the war. Of the approximately 40,000 teachers in the Soviet Zone in 1945, three-fourths had belonged to the NSDAP and many of the rest had been involved in some way with fascist organizations. Recognizing the influence of the school on the intellectual, political, and moral attitudes of young people, the Soviet occupation authorities and the anti-fascist German administrators expelled most of these Altlehrer from their positions and began an intensive recruitment of Neulehrer whose pasts were untainted by Nazi ideology. Already in the fall of 1945, 15,000 new teachers began instructing, and they were joined by 25,000 new colleagues in the fall of 1946.[1] In her essay "Der Lehrer" (1951) Anna Seghers contrasted these efforts in the East with the re-establishment in West Germany of an educational system designed, in her opinion, to produce Untertanen who had learned nothing from the past and who therefore could be manipulated to serve the militaristic interests of those in power. At this point in German history, she argued, teachers had to decide to educate their pupils about the horrors of war, which would mean awakening in them a feeling for the unity of Germany, its history, language, and culture, and its profound need of peace. Finally, she compared the work of the teacher in educating youth to that of the writer and stated: "Wer ist denn so wichtig wie ein Lehrer unter den Schaffenden? Er schafft ja am Menschen."[2]

In spite of this general realization of the teacher's importance in creating a peaceful, socialist society, Johannes R. Becher noted a year later, in

199

1952, that the figure of the teacher had been largely neglected by socialist writers: "Es ist eine merkwürdige Erscheinung, und man müßte viel darüber nachdenken, warum von allen Berufen ausgerechnet der Lehrer von der Literatur so kümmerlich behandelt wird."[3] This remained true throughout the fifties, but, after the mid-sixties, the educational system in the established socialist state became a popular literary topic. Socialist teachers are the central characters in several novels from the late sixties, including Egon Richter's Zeugnis zu dritt (1967) and Alfred Wellm's Eine Pause für Wanzka (1968). Günter Görlich has focused on the school environment in several of his works, including the novel for young readers, Den Wolken ein Stück näher, which won the National Prize in 1971, and his widely-read short novel, Eine Anzeige in der Zeitung (1978). Furthermore, the school milieu is central in other works of fiction such as Erich Loest's short story "Eine Falte spinnwebfein" (1974) and Erik Neutsch's novella Zwei leere Stühle (1979). Finally, several authors who have left the GDR formulate sharp criticisms of the educational system in books published in the West, most importantly, Jurek Becker in his novel Schlaflose Tage (1978).[4]

This substantial volume of literature dealing with education led Wolfgang Emmerich to note in 1981: "Es macht stutzig, daß es in der DDR neuerdings ein Genre gibt, das man eigentlich mit dem wilhelminischen Untertanenstaat um 1900 verbindet: die Schulgeschichte."[5] But is this really a valid comparison? Literary works concerning pupils, teachers, and the school milieu around the turn of the century were characterized primarily by their criticism of authoritarian, pedantic pedagogical methods aimed at creating obedient, "loyal subjects of the Kaiser" and by their decided partiality for the pupils who were sometimes driven to rebel against their oppressive teachers.[6] We will investigate the literary portrayal of GDR teachers in order to determine the differences between them and the depiction of teachers in Wilhelminian literature. Three predominant themes emerge in this discussion: 1) conflicts between teachers in the methodological, ideological, or personal spheres; 2) the teacher as socialist role model and the relationship between teachers and pupils; 3) the qualities teachers encourage in their pupils, which often reflect differing views on the nature of the "socialist personality," and, in particular, the question of Aufrichtigkeit in education.

A striking feature of several of these works is the fact that the central conflict does not pit students against teachers, but rather teachers against other teachers. In Richter's and Wellm's novels and in Görlich's Eine Anzeige in der Zeitung, the plots develop antagonisms and disagreements between faculty members or school administrators which illuminate issues of education and social policy. As a consequence, the dramatic confrontations in these GDR works unfold more frequently in the faculty lounge or in staff meetings than in the classroom.

For example, although we are told that Elisabeth Möbius, the central figure in Richter's Zeugnis zu dritt, is a fine teacher, we never actually see her act in this capacity.[7] After a series of conflicts with her colleagues, she is relieved of her duties as an assistant director in her school and later as a teacher as well. Subtle tensions between her and the other administrators reach an initial crest over the case of a bright student with high grades who is nonetheless not recommended for the university on the grounds that he is arrogant and lacks social responsibility. Elisabeth strongly rejects this political reasoning and argues that the boy should be evaluated solely on his academic performance. Her stubbornness on this issue, combined with her indiscretion in prematurely informing the boy's father of the faculty decision, results in her first demotion. When her son defects to West Berlin and she visits him there in a vain attempt to talk him into coming back, her director feels justified in compelling her to leave the school, since her credibility as a socialist model has been severely undermined. Richter contrasts the politically "correct," but personally harsh and uncompassionate view voiced by Elisabeth's director with the testimony of two other individuals involved in her case, her psychiatrist and her former pedagogy professor. The debate between these two men over the causes of Elisabeth's difficulties and the cure for her subsequent deep depression give interesting insights into the theoretical relationship between psychiatry and social policy in the GDR. By exploring the personal and emotional circumstances which influenced Elisabeth and, at the same time, by criticizing the insensitivity of her colleagues to her need for moral support, Richter succeeds in evoking sympathy for Elisabeth's plight. Though he does not vindicate her actions, he does make a convincing argument for the necessity of considering extenuating circumstances which may be totally personal, while at the same time he makes it clear that the individual's mental health is a collective responsibility.

Although Elisabeth suffers from disagreements with her fellow teachers and administrators over specific policy matters, her profession is in fact not essential to the nature of her troubles. The dynamics in the relationship between an individual and the collective in Zeugnis zu dritt do not seem unique to teachers, and no doubt Richter intended that Elisabeth's case should be relevant for socialist society in general. Gustav Wanzka, the first-person narrator of Alfred Wellm's novel Pause für Wanzka, likewise experiences sharp disagreements with his fellow teachers.[8] Here, however, the conflicts do relate specifically to education, for the tensions between Wanzka and his colleagues stem from opposing teaching methods and goals. A sincere love of children, a strong curiosity about their latent skills, and a genuine desire to help them realize their potential characterize Wanzka as a passionately committed teacher. An enthusiasm for learning permeates his classroom, and the curiosity and spontaneity he encourages in his pupils occasionally even result in breakdowns of discipline. As Wanzka tells his supportive young colleague Marlott, a teacher needs to wield a kind of "divining rod" to seek out the intellectual gifts of a child that often lie buried beneath the surface. Such a boy is Norbert Kniep, a headstrong youngster who frequently gets into trouble with the other teachers, but who has remarkable ability in mathematics. Wanzka patiently conquers Norbert's initial distrust and thereafter spends hours of his free time instilling in the boy a love for mathematics and honing his natural talents. In contrast he speaks disparagingly of the best student in the class, Klausgünther, a typically obsequious Streber who invariably volunteers the correct answer in his eagerness to please the teacher, but who essentially lacks creativity.

A majority of his colleagues do not share Wanzka's views. They interpret the time he devotes to Norbert as favoritism and resent the fact that he does not impose stricter discipline on his class. As a consequence, they force him to relinquish his duties as "class teacher" (Klassenlehrer) with the justification that he has arrogantly neglected his responsibilities to the collective. Wanzka compensates for this disappointment by placing even greater hopes in his young protégé, firmly convinced that Norbert's future accomplishments will ultimately vindicate him.

Inexorably the conflict between Wanzka and his detractors builds to another crisis, this time occasioned by debate over who should represent the school at the regional competition (Kreisolympiade) for young mathematicians. The opposition to Norbert's participation is led by Seiler, Wanzka's replacement as Klassenlehrer and his exact counterpart in terms of educational philosophy. Throughout the novel Seiler appears as a strict disciplinarian and a calculatingly efficient teacher who shows no confidence whatsoever in Norbert. At the faculty meeting to choose the school's representatives, Seiler cites a long list of the boy's disciplinary infractions, but from the outset it is clear that the true object of his criticism is Wanzka, whom he accuses of promoting egotism and petit-bourgeois individualism. At this point Wanzka receives support from his young colleague Marlott, who sharply denounces Seiler's arguments as pedagogical hypocrisy and hot air. Never has she heard him mention his students with the slightest affection, and his harping on the "collective person" as the goal of education was in fact nothing but an empty phrase to stifle individuality.

Pause für Wanzka ends on an optimistic note. Although Norbert fails once again to get a recommendation from his teachers--this time to attend the Erweiterte Oberschule--he attracts the attention of a professor at a competition for young mathematicians in Berlin who recognizes his promise and guarantees him entrance to the Oberschule. Despite this harmonious conclusion, Wellm's novel leaves unresolved certain disturbing implications about the educational system in the GDR. Young Norbert possesses a rare mathematical intelligence, but it is only due to the tireless efforts of an exceptionally devoted teacher--himself besieged by unsympathetic colleagues--that the boy is allowed to develop his gifts, and even then he succeeds only because of a sequence of highly fortunate coincidences. Seiler and Klausgünther, Wellm seems to suggest, represent the rule. Rather than encouraging teachers to nurture the potential of individual pupils, the GDR school system as depicted in this novel fosters obedience, ideological conformity, and an opportunistic preoccupation with personal advancement. [9]

At first glance it seems that the conflict between individual teachers in Günter Görlich's Eine Anzeige in der Zeitung is responsible for more tragic consequences than such conflicts in the previous two works. [10] Throughout most of the book the narrator,

Herbert Kähne, feels troubled by the thought that
tensions with the school's director perhaps contributed to the suicide of his friend and colleague, Manfred Just. As Kähne mulls over the past two years,
trying to find out what motivated his friend's death,
he returns again and again to clashes between the two
men's personalities and outlooks on teaching. Karl
Strebelow, a veteran Neulehrer from the difficult
postwar years, is a serious, hard-working, and competent director, proud of the orderly, disciplined way
his school runs. A man of unswerving commitment to
principle and practicality, he dismisses pedagogical
innovations and curricular reforms as "unfruchtbares
Spinnen" (p. 19). From the outset he views with sus-
picion Just's easy-going, slightly sarcastic, and open
manner; his longish hair, bright-colored shirts, and
Polish bookbag impress him as rather frivolous and ir-
responsible. The conflict between the two men goes
much deeper, however, and concerns fundamental issues
of educational policy at the school. The tension Just
introduces into the faculty collective with his frank
criticism of longstanding procedures exposes the director's inflexibility and his defensive avoidance of
sensitive, difficult issues.

Just's influence at the school does not disappear
with his suicide. In fact, the unexplained circumstances surrounding his death and Strebelow's directive that the students must be shielded from the truth
create serious repercussions for the relationship between the director and his staff. Pressed by Just's
admiring students for an explanation of his death, one
of the teachers fears that she will lose all credibility with her class if she continues to hide the truth.
She therefore defies Strebelow's directive, and when
he threatens to initiate a disciplinary procedure
against her, Kähne, the narrator, must also take
sides. As the book closes he decides against the director in favor of a policy of honesty with the students:

> Da darf ihnen nichts erspart bleiben
> an Problemen und Kämpfen. Wie sollen
> sie diese Welt sonst verändern? Und
> um Veränderung in Richtung unserer
> Ideale geht es immer. . . . Ich werde
> unbequem werden müssen, auch wenn es
> mir manchmal schwer fallen wird. Das
> weiß ich jetzt schon, es wird mir
> meistens schwer fallen. Jede Erstar-
> rung muß aufgebrochen werden im In-

teresse unserer Sache. Gegen Still-
stand und Routine gilt es anzutreten.
(p. 199)

Unfortunately, Görlich himself undermines somewhat
this resolution to be forthright and outspoken.
Through a series of Just's letters introduced at the
end of the work, we discover that he was suffering
from an incurable disease which would have left him an
invalid and ended his career, a prospect he could not
endure. In the letters he also reflects upon his
dealings with Strebelow and concedes that he himself
could well afford to adopt some of his director's
practicality and solidity. Thus, Görlich essentially
retreats from the more serious implication--suggested
throughout most of the novel--that Just's suicide is
directly connected to Strebelow's stubborn narrow-
mindedness and outdated pedagogical ideas.

With respect to how the relationship between
teacher and pupil is portrayed in recent GDR fiction,
what immediately catches the eye is that, with the exception of Loest in "Eine Falte spinnwebfein," all
these writers show the goals and conflicts of socialist education primarily from the teacher's point of
view. This identification with the teacher's perspective means that these writers often depict teachers as
role models in regard to their command of subject matter, their political standpoint, and their moral uprightness. However, these writers do not present the
best teachers as paragons of virtue, or as "positive
heroes." In fact, the works depict complex situations
in which the notion of teachers as flawless appears
outdated; those teachers who are more flexible are, on
the other hand, sympathetic characters. In Zeugnis zu
dritt, for example, the school director who forces
Elisabeth's resignation is portrayed as narrow-minded
and rigid, for he bases this decision on the premise
that she is no longer fit to be a role model for children who are to become good socialists. In Eine Anzeige in der Zeitung the older school director insists
that Just's suicide be kept from the pupils because it
contradicts his traditional notion that the actions
of a teacher must always be exemplary. The director's
rigid position leads to a confrontation with the other
teachers in the school who believe the pupils deserve
to know the truth.

Although such disagreements over the proper image
teachers should project are usually shown from the
teacher's perspective, occasionally the pupils them-

selves call their teachers' attitudes into question. In Erik Neutsch's Zwei leere Stühle, a school director reflects on unexpected developments in the lives of two former pupils who did not attend a class reunion. 11 Wolfgang, the best student in the class and the teachers' favorite, became an opportunistic physician and fled the Republic, whereas Uwe, the black sheep of the class who often asked difficult questions, became an army-officer and died trying to rescue one of his comrades from a wrecked tank during a maneuver. Shortly before his death, Uwe visited the director and reminisced about his feeling in school that teachers did not treat the pupils fairly or trust them, and that they viewed the pupils as their enemies. After he spoke of his dislike of school and his frequent desire to stay away from it, the director remarked sagely that this attitude surely had to do with "how one learns." Uwe replied that it was also a matter of "how one teaches." Whereas teachers tended to view rebelliousness and a questioning attitude as indicative of character defects which pupils should overcome, Uwe felt that they were caused in part by teachers' insensitivity to young people's concerns. This reply led the teacher to remember how he had handled Uwe's question about Czechoslovakia in 1968. Uwe had asked how the foreign policy of the Soviet Union could still be defended after it had sent its tanks to quell unrest in another socialist country. The teacher had not wanted simply to threaten Uwe with failing him because of his provocative questions, but, rather than dealing with the issue, he had chosen to call on Wolfgang to furnish a flawless ideological explanation for these events. Wolfgang had rattled off a discourse on the difference between socialist democracy and democratic socialism, which the teacher had of course agreed with, but which had left Uwe unconvinced.

Looking back on such classroom situations years later, the director recognizes that he and other teachers often took the comfortable way out when they encouraged pupils like Wolfgang at the expense of more difficult pupils like Uwe. He now sees that rather than placing their sole emphasis on grades and the ability to memorize slogans, teachers should try to judge and develop the entire personality of their pupils and to deal forthrightly with the moral conflicts confronting both teachers and pupils. Yet Neutsch retracts somewhat the critical thrust of these important problems at the end. Although the author urges greater trust and openness between teachers and pupils, his exclusive emphasis on the motives behind probing questions assumes both that teachers can always determine these motives and that the questioners themselves are clear about them. Neutsch seems to propose that the character of a young person is fixed and constant, thereby ignoring that it is the task of the teacher to shape and nurture that character.

Such portrayals of the interaction between teacher and pupil point to the third major theme in these works, the qualities teachers encourage in their pupils, qualities which often reflect differing views on the nature of the "socialist personality." In Wellm's and Neutsch's works the different approaches to integrating the individual pupil into the socialist collective focus on the contrast between the Primus, the best pupil in the class in the opinion of the stricter teachers, and another gifted but less compliant pupil whom the more flexible teachers wish to help. [12] Even though these authors are concerned with the development of the "socialist personality" and with participation in and responsibility for the collective, they rarely depict interaction among pupils with respect to grades, standing in class, or the privilege of going on to higher education. Rather, these competitive situations are seen from the teacher's point of view--for example, when the teachers have to decide as a group who will be admitted to the Erweiterte Oberschule and when they express different opinions on how much to take grades, family background, and attitude towards socialism into account.

An interesting exception in this is Erich Loest's short story "Eine Falte spinnwebfein." [13] Told from the perspective of a tenth-grade girl, this story recreates the stifling, anxiety-producing atmosphere of competition for grades among pupils trying to get into the Erweiterte Oberschule. From Monika's class, two of the top three pupils will be selected. One boy who is planning to be an army officer is certain of a place, and so the competition intensifies between Monika with her 1.21 average and her best friend, Angi, slightly ahead with 1.19. During the math test which will decide the outcome, Monika slides a "cheat sheet" with the wrong answer to a problem over to Angi to copy from. Although Angi believes Monika afterwards when she says that she did not mean to trick her, Monika knows that she has started on the way to university studies through deception. By focusing on the experiences of pupils, Loest is able to show some of the intense pressures which can lead to a competitive, individualistic attitude, as well as to feelings of guilt and inadequacy among pupils who are forced by social conditions to act in this way.

One particular aspect of educational life seems central to several of these works, the aspect of "forthrightness" (Aufrichtigkeit). In GDR society, which sets as an official goal of its educational system the development of the socialist personality, teachers seem confronted with the dilemma of encouraging genuine commitment to socialism out of conviction rather than convenience. While the schools may praise honesty and forthrightness in theory, they may simultaneously promote the opposite behavior in practice. The schoolgirl in Loest's story, for example, is compelled by the pressures of competition to betray her best friend in order to advance herself. In a general sense, the conflict between Wanzka and Seiler in Wellm's novel likewise turns on the complex of intellectual honesty and sincerity. Seiler uses catchwords with a ring of unimpeachable authority, such as the "collective person," to justify an approach to education which rewards unquestioning obedience to authority, a servile eagerness to please, and a diligent, but uncritical studiousness. Wanzka's protégé, Norbert, on the other hand, possesses an admirable, upright character, and, on more than one occasion, disobeys his teachers and faces the consequences rather than sacrifice his principles.

The issue of intellectual honesty and political sincerity in education and the negative consequences for society when these qualities are not fostered are even more central concerns in Görlich's Eine Anzeige in der Zeitung. For Manfred Just, unshrinking candor in the face of awkward and difficult problems guides his behavior both in faculty meetings and in the classroom. As he states, "Ich bin gewohnt, meine Meinung zu sagen. Ich hasse Unaufrichtigkeit. Besser Streit im Lehrerkollektiv als eine Ruhe, die alle Widersprüche verdeckt" (p. 37). On one occasion, the narrator Kähne reports his observations of a lesson in which Just encouraged his pupils to express their true feelings on an issue of social morality. The teacher had wisely chosen a situation in which the options were not clear-cut, but required considered judgement. Instead of dictating abstract principles of socialist behavior, Just wanted the pupils to develop their own critical understanding of these principles. It is Just's legacy that Kähne ultimately decides to defy the director's order not to answer the students' ques-

208

tions about their teacher's death, but henceforth to face even such tough issues with courage and honesty.

The treatment of the Aufrichtigkeit theme in Erik Neutsch's novella Zwei leere Stühle adds another dimension to the issue. Whereas in Görlich's work a teacher is willing to take the consequences of bluntly stating his mind on sensitive matters, here a student encounters censure and injustice at the hands of his teachers for voicing his opinions and doubts. Pondering the fate of Uwe and Wolfgang, the narrator and director of the school ultimately realizes: "Wir haben Zensuren auf Antworten gegeben, aber nicht darauf, was hinter den Antworten stand, Überzeugung oder nicht doch Heuchelei" (p. 46). By side-stepping the doubts and concerns of their students and dismissing their difficult questions with pat answers and simplistic slogans, teachers foster conformism and discourage genuine socialist convictions. Though his message comes through clearly, Neutsch's novella remains flawed and unconvincing. It is troublesome that both Uwe and Wolfgang make a complete about-face after leaving school, a transformation that seems unmotivated in each case. Why does Uwe, who has been critical of the military action in Czechoslovakia, decide upon an army career, of all things? Similarly, why does Wolfgang, who heretofore has enjoyed the fruits of success in this society, suddenly choose to leave the country? Would it not have been more convincing, albeit more disturbing, to have avoided this abrupt turnabout and to have extended Uwe's and Wolfgang's lives in the pattern established at school, in which case, of course, Uwe would have ended a social failure and Wolfgang a social success?

The theme of Aufrichtigkeit is central in Schlaflose Tage, Jurek Becker's novel about the teacher Karl Simrock, published in the Federal Republic in 1978. 14 At the beginning of the novel, Simrock feels a pain in his chest one day while teaching, and a somewhat hypochondriac fear that his days are numbered leads him to resolve to eliminate routine and complacency from his life, to live authentically, and to take chances. Not only does he decide to end his boring marriage, but he also decides to encourage critical thought and honesty among his pupils, as he states: "Sich mühen, aufrichtig zu sein. Nicht nur in Zeiten, da Aufrichtigkeit erlaubt ist, sondern immer. Oder fast immer, oder so oft wie möglich. Sooft es die Kraft erlaubt" (p. 29). After a number of unsettling incidents in his classes when he begins to put his convictions into practice,

Simrock's resolution precipitates a crisis when an officer of the National People's Army visits his class
to encourage pupils to go into officer training. Simrock asks the officer probing questions about his pay
and restrictions on his personal life, and as a result, Simrock is dismissed from the school. He goes
to work delivering bread and soon realizes how little
he as an intellectual knows about manual labor. The
school authorities finally decide that he can be re-
instated if he apologizes and promises never again to
create such confusion in his pupils' minds. But rather than compromise what he believes to be morally
right, he prefers to continue driving the bread truck
and relinquish any influence he might have on changing
the school system. Becker clearly views schools in
the GDR extremely pessimistically and implies that
there is no possibility for the individual teacher to
effect positive change in the classroom.

The depiction of school life in the works discussed clearly differs fundamentally from the depiction of school life in Wilhelminian literature. Writers around the turn of the century focused on the
school milieu in order to criticize repressive teachers as representatives of a militaristic, authoritarian, and reactionary society. Their perspective and
sympathies invariably sided with the students. These
GDR writers, in contrast, do not denounce the educational goals of their society. Integration into socialism is not questioned, but rather how best to ac-
complish this aim. The conflicts in these works do
not generally pit students against teachers. Instead,
the writers concentrate, for the most part, on methodological differences among teachers who, on the surface at least, subscribe to the same ends. Whereas
Wilhelminian teachers were depicted as demanding
strict, unquestioning adherence to repressive social
norms, these GDR writers consider it the primary task
of the teacher to encourage genuine socialist convictions, not uncritical conformism. However, these works
often do not resolve in a totally convincing and consistent manner the dilemma of how best to foster this
sincerity and Aufrichtigkeit. Görlich and Neutsch
seem to draw back from the critical problems they themselves raise, whereas Becker carries the issue to an
ultimately bleak and pessimistic conclusion. Insofar
as these works stimulate discussion of the aims and
current problems of the educational system in the GDR,
they can heighten awareness of necessary improvements.

Mass. Inst. of Tech. / Brown University

Notes

1 Akademie der Pädagogischen Wissenschaften der DDR, Das Bildungswesen der Deutschen Demokratischen Republik (Berlin: Volk und Wissen, 1979), p. 87.

2 Anna Seghers, "Der Lehrer," in her Über Kunst und Wirklichkeit (Berlin: Akademie, 1971), III, 258.

3 Johannes R. Becher, Verteidigung der Poesie (Berlin: Aufbau, 1960), p. 401.

4 Other GDR works on this general theme which we have omitted from this discussion for reasons of space are Anna Seghers' Die Entscheidung (1959) and Das Vertrauen (1968), and Hans Weber's Sprung ins Riesenrad (1968). Two more examples of works touching on the GDR educational system by writers who have left the GDR are Reiner Kunze's Die wunderbaren Jahre (1976) and Jürgen Fuchs' Pappkameraden (1981).

5 Wolfgang Emmerich, Kleine Literaturgeschichte der DDR (Darmstadt/Neuwied: Luchterhand, 1981), p.199.

6 See Robert Holub, "Das Stereotyp des Lehrers in der Literatur des Kaiserreichs," in Stereotyp und Vorurteil in der Literatur, ed. James Elliott et al. (Göttingen: Vandenhoeck und Ruprecht, 1978), pp. 33-49.

7 Egon Richter, Zeugnis zu dritt (Rostock: Hinstorff, 1967).

8 Alfred Wellm, Eine Pause für Wanzka (Berlin: Aufbau, 1968).

9 Not surprisingly, certain critics in the GDR have praised Wanzka's evident passion for teaching, while at the same time they have faulted him for insufficient cooperation with the faculty collective. See Anneliese Große, "Alfred Wellm's Pause für Wanzka," in Kritik in der Zeit, ed. Klaus Jarmatz (Halle: Mitteldeutscher Verlag, 1970), pp. 874-886.

10 Günter Görlich, Eine Anzeige in der Zeitung (Berlin: Neues Leben, 1978).

11 Erik Neutsch, Zwei leere Stühle (Halle, Mitteldeutscher Verlag, 1979).

[12] See also Görlich's book for young readers, Den Wolken ein Stück näher (Berlin: Kinderbuchverlag, 1971), in which the Klassenbester is portrayed as a model for his classmates. Although he goes through a period of neglecting his duties as Gruppenleiter of the class out of resentment toward the new, young, female teacher (who, he thinks, does not act forcefully enough), he comes around in the end.

[13] Erich Loest, "Eine Falte spinnwebfein," in his Pistole mit Sechzehn (Hamburg: Hoffmann und Campe, 1979).

[14] Jurek Becker, Schlaflose Tage (Frankfurt/M: Suhrkamp, 1978).

Erbe and Its Vicissitudes:
Günter de Bruyn's Re-examination of Jean Paul

James Knowlton

Much of Günter de Bruyn's writing has been concerned with questions of literary reception in the
GDR. It is no coincidence that the protagonist of his
first widely-read novel, Buridans Esel (1968), a librarian by profession and the director of a large library in Berlin, is named Erp, a slight deformation of
the word "Erbe." As a librarian, Karl Erp is a guard-
ian of the literary tradition, a tradition which is
underscored by the many literary quotes woven into
this early novel: quotes from Jean Paul, Fontane,
Goethe, and Arno Holz, to name a few. Questions of
private literary reception in conflict with systems of
political domination pervade de Bruyn's next two
works, Preisverleihung (1972) and Märkische Forschungen (1978). Both books have literary scholars as key
figures; both ask questions about the function of literary texts—historical as well as contemporary—in
the highly charged political atmosphere of the GDR.
Is literary reception a private process of communication between writer and reader? If so, what role do
professional literary critics and scholars play?

De Bruyn's novels pose these questions without
answering them, but his essayistic writings go a long
way toward clarifying his position. In "Der Künstler
und die anderen," a 1975 essay on Thomas Mann, de
Bruyn wrote:

> Weder Entstehung noch Aufnahme von
> Literatur haben etwas mit Wissen-
> schaft zu tun. Da aber die Wissen-
> schaftler die Literatur verwalten,
> schieben sie sich gern zwischen das
> Buch und die Leser, fördern zwar Wis-
> sen, mindern aber die Wirkung. Manche

213

> Interpretation wirkt wie eine Warnung
> vor der Unmittelbarkeit des Kunster-
> lebnisses. Die Furcht vor "falscher
> Aktualisierung" ist eine vor der Le-
> bendigkeit der Kunst. Man entschärft
> sie, wenn man sie auf ihre Zeit zu-
> rückverweist. Manche Förderung der
> Literatur ist wie eine Verbannung ins
> Museum.[1]

In taking up the cudgels against official positions on literary reception and in favor of a personal
comprehension of literature, de Bruyn echoes the Sinn
und Form debate of 1971-72 on questions of authoritarian domination of the literary scene in the GDR.[2]
As de Bruyn sees it, literary reception is a private
process in which the reader's horizons of expectation
and experience are challenged and expanded. Reading
contemporary and particularly past literary works can
offer individuals experiences, insights, and knowledge
not available in everyday life; the reader is encouraged to compare his own reality with that which he has
subjectively experienced through literature. By reading literary descriptions of the past, the reader
gains new modes of perception with which he can better
comprehend his society as a continuing process subject
to the same kinds of change visible in these works.
The GDR critic and scholar Dietrich Sommer noted this
linkage of past and present in regard to de Bruyn's
approach to the times of Jean Paul:

> Dieser Aneignungsstandpunkt . . .
> läßt Fremdes und anscheinend längst
> Vergangenes als vertraut und aktuell
> erscheinen, ruft die Einheit von Kon-
> tinuität und Diskontinuität der Lite-
> ratur- und Gesellschaftsentwicklung
> und nicht zuletzt die Widersprüche
> einer auf Literatur eingeschworenen
> Lebensweise ins Bewußtsein.[3]

De Bruyn steadfastly refuses to distinguish between reading, literary reception, and Erbeaneignung
as it concerns literature, thus contradicting the view
of the Party and governmental institutions which have
insisted on an ideological-political distinction between current literary production in the GDR and literature of the past (Erbe). De Bruyn's position on
reception and Erbe differs substantially from the officially touted Erbepflege mandated by the GDR's cultural policy, which sees in the appropriation of the

truly humanistic cultural heritage the possibility of revitalizing the liberal-democratic German tradition and legitimizing the GDR state as heir to this tradition. This view entails the creation of a semi-official interpretive arm of Party policy which forms and executes policy decisions regarding useful and useless Erbe, establishing, as it were, an apparatus which accords stamps of approval to certain works and authors while discarding or denouncing others. Within this framework of restricted literary discourse, literary reception takes on a repressive character because of the implicit attempt at domination inherent in the system of promoting books and authors representing a world view which corresponds to Party interpretations of social and historical reality. Thus writers like Goethe, Schiller, and Heine have been decreed to be legitimate heritage, while others, such as Jean Paul, Kleist, and Kafka, have been deemed to be of limited legitimacy. The result of this has been the creation of an official canon carrying normative force. To contradict its views is to oppose the official position represented by literary administrators, critics, and scholars.

In essays on Thomas Mann, Arnold Zweig, Theodor Fontane, Karl May, and Jean Paul, to name a few of the authors he has studied, de Bruyn has delineated his own position on Erbe--a position which has underscored the necessity for readers to establish a private, subjectively productive relationship with these and other authors, to cull what is individually and subjectively useful for them. In 1975 de Bruyn published his essayistic opus magnum, a ca. 400-page examination of Jean Paul's life and works entitled Das Leben des Jean Paul Friedrich Richter. Eine Biographie.4

Although maligned by literary historians under the sway of Georg Lukács' condemnation of Jean Paul as a mediator of "kleinbürgerliche Versöhnung mit der elenden deutschen Wirklichkeit,"5 Jean Paul has, as de Bruyn points out, had an effect on numerous GDR writers, among them Fritz Rudolf Fries, Friedemann Berger, Franz Fühmann, Irmtraud Morgner, and Helga Schütz. One can add of course de Bruyn himself, whose narrative stances have been greatly influenced by Jean Paul's novels. The ironically detached narrative style de Bruyn employed in Buridans Esel and Märkische Forschungen to expose and castigate petit-bourgeois attitudes rampant in the GDR harks directly back to Jean Paul's similar use of irony to at once criticize and humoristically affirm the many contradictions evident in his own society. As if to underscore this fruitful use of Jean Paul, de Bruyn employs direct quotations from Jean Paul's works in both of these novels. [6] The rather private appropriation of Jean Paul by GDR authors, however, has taken place, if not in contradiction to, then at least in disagreement with official positions, which have tended to stress the classical tradition of Goethe's Weimar over Jean Paul's "kleinbürgerlich-plebejische Opposition." [7]

In 1974, Wolfgang Harich, newly rehabilitated after years of incarceration for anti-state activities ("die Harich-Gruppe"), published his seminal <u>Jean Pauls Revolutionsdichtung. Versuch einer neuen Deutung seiner historischen Romane</u>, an attempt to ideologically resurrect Jean Paul. In his rather bombastic academic prose, Harich endeavors to salvage and actualize Jean Paul for the GDR as a "demokratischer Revolutionär," a "jakobinischer Revolutionär," even a "Girondist."[8] Under Harich's sleight of pen, the deeply contradictory ironist is transformed into a revolutionary polemicist. Here Jean Paul's work becomes a political rather than a literary entity; his value as a writer is demonstrated with ideological, not aesthetic, criteria, by which Harich attempts to integrate him into the prevailing apparatus of acceptable and useful <u>Erbe</u>.

In a 1975 essay, de Bruyn countered:

> hier [wird] Jean Paul sozusagen rehabilitiert . . . aber mit den Methoden dessen, der ihn vorher verdammte. Keine Lösung von Lukács liegt hier vor, sondern eine Berichtigung in diesem einen Punkt. Mit Recht wird hier das bürgerlich-biedermeierliche Bild Jean Pauls (das Lukács ja nur auf seinen anderen Standpunkt mit hinüber nahm ohne es zu ändern) entscheidend revidiert. Statt aber die schon zu lange einseitig belastete Waage des Urteils ins Gleichgewicht zu bringen, wird sie auf der anderen Seite überlastet. [9]

In salvaging Jean Paul from Lukács' one-sided evaluation, Harich had indeed created "ein festes Ufer . . . von dem sich abzustoßen für die Literaturwissenschaft lohnend ist,"[10] de Bruyn conceded, but Harich's work was guided by a central intelligence which selected

216

information useful for its thesis and ignored contradictory aspects. The result is a distorted and falsified image of Jean Paul, perhaps useful for the ideological orientation of GDR school books, but detrimental to those seeking a personal understanding of Jean Paul. In a 1976 foreword to Das Leben des Quintus Fixlein, de Bruyn pointedly argued: "Jeder Versuch, die Worturwälder Jean Pauls durch Ausholzen zu Parks umzuformen, wird zur Verfälschung." [11]

Thus de Bruyn's Jean Paul book, published one year after the appearance of Harich's study, is, de Bruyn admits, to some extent a polemic aimed at correcting the GDR's official comprehension of Jean Paul and freeing it from ideologically motivated distortions. As he comments in the work: "Auf den von Biographen gesponnenen roten Faden läßt sich ein Genie wie dieses nicht ziehen, in das Glanzpapier der Verehrung nicht wickeln. Wenn Biographie mehr sein will als Denkmalsbau, darf sie die Widersprüche nicht zudecken" (p. 113). De Bruyn's enormously entertaining book vividly recreates Jean Paul's life and times, placing his extensive oeuvre solidly within the sociopolitical and aesthetic context of his age; it portrays a writer--at times brilliant, at times eccentric --struggling to gain recognition in a literary world largely dominated by the cultural Olympus of Goethe's Weimar. Unlike Harich's highly theoretical treatise, de Bruyn's biography introduces a thoroughly and fanatically private man, a workaholic who, when his strength flagged, found recourse to stimulants which allowed him to maintain his grueling eighteen-hour days. At first, coffee and, later, sturdy brown beer became Jean Paul's daily companions--he referred to them as his "vorletzte Ölung," his "Weihwasser" (p. 245)--without which he could not work. De Bruyn quotes from a letter Jean Paul's wife wrote to a friend describing her husband's nervous anticipation of the periodic arrival of his beer order:

Bei der Einfahrt eines Bierfasses . . . läuft er seliger umher als bei dem Eintritt eines Kindes in die Welt. . . . Mit solcher Ungeduld werden die Stunden gezählt und schon im Voraus mit Trinken gefasstet. Ist er [der Kutscher] endlich angekommen, dann wehe ihm, wenn er zu lange ausruht; gleich muß das Bier ins Haus, um einen frischen Krug mit einem Heber herausziehen zu können. (p. 245)

This quotation and similar sections of the book demonstrate de Bruyn's underlying intention: to revitalize Jean Paul's life, work, and times, to free this great humorist from what Thomas Mann has called "historischen Edelrost";[12] to make Jean Paul accessible and interesting to today's readers. The motivation for de Bruyn's work on Jean Paul lies less in his admittedly great affinity for Jean Paul's writing than in a desire to open up an alternative realm of literary discourse untainted by ideological dictates from above.

In addition to providing fascinating reading even for those not particularly interested in Jean Paul, de Bruyn's book is studded with observations on various aspects of literary life in the GDR. Jean Paul, who, especially following the Restoration in the early nineteenth century, suffered under the heavy hand of censors, railed against all forms of censorship; at one point, he sardonically proposed that he--as the greatest expert in the field--be appointed a censor of his own books, a point de Bruyn quickly picks up to comment obliquely on a similar practice in his own society, i.e., self-censorship:

> Denn mit dem, was er [Jean Paul] "Selbst-Zensierung" nennt, beschreibt er, was zur wirklichen Gefahr für den Wahrheitsgehalt von Literatur werden könnte: den unter Zensurdruck und geistiger Manipulation einsetzenden Vorgang, der aus einem sozialen Hemmnis ein psychisches macht, äußere Grenzen vorverlegt ins Innere des Schreibenden und zwar den Zensurbeamten entlastet, die Literatur aber von Wirklichkeit entleert. (p. 273)

The anticipated authoritarian response to critical literary texts, de Bruyn claims, can intimidate sensitive writers before they submit their texts to the rigorous screening process characteristic of the GDR's literary scene: "Daran scheitert manchmal eine heutige Verlagsarbeit, bei der kritische Zeigefinger schon gehoben werden, ehe das erste Wort geschrieben ist" (p. 171). But this fear of repressive criticism also explains the susceptibility of many GDR authors to opportunism and conformity: "Wenn der Beifall von unten ausbleibt, nimmt man mit dem von oben vorlieb" (p. 171).

As disturbing and dangerous as censorship can be for individual authors, de Bruyn argues, it has little lasting effect on preventing the communication of ideas and trends. Censors attempt to dam up intellectual currents and fail miserably, appearing as fools to future generations. "Zu hoffen ist," he writes, "daß auch für kommende Jahrhunderte der Eindruck bleibt, den unseres von der Zensur der vergangenen hat: so lästig und hemmend sie auch auf jeder Gegenwart lastete, blieb sie letzten Endes auch wirkungslos. Die Geschichte der Zensur in Deutschland ist eine ihrer Ohnmacht, die vom Negativen her die Macht des geschriebenen Wortes verdeutlicht" (p. 262).

Censorship, de Bruyn and Jean Paul argue, is both ineffectual and harmful to the political system enforcing it. It prevents the dissemination of useful knowledge in the society that generates it, often leaving more liberal societies to cull useful information for their own use from works censored elsewhere. Knowledge is present for all, but it can only be achieved through free discourse. "Der Erkenntnisbaum wächst nur als Freiheitsbaum," de Bruyn says (p. 273). He asks, moreover, what right censors can invoke to justify their existence. In whose name do they perform their activity? In the name of truth? "Das setzte voraus, der Zensor hätte sie. Dann wäre alles Suchen nach ihr, jede Wissenschaft also unnütz" (p. 272).

In a stunningly provocative passage remarkable for its subtlety as well as for its pointedness, de Bruyn touches on a theme very much at the heart of the censorship question in the GDR: "Mauern schützen zwar, versperren aber auch die Sicht. Der einzige Ausweg aus diesem Dilemma ist immer der, zu den schon vorhandenen Privilegien ein neues zu schaffen: das der Information" (p. 265). This comment mirrors current discussion in the GDR--perhaps inspired by Rudolf Bahro's Die Alternative--concerning the accessibility of information, a vital issue in a hierarchically structured society like the GDR. Control of information means power, Bahro pointed out, and this is the reason why the Party and government officials so carefully shepherd its flow, thus assuring their solid grip on social processes. Consequently, de Bruyn, speaking through Jean Paul, suggests that censorship is as misused today as in the nineteenth century. The danger inherent in the printed word lies less with the populace as a whole, which has little control over sociopolitical developments, than with the ruling elite:

"Die Zensoren müßten auch den Fürsten Bücher zu lesen verbieten, weil deren Möglichkeiten, Unheil zu stiften, viel größer sind" (p. 273).

In sketching Jean Paul's life and work, de Bruyn shows distinct parallels to literary life in the GDR. This, after all, is what Erbeaneignung should be all about: the appropriation of the cultural heritage not solely as an object of scholarly study, but rather as something concretely and subjectively useful for today. Dietrich Sommer recognizes this aspect of de Bruyn's book when he writes: "Vor allem aber wird in de Bruyns origineller Darstellung Jean Paul zu einem Medium der künstlerischen Selbstverständigung des sozialistischen Autors über den Sinn literarischen Arbeitens, über die gesellschaftliche Funktion der Literatur, über die Beziehungen zwischen Literatur, Politik und Philosophie." [13]

What is important in approaching the cultural heritage is not the tradition itself, but rather our relationship to it--what writer Fritz Rudolf Fries in a striking formulation calls "Tradition als unabgegoltene Gegenwart." [14] This fascinating thought, perhaps conceived as a correlate to West Germany's concept of Vergangenheitsbewältigung, assumes the object of contemplation not to be the tradition per se, but rather present-day society. "Die Kultur und Literatur vergangener Epochen," says Sigrid Damm, varying a formulation of Engels, "machen wir aus einem 'Ding an sich' zu einem Ding 'für uns.'" [15] Lukács, Harich, and de Bruyn have all approached Jean Paul with different presuppositions, placing differing demands upon their author as an element in the GDR's cultural heritage. Each has arrived at strictly dissimilar conclusions, none of which possesses absolute validity. Harich, following Lukács' lead, stresses the political side of Jean Paul's writing. But unlike Lukács, who had rejected Jean Paul as hopelessly and apolitically petit-bourgeois, Harich's ideologically motivated reading of Jean Paul's novels allows this great writer to be assimilated as a bourgeois revolutionary into the prevailing academic-historical view of the cultural heritage. De Bruyn, on the other hand, emphasizes Jean Paul's subjective value to readers seeking the personal experience de Bruyn sees as the key to literary reception. Each of these authors is ultimately using his portrayal of Jean Paul to express his own views on present-day society. De Bruyn's book underscores this ambivalent relationship of present to past when he writes:

> Für die Erinnerung ist Vergangenheit
> nichts Unabänderliches. Nie hat sie
> ihren Zweck in sich selbst, immer
> dient sie gegenwärtigen Zwecken.
> Durch Vergessen, Verfälschen, Korri-
> gieren, Deuten, Idealisieren paßt die
> Erinnerung vergangene Tatsachen der
> Gegenwart an. Mit Unehrlichkeit hat
> das nichts zu tun, nur mit veränder-
> lichen Standpunkten. (p. 16)

Dietrich Sommer, known for his work on the reception and function of literature, confirms "daß Erbeaneignung um so produktiver verläuft je vielfältiger
und genauer das Verhältnis zwischen dem historischen
Gegenstand und den gegenwärtigen Aneignungsbedingungen
reflektiert wird."[16] This presumes, Sommer concludes,
a well-developed consciousness of history and tradition that is not guided by highly theoretical abstractions, but rather by "Funktionsvorstellungen in bezug
auf die gegenwärtigen Erfordernisse der Kunst- und Ge-
sellschaftsentwicklung."[17] This is indeed the point
de Bruyn is trying to make, i.e., that the renewed interest among GDR writers in previously unacceptable
authors such as Jean Paul, Kleist, Kafka, and Joyce
clearly reflects altered conditions in the production,
distribution, and reception of literature. The gradual demise of dogmatic conceptions of socialist realism
coupled with the proclaimed relaxation of previous
taboos have stimulated lively discussion on form and
content issues in literature. Conceptions of realism
have been greatly expanded; irrational aspects of existence such as dreams, fantasy, influence of the sub-
conscious, even death and dying have become accepted
themes of GDR literature, themes which, de Bruyn suggests, can only be treated with the help of formal
means such as stream-of-consciousness and montage
techniques combined with a renewed emphasis on subjectivity. This explains in part the newly awakened
interest among GDR writers in past literary figures
and techniques. As de Bruyn points out:

> Die Aneignung Jean Pauls geht in der
> DDR einher mit einer allgemeinen Er-
> weiterung des Realismus-Begriffs. . .
> Man entdeckt das Individuum in allen
> seinen Erscheinungsformen. Man bringt
> vor allem die eigne Individualität
> ins Spiel, entdeckt mit wachsender
> Souveränität wieder das Spielerische
> in der Kunst, das Groteske auch, be-

greift, daß Wirklichkeit nicht nur
mit Elementen der Wirklichkeit wie-
dergegeben werden kann. [18]

To be sure, the ferment de Bruyn sees in current GDR
literature is not a product of the rediscovery of Jean
Paul. On the contrary, "die Beschäftigung mit ihm ist
vielmehr Produkt dieser Bewegung, die mehr ist als Reaktion auf eine Literatur, die stärker Absichten als
Wirklichkeit verpflichtet war. . . ."[19]

Thus de Bruyn's biography of Jean Paul is to some
extent a polemic against Harich's attempt to manipulate Jean Paul to fit officially espoused ideological
concepts. In Harich's treatment, Jean Paul becomes a
useful historical figure in the developmental line
drawn by GDR ideologues. This kind of "Geste der Ge-
wißheit,"[20] characteristic of many academic-historical
evaluations of literature, robs literature of its direct effect upon the reader. It mediates a view of
art as dead nature, encouraging readers to see important writers such as Kleist, Goethe, or Jean Paul as
estranged and remote historical objects. This is, of
course, the dilemma of many of the GDR's politically
guided historians--in his Jean Paul book de Bruyn
calls them "Traditionslinienentwerfer": "Der Anschau-
lichkeit wegen brauchen sie Konkretes, das aber, so
wie es ist, nicht paßt. Meist wird dann das Hinken
durch Amputieren beseitigt" (p. 275). De Bruyn warns
of such situations, "wo von den gleichen Ereignissen
und Personen aus Traditionslinien in die verschieden-
sten Richtungen gezogen werden, immer dem gleichen
Schema der Einseitigkeit folgend. Man zeigt die Seite, die man für die helle hält und unterschlägt mit
der dunklen die Widersprüchlichkeit der Zeit" (p.275).

The result is a dogmatic view of past literary
creations, offering readers little personal experience, indeed making these works seem alien to a large
reading public. And the quest for relevant personal
experience, for self-experience, are the primary
reasons why the readers select the book they read:
"[Dem Leser] gelten individuelle Maßstäbe. Bei ihm be-
stimmt der Rang [eines Buches] sich aus dem Platz, den
es in seiner persönlichen Entwicklung einnimmt. Das
Erleben erteilt Zensuren, nicht die Wissenschaft. Die
darf nur hilfreich Hand anlegen zum besseren Verständnis." [21]

Thus de Bruyn's "radikale Demokratisisierung des
Erbes"[22] points toward a comprehension of literature

as a vital mediator between subjective individuality and objective reality. Reading subverts prevailing norms and provides, through the experience of others, access to expanded perception and self-comprehension unfettered by ideologically grounded interpretations of reality.

Rutgers University

Notes

[1] Günter de Bruyn, "Der Künstler und die anderen. Nachwort zu Thomas Manns Tonio Kröger," in his Im Querschnitt. Prosa, Essay, Biographie (Halle/Leipzig: Mitteldeutscher Verlag, 1979), p. 356.

[2] In the initial contribution to this discussion poet Adolf Endler accused the GDR's professional literary critics and scholars of approaching literary texts with heavy-handedly normative and brutally dogmatic methods. Endler argued that literary scholarship, rather than mediating between the text and the reader, intruded in the process of reception with politically conceived norms based on axioms of Marxism-Leninism, rendering political verdicts rather than aesthetic analyses and thus disturbing the communicative flow between the writer and his readers. In his vociferous attack, Endler accused the GDR's Germanists of "Nebelreiterei," "Willkür," "brutaler Dogmatismus," and "Unfähigkeit zum Kunstgenuß." Adolf Endler, "Im Zeichen der Inkonsequenz: Über Hans Richters Aufsatzsammlung Verse Dichter Wirklichkeiten," Sinn und Form, 23, No. 6 (1971), esp. pp. 1363-64.

[3] Dietrich Sommer, "Günter de Bruyn: Das Leben des Jean Paul Friedrich Richter," Weimarer Beiträge, 23, No. 9 (1977), 131-32.

[4] Günter de Bruyn, Das Leben des Jean Paul Friedrich Richter. Eine Biographie (Frankfurt/M: Fischer, 1978). The original edition was published by Mitteldeutscher Verlag in 1975. Page citations refer to the Fischer edition.

[5] Georg Lukács, Skizze einer Geschichte der neueren deutschen Literatur (Berlin: Aufbau, 1953), p. 39. As de Bruyn commented on Lukács' influence on the GDR's comprehension of Jean Paul: "Die Kanonisierung,

die das Werk dieses bedeutenden marxistischen Literaturwissenschaftlers (wie ich annehme: gegen seinen Willen) erfahren hatte, wirkte sich für die Jean Paul-Rezeption ungünstig aus." Günter de Bruyn, "Jean Paul und die neuere DDR-Literatur," Jahrbuch der Jean-Paul-Gesellschaft, 10 (1975), 206.

[6] For a more detailed discussion of this use of literary quotations, see Bernd Allenstein, "Günter de Bruyn," in Kritisches Lexikon zur deutschsprachigen Gegenwartsliteratur, ed. Heinz Ludwig Arnold (Munich: edition text + kritik, 1978 ff.), esp. pp. 6 and 9.

[7] Hans-Dieter Dahnke, et. al., Geschichte der deutschen Literatur 1789 bis 1930, Vol. 7 of Geschichte der deutschen Literatur (Berlin: Volk und Wissen, 1978), p. 436.

[8] Wolfgang Harich, Jean Pauls Revolutionsdichtung. Versuch einer neuen Deutung seiner historischen Romane (Reinbek: Rowohlt, 1974), esp. pp. 92 and 122.

[9] "Jean Paul und die neuere DDR-Literatur," p. 206.

[10] "Jean Paul und die neuere DDR-Literatur," p. 207.

[11] Reprinted as "Lesefreuden mit Jean Paul," in Im Querschnitt, p. 344. De Bruyn's work Märkische Forschungen was conceived as a satire of Harich's treatment of Jean Paul.

[12] Thomas Mann, Der Zauberberg (Frankfurt/M: Fischer, 1952), p. 5.

[13] Sommer, p. 131.

[14] Fritz Rudolf Fries, "Jean Paul unter uns," Sinn und Form, 28, No. 3 (1976), 688.

[15] Sigrid Damm, ". . . setzen der Menschlichkeit neue Maßstäbe, " Neue Deutsche Literatur, 24, No. 10 (1976), 150.

[16] Sommer, p. 132.

[17] Sommer, p. 132.

[18] "Jean Paul und die neuere DDR-Literatur," p. 209.

[19] "Jean Paul und die neuere DDR-Literatur," p. 209.

[20] "Der Künstler und die anderen," p. 357.

[21] "Der Künstler und die anderen," p. 357.

[22] Damm, p. 150.

Friedrich Nietzsche in the GDR:
A Problematic Reception

Denis M. Sweet

The kind of interest taken, again and again, in Nietzsche in the West, most prominently by Michel Foucault, Gilles Deleuze, Jacques Derrida, and Jürgen Habermas beginning in the late 1960s,[1] has no counterpart in the GDR. Indeed, it is difficult to speak of a Nietzsche reception there at all if by reception is meant an interest in, and an attempt to come to terms with, a primary text. No Nietzsche texts have been published in the GDR.[2] There, with an almost mirror-image exclusivity, concentration has not been upon the ideas, the text itself, but upon their actual, political effects in the society receptive to them. The attempt has never been made in the GDR to analyze Nietzsche's works as such. Nietzsche hermeneutics has always been a subordinate part of a larger process: a functional analysis of the part his thought has played and continues to play in the formation of the ideology of the bourgeois state. To put it quite simply: Nietzsche reception in the GDR is the chronicle of Nietzsche reception elsewhere. It is the reception of a reception: in the imperialist era, in the Nazi state, among the Right in the West today. The framework for such analysis was set, and continues to be dominated by, Georg Lukács.[3]

The year is 1935. Three Marxist writers publish texts in exile, in Moscow and Zurich, dealing with the philosopher Friedrich Nietzsche: Ernst Bloch, Erbschaft dieser Zeit; Hans Günther, Der Herren eigner Geist and "Der Fall Nietzsche"; and Georg Lukács, "Nietzsche als Vorläufer der faschistischen Ästhetik."[4] All these works sprang from the immediate need to analyze and combat German fascism.

First, Bloch's Erbschaft dieser Zeit. This long

and difficult book possesses an implacable fury wielded with such sovereign precision that it assumes an unique place in German letters. Bloch's postulate of "Ungleichzeitigkeit" at the center of his argumentation represents a far-reaching attempt to uncover strands of social and mental life running counter to late capitalism that could be co-opted by the Nazis for their own purposes, or reclaimed for revolutionary Marxism, or, at the very least, neutralized. Bloch was consequently open to a large scale, critical inventory-taking of the cultural phenomena of late capitalism for the purposes of a possible Erbfolge: "Daß die jeweils letzte Maschine, welche die spätbürgerliche Technik erzeugt, die beste sei, wird marxistisch nicht bestritten. Jedoch fast gar kein Erbe wird an den ideologischen Erscheinungen und Produkten der Spätzeit anerkannt" (p. 17). Bloch's work immediately received a lengthy criticism by Hans Günther entitled "Erbschaft dieser Zeit?" that appeared in the Moscow journal Internationale Literatur in 1936. In it the advisability of openness to the cultural heritage of late capitalist society is questioned, as is the entire concept of Ungleichzeitigkeit. Günther questioned even whether such a notion is compatible with Marxism. Bloch thereupon issued a polemical defense in the same journal; Günther answered with an "Antwort an Ernst Bloch." So began a controversy of an important political and historical nature. The problems of cultural heritage discussed here in connection with a theory of fascism and a critique of fascist ideology led into the discussion of the politics of the popular front of those years.

Yet as momentous as Bloch's work was, I can find no trace of it in the discussion of Nietzsche in the GDR.[5] And, unlike Bloch's Das Prinzip Hoffnung, it has never been published there.

Hans Günther wrote and published in Soviet exile in the 1930s. He was a member of the KPD, was delegated to Moscow in 1932 to serve on the board of the International League of Revolutionary Writers, and died in Vladivostok en route to a detention camp, the victim of a purge.[6] Günther was an exceedingly prolific anti-fascist writer of great verve and barbed wit. His book, Der Herren eigner Geist, was the first major detailed analysis and criticism of the ideology of National Socialism. The Nietzsche chapter contained in this book and his study "Der Fall Nietzsche" are the only writings published in the GDR (to my knowledge) which trace the pattern of development in his writings, distinguish stages in his thought, and have every appearance of offering an original analysis. Yet it was not until 1981 that these and others of Günther's writings were rescued from oblivion and reprinted by Aufbau Verlag in a 900-page volume, Der Herren eigner Geist. Ausgewählte Schriften.

Nonetheless Günther's argumentation has what will be a familiar ring. The charge is leveled at Nietzsche as the critic of decadence, nihilism, and modernism that he simply chastises the spirit of the times, the cultural symptoms of capitalism, with no understanding of their social and economic foundations (p. 264) and that this functions merely as a distraction from and defense of the existing order. Posing as a revolutionary without being one, Nietzsche acts to defuse real revolutionary activity (p. 152). This sums up Günther's criticism of Nietzsche in his own era. The next step is a discussion of Nietzsche and National Socialism. Günther criticizes those aspects of Nietzsche's philosophy that came to the aid of the fascists in their attempts at mass manipulation:

> An Nietzsches Schema haben aber auch, bei allen inhaltlichen Änderungen, die Faschisten angeknüpft, und dies aus verständlichen Gründen. War es doch ihre besondere Aufgabe, ein Schreckensregiment gegen die Massen mit Hilfe der Massen zu errichten. Sie mußten den Kapitalismus "retten" und doch auch ihrer überwiegend antikapitalistisch eingestellten Gefolgschaft die Aufhebung des Kapitalismus versprechen. Sie hatten die brutalste Reaktion als radikalste Revolution zu tarnen. Und welche Ideologie hätte für diesen konträren Doppelzweck besser zum Vorbild dienen können als die paradoxe Philosophie Nietzsches mit ihrem "Erneuern" und Bewahren in einem, mit ihrem "Jasagen auf Grund eines Nein!" (p. 290)

But it falls to Lukács to provide a far more sweeping and telling criticism. In his article "Nietzsche als Vorläufer der faschistischen Ästhetik," Lukács views Nietzsche, on the one hand, as a romantic, and consequently reactionary, critic of late nineteenth-century capitalist society who shares with the romantics a longing for a return to pre-capitalist life, and, on the other hand, as the constructor of a visionary utopian future where all the contradictions of capitalist society, while remaining capitalist, have been resolved. Nietzsche thus becomes, in his analysis, indissolubly linked to the two entirely re-actionary elements which overtake German history. I mean, of course, imperialism and fascism. Lukács' analysis brings to the fore the pernicious aspects of Nietzsche's thought and, in one grand stroke, distinguishes him from all the other romantic critics of capitalist, industrialized society. They emphasized the good side of modern society while condemning the bad and yearning for a return to a pre-capitalist state. Nietzsche does just the opposite. He praises the bad side of capitalism (domination, constant struggle for a living, elitist ideology of a master race, social Darwinism) while positing an extrapo-lated version of this society in the future where all the contradictions have been resolved through intensi-fication of precisely this bad side. As if to make this entire process more seductive, Lukács argues, Nietzsche's attack on the society of his times takes on the appearance of a revolutionary stance and prom-ises a radically new world: "die Verteidigung der Prinzipien des Kapitalismus bekommt die Geste eines radikalen Anstürmens gegen die gegenwärtige Gesell-schaft, sie wird eine scheinrevolutionäre Attitüde (p. 334). Nietzsche uncovers, Lukács concedes, a whole series of important manifest forms of capitalist de-cline, but this uncovering of symptoms of malaise and Nietzsche's immanent activism do not point the way to a better world based on an analysis of the actual eco-nomic forces of inequality and domination at work in Wilhelmine capitalism. Quite the contrary. Nietz-sche's non-dialectical and non-materialist analysis, while pointing out forms of decadence along the way, only leads to, and can only lead to, mythic solutions.

A growing exasperation in the face of Nietzsche's inability to overcome the limitations of a subjective, idealist critique that itself becomes swallowed up by the objective turn of events in Germany, i.e., the on-surge of imperialism, breaks forth again and again in the Marxist Lukács' analysis: "Objektiv steckt hinter dem Erlebnis Nietzsches nichts weiter als die Illu-sion, die Widersprüche des wirklichen Kapitalismus durch den Mythos eines erdichteten entwickelteren Ka-pitalismus, des Imperialismus, überwinden zu können" (p. 333). The mythic figurations proffered by Nietz-sche and directed against the capitalist society of his day only lead to an even more developed and more

brutal capitalism, and can furnish mythological under-
pinings for the state, Lukács concludes.

This first step in his argumentation focusing on
Nietzsche as the "herald and prophet of imperialist
genesis" (a variation of Franz Mehring's phrase describing Nietzsche as "der Herold und Opfer des Großkapitals"),[7] is put forward more and more energetical-
ly in Lukács' later writings: in the article "Der
deutsche Faschismus und Nietzsche," which appeared in
Moscow nine years later, at the height of the war; and
in the most decisive, and most pointed, Auseinandersetzung of all, the key chapter "Nietzsche als Begrün-
der des Irrationalismus der imperialistischen Perio-
de," in Lukács' famous book Die Zerstörung der Vernunft.[8]

The identification with imperialism leads directly to another: that of Nietzsche with fascism. If one
follows the definition of fascism set down by the Kom-
intern in 1933 ("Fascism is the open terrorist dicta-
torship of the most reactionary, most chauvinistic,
most imperialistic elements of finance capital."),[9]
there is little to distinguish specifically Nazi characteristics from the preceding phase of imperialism.
This epistemological difficulty is compounded by another: the fascists, from Mussolini to the Berlin university professor, National Socialist ideologue, and
Nietzsche scholar, Alfred Baeumler, to Hitler himself,
openly claimed Nietzsche as a source of inspiration
and their forerunner. So the prophet and herald of
imperialist genesis is also viewed by Lukács and the
GDR writers after him (just as he was in a less immediate sense by Günther) as an inspiration and ideological source for later National Socialist theory and
practice.

These two criticisms are joined by a third after
the war. To the question of Nietzsche reception by
the bourgeoisie in the earlier part of this century,
and to the enormously problematical Nietzsche reception by the Nazis, comes a third element, which GDR
writers see as an active continuation of the anti-socialist tradition of the first two (and one more reason for these older receptions remaining so worri-
some): namely the Nietzsche reception in Cold War West
Germany.

It comes as no surprise that the longest study
ever to appear in the GDR on Nietzsche is a comprehensive registration of Nietzsche reception in the Feder-

al Republic. Indeed, the writings produced in the FRG in the late forties and early fifties gave cause for alarm. To put it simply: the attempt was now being made not only to dissociate Nietzsche from the Nazi past, but also from any serious connection with the social make-up of his own times. In this analysis everything becomes individualized, psychological, and, at worst, pathological. Nietzsche's ideas are now, whether the products of genius or neurosis or disease, the works of one individual, idealized, disembodied of a larger, more telling, social context. In this way, the part they played in Nietzsche's own era and the part they came to play in Nazi ideology are never examined, are ignored, nullified. Bernhard Kaufhold, the GDR commentator on this turn of events, is filled with exasperation and foreboding over just what role such "laundered" Nietzsche thinking will play in the future.[10] It is important to remember here that for Kaufhold Nietzsche is primarily an anti-socialist. Nietzsche's rehabilitation in West Germany, seen from this angle, is therefore only one more undertaking in the intensifying Cold War. Indeed, it was precisely the conservative and Christian elements in Cold War West Germany, those factions most antagonistic to the GDR, who were behind the denazified, new interpretation of Nietzsche.

In the vast range of postwar German Nietzsche literature that Kaufhold surveys, the attempt to mystify history rears up again and again. Alfred Weber and particularly Alfred v. Martin, authors he cites at length, dramatically exemplify the fundamental illicitness of creating a demonic and inhuman realm as the supra-historical explanation for the German character. By so doing, Nietzsche's philosophy becomes simply a point of contact with the demonic sphere such as has always been a part of the eternal German being ("gehört zu des ewigen Deutschen Wesen, ist wiederkehrendes deutsches Schicksal. Immer wieder zeigt sich der Deutsche bereit mit dem Teufel zu paktieren . . ." in Martin's terminology.)[11] Nietzsche is thus "ein extrem deutscher Fall," a Faust-figure. This undertaking projects fascism into a mythical realm of "German being" so as to veil over its economic and historic roots. In like fashion, fascism for Alfred Weber was "a sudden darkening . . . the beating wing of dark and demonic powers."[12]

The survey ends with the discussion of a work that provides an even starker notion of the murky and pestilential atmosphere of the Cold War period than

Wolfgang Koeppen's Tod in Rom, namely Ernst Schwarz'
Weltbild und Weltgeschichte. Here the incredible
claim is made that working-class socialism was the
precursor of National "Socialism" and that Nietzsche's
struggle against the working class was, therefore,
"anti-fascist"! [13]

Kaufhold's concern in the late 1950s that Nietzsche was being mined for the purposes of Cold War confrontation seems prescient. [14] The response in the GDR,
again and again, has been to close off that possibility. Here there is no rehabilitation. Nietzsche sig-
nifies anti-socialism and remains fastened to the background of previous receptions. The spectrum ranges
from the strident rejection found in the representative reference work Deutsche Literaturgeschichte in
einem Band, [15] to the cool criticism in Hans Kaufmann's
more recent Krisen und Wandlungen der deutschen Literatur von Wedekind bis Feuchtwanger. [16] In the former,
Nietzsche is depicted as a "seductive surrogate for
decadents of all shades" (p. 464) who is particularly
adept at feigning revolutionary fervor only to attack
socialism. His "superman" and "blond beast" are portrayed as ideological waystations on the way to fascism. For Kaufmann, Nietzsche is only of interest as
a "symptom of the 'intellectual lay of the land' in
the literary world of that era"(p. 41); his persistent influence, a manifestation of the general crisis
situation for art. In like vein, Frank Rupprecht
writes that "Nietzsche merely announced with his 'new'
values the ideology of the imperialist epoch, capitalism's changeover to reaction and violence along the
whole line." [17]

None of these discussions moves beyond the
groundwork laid down by Lukács; and even more recent
work offers little prospect of this either. By virtue
of the sheer size of his output, current Nietzsche reception in the GDR seems the province of one man,
Heinz Malorny, "wissenschaftlicher Arbeitsleiter" at
the Academy of Sciences of the GDR, who since 1978 has
published annually on Nietzsche.[18] This in itself is
noteworthy since up to that time writings dealing directly with Nietzsche appeared on a rather sporadic
basis. Yet the tenacity of publication bespeaks no
novelty of approach. The argumentation of Malorny's
most significant work, his contribution to the highly
differentiated and very detailed collection of essays
on fascism that appeared in 1980, Faschismus-Forschung. Positionen, Probleme, Polemik, marks off the
stations of a well-trodden path: imperialism, fascism,

Nietzsche reception in the FRG. The first two sections figure simply as repetitions of the argumentation familiar from Lukács: "Wir sehen allerdings in Nietzsche einen der wichtigsten geistigen Vorläufer und Wegbereiter der Philosophie und Ideologie des Imperialismus, darunter auch der faschistischen Ideologie in Deutschland" (p. 283). The final section displays the same kinds of concern voiced by Kaufhold twenty-five years earlier, namely a denunciation of the mystification of fascism by West German writers that deprives it of historical roots and thus makes it seem an anomaly. To my mind this is a justifiable concern, but Malorny's conclusion, which bears quoting in full, is characterized by an intransigence that offers little prospect that the "Sehschlitz" of GDR real socialism will ever acquire more depth of vision vis à vis Nietzsche:

> Die Spannweite der Berufung auf Nietz
> sche reicht heute von den alten und
> neuen Nazis und den Neokonservativen
> bis zu den Versuchen einer Synthese
> von Marx und Nietzsche bei den moder-
> nen Revisionisten. Die marxistisch-
> leninistische Philosophiegeschichts-
> schreibung wird sich auch in Zukunft
> allen derartigen Versuchen einer Wie-
> dererweckung der Ideen Nietzsches ge-
> genüber unversöhnlich verhalten, wie
> sie bisher Nietzsche stets als phi-
> losophischen Gegner behandelt hat.
> (p. 301)

Malorny's contribution to the Philosophen-Lexikon (1982) follows along the exact same lines but includes the following update: "Gegenwärtig reicht die Skala der Nietzsche-Rezeption von den Anhängern der äußersten Rechten und des Konservativismus (Mohler, Rohrmoser) über die Vertreter des Linksliberalismus (Frankfurter Schule) bis zu den Ideologen des zeitgenössischen Revisionismus (Praxisphilosophie)" (p. 697)--the implication being that all those listed are in error.

And yet there have been other voices. One work to appear in the GDR that makes its own original contribution to an understanding of Nietzsche is Richard Hamann and Jost Hermand's Gründerzeit.[19] Although it appeared four years after Hamann's death, Jost Hermand ascribes the chapters on Nietzsche to Hamann, who had been a professor of art history at Humboldt University and a member of the German Academy of Sciences. Over and beyond the chapter or two that deal with him, this book is suffused with Nietzsche. Here he is the figure central to the Gründerzeit and is used to demonstrate every single one of its essential characteristics. Passage after passage is quoted in illustration, especially from Thus Spoke Zarathustra. Even though this book went through two printings in the GDR, it comes as no surprise that it was never reviewed there. As Jost Hermand put it in private conversation, perhaps the book was "too uncritical" of Nietzsche.[20] Yet it is altogether characteristic that Nietzsche should surface first in connection with discussion of art and literature, in connection with those progressive bourgeois writers and artists who had come under his influence. As in Hamann and Hermand's discussion of Nietzsche in Gründerzeit, so does Nietzsche reappear in a positive sense in Diether Schmidt's Otto Dix im Selbstbildnis.[21] Dix had been galvanized early on in life by Nietzsche, and it is to the credit of Diether Schmidt that this book makes no bones about it.

I wish I could say that new ground is being broken; at least I can say that preparations are being made. The most differentiated discussion of Nietzsche to appear in the GDR to date is also the most recent. Renate Reschke's article on Nietzsche reception in the West enjoys the advantage of concentrating on recent developments.[22] It does not trip over the first two steps of usual GDR criticism, imperialism and fascism. Indeed, the point of view offered here sees Lukács' analysis as an important contribution--an understanding of "the line of tradition of irrationalist philosophy" with Nietzsche as "key figure" (p. 1194)-- in the context of Lukács' own time. That said, Reschke focuses on various currents of contemporary Nietzsche reception in the West. This has become a subject of interest since a result of the post-war editorial work by Schlechta in the 1950s, and especially by Colli and Montinari more recently, has been to weaken the position of the Right that had fed off a mythic view of the man and falsified texts. Furthermore, the Left has itself renewed an interest in Nietzsche. It is not necessary here to follow Reschke through the critical inventory of leftist Nietzsche reception, from anarchist to structuralist, that ensues. What is new here, and of interest to the concern of this paper, is an openness, even encouragement, of a comparative study of Marx and Nietzsche within the society of their day. The concluding paragraph articulates the point quite clearly: "[V]ielmehr muß die marxistische

Kritik in stärkerem Maße sich nicht nur Nietzschescher Positionen differenzierter vergewissern, sondern auch das gesamte Spektrum der eigenen Auseinandersetzung mit seinem Denken zum Gegenstand ihres Selbstverständnisses hinsichtlich des umstrittenen Philosophen machen" (p. 1211).

It was Renate Reschke who, as a participant in the International Nietzsche Conference on the theme "Reception and Critique" ("Aufnahme und Auseinandersetzung") held in Reisenburg in 1980, underscored the most recent efforts in the GDR to approach the problematic Nietzsche in a less constrained fashion than heretofore. Responding to Ernst Behler's paper on Nietzsche in Eastern European Marxist criticism, Reschke cited the new interest in Nietzsche as a lyric poet, the renewed, more differentiated attempt to think through cultural heritage--particularly avantgarde and leftist--, and the new Marxist interest in Nietzsche's cultural critique, as evidence of a growing, more sophisticated Nietzsche reception in the GDR.[23]

In the meantime, Reclam Verlag in Leipzig has approached Friedrich Tomberg at the University of Jena with the proposal that he edit a Nietzsche anthology. This would be the first Nietzsche publication of any sort in the GDR. Friedrich Tomberg has, as he has assured me, written a first draft of an introduction to the anthology, has even read papers and held Streitgespräche in Berlin on the subject of Nietzsche's place in the humanist tradition. When I spoke to him in the summer of 1982 he promised xerox copies of all these writings, but wrote me in March, 1983 that the time was not yet ripe for their distribution, that there needs to be a general rethinking of Nietzsche from the ground up, otherwise his efforts would only serve confusion. "So in the meantime my desk drawer remains locked," he concluded.[24]

The Goethe-Schiller Archive in Weimar (where the former Nietzsche Archive is now housed) has its own publishing plans. In the summer of 1982 its director, Karl-Heinz Hahn, spoke to me of plans to publish a facsimile edition of Ecce Homo with a lengthy introduction by the Schelling specialist Steffan Dietzsch, which would place the work in philosophical and historical perspective. But this too seems to have changed somewhat in the meantime. Instead, Hahn himself and Montinari, the editor of the historical-critical edition of Nietzsche's works, will supply a history of the origination of Ecce Homo (a philological Entwicklungsgeschichte) to figure as the introduction. This book is forthcoming. Steffan Dietzsch's analysis is to appear elsewhere.[25]

What we see, scattered here and there, are first, tentative signs of a rethinking of Nietzsche in the GDR. As Friedrich Tomberg put it in a letter to me:

> Je mehr sich . . . unsere Literatur-wissenschaftler mit der modernen bür-gerlichen Literatur beschäftigten, umso mehr gerieten sie in Verlegen-heit: Überall stießen sie auf den Einfluß Nietzsches. Hochgeschätzte Autoren, so bemerkte man, standen--trotz aller Kritik--im ganzen er-staunlich positiv zu ihm. Mithin sind wir jetzt in einem Dilemma: Die Philosophen haben bisher fast einzig den Quasi-Faschisten zur Kenntnis ge-nommen, die Literaturwissenschaftler haben den bedeutenden Literaten vor Augen. Es bleibt nichts anderes üb-rig, als daß wir uns alle zusammen-setzen, nachdem wir das Gesamtwerk erst einmal studiert haben. Das steht aber noch bevor. [26]

Indeed, I think that this hits the nail on the head. Werner Mittenzwei, the eminent Brecht scholar, reports that Eike Middell is preparing an extensive study of German literature and Nietzsche, and Renate Reschke a B-Dissertation on Nietzsche's aesthetic conceptions.[27] Even if no clear contours have yet emerged, it is nonetheless already apparent that the official rele-gation of Nietzsche to "unbrauchbares Erbe" (useless cultural heritage) has become less adamant.[28]

The anathematization of Nietzsche by earlier Marxist writers makes reassessment extremely arduous. It may be that for the foreseeable future there can be no other way but that Nietzsche in the GDR, like Janus in Rome, will have two faces, one looking back to and serving reaction, the other pointing to a scathing, if individualist, critique of bourgeois society. This duality was foreshadowed long ago: Heinrich Mann ("the primary anti-fascist writer of Western Europe")[29] writing a paean to the individualist philosopher Nietzsche in Thomas Mann's exile journal Maß und Wert [30] at the very same time (1939) that, in Moscow,

Fritz Erpenbeck, the editor of the exile journal Das Wort, was refusing an article on Nietzsche by Hans Natonek, giving as reason: "we cannot agree with your introductory assessment of Nietzsche . . . We do indeed see in Nietzsche (considering his entire work) the father of Nazi philosophy."[31]

There are many receptions at work here, and they need to be sorted out, and thought through, da capo. There are signs that that is just what is going on in the GDR at the moment.

University of New Hampshire

Notes

[1] See, for example, Michel Foucault, "Nietzsche, Freud, Marx," Cahiers de Royaumont--Philosophie, 6 (1967), 183-92; "Nietzsche, Genealogy, History," in Language, Counter-Memory, Practice (Ithaca: Cornell University Press, 1977); and the contributions by Deleuze and Derrida in Nietzsche aujourd'hui?, 2 vols. (Paris: Union Générale d'Editions, 1973).

[2] The sole exception will be Nietzsche's Ecce Homo planned for publication in 1984 by Verlag Edition Leipzig. See the remarks at the end of this paper.

[3] Marxist Nietzsche reception actually dates back to Plekhanov and Franz Mehring, who both wrote on the correspondence of Nietzsche's thought with the practice of an expansive capitalism. Mehring apostrophized Nietzsche in Die Lessing-Legende as "den Philosophen des Großkapitals" (Die Lessing-Legende, Vol. IX of Gesammelte Schriften [Berlin: Dietz, 1963], p. 363).

[4] Ernst Bloch, Erbschaft dieser Zeit, Vol. IV of Gesamtausgabe (Frankfurt: Suhrkamp, 1962). Originally published in Zurich in 1935. The works by Hans Günther, originally published in Moscow in 1935, are now all to be found in Der Herren eigner Geist. Ausgewählte Schriften (Berlin/Weimar: Aufbau, 1981). Georg Lukács' Nietzsche essay, originally published in Internationale Literatur in Moscow in 1935, is in his Probleme der Ästhetik, Vol. X of Werke (Neuwied/Berlin: Luchterhand, 1969). Subsequent page references to these writings will be given parenthetically in the

text.

[5] The one exception is the mention given by Renate Reschke; cf. Note 22 below.

[6] David Pike, German Writers in Soviet Exile, 1933-1945 (Chapel Hill: University of North Carolina Press, 1982), pp. 315-17, 347.

[7] Lukács' phrase is in "Nietzsche als Vorläufer der faschistischen Ästhetik," p. 317; Mehring's in Die Lessing-Legende, p. 364. Here and throughout the paper, all translations are my own.

[8] Georg Lukács, "Der deutsche Faschismus und Nietzsche," Internationale Literatur, 12 (1943), pp. 55-64; Die Zerstörung der Vernunft. Der Weg des Irrationalismus von Schelling bis zu Hitler (Berlin: Aufbau, 1954).

[9] Bernhard Blanke, Reimut Reiche, and Jürgen Werth, "Die Faschismus-Theorie der DDR," Das Argument, 7, No. 33 (1965), 35. See also Iring Fetscher, "Faschismus und Nationalsozialismus. Zur Kritik des sowjetmarxistischen Faschismusbegriffs," Politische Vierteljahresschrift, 3, No. 1 (1962), 42-63.

[10] Bernhard Kaufhold, "Zur Nietzsche-Rezeption in der westdeutschen Philosophie der Nachkriegszeit," in Beiträge zur Kritik der gegenwärtigen bürgerlichen Geschichtsphilosophie, ed. Robert Schulz (Berlin: Deutscher Verlag der Wissenschaften, 1958), pp. 279-409.

[11] Kaufhold, p. 326. Kaufhold quotes from Alfred v. Martin, Der heroische Nihilismus und seine Überwindung (Krefeld: Scherpe, 1948).

[12] Kaufhold, p. 326. The quotation is from Alfred Weber, Abschied von der bisherigen Geschichte (Hamburg: Claassen & Goverts, 1946), pp. 225-26.

[13] Kaufhold, p. 395. The reference is to Ernst Schwarz, Weltbild und Weltgeschichte (Stuttgart: Deutsche Verlagsanstalt, 1946), p. 26.

[14] The deliberate historical dislocations described by Kaufhold are being repeated just as facilely today. Werner J. Dannhauser, a professor of political science at Cornell University, put forth the proposition that "the final stamp of approval for a

denazified Nietzsche in the postwar era had to come from the Left. . . . How and why did the Left need Nietzsche? That question has a simple, though admittedly inadequate answer: Marx was not enough." The implication is that the Left, first of all, pursues an inadequate analysis of contemporary society, i.e., Marxism, that it must supplement elsewhere--with Nietzsche--and, second, that the Left is fundamentally dishonest in calling itself Marxist when it actually has need of a rehabilitated protofascist to keep itself going. Here once again the confabulation of Nietzsche and Marx for the benefit of the Right. "The Trivialization of Friedrich Nietzsche," The American Spectator, 15, No. 5 (May 1982), 9.

[15] Deutsche Literaturgeschichte in einem Band, ed. Jürgen Geerdts (Berlin: Volk und Wissen, 1965).

[16] Hans Kaufmann, Krisen und Wandlungen der deutschen Literatur von Wedekind bis Feuchtwanger (Berlin/Weimar: Aufbau, 1976).

[17] Frank Rupprecht, "Der Pessimismus und die Krise der gegenwärtigen bürgerlichen Philosophie," Deutsche Zeitschrift für Philosophie, 27, No. 8 (1979), 950.

[18] Heinz Malorny, "Friedrich Nietzsche gegen den klassischen bürgerlichen Humanismus," in Philosophie und Humanismus. Beiträge zum Menschenbild der deutschen Klassik (Weimar: Böhlau, 1978), pp. 220-234; "Tendenzen der Nietzsche-Rezeption in der BRD," Deutsche Zeitschrift für Philosophie, 27, No. 12 (1979), 1493-1500; "Friedrich Nietzsche und der deutsche Faschismus," in Faschismus-Forschung. Positionen, Probleme, Polemik, ed. Dietrich Eichholtz and Kurt Gossweiler (Berlin: Akademie, 1980), pp. 279-301; "Nietzsche-Renaissance in der Welt von Gestern," Einheit, 10 (1981), 1038-1045; Friedrich Nietzsches Kritik an der Bourgeoisie und der bürgerlichen Gesellschaft," in Ludwig Elm, Günter Rudolph, and Heinz Malorny, Traditionen des Konservativismus (Berlin: Akademie, 1982); "Friedrich Nietzsche," in Philosophen-Lexikon, ed. Dietrich Alexander and Erhard Lange (Berlin: Dietz, 1982), pp. 693-698.

[19] Richard Hamann and Jost Hermand, Gründerzeit, Vol. I of Deutsche Kunst und Kultur von der Gründerzeit bis zum Expressionismus (Berlin: Akademie, 1965).

[20] Private conversation with Jost Hermand during

the "Women, Fascism, Everyday Life" conference at Ohio State University, 30 April 1983.

[21] Diether Schmidt, Otto Dix im Selbstbildnis (Berlin: Henschelverlag, 1981).

[22] Renate Reschke, "Kritische Aneignung und notwendige Auseinandersetzung. Zu einigen Tendenzen moderner bürgerlicher Nietzsche-Rezeption," Weimarer Beiträge, 29, No. 7 (1983), 1190-1211.

[23] Ernst Behler, "Nietzsche in der marxistischen Kritik Osteuropas," Nietzsche Studien, 10/11 (1981/82), 80-96. Renate Reschke's remarks are contained in the "Diskussion" immediately following, pp. 98-100.

[24] Letter received from Friedrich Tomberg, 11 March 1983.

[25] This information is contained in two letters to me from Karl-Heinz Hahn, one dated 25 March 1983, the other undated (postmarked 22 September 1983). For a detailed account of the new critical Nietzsche edition by Colli and Montinari, see Mazzino Montinari, Nietzsche lesen (Berlin/New York: de Gruyter, 1982), esp. "Die neue kritische Gesamtausgabe von Nietzsches Werken," pp. 10-21. See also Montinari's critique of Lukács: "Nietzsche zwischen Alfred Baeumler and Georg Lukács," pp. 169-206.

[26] Letter received from Friedrich Tomberg, 11 March 1983.

[27] Letter received from Werner Mittenzwei, 17 November 1983.

[28] "Wer erbt, der erbt auch Unbrauchbares. Zur Auseinandersetzung mit ideologischen Positionen, deren Verführungsgewalt und Gefährlichkeit sich tagtäglich noch offenbart. Ein Beitrag von Genossen Prof. Dr. Karl-Heinz Hahn," Das Volk, 26 August 1981, no page number.

[29] Nigel Hamilton, The Brothers Mann (New Haven: Yale University Press, 1979), p. 288.

[30] Heinrich Mann, "Nietzsche," Maß und Wert, 2, No. 3 (1939), 277-304.

[31] Quoted from David Pike, German Writers in Soviet Exile, 1933-1945, p. 222, footnote.

Geschichte als Denk- und Spielraum:
Die DDR-Historiker im Lutherjahr

Wolfgang Büscher

Das Jahr 1983 wurde von der offiziellen DDR als doppeltes Gedenkjahr apostrophiert: Der Tod von Karl Marx lag einhundert, die Geburt Martin Luthers fünfhundert Jahre zurück. Fragt man nach den Ergebnissen von "Lutherjahr" und "Marxjahr," so fällt die Antwort leicht. Zahlreiche neue und interessante Entwicklungen haben mit Person und Werk des Reformators zu tun. Zu Marx bekannte man sich in der gewohnten Weise, mit Luther setzte man sich neu auseinander.

Dieser Unterschied ist nicht untypisch für die geistige Lage der sozialistischen deutschen Republik am Beginn der achtziger Jahre. Neue Impulse kommen von der Peripherie, vor allem aus dem kirchlichen und jugendlichen Milieu. Das Zentrum, das herrschende Denken, verhält sich gegenüber den eigenen Inhalten und zur eigenen Geschichte strikt konservativ. Das Verhalten gegenüber den neuen Impulsen ist sehr unterschiedlich: Während explizit politische Initiativen wie die der Friedens- und Umweltgruppen häufig abgeblockt und so gut wie immer mit Mißtrauen betrachtet werden, ist der Beitrag der lutherischen Christen zu einer breiter als früher angelegten Traditionspflege und geschichtlichen Verwurzelung der DDR durchaus erwünscht.

Die SED hatte auf das Lutherjahr nicht nur städtebaulich, touristisch und publizistisch hingearbeitet, sie hatte das Jubiläum am 10. November 1983 nicht zuletzt geistig vorbereitet. Vor allem den Historikern und Künstlern in der DDR bot das Lutherjahr Raum für eine intensive Beschäftigung mit der Reformation und ihren Charakteren.

Unter den einhundert Angehörigen der politischen

243

und kulturellen DDR-Elite, die am 13. Juni 1980 in Ost-Berlin das staatliche "Martin-Luther-Komitee der DDR" gründeten, war auch der inzwischen verstorbene Alexander Abusch in seiner Funktion als Ehrenpräsident des DDR-Kulturbundes. Erich Honecker, der den Vorsitz des Luther-Komitees übernahm, bezeichnete gleich im ersten Satz seiner Rede Luther als einen "der größten Söhne des deutschen Volkes."[1] Ob sich Abusch, als er dies hörte, an sein eigenes Buch erinnerte, das er fast vier Jahrzehnte zuvor im mexikanischen Exil geschrieben und 1946 im neugegründeten (Ost-)Berliner Aufbau Verlag unter dem Titel "Der Irrweg einer Nation" veröffentlicht hatte? Darin hatte er Luther auch superlativisch beschrieben--nur andersherum als sein Parteivorsitzender 1980. Abusch schrieb damals: "Martin Luther wurde zur größten geistigen Figur der deutschen Gegenrevolution für Jahrhunderte."[2] Und er ging noch einen Schritt weiter, denn er meinte nicht nur das Haupt, sondern die ganze Richtung: "Die wesentliche Schuld an der Niederlage der Bauern und daran, daß kein großes Volksbündnis von Stadt und Land für ein gemeinsames Freiheitsprogramm zustandekommen konnte, trägt die deutsche Reformation" (S. 22).

Die deklamatorischen Pointen, in denen Abusch 1946 und Honecker 1980 ihr jeweiliges Urteil über Luther zusammenfaßten, bezeichnen den extrem veränderten Umgang der DDR mit diesem Teil ihres Erbes von den Gründerjahren bis heute. Bei Abusch verband sich die radikale Kritik an Luther, die Verurteilung der von ihm geprägten Reformation als eine der Quellen des deutschen Militarismus und Faschismus, mit der vorbehaltlosen Wertschätzung des Thomas Müntzer. Dieser sei der "erste Stratege des Volkskriegs in Deutschland" gewesen, ihm habe "ein Kampfbündnis von Bauern und Städtebürgern mit den ersten Proletariern, den Zwickauer Tuchknappen und den Mansfelder Bergknappen" vorgeschwebt, kurz--Müntzer war für Abusch "die gewaltigste revolutionäre Persönlichkeit seiner Zeit: der Verkünder der irdischen Gerechtigkeit im Namen der 'reinen Furcht Gottes'" (S. 21-22).

Eine solche Sicht der Geschichte wird heute von DDR-Historikern als unwissenschaftlich verworfen. Damals "dominierte die Polemik," resümierte der Ost-Berliner Historiker Günter Vogler 1983.[3] Schriften wie die von Alexander Abusch waren eher Ausdruck der aktuellen politischen Auseinandersetzung mit der Rolle des Protestantismus (und anderer Kräfte) in den dreißiger und vierziger Jahren als wissenschaftliche Versuche. "Der positive Zugang zu Luther," so Vogler weiter,

244

"wurde mit der nationalen Frage gefunden, wie sie durch die Spaltung Deutschlands im Gefolge des Zweiten Weltkrieges als aktuelles politisches Problem existierte" (S. 55).

Damit ist die positive Einstellung der auf Wiedervereinigung bedachten DDR in den frühen fünfziger Jahren gegenüber einem weitgefaßten gesamtdeutschen kulturellen Erbe gemeint. Das nationale historische Motiv stand jedoch damals im Kontrast zur sozialgeschichtlichen Denktradition der Kommunisten. Dies zeigte der Streit um die Bewertung Luthers auf einer Tagung, die 1952 im Museum für deutsche Geschichte in Ost-Berlin stattfand. Die traditionell-marxistischen Kritiker der Reformation hielten den Bauernkrieg hoch, während andere--unter ihnen das heutige Politbüromitglied Kurt Hager--aus nationalpolitischen Gegenwartsinteressen heraus für eine mildere Behandlung von Luthers Werk plädierten.[4] Mit der Losung "Deutsche an einen Tisch" verschwand jedoch bald auch ein politisches Interesse der SED an Luther.

Die sechziger Jahre brachten eine vorsichtige Annäherung der DDR-Historiker an den Reformator; der Begriff der "frühbürgerlichen Revolution in Deutschland" sollte die bisherige Einengung des marxistischen Blicks auf die Bauernkriege überwinden helfen.[5] Politisch interessant wurde dies alles erst wieder im Vorfeld des 500. Geburtstags von Martin Luther. Wiederum steht die SED einem weitgefaßten kulturellen Erbebegriff positiv gegenüber, allerdings nicht mehr aus dem Wunsch nach gesamtdeutscher Politik heraus, sondern--eher im Gegenteil--in dem Bestreben, nach mehr als dreißig Jahren die eigene Identität in der deutschen Geschichte stärker als bisher zu verwurzeln. Eben diese Vermutung sowie die Beobachtung einer Umwertung der beiden Symbolfiguren Luther und Müntzer standen zunächst im Mittelpunkt westdeutscher Kommentare zu der als gigantisch empfundenen Lutherehrung der DDR.

Die Ende der siebziger Jahre bei uns als sensationell wahrgenommene Verkehrung der Rangfolge Müntzer/Luther war jedoch nichts weiter als eine Begleiterscheinung des neuen Lutherbilds in der DDR, die, indem sie vollzogen wurde, sogleich ihre Bedeutung verlor. Die wirkliche Sensation ist das neue Lutherbild selbst, ist die Integration der geistig-geistlichen Dimension der Reformation in das marxistische Geschichtsverständnis.

Die "Thesen über Martin Luther," die die SED im

September 1981 veröffentlichte, konzidieren die "zentrale Bedeutung der Theologie" für jene Epoche der "frühbürgerlichen Revolution," als die die Reformationszeit bezeichnet wird. [6] Historiker wie Gerhard Brendler und Adolf Laube, die zu den Autoren der SED-Thesen gehören, haben den Primat des Religiösen für Person und Zeit Luthers immer wieder betont. [7]

Seit dem Beginn der achtziger Jahre entfaltet die These von der "frühbürgerlichen Revolution" ihre Wirkungen: Erstens überwindet sie die Trennung von Bauernkrieg und Reformation, den Dualismus von politischer Bewegung und Glaubenskampf, indem sie die Reformation als Gesamtprozeß interpretiert. Zweitens enthebt sie damit die marxistischen Historiker der Notwendigkeit, sich zum jeweils radikalsten Flügel einer historischen Epoche bekennen zu müssen--Müntzer und der Bauernaufstand können als partikular erklärt werden, ohne sie länger zum Kriterium der Beurteilung der anderen reformatorischen Strömungen erheben zu müssen. Drittens erlaubt sie eine umfassende Würdigung Luthers. Die Scheidung in den frühen progressiven und den alten reaktionären Luther kann aufgegeben werden, drückte doch der Reformator das zu seiner Zeit mögliche Maß des Fortschritts--und eben nicht eine unzeitgemäße Utopie--aus. Die frühbürgerliche Revolution stand auf der Tagesordnung und nicht ein kommunistisch-utopisches Himmelreich der Bauern auf Erden.

"Auch bei einer versöhnlicheren Haltung Luthers [gegenüber den Aufständischen] hätte der Bauernkrieg nicht siegen können," schrieb Max Steinmetz 1982. Seine Erklärung: "Der radikalste Akt bürgerlicher Revolutionen muß gesetzmäßig über das Erreichbare hinausgehen: nur so kann der Erfolg der gemäßigten Kräfte gefestigt und zugleich ein Vorgriff auf zukünftige revolutionäre Kämpfe ermöglicht werden." [8] Sein Kollege Ernst Engelberg hatte drei Jahre zuvor von der "objektiven Funktion" des Bauernaufstandes für das "Ganze" gesprochen. Dieses "Ganze" nennt Steinmetz den "Erfolg der gemäßigten Kräfte." Bei Engelberg ist es das Ziel, "die Resultate der kirchlich-institutionellen und ideologischen Umwälzung zu sichern." [9]

Bis hierhin bleibt die neue Argumentation klassisch-marxistisch. Ein Rest von unhistorisch-idealistischem Umgang mit einer Epoche der deutschen Geschichte wird getilgt--man erklärt die Reformation und ihre Charaktere aus der Zeit heraus, man läßt vordergründige Polemiken und Projektionen beiseite. Soweit handelt es sich um ein Geraderücken des Geschichtsbildes, um eine späte Entstalinisierung des historischen Denkens.

Die SED hat erst relativ spät, in den letzten Jahren nämlich, die längst vorliegenden neuen Erkenntnisse ihrer Historiker aufgegriffen--um damit Politik zu machen: Kirchenpolitik, Außenpolitik, DDR-Nationalpolitik. Den Luther-Spezialisten selbst diente das neue Bild der Reformation als Plattform, von der aus weitergedacht wurde. Mit Spannung war die neue Luther-Biographie von Gerhard Brendler erwartet worden. Kurz vor dem Abschluß des Lutherjahres, im Herbst 1983, erschien sie unter dem Titel "Martin Luther. Theologie und Revolution" im VEB Deutscher Verlag der Wissenschaften. Den ersten Versuch einer DDR-marxistischen Luther-Biographie hatte im Jahre 1967 Gerhard Zschäbitz veröffentlicht.[10] In seinem Vorwort unterscheidet Brendler sein eigenes Werk von Zschäbitz' Biographie so: dieser habe sich darauf konzentriert, "das gesellschaftliche Umfeld, in dem Martin Luther wirkte, darzustellen," da das auch anderweitig ausführlich geschehen sei, "konnte ich mich . . . mehr Luthers geistiger Entwicklung und seinem individuellen Verhalten zuwenden."[11]

Nach allem, was dem Erscheinen von Brendlers Buch vorangegangen war, mußte erwartet werden, daß eine solche Akzentuierung nicht nur das rein sachlich begründete fortschreitende Eindringen in die Materie ausdrückte, sondern auch eine veränderte Sicht. Steinmetz hatte die von allen Seiten geforderte "vertiefte Behandlung des weltanschaulich-religiös-theologischen Komplexes" mit einem Verdikt gegen die klassisch-marxistische Religionskritik begründet: "Das Wort von der religiösen 'Verkleidung' der Klassenkämpfe ist abgegriffen und klingt nach Maskerade und Mummenschanz. Im Grunde ist alles um einige Grade ernster und schwieriger."[12]

Brendler hat keine reine Luther-Biographie geschrieben. Er versucht zugleich, dem Untertitel seines Buches gerecht zu werden--"Theologie und Revolution." Seine Schilderung der Entwicklung und der Lebensumstände des Reformators unterbricht der Autor immer wieder mit allgemeinen Erörterungen über Religion und mit Schlußfolgerungen für die marxistische Theorie. Dabei nimmt er unter anderem--sein Text von 1979 deutet es schon an[13]--den Begriff der Legitimation von Macht zuhilfe: "Mit der Forderung, aus der Bibel widerlegt zu werden, brachte Luther ein anderes Legitimationsprinzip zur Geltung als das in der Kirche faktisch herrschende Prinzip der etablierten Autorität" (S. 127). Brendler kommt immer wieder auf dieses Argument zurück.

Luthers Primat des rechten Glaubens gegenüber dem rechten Leben, sein Setzen auf den Glauben als Geschenk, kann mit Hilfe des Legitimationsarguments positiv aufgegriffen werden. Immerhin umschloß diese Luthersche Auffassung die "Aufforderung zur Predigt und zur Verbreitung der rechten Lehre." Damit aber traf Luther "genau die Aufgabe . . . , die in der Vorbereitungs- und Aufschwungphase einer jeden revolutionären Bewegung gelöst werden muß: die Ausstattung der veränderungswilligen Kräfte mit einem neuen Bewußtsein" (S. 185). Mit einer solchen funktionalen Betrachtung des neuen Glaubens wird das traditionelle marxistische Basis-Überbau-Modell entflochten--Glaube und (Klassen-)Interesse werden als jeweils eigene Sphären anerkannt. Der Glaube muß in diesem Fall nicht mehr in allen seinen Fasern als ideologischer Reflex der bäuerlichen oder bürgerlichen Interessen nachgewiesen werden; es reicht, daß sich beides traf und zusammenwirkte. "Luther kritisierte die Kirche nicht als Bürger," schreibt Brendler, und seine Motive "koinzidieren" nur mit "gesellschaftlichen Interessen." Die reformatorische Theologie wirkt demnach "als Ferment oder Katalysator in den ideologischen Prozessen des Bürgertums, ohne selbst je ganz in bürgerlicher Ideologie aufzugehen oder sich auf eine solche reduzieren zu lassen" (S. 204-05).

"Revolutionstheoretisch," so folgert Brendler im Kapitel über Luthers Auftreten in Worms 1521, "handelt es sich hierbei um eine wichtige Phase der Rebellion. Den historisch gewachsenen und hierarchisch etablierten Autoritäten wird die Entscheidungsbefugnis über die Kriterien der Legitimität aberkannt" (S. 228).

"Neues Bewußtsein," "Legitimität" als Grundlage von Macht und Machtwechsel, Luther selbst als "Symbol" (S. 245) für disparate weltliche Interessen--dieses funktionale Strukturmodell ist zwar an sich keineswegs neu, innermarxistisch entlastet es aber das Denken von dem Druck, jedwede Idee als Ausgeburt irgendeines ökonomischen oder davon abgeleiteten Interesses überführen zu müssen.

Diese neugewonnene Souveränität erlaubt es Brendler auch, die sprachschöpferische Rolle Luthers in einer anderen als der zuvor in der DDR üblichen Weise zu würdigen. Selbst die schärfsten Luther-Kritiker unter den DDR-Marxisten hatten diesen Aspekt gelten lassen. "Darüber sind wir uns alle einig," hatte Hermann Duncker in einem Streitgespräch 1952 zugestanden. 14 Brendler geht nun über dieses wohlfeile, weil isolierte Zugeständnis hinaus. "Luther war kein 'Sprachschöpfer,' wie man das immer wieder hören kann," schreibt er und wendet sich dagegen, die "Bibelübersetzung nur oder vor allem als sprachliche Leistung zu verstehen." Luther habe sich seinem Deutsch so unbefangen hingeben können, "weil er sich seiner Auffassung von der Mitte der biblischen Botschaften sicher war und auch längst die Erkenntnis gewonnen hatte, daß diese Botschaft nur aus dem verständlichen Wort in das Ohr gelangen und von da aus den Glauben im Herzen bewirken könne" (S. 286). In diesem Zusammenhang weist Brendler auf einen interessanten Punkt hin. Am Beginn der Reformation habe "nicht der Wunsch nach etwas Neuem" gestanden, sondern "das Verlangen nach etwas Altem." Luthers "Biblizismus" sei sein "geistiger Rettungsanker in der Autoritätskrise gewesen. Dies korrespondiere auffallend mit der Forderung der bäuerlichen Bewegung "nach dem 'alten Recht'" (S. 290-91).

Eine zentrale Feststellung, die sich durch Brendlers Luther-Biographie zieht, ist die Spannung zwischen dem existentiellen und dem institutionellen Reformator, zwischen Glaube und Gesetz und--damit zusammenhängend--auch zwischen Theologie und Politik. Bendler versucht nicht, das eine gegen das andere auszuspielen, er polemisiert explizit gegen die--früher übliche--scharfe Trennung des jungen vom alten Luther, also gewissermaßen der lutherischen Frühschriften von dessen Spätwerk (S. 388).

Als politisch denkenden Historiker fasziniert Brendler die Zwei-Reiche-Lehre. Weit ausholend schildert er den Konflikt zwischen Ideologie und Realität als ein Grundproblem aller aus Umwälzungen hervorgegangenen Gesellschaften. "Die Bewegung verändert den bestehenden Zustand, die Institution erhält das Erreichte"--, so faßt er diese Regel der Geschichte bündig zusammen und fügt hinzu, der Glaube sei etwas für Oppositionszeiten, in denen es gelte, bestehende Ordnungen zu erschüttern. Im Erfolgsfalle jedoch müsse die ehedem glaubensbeflügelte Rebellenschar "mit Gebot und Gesetz für Zucht und Ordnung sorgen" (S. 391). Es fällt dem Historiker leicht, diesen Wandel der "Funktion des Glaubens" anhand der Reformationsgeschichte schlüssig zu belegen.

Aktuelle Bezüge klingen an, wenn Brendler Luther zugute hält, er habe mit seiner Zwei-Reiche-Lehre, seiner Unterscheidung des weltlichen und des geistlichen Regimentes Gottes, die eigentliche "politische Theorie der Reformation" geschaffen: "Sie errichtete einen geistigen Damm dagegen, aus dem Christentum einen Islam zu machen, das Evangelium 'fleischlich' zu deuten und es zum 'Gesetz' zu erheben" (S. 303).

Während einer Podiumsdiskussion im Rahmen des Wittenberger Kirchentages im September 1983, an der Brendler teilnahm, nahm er Luther gegen dessen Bezeichnung als selektiver Pazifist in Schutz. Nichts dergleichen sei an Luther zu entdecken, meinte Brendler, der Reformator habe "ganz vernünftig im Rahmen der kursächsischen Politik" operiert.

Diese Art von Vernunft besteht in dem Verzicht auf die Versuchung der Totalisierung des neuen Glaubens. Luther habe "die Politik Politik sein" lassen, die zwar vom Glauben her "prinzipiell vertretbar" sein, nicht jedoch ihre Eigenständigkeit aufgeben müsse. Wie bei der Wittenberger Diskussion mit evangelischen Theologen, führt Brendler auch in seinem Buch den Klassiker des zweckrationalen Staatsegoismus, Niccolo Macchiavelli, an, der mit der Zwei-Reiche-Lehre gemein habe, daß die Politik als "ein selbständiges Betätigungsfeld mit eigenen Regeln" betrachtet und geachtet werde (S. 410-11).

Kurz: der Protestantismus ist eine Größe, mit der es sich--von Staatsinteressen aus betrachtet--gut und gerne leben läßt. Hier werden politische Konsequenzen aus dem geschichtsphilosophischen Umdenken deutlich. Ist das Basis-Überbau-Modell erst einmal entflochten und eine funktionale Sicht von Ideologie/Religion/Glaube an die Stelle der Widerspiegelungstheorie getreten, kann die ganze ideologisch-verkrampfte und politisch-konfliktträchtige Fragestellung nach dem Absterben der Religion und der Durchsetzung des wissenschaftlichen Atheismus als unangefochtener Bewußtseinsform aufgegeben werden. Im neuen Koordinatensystem der zwei Reiche können nunmehr zwei "abgesackte Revolutionskurve[n]" (Brendler)--die eine ist es seit Jahrhunderten, die andere seit Jahrzehnten--an einem Aufschwung ihrer neu geordneten Beziehungen arbeiten.

Die "Politik des 6. März 1978" kann sich nach dem Lutherjahr auf eine tiefgestaffelte ideologische Grundlage stützen. Was Macchiavelli und der Reforma-

tor mangels Gelegenheit nicht zuwege brachten--Honek-
ker und ein evangelischer Bischof haben es nachgeholt.

Neben der eminent politischen Dimension des neuen
Bildes von Luther und seiner Reformation tritt bei
Historikern wie bei Künstlern in der DDR eine nicht
minder interessante weitere Bezugnahme auf Luther
hervor.[15] Es ist die Faszination seines an und um die
eigene Existenz--im physischen und geistlichen Sinne
--gehenden Glaubenskampfes. Die trockene Formel vom
Ernstnehmen der Theologie läßt Gerhard Brendler weit
hinter sich, wenn er auf Luthers Glaubenskrisen zu
sprechen kommt. Die "philosophisch gewordene Gottes-
idee" der mittelalterlichen Kirche habe an den Widersprüchen ihrer Unersättlichkeit gekrankt (S. 67). Sie
schließe das Böse in sich ein, teile die Gläubigen in
vorherbestimmte Himmels- und Höllenexistenzen ein und
habe sich Luther als "ein gespaltenes Wesen, ein
schillerndes Monstrum, ein Wesen im Widerspruch zu
seiner Idee, ein Gott, der den Teufel in sich hat,"
präsentiert (S. 68). "Urhaß" nennt Brendler die Auf-
wallungen gegen "dieses Untier, das den Menschen
opfert und in die Hölle stößt" (S. 69). Und von einer
"scharfen psychologischen Beobachtungsgabe" spricht er
im Zusammenhang mit der Römerbriefvorlesung--Luther
habe die für den Glauben destruktiven Wirkungen der
nur dem Gesetz folgenden Werke erkannt (S. 66). Wo
DDR-Philosophen die "negative Einstellung Martin
Luthers zur Philosophie" konstatieren und darauf hin-
weisen, daß es schließlich auch noch Renaissance und
Humanismus gegeben habe,[16] findet Brendler seinen
Stoff: "Was bleibt und aus dem Entsetzen herausführen
kann, ist der nackte . . . Glaube daran, daß auf einen
Karfreitag das Ostern folgt, auf den Kreuzestod die
Auferstehung. Hier helfen keinerlei Vernünfteleien
und Begriffskrücken der Philosophie mehr, das muß ge-
glaubt werden ohne Wenn und Aber, sonst reduziert sich
der Bericht auf eine interessante Tragödie aus der An-
tike" (S. 69).

Der Historiker bemerkt zwar, daß letztere Lesart
heutzutage für immer mehr Menschen die noch einzig annehmbare geworden sei, räsonniert jedoch bereits auf
der folgenden Seite über die Funktion des Glaubens im
Alltag: "als Vertrauen" sei er "die unerläßliche Voraussetzung eines auch nur einigermaßen erträglichen
Zusammenlebens zwischen den Menschen."

Das gilt auch generell für die Bereiche der Existenz, die nicht von der Vernunft abgedeckt sind: eine
"Fluchtburg des Nichtwissens," seiner Herkunft nach

eventuell sogar ein Vorurteil, ist der Glaube doch
existentiell unverzichtbar. "Psychologisch," mutmaßt
Brendler, "dürfte er wohl so etwas Ähnliches sein wie
ein Weitermachen im Ungewissen mit der Hoffnung auf
ein gutes Ende" (S. 70). Brendlers paradoxe Bemerkungen über Säkularisierung und Rolle des Glaubens scheinen selbst vom Umgang mit jener Weisheit berührt worden zu sein, die er dem Glauben attestiert: "die halb
trotzige, halb verschmitzte Weisheit des credo, quia
absurdum est - ich glaube, weil es absurd ist" (S. 70).

Anmerkungen

[1] Martin Luther und unsere Zeit. Konstituierung
des Martin-Luther-Komitees der DDR am 13. Juni 1980 in
Berlin (Berlin/Weimar: Aufbau, 1980), S. 11.

[2] Alexander Abusch, Der Irrweg einer Nation. Ein
Beitrag zum Verständnis deutscher Geschichte (Berlin:
Aufbau, 1946), S. 23.

[3] Günter Vogler, "Der Platz Luthers in der Ge-
schichtsschreibung der DDR," in Martin Luther in beiden deutschen Staaten, Helmstedter Beiträge, Hrsg.
Politische Bildungsstätte Helmstedt, e.V., 1983, S.
53.

[4] Diesen Streit beschreibt Steinmetz in seinem
Artikel "Betrachtungen zur Entwicklung des marxistischen Lutherbildes in der DDR," Mühlhäuser Beiträge,
5/1982, pp. 3-8.

[5] Steinmetz veröffentlichte 1960 entsprechende
Thesen: Max Steinmetz, "Die frühbürgerliche Revolu-
tion in Deutschland (1476 - 1535)," Zeitschrift für
Geschichtswissenschaft, 8, No. 1 (1960), 113 ff.

[6] "Thesen über Martin Luther. Zum 500. Geburts-
tag," Einheit, 36, No. 9 (1981), 891.

[7] Gerhard Brendler, "Martin Luther - Erbe und
Tradition," Wissenschaftliche Mitteilungen der Histo-
rikergesellschaft der DDR, Nos. 1/2 (1979), S. 36;
Adolf Laube, "Martin Luther in der Erbe- und Tradi-
tionsauffassung der DDR," Vortrag am 3.11.1982 in der
Evangelischen Akademie in Tutzing.

[8] Steinmetz, "Betrachtungen," S. 6.

[9] Ernst Engelberg, "Was hat Luther mit Marx zu tun?" Forum, 33, No. 13 (1979).

[10] Gerhard Zschäbitz, Martin Luther. Größe und Grenzen. Teil 1 (Berlin: Deutscher Verlag der Wissenschaften, 1967).

[11] Gerhard Brendler, Martin Luther. Theologie und Revolution (Berlin: Deutscher Verlag der Wissenschaften, 1983), S. 7.

[12] Steinmetz, "Betrachtungen," S. 7.

[13] Brendler, "Martin Luther - Erbe und Tradition," S. 36. Vgl. auch Adolf Laube, "Martin Luther in der Erbe- und Traditionsauffassung der DDR."

[14] Zitiert nach Max Steinmetz, "Betrachtungen," S. 5.

[15] Die Ostberliner Schriftstellerin Helga Schütz ging hier wohl--im Wortsinne--am weitesten. Im Zuge ihrer Arbeit an einem Drehbuch für einen Lutherfilm wanderte sie "per pedes apostolorum" von Erfurt nach Wittenberg. Ihre Filmerzählung dringt stärker als das schließlich vom DDR-Fernsehen realisierte Drehbuch von Hans Kohlus (vgl. "Ich wußte über Luther ganz wenig. Gespräch zwischen dem DDR-Schauspieler Ulrich Thein und Wolfgang Büscher," Kirche im Sozialismus, 8, No. 6 [1982], 15-19) in Luthers existentielle Krise und überhaupt in seine persönliche Existenz ein (Helga Schütz, Martin Luther. Eine Erzählung für den Film [Berlin/Weimar: Aufbau, 1983]).

[16] Vgl. Alexander Kolesnyk, "Zu philosophischen Problemen bei Martin Luther," Deutsche Zeitschrift für Philosophie, 31, No. 12 (1983), 1400 ff.

Beyond the Crisis of Marxism?
An Emerging Cultural Marxism in the GDR

Volker Gransow

The 100th anniversary of the death of Karl Marx could only be celebrated because word had not spread that Marx is still alive. In 1882 Marx made contact with extra-terrestrials who enabled him to leave this planet in 1883 and explore various types of communist cultures in outer space. This experience strengthened his interest in ecological and anarchist concerns as well as his distrust of Engles' interpretations of his works. Now and then Marx meets with terrestrials to give them support in their efforts to find new communal ways of living together. Information about Marx' whereabouts is revealed by an author called P.M. in a book entitled Weltgeist Superstar.[1]

One can assume that Marx is sitting in his spaceship laughing about the crisis of Marxism. As one of his adherents recently remarked, Marxism has a history of being like the man with the sandwichboard saying: Beware thy end is nigh! When the end of capitalism doesn't arrive within the expected timespan, Marxists go back to the drawing board; they examine the past and often provide quite good explanations as to why capitalism has managed to survive.[2] And, one might add, they are equally good at explaining why democratization has not yet come about in the countries of "real socialism."[3] They have severe difficulties, however, in analyzing what is happening within Marxism itself. The "Marxism of Marxism" is one of the main problems Marxists have.[4]

Thus it is not very surprising that the tendency towards political divergence should be perceived as a crisis of Marxism. And, contrary to the widely-held view, it was not Louis Althusser who first defined this crisis. Otto Bauer wrote about the crisis of

Marxism, which he regarded as already the second, in 1923:

> Aus ihrem geschichtlichen und systematischen Zusammenhang herausgerissen, wurden Marxens Sätze zu starren Formeln, zu erstarrten Schlagworten, die nun in ganz anderer geschichtlicher Situation, als Marx sie gekannt, in ganz anderem Zusammenhang, als Marx sie gesprochen, den Streit der Parteien entscheiden sollten. Als die Revolution die Revolutionäre in feindliche Parteien schied, beriefen sie sich hüben wie drüben auf Marxens Worte als die höchste, von allen unbestrittene Autorität; und der Streit um die Deutung von Marx-Zitaten endete in blutigem Straßenkampf, endete mit Todesurteilen der Revolutionsgerichte. Der Streit um den Sinn von Marx-Zitaten ward zur ideologischen Verhüllung der Klassen- und Parteikämpfe des 20. Jahrhunderts . . . So wurde Marxens Schule zerrissen. Gerade durch seine gewaltigste Expansion ist der Marxismus in eine viel wesentlichere Krise gestürzt worden, als es die vielbesprochene Krise des Marxismus in der Zeit des Streites um den Revisionismus war. [5]

Bauer added an additional aspect to this predominantly political interpretation of the crisis of Marxism: the ever changing historical situation. He pointed out that capitalism, working class, and revolution were different in 1923 than in 1847 or 1867, and concluded: "Was heute eine Krise des Marxismus zu sein scheint, es ist nichts anderes als der schmerzhafte Prozeß der Anpassung des Sozialismus an eine von Grund aus umgewälzte Welt" (p. 50). The task of the Marxian school was, therefore, to go beyond Marx:

> Diese Umwälzung selbst mit Marxschen Arbeitsmitteln zu begreifen und dadurch den Marxismus weiterzuentwikkeln, ihn über Marx selbst hinauszuführen, das ist jetzt die Aufgabe der Marxschen Schule. (p. 51)

These two elements of the crisis of Marxism, as

Bauer perceived them in 1923, can be found again--although not as clearly pronounced--in Louis Althusser's famous book, Sur la crise du Marxisme (1978). According to Althusser, the crisis of Marxism is, first, a crisis of revolutionary organizations, and, secondly, a crisis of theory. He identifies a special need for a theory of the state and for a theory of organizations, especially the party.[6]

Five years after the first appearance of Althusser's book I am very much reminded of the man with the sandwichboard. First, because "crisis of organizations" is a very mild metaphor for the breakdown of the international communist movement. Secondly, because the emphasis on political theory is much too narrow. Althusser mentions neither the indivisible conjunction of politics and culture in the present world crisis nor--and this is especially important--the conflict between the old paradigm of the political and the new one. According to Claus Offe, the conventional paradigm is characterized by themes and issues centered around economic growth, military and social security, and by a highly representative type of mass-involvement, while the new, emerging paradigm of the political, advanced by the "new social movements" of women, gays, squatters, ecologists, etc., deals with the "non-reproducible parameters of human life, that is, with conditions that can only be destroyed and disorganized, but not created by either economic activity or acts of political authority."[7] Offe finds it problematic to speak of these issues and themes as being "political" at all, given the fact that the usage of the word "politics" is ordinarily restricted to those conditions of human life that can be shaped and altered by means of power and authority:

> These issues are political only in a negative, if not paradoxical sense, namely in the sense of "anti-political" politics. It is a politics that tries to establish firm limits for the conventional range or reach of politics by asserting "private" ways of life and identities in a political way. The substance of private life turns into political action. (pp. 13-14)

This leads to the question of a theoretical framework which can grasp both the subjective aspect and also the quasi-natural aspect of social systems

which are not immediately accessible to the consciousness of the actors.[8] This can be understood as a
call for a "cultural Marxism" in general[9] or as a plea
for a "culturalist turn"[10] in special fields of research. The new kind of "cultural materialism" concerns even "our fundamental physical-material existence."[11]

All of this taken for granted, one can ask why I
am raising these points at a conference on the GDR.
According to the Central Committee of the Socialist
Unity Party, there is no crisis of Marxism:

> Die neuerlichen Behauptungen von ei-
> ner "Krise des Marxismus" stellen
> nichts anderes dar als ideologische
> Reaktionen auf den Vormarsch der
> Kräfte des gesellschaftlichen Fort-
> schritts. Sie dienen dem Ziel, die
> Lebenskraft und Ausstrahlung des rea-
> len Sozialismus einzudämmen und von
> der tatsächlichen tiefen und unauf-
> hebbaren Krise des Kapitalismus abzu-
> lenken.[12]

If there is no such crisis, there is no need to
look for possibilities of finding a solution. - As a
matter of fact, the theses of the Central Committee
are representative of a kind of Marxism which is reduced to the political legitimation of the ruling Party. The same can be said of most GDR political theory
--with notable exceptions.[13] To go beyond the crisis
of Marxism it is not necessary to demonstrate in detail the differences between, say, Marx and the party,
Marx and the state, and Marx and communist society.[14]
This honorable endeavor is mostly boring, because
proving the legitimating function of GDR political
theory doesn't bring us a single step further, even if
it points out the ambiguity of official Marxism, which
could be used to legitimate a profound transition in
the quality of "real socialism." This is only a legitimation of another kind.[15]

I think it is much more useful to consider instead GDR cultural theory, which does not have these
clear political functions. The questions which I
have derived from Western debate are: 1) Is it possible to develop a broad notion of culture without
losing the differentia specifica of the term? 2) Is
there a tendency to comprehend the new relationships
between the public and private spheres? In short, is

there an emerging cultural Marxism in the GDR?

The discussion about cultural theory in the GDR started, strictly speaking, at the beginning of the sixties, when political-cultural measures such as the collectivization of agriculture and the creation of polytechnical comprehensive schools had been carried out, and the Bitterfeld Way (a program calling for closer links between workers and artists) had been proclaimed. As early as 1960 the Leipzig scholar Fred Staufenbiel sharply attacked Hans Koch's position that ideology and culture are the same field and that culture is a part of the superstructure. Staufenbiel defined culture as the sum of the products of human work, "als Summe der materiellen und geistigen Erzeugnisse menschlicher Arbeit."[16] Walter Besenbruch criticized the view that culture is only a certain area ("Bereich").[17] These arguments led Hans Koch to rethink his position. In an article written with Erika Hinckel in 1962, he distinguished between material and intellectual culture, i.e., between the material products of human labor and culture in a narrow sense: arts, literature, science.[18] This position was attacked by Dietrich Mühlberg, who criticized it as an unnecessary parallel to the "basic question" of philosophy and as an underestimation of the relationship between material and intellectual labor. He suggested instead a distinction between objective and subjective culture. Objective culture was defined as the totality of all creative possibilities given to a society as a result of the activities of past generations; subjective culture, as the ability of social individuals to appropriate and develop the objective culture: "die Fähigkeit der gesellschaftlichen Individuen, die objektive Kultur anzueignen und schöpferisch weiterzubilden."[19]

Mühlberg's introduction of the subject-object dialectic into cultural theory was a major breakthrough. It implies, on the one hand, a broad notion of culture, which, on the other hand, cannot be identified with either "society" or "way of life" because the cultural process is located in the appropriation of objective conditions of life by means of subjective activities.[20] After 1971, when Walter Ulbricht was replaced by Erich Honecker as First Secretary, the main task of politics in the GDR was satisfying the needs of all working people. This orientation towards the living conditions of the population furthered the "official" acceptance of this broad notion of culture. The distinction between subjective and objective culture was used as a means of describing the pragmatism and realism of cultural policy. The insight was reached,

> daß sozialistische Kulturrevolution nicht auf das Heranführen der Massen an eine - vorgegebene - Kultur zu reduzieren ist, sondern als objektive Kultur letzten Endes nur das zu bewerten ist, was in den Lebensbedingungen der Klassen-Individuen real vergegenständlicht ist, und was - wenn auch nur in ersten Ansätzen - in den tatsächlichen Aneignungsprozeß einbezogen, zur subjektiven Kultur ausgebildet wird. [21]

This position has a certain ambiguity because it implies the possibility of adapting individuals to circumstances they cannot change. But people in the GDR have a good feeling for subject-object relationships:

> Es gibt immer so etwas wie eine offizielle Anschauung von der Welt, die in der Schule, durch die Zeitung, durch das Fernsehen vertreten wird, und die bei uns heißt: Der Mensch kann seine Umstände verändern, ist Subjekt. - Und dann machen wir jeden Tag die Erfahrung, daß er Objekt ist. Das ist die andere Wahrheit. [22]

The acceptance of the broad notion of culture by the Honecker administration was by no means a complete victory.[23] The separation of material and intellectual culture is still very common, even in the social sciences and politics. And in everyday life an understanding of culture prevails which reduces culture to mere decoration. Nevertheless, this acceptance brought the theoretical discussion of the subject of cultural theory to a preliminary end.[24] A study group around Dietrich Mühlberg started an ambitious project of rewriting the cultural history of the German proletariat. One political goal of the project was to provide evidence of the ability of the working class to rule: "Das große Engagement für diese Seite der Proletariatsforschung dürfte auch darauf zurückzuführen sein, daß hier weitergehende wissenschaftliche Nachweise für die Herrschaftsfähigkeit der Arbeiterklasse geliefert werden." [25] It may be noteworthy that the abilities of the working class are mentioned--not those of its vanguard. The discussion of the works of Western Marxists stressed the impulses they gave to cultural history in the GDR, not only the differences:

> Bezogen auf E. P. Thompson, Pierre Bourdieu, Raymond Williams u.a. wurden die Einheit von klassenspezifischen und gesamtgesellschaftlichen Merkmalen, der Doppelcharakter proletarischer Lebensbedingungen und Verhaltensweisen als das Kapitalverhältnis stabilisierende und zugleich sprengende Momente hervorgehoben. [26]

Whereas Isolde Dietrich and Dietrich Mühlberg turned their attention to cultural history, Helmut Hanke focused his interest in a broadly understood concept of culture on way of life. He stressed way of life as the basic sphere of cultural development, showed understanding for an "alternative" way of life in the West, and tried to explain the similarities between the capitalist and socialist ways of life.[27] In spite of his technological optimism, Hanke prefers the term "Lebensweise im Sozialismus" to "sozialistische Lebensweise," a preference which exhibits a certain pessimism in regard to the chances of real socialism. But even in his latest publications, Hanke does not go as far as the old historian Jürgen Kuczynski, who bluntly stated:

> Die Lebensweise der Menschen in den Ländern des realen Sozialismus ist heute noch das Produkt einer Mischung verschiedenster Gesellschaftsformationen: der sozialistischen, der kapitalistischen, der religiös-feudalen. [28]

Hanke's and Kuczynski's realistic attitudes vis-à-vis the actual way of life are shared by Irene Dölling; unlike them, however, she introduced another possibility for making the broad notion of culture more concrete. She is dealing with an experience which Stephan Hermlin describes as follows:

> Längst schon glaubte ich, es [das "Kommunistische Manifest"] genau zu kennen, als ich, es war etwa in meinem fünfzigsten Lebensjahr, eine unheimliche Entdeckung machte. Unter

den Sätzen, die für mich seit langem
selbstverständlich geworden waren,
befand sich einer, der folgendermaßen
lautet: "An die Stelle der alten bürgerlichen Gesellschaft mit ihren
Klassen und Klassengegensätzen tritt
eine Assoziation, worin die freie
Entwicklung aller die Bedingung für
die freie Entwicklung eines jeden
ist." Ich weiß nicht, wann ich be-
gonnen hatte, den Satz so zu lesen,
wie er hier steht. Ich las ihn so, er
lautete für mich so, weil er meinem
damaligen Weltverständnis auf diese
Weise entsprach. Wie groß war mein
Erstaunen, ja mein Entsetzen, als ich
nach vielen Jahren fand, daß der Satz
in Wirklichkeit gerade das Gegenteil
besagte: " . . . worin die freie Entwicklung eines jeden die Bedingung
für die freie Entwicklung aller ist."
. . . Dennoch mischte sich in mein
Entsetzen Erleichterung. Plötzlich
war eine Schrift vor meinem Auge erschienen, die ich lange erwartet, auf
die ich gehofft hatte. [29]

Irene Dölling analyzed this experience in a more
scholarly way. During the seventies she was a member
of a study group on cultural theory which investigated
Marx and Engels' understanding of culture. The study
group stressed the notion of "Individualitätsformen"
as a conjunction between objective and subjective culture:

Mit dem Auffinden historischer Individualitätsformen ist die Möglichkeit
gegeben, Kriterien für das geschichtliche Maß, das Niveau der subjektiven
Kultur einer Gesellschaft oder Klasse
zu gewinnen und Lebensweise als Re-
sultat der schöpferischen Auseinandersetzung der (Klassen-)Individuen
mit ihren Lebensbedingungen (der objektiven Kultur) in ihrer Gesetzmäßigkeit zu fassen. [30]

Dölling developed this position in her book on
human beings and their biological constitution, using
sexuality as an example. She points out that a vast
majority of GDR scholars fail to grasp sexuality as a

262

social relationship:

> Wird Sexualität nicht im grundlegen-
> den Sinne als soziales Verhältnis be-
> griffen, so bleiben die Bemühungen um
> Sexualaufklärung im wesentlichen in
> der Information über biologische Ab-
> laufprozesse, sexuelle Techniken, Or-
> gasmusfähigkeit usw. stecken . . . .
> Im Grunde wird damit - ungewollt -
> die theoretische Konzeption der ab-
> strakten Gegenüberstellung von Indi-
> viduum und Gesellschaft beibehalten.[31]

All of Dölling's writings can be understood as a
fight against this abstract opposition of individual
and society, and as a plea for taking into account the
concrete conjunctions, the "Individualitätsformen."
As early as 1974 she asked--relatively cautiously--
whether the ideal of the universally developed socialist personality was not an unrealistic wish;[32] by 1980
she seems to regard the universally developed personality as impossible.[33] A consequence for the interpretation of cultural theory is her development of a
theory of personality which concerns itself with the
individual and avoids the pitfalls of psychoanalysis
by understanding the forms of individuality as general
contradictions of the individual being.[34]

It is noteworthy that Dölling always uses the experiences of women as examples for her theories. She
was the first and only social scientist in the GDR who
dealt with Maxie Wander's interviews in Guten Morgen,
Du Schöne in a general way. In her essay on the analysis of gender relationships, Dölling attacks the
neutralization of sex roles, male rule in all its
forms--from general values to body language--and the
common "double bind" situation of women in the GDR.
One of her conclusions may sound familiar to a Western
audience:

> Um die Tendenz abzubauen, daß Frauen
> die Widersprüchlichkeit des Kultur-
> prozesses nur auf der Ebene der Un-
> mittelbarkeit erleben, psychisch die-
> se Widersprüchlichkeit durch das Ge-
> fühl der Minderwertigkeit, des sub-
> jektiven Versagens im Beruf, als Mut-
> ter, als Partnerin "verarbeiten", ist
> es notwendig, sich öffentlich über
> die gesellschaftlichen Ursachen sol-

cher als "privat" erlebten Konflikte
zu verständigen.[35]

The thesis that private issues are political is
well-known in the West. In this respect Dölling's
view reflects the Western discussion. But her stress
on the need for a general theory of society in conjunction with an analysis of the contradictions of the
individual is something which has not been regarded in
this special way, not even by Western Marxists such as
Lucien Seve or Klaus Kolzkamp.[36]

To sum up, there is reason to believe that the
GDR is contributing to the emergence of a cultural
Marxism. Its contribution has specific advantages and
restraints. A main strength is its developing of a
broad concept of culture without identifying it with
either way of life or society. A main disadvantage is
its lack of interest in viewing culture as the relationship between conditions of life and activity, and
as a significant system through which a social order
is communicated, reproduced, experienced, and explored.[37] By going beyond established Marxism, Marx
may gain back a position even in real socialism, which
was described by Volker Braun in the following:

> Aber was hat er [Marx] uns überlassen!
> Welchen Mangel an Illusionen.
> Welchen weltweiten Verlust
> An sicheren Werten. Welche verbreitete
> Unfähigkeit, sich zu unterwerfen!
> Und wie ausgeschlossen, unter uns
> Nicht an allem zu zweifeln. Seither
> All unsre Erfolge: nur Abschlagszahlungen
> Der Geschichte. Dahin die Zeit
> Sich nicht hinzugeben an die Sache
> Und wie unmöglich, nicht ans Ende zu gehn:
> Und es nicht für den Anfang zu halten![38]

In other words, Marx will continue to leave his spaceship now and then.

Universität Bielefeld / FU Berlin

Notes

[1] P.M., Weltgeist Superstar (Basel: Stroemfeld/
Roter Stern, 1980).

^{2} Eric Hobsbawm, Ralph Milliband, Bob Rowthorn, and Anne Sassin, "Karl Marx: 100 Not Out," Marxism Today, 27, No. 3 (1983), 9. The quotation is from Hobsbawm.

^{3} See for example Agnes Heller, Ferenc Feher, and György Markus, Der sowjetische Weg. Bedürfnisdiktatur und entfremdeter Alltag (Hamburg: Verlag für das Studium der Arbeiterbewegung, 1983).

^{4} See Alvin W. Gouldner, The Two Marxisms. Contradictions and Anomalies in the Development of Theory (New York: Seabury, 1980), p. 10.

^{5} Otto Bauer, "Marx als Mahnung," in Bauer's Werkausgabe (Vienna: Europa, 1980), IX, 49.

^{6} Louis Althusser, Die Krise des Marxismus (Hamburg: Verlag für das Studium der Arbeiterbewegung, 1978), esp. pp. 54, 56, 66.

^{7} Claus Offe, "The Emerging Coexistence of Two Paradigms of the Political," unpublished paper read at conference of the Joint Committee on Western Europe in Florence, Italy, 1980, pp. 13-14.

^{8} Jürgen Habermas, "Habermas Talking," Theory and Society, 1, No. 1 (1974), 48.

^{9} See Richard R. Weiner, Cultural Marxism and Political Sociology (London/Beverly Hills: Sage, 1981).

^{10} See Birgit Mahnkopf, "Das kulturtheoretische Defizit industriesoziologischer Forschung," Probleme des Klassenkampfes, 12, No. 46 (1982), 48.

^{11} Raymond Williams, Problems in Materialism and Culture (London: Verso, 1980), p. 108.

^{12} Thesen des Zentralkomitees der SED zum Karl-Marx-Jahr 1983 (Berlin: Dietz, 1982), p. 36.

^{13} For example, Uwe Jens Heuer, Recht und Wirtschaftsleitung im Sozialismus (Berlin: Akademie, 1982).

^{14} See Karl Marx und die DDR, ed. Friedrich-Ebert Stiftung (Bonn: Neue Gesellschaft, 1982).

^{15} See Fred Oldenburg, "Marx über die Partei - Zur Legitimationsproblematik der SED-Herrschaft," Berichte des Bundesinstituts für ostwissenschaftliche und internationale Studien, No. 47 (1982).

[16] Fred Staufenbiel, "Grundfragen der Leninschen Theorie von der sozialistischen Kulturrevolution und die kulturelle Entwicklung in der DDR," Deutsche Zeitschrift für Philosophie, 8, No. 8 (1960), 910.

[17] Walter Besenbruch, "Über die Einheit von Politik, Ökonomie und Kultur," Deutsche Zeitschrift für Philosophie, 8, No. 8 (1960), 940.

[18] See Hans Koch and Erika Hinckel, "Zur marxistisch-leninistischen Theorie der Kultur," Einheit, 16, No. 6 (1962).

[19] Dietrich Mühlberg, "Zur marxistischen Auffassung der Kulturgeschichte," Deutsche Zeitschrift für Philosophie, 12, No. 9 (1964), 1042. The so-called "basic question" of Leninist philosophy is the distinction between a materialist and an idealist approach.

[20] See Kulturpolitisches Wörterbuch, 2nd ed. (Berlin: Dietz, 1978), p. 364.

[21] Irene Dölling, "Kulturtheorie als angewandter historischer Materialismus," Deutsche Zeitschrift für Philosophie, 23, No. 3 (1975), 449.

[22] From a talk with young writers: "Vorbild - Leitbild," Weimarer Beiträge, 25, No. 7 (1979), 18.

[23] See Kurt Hager, Zu Fragen der Kulturpolitik der SED (Berlin: Dietz, 1972).

[24] See Isolde Dietrich and Dietrich Mühlberg, "Zur Kulturgeschichte der Arbeiterklasse," Jahrbuch für Volkskunde und Kulturgeschichte, 22 (1979), 50.

[25] Isolde Dietrich, "IX. Kulturtheoretisches Kolloquium in Berlin," Mitteilungen aus der kulturwissenschaftlichen Forschung, No. 9 (1981), p. 7. First results of this project are: Dietrich Mühlberg, ed., Arbeiterleben um 1900 (Berlin: Dietz, 1983); Dietrich Mühlberg, Woher wir wissen was Kultur ist (Berlin: Deutscher Verlag der Wissenschaften, 1983).

[26] Dietrich, "IX. Kulturtheoretisches Kolloquium in Berlin," p. 8.

[27] Helmut Hanke, "Kultur und Lebensweise," in Zur

Theorie der sozialistischen kultur (Berlin: Dietz, 1982), pp. 223-331.

[28] Jürgen Kuczynski, "Zur Soziologie des Alltags: ein Anlaß zur Diskussion," Jahrbuch für Soziologie und Sozialpolitik, 3 (1982), 120.

[29] Stephan Hermlin, Abendlicht (Berlin: Wagenbach, 1980), pp. 21-22.

[30] Dietrich Mühlberg, ed., Der Beitrag von Marx und Engels zur wissenschaftlichen Kulturauffassung der Arbeiterklasse (Berlin: Humboldt Universität, 1980), Part VI, p. 19.

[31] Irene Dölling, Naturwesen - Individuum - Persönlichkeit. Die Menschen und ihre biologische Konstitution in der marxistisch-leninistischen Kulturtheorie (Berlin: Deutscher Verlag der Wissenschaften, 1979), p. 57.

[32] Irene Dölling, "Biologische Konstitution und sozialistische Persönlichkeitsentwicklung," Weimarer Beiträge, 20, No. 11 (1974), 114.

[33] Irene Dölling, "Kulturtheoretische Überlegungen zur Lebensweise und zur Persönlichkeitsentwicklung älterer Menschen in der sozialistischen Gesellschaft," in Studien zum Altern in der sozialistischen Gesellschaft (Berlin: Gesellschaft für Gerontologie, 1980), p. 190.

[34] See Irene Dölling, "Zur Vermittlung von gesellschaftlichem und individuellem Lebensprozeß," Weimarer Beiträge, 27, No. 10 (1981), esp. pp. 100-106.

[35] Irene Dölling, "Zur kulturtheoretischen Analyse von Geschlechterbeziehungen," Weimarer Beiträge, 26, No. 1 (1980), 79. See also Dölling's contributions in Mitteilungen aus der kulturwissenschaftlichen Forschung, No. 11 (1982).

[36] See Dölling, "Zur Vermittlung von gesellschaftlichem und individuellem Lebensprozeß," pp. 98-100 and 120 (notes).

[37] See Raymond Williams, Culture (Glasgow: Fontana, 1981), p. 13.

[38] Volker Braun, "Karl Marx," in Gegen die symmetrische Welt (Frankfurt/M: Suhrkamp, 1974), p. 47.

The GDR's Heftreihenliteratur
as a Channel of Political Socialization

Anita M. Mallinckrodt

As many students of the GDR have found, its literature offers an unusually clear mirroring of that society. This is true not only for its Belletristik, which has been the focus of most studies, but also for its Unterhaltungsliteratur, or popular literature, which has not yet received much critical attention. And among the various forms of popular literature there are the brochure series, or Heftreihen, about which very little was known. These are what German tradition refers to as Groschenhefte, i.e., as "penny" or "dime" novels.

About 500,000 copies of such Hefte are put on sale at GDR newspaper kiosks each month by three major publishing houses which together turn out five series. Their readers are primarily youth or young adults; the stories are chiefly adventure or crime stories (Krimis); the covers promise "action"; the price is small. In the FRG, literature specialists would assume that the series are "triviale Literatur," and literature sociologists would presume they are "Trivialliteratur," while Americans might call them "formula fiction." But are they? That was the issue which this study set out to examine, based on a political-science interest in socio-political values and norms conveyed by Heftliteratur, rather than literary science's concern with its aesthetic qualities.

The theoretical approach was that of political socialization, or the process of orienting citizens' beliefs, information, and attitudes toward their political world. Since Heftreihenliteratur is published in the GDR to educate as well as to entertain, it was assumed to be part of the political socialization process. Based on these premises, the hypothesis of the

study was 1) that, while the Heftreihenliteratur of
the GDR might externally look like brochure literature
published in the West and share its general characteristics, it also would be dissimilar because it would
reflect the different socio-political system in which
it was produced; and 2) that this would be reflected
especially in the presentation of literary characters,
or Leitbilder. Thus, the specific research questions
to be answered were to what extent the Heftreihenliteratur reflected the values/norms of socialism and how
they were presented. Content analysis was the methodological tool chosen to test the hypothesis and answer
the research questions.

The genesis and development of Heftliteratur are
essential to understanding its social function and political role in the GDR today. The origins go back to
the late 1920s, to German socialism. Although a full
account of the cultural theory and practice of the
Arbeiterbewegung during that period has not yet been
written,[1] some roots of socialist brochure literature
can be traced.

For instance, in the 1920s, Wieland Herzfelde,
head of the progressive Malik Verlag, often complained
in print, as did others, about the "Schundliteratur"
being offered the masses as popular reading. The
question of what should replace bourgeois literature
was a subject of intense debate. The revolutionary
wing of the German workers' movement found some answers in the Proletkult of post-revolutionary Russia.
Thus, the Malik Verlag, too, began to publish inter-
nationally known authors, such as John Dos Passos and
Upton Sinclair, in the Rote-Roman-Serie. Inexpensive
series of documents, essays, and poems were turned out
in the Kleine revolutionäre Bibliothek. The Reportage
form of writing became popular with the works of Egon
Erwin Kisch and John Reed; "worker authors" were "discovered" and encouraged. The magazine Linkskurve,
published in the KPD's Internationaler Arbeiter-Verlag
in Berlin, sponsored contests to stimulate proletarian
revolutionary literature, and in 1930 the Eine-Mark-
Serie of novels was born.

Inexpensive brochure literature, however, remained a problem. Thus a special appeal went out to
authors for "Groschen- und 20-Pfennighefte" stories
which could counter "die Ströme von widerlichen Detek-
tivnovellen, süßsauren und verhetzenden Missionsge-
schichten, bürgerlichem Hintertreppenkitsch."[2] Such

series were indeed begun, for instance, the Rote Reihe in 1931/32. But it was too late. It was 1933. The hopeful development of socialist literature and art for the working class was interrupted by twelve years of Nazi rule.

When the war was over, the hunger for information was great. In the Soviet Zone some cultural leaders wanted to use the traditional popular literature to educate people to a new way of life, that of socialism. But others wanted to first concentrate on overcoming fascism, and so the literature of the antifascist emigration was introduced and emphasized. At the same time, however, "Schund und Schmutzliteratur" was coming across the border from the West. To counter it and simultaneously meet the demand for popular reading material, authors were recruited, somewhat as in the 1920s, to write proletarian novels for inexpensive series. And so by 1949 the first of the brochure series, Das Neue Abenteuer, from the publishing house for youth, Verlag Neues Leben, was on the newsstands.

The 1950s saw the introduction of more series, some quite strident and polemic. Academicians began to take an interest, often critical interest, in the quality of the writing, and by the late 1950s a number of the series had been dropped and an official review of Heftliteratur was underway. The 1960s brought a stabilization of literary production in the GDR and a reduction in the flow of competitive Western Groschenhefte after the building of the Wall. Thus, by the 1970s there were six major series: Das Neue Abenteuer from Verlag Neues Leben; the Krimi series Blaulicht from Verlag Neues Berlin; KAP, or "Krimis, Abenteuer und Phantastik," (now defunct) from Verlag Kultur und Fortschritt; and Meridian, Erzählerreihe, and the Reportage series Tatsachen from Militärverlag der DDR. (So-called Liebesromane or Eheromane are deliberately excluded from Heftliteratur in the GDR.) The 1970s also brought significant academic research focused on Heftreihenliteratur, especially at the Pädagogische Hochschule in Potsdam[3] and at the University of Halle.[4] The approach of these studies was not literary but pedagogical and functional, i.e., they assessed how specific Heft series fulfilled their twofold task of entertaining and educating.

As noted above, the Heft series can also be seen from a political-science point of view, that is, as a channel of political socialization. This was the approach that led the author to gather more than 9000 facts about 59 Hefte and 47 short stories from magazines for women (used as a contrast to the presentation of women in the Heft stories) and interpretative background information from GDR colleagues who edit the series or study them academically. The random sample of publications was drawn from the 1970 and 1978 publishing periods, i.e., before and after Erich Honecker's assumption of SED leadership.

Data were collected via content analysis methodology incorporated into a seven-page evaluation form which focused on two units of analysis: the Heft as a literary item; and its literary characters as models (Leitbilder). In regard to the Hefte as individual items, the data collected included the sex and nationality of the author, the broad subject-matter context (war, crime, adventure, polit-history, social action, family life, biography/memoir), the thematic conflict central to the story (e.g., morality, power, love, career/performance), the geographical "where" and the temporal "when" setting, the socio-economic system (e.g., capitalism, socialism, non-capitalist development), the political system (e.g., constitutional democracy, people's republic, revolutionary democracy), the political "in/out" structure of the context (Machthaber vis-à-vis Machtlose), etc. Concerning the literary figures (the protagonist, or leading character of the story, and up to five antagonists, or reacting secondary characters), the data collected included their regional identity, sex, race, marital status, age group, socio-economic status, profession, political "in/out" position, general image, and the socio-political values, personal intellectual behavioral norms, and personal emotional behavioral norms which they reflected as they moved across the pages of the Hefte.

The total frequency and correlation findings were then divided into three broad areas: Weltanschauung; GDR society; and socialist personality, as represented in the sampled Hefte. The areas are presented here in narrative, summary form, rather than burdening such a short text with the documentary statistics and illustrations available in the longer version.[5]

Weltanschauung. The Hefte showed socialism engaged in a constant and intensifying world-wide class-struggle of power- and morality-motivated confrontations with other ideologies, especially capitalism. (Thirty-nine of the 59 Hefte stories in the sample

272

were set outside the GDR.) The conflicts were based primarily on actual political events from history and the present: German anti-fascists versus the Nazis, Sicilian farmers versus the Mafia, Angolans versus Western mercenaries, Guatemalan revolutionaries versus American interventionists, pro-Allende Chilean truckdrivers versus putschists. Socialism was preeminent, accounting for 41% of the systemic contexts. Capitalism, used for 34% of the socio-economic contexts, was shown as a system involved in exploitation (as in Guatemala) and intervention (as in Vietnam) and leading to the perversion of society (e.g., social injustice in Sicily or orchestrated destruction of leftist labor organization efforts in the United States). The Third World (12% of all regional settings) was presented as struggling toward non-capitalist development (e.g., Egyptian nationalization of the Suez Canal or Sicilian land reform). The case against traditional colonialism was made, for instance, by Jack London, one of the numerous classical authors included in the Das Neue Abenteuer series.

War, which was treated in about one-fourth of the stories, was presented not only in the form of wars of liberation but also as the struggle against Nazi fascism, World War II. Here the socialists fighting on the front lines were portrayed as courageous and dedicated anti-fascists; they were primarily Soviet military personnel and Germans in partisan units, while socialists behind the lines were shown as active resistors of fascism in organized groups, factories, concentration and POW camps. The focus was on individuals more than on armies or battles. Typical of the tone of such stories is the following quote:

> alle friedliebenden Menschen blicken auf die Männer, die sich von Hitler abgewendet und ihm den Kampf angesagt haben. Sie verkörpern bereits das neue Deutschland, das nach der Niederlage Hitlers kommen wird. [6]

In the class struggle on all these levels, socialism was shown to be supported by primarily positive persons, i.e., by people who were socially active and responsible, intellectually alert and professionally competent, and emotionally humanistic and "good." In socialist countries, such as the USSR, they were dedicated to maintaining and developing that sociopolitical system; in the Third World they struggled to establish socialism (as in Angola); in pre-war Germany they worked and organized for the evolution of socialism and elimination of fascism; in World War II they fought for fascism's defeat; in Western capitalist settings (Sicily, United States, Guatemala, Chile) they struggled to mitigate the harshest aspects of injustice and exploitation. As a Sicilian worker says, "Wir wollen doch nur, daß wir wie Menschen und nicht wie Tiere leben."[7] The reality of such struggles was not diluted by the sensationalized and distracting presentation of violence.

The revolutionary tradition of the German people was emphasized, too, in stories about the Weimar Republic (Spartacist youth struggling for apprentice rights, for example) and especially about the Nazi period. For instance, in a story about factory sabotage, the leader of the Anti-Fascist Action Committee says, "Trotz der ungeheuren Gefahr war die Ehre der deutschen Arbeiterklasse auch in der Gießerei . . . reingehalten worden."[8] In such World War II stories, the military as a socio-economic group included sympathetic anti-fascist Wehrmacht soldiers and unsympathetic Nazi officers, the latter always cast in secondary, or antagonist, roles. In presenting fascism, the authors concentrated on various aspects, including the need to be informed about it. For instance, a naive German Pflichtjahrmädchen is told:

> Du bist 16 Jahre alt. Du hast Augen im Kopf. Wie es bei dir zu Hause ist, weiß ich nicht. Aber ich kann es mir vorstellen. Hier hattest du allerdings genug Gelegenheit, Dinge zu bemerken, die deinen Denkapparat hätten in Bewegung setzen können. Man muß nicht immer warten, bis einem alles haarklein erklärt wird. Nicht in dieser Zeit.[9]

And in another story one Arbeitsdienst youth tells another that the essence of fascist evil is the "Abtötung des Geistes zu dem Zwecke, die Menschen zu willfährigen Mördern zu machen."[10] Also emphasized were the need to resist fascism, the urgency of active resistance, the need to organize that resistance and lead it carefully and courageously, and the relationship between active, organized anti-fascism and communism.

The positive non-GDR protagonists offered by the Hefte as Leitbilder of socialism included not only Red

Army military figures of the war stories but also a contemporary Soviet test pilot, a geologist, and a harbor pilot on loan to Egypt. In the non-socialist context, the protagonist Leitbilder included the Sicilian and Chilean workers mentioned above and also ten protagonists representing Germany before 1945: the resistors, camp prisoners, a KPD courier, along with the Spartacists, Arbeitsdienst youth, and Pflichtjahr youth discussed previously. The stories set in the Third World featured a West European reporter in the Vietnam war story, as well as a British mercenary involved in the Angolan conflict.

GDR society. Most of the twenty Hefte dealing with the GDR itself were Krimis (18 out of 20 or 90%). Most of them presented crime as a morality conflict between those who enforce and uphold the law and those who break it, with a happy-end when legality prevails. (Power was the theme when the crime was foreign espionage.) Thus, most of the protagonists were from the political intelligentsia, the police, and the military. On the other hand, workers made up about a third of the antagonists, many cast as the criminals or suspects. Youth characters fell into similar roles. The kinds of crime troubling the society, as presumed by brochure authors, reflect quite accurately the statistics of the real GDR world: dominance of property crimes, significantly high rates of youth crime, of alcohol-related crime, etc. In short, the GDR crime depicted was not that of gangsters and the organized underworld or of sadistic, brutal street and drug criminals, but rather instances of theft, robbery, fraud, blackmail, arson, espionage, and rowdyism. And the causes of crime were found in the nature of society, not in the nature of man. As Oberleutnant Maronde says about a young female criminal:

> Mit solchen egoistischen Lebensauffassungen . . . wird kein Mensch geboren. Wir müssen herausfinden, wieso da in ihrem Leben eine Weiche verkehrt gestellt wurde und sie auf eine so schiefe Bahn geraten konnte.[11]

The rehabilitation of criminals was emphasized. For instance, a director says about a worker:

> Er arbeitet exakt und sorgfältig, wir hatten bisher keinen Grund zur Klage. Und sie wissen ja, wenn nicht vom Gericht ausdrücklich ein Berufsverbot

> ausgesprochen wird, hat jeder nach
> Verbüßung der Strafe das Recht, sei-
> nen erlernten Beruf wieder auszu-
> üben.[12]

Violence, on the other hand, was greatly played down.
For instance, the appearance of a drowned corpse was
limited to this brief description:

> Es war kein Anblick für schwache
> Nerven; das Antlitz gedunsen, ver-
> unstaltet, die einstige Schönheit
> gräßlich zerstört, die Augen aufge-
> rissen und verzerrt im Todeskampf.[13]

And when blood did flow, as in the rare case of the
machine-gun death of an ex-SS man, that was told in
nine simple words: "Rote Flecke auf seiner Brust. Sie
vergrößerten sich schnell."[14]

The police and military protagonists were clearly
"good guys," just and fair representatives of state
authority. In the stories sampled, they frequently
came from worker backgrounds, had close and friendly
relations with the people, and elicited public cooperation in solving the law-and-order problems of society. They were relaxed with each other, i.e., non-
elitist, and worked collectively. And they worked
very hard, indeed. In fact, the GDR's work world was
shown as motivated by Arbeitsfreude and Leistung among
all professional groups.

The brochures studied showed relationships among
GDR citizens as sensitive and warm. However, family
or romantic relationships were infrequently presented,
and sexuality was a rarity. Some demographic groups
were also scarce: the aged, widowed, divorced, or sep-
arated. The presentation of GDR women was a mixed
picture. First of all, not many women were to be
found (5.2% of the GDR protagonists and 20.8% of the
antagonists), and those depicted were male-created;
the sample included only two women authors. At the
same time, women were not presented as objects, but
the most emancipated women figures in the stories set
in the GDR were the creation of one woman author.[15]

Societal critique was neither emphasized nor entirely omitted in the Hefte. However, since so many
of the stories taking place in the GDR were Krimis,
much of the presented criticism concerned conditions
relating to crime. In the 1978 publishing period,

societal criticism seems to have been more substantive. For instance, one Krimi, written from the perspective of youth, questioned non-creative thought, conformity, and the pressure to perform:

> Ich habe nichts gegen Lernen und Diskutieren, im Gegenteil. Nur mußte ich mich neulich fragen, ob sich ein gutes Kollektiv dadurch auszeichnet, daß alle das gleiche gleich gut und gleich begeistert tun. Man könnte doch beispielsweise statt der Themen des FDJ-Studienjahres . . . mal Engels' ganzen "Ludwig Feuerbach und der Ausgang der klassischen deutschen Philosophie" lesen. Nicht nur die paar Seiten, die im Unterricht verlangt werden. Vielleicht in Gruppen, die einen den "Feuerbach", die anderen den "Anti-Dühring", jeder das, was ihn interessiert, und dann darüber reden.[16]
> Woher nehmen sie eigentlich die Gewißheit, daß das, was sie für richtig halten, tatsächlich auch das Richtige für mich ist? Vater mit seinem Maschinenbaustudiumtick, die Klasse mit ihrem "Kollektivgeist". Auf die Idee mich zu fragen, was ich davon halte, kommt niemand. Verdammt noch mal, warum kann man denn mit keinem so reden, wie einem gerade zu Mute ist, ohne daß immer einer gleich denkt, man will das FDJ-Studienjahr schmeißen oder gar Schlimmeres. (p. 9)
> Bin ich nicht imstande, eine bestimmte Leistung zu vollbringen, blamiere ich mich. Schaffe ich sie, imponiert das. Immer nur Leistungen, Leistungen. In der Schule und zu Hause. Sogar bei Ede und seinen Kumpeln [workers] ist es nicht anders. Nur eine andere Ebene. (p. 15)

Socialist Personality. Much has been written in the GDR about the socialist personality, the need to develop it, and the definition of specific problem areas. The arts are supposed to offer models, or Vorbilder. To assess whether socialist values were indeed reflected in the protagonist and antagonist Leitbilder which the Hefte authors offered their readers, two main kinds of criteria were applied: exemplary values and norms specified in the GDR Youth Law and some values and norms which the University of Halle collective used in surveying GDR reader expectations in regard to literary figures.[17] In reporting the findings, precise percentages and proportions cannot be used; assigning values and norms to literary statements is an admittedly subjective exercise. Nevertheless, overall assessments, such as "frequent," "infrequent," or "modest" reflections of values give some general indication of what was presented in the brochure literature studied.

For instance, socio-political values (Parteilichkeit, Internationalismus, Kollektivität, etc.) were less frequently found (about one-fourth of the total volume noted) than were norms of intellectual and emotional behavior. And concerning these last two sets of norms, there was a difference between protagonists and antagonists: the protagonists reflected more intellectual behavioral norms and the antagonists more emotional behavioral norms. Overall, about two-thirds of all values/norms registered were positive and one-third negative. Some of the former are set down in the Youth Law, but others, such as justice, which found expression in the Hefte are not specifically mentioned there.

Among the protagonists, the most frequently reflected socio-political values were justice, work productivity, and social activism/sense of duty. The most frequent intellectual behavioral norms were critical/factual/rational thought, capability/competence/performance, and alertness/intelligence/self-development. The most frequent emotional behavioral norms were sensitivity/empathy/lovingness and confidentiality/politeness. The antagonists generally demonstrated these same characteristics with slightly different emphases.

Interesting was the fact that very few negative values/norms were ascribed to protagonists, for instance, the police and military personnel who dominated the cast of leading characters. On the other hand, where negative references to antagonists were found, they sometimes seemed to be used as reinforcement of specific positive values. For example, the value of social responsibility is highlighted when an incompetent brigade leader says: "So eine Brigade ist schließlich keine Erziehungsanstalt für komplizierte Charaktere." [18]

on the side of progress and justice in a constant and intensifying class struggle, a system supporting significant causes throughout time and around the world, a community of cooperating states whose strength included collective/cooperative work and achievement rather than counter-productive egoistic individualism and competition. Socialism was depicted as a viable system--despite serious challenges (e.g., counter-revolution)--based on enduring socio-political concepts, a system honoring work and workers and supporting the cause of human liberation, including women's emancipation (especially in developing countries), and as an achieving, positive system inspiring dedication and loyalty and offering hope and optimism.

Within the GDR context, socialism was presented as a superior German system, capable of supporting a sovereign nation state, fulfilling the historical goal of the German Arbeiterbewegung, and creating a stable society and way of life affirmed by most of its people. Moreover, the system was shown as fostering a way of life in which people are generally good and kind to each other (but without intimate relationships) and women are accepted as economically and politically equal to men. At the same time, women were not depicted as major actors in society or as people whose fuller psychological/emotional emancipation is significant. In addition, GDR socialism was portrayed as a system concerned about coping with crime, focused on state authority figures, emphasizing Leistung, and encouraging collectivity and quality leadership. Finally, it was pictured as a system increasingly engaged in substantive, though system-accepting, self-criticism.

Heftreihen editors and writers emphasize that in presenting such socio-political overviews via literature they do not mechanically parrot the "Party line," as is widely assumed abroad. On the other hand, there are of course recognized taboos and internalized "rules of the game" (or self-censorship), especially for literature which is educational and affirmative, or system-maintaining. Thus it was interesting to find that certain Party values (as stated in the 1976 Party Program) such as internationalism, Third World importance, women's emancipation, centrality of workers in socialism, attention to the aged (and to some extent to youth), the essentiality of criticism/self-criticism, and iron discipline within the military were not emphasized in the Hefte. Specifically, GDR readers might wonder about the incongruity between

Thus, in conclusion, it seems clear that the publication of Heftreihenliteratur in the GDR, because of the educational half of its task, is part of that country's political socialization. As in all countries, that socialization process includes efforts to orient citizen attitudes and values to: 1) the political system as a whole (e.g., existence of the GDR as a sovereign state); 2) particular political roles or structures (e.g., SED, Nationale Volksarmee, Volkspolizei); 3) individuals or groups filling such roles (e.g., border guards, city police); and 4) specific public policies and issues (e.g., national defense/security, work productivity, crime).[19]

Moreover, the life-long political socialization process carried out by all governments is intended either to establish a new political system or to maintain an existing one. For the GDR, it seems to be a bit of both. "System establishment" apparently is still necessary vis-à-vis the constant challenge represented by the existence of the FRG and family ties to it; "system maintenance" is relevant, as in all systems, for persuaded citizens whose earlier socialization nevertheless is tested by their personal encounter with political realities. Because of the two-Germanies factor, the Marxist/Leninist emphasis on political education, and the centralized governance/ guidance of the socio-political system, the GDR's political socialization is intense, regulated, and largely direct. That is not, however, to suggest that it is total in impact.

Thus, Heftreihenliteratur is a significant, if not central, part of the GDR's political socialization process. Reflecting in form and intent the 1920s and 1930s' approach to socialist mass literature, present Heftliteratur is optimistic, "in tune" with history, and addressed to real interests and needs. In short, the hypothesis that Heftliteratur in the GDR is a socialist literature was confirmed: many stories from the sample were set in the socialist socio-economic system and the people's republic political system; over half had Eastern Europe as their regional setting; over half of the protagonists and antagonists expressed primarily values and norms considered significant to the "socialist personality."

The data show that socialism was presented as overwhelmingly positive, both on the international scene and in the GDR itself. Worldwide, socialism was shown as a socio-political system dynamically involved

280

officially stated values and the emphasis placed by the Hefte on police and military rather than workers and farmers, on production-related Leistung rather than on creative activity, about the limitation of social issue criticism largely to economic conditions, the apparent lack of concern for the reading interests of female youth and young female adults, and the general lack of support for the non-economic dimensions of women's emancipation. At the same time, the Hefte sampled mirrored other objective conditions quite accurately. For instance, stories about Egypt, Vietnam, Angola, and Chile were published at times when these countries were of current foreign policy concern to the GDR. Changed perceptions among GDR legal specialists and criminologists about criminal causality were taken into account in the Krimis, as were the kinds of crime the statistics reported.

Thus, while basically conservative, that is, reflecting to a large extent existent official and dominant values and norms of the political system, the brochure literature was neither alienated from reality nor escapist. The themes and plots were not trite but were taken primarily from the real world of national and international politics and history, as seen from the socialist point of view. While the conflicts were usually resolved happily, this was not always so.

The protagonists and antagonists were largely positive figures. Depending on author and series, they sometimes were stereotyped and not fully developed; sometimes, however, they were rounded figures, relative, of course, to the restrictions on character development inherent in the short-story literary form. The figures lived and moved in a world of conflict, social action, hard work, and achievement, with little time to laugh and be happy or to engage in personal emotional involvements. When women figures were presented, they were not objects or negative characters, and their professional achievements were not ignored; however, women characters were not numerous in the brochure literature, and the emancipation process went largely untreated.

The GDR's Heft authors, who are mostly male (in this sample 56 of 59), are neither assembly-line writers nor "hacks." Classical writers are included among them, along with well-known contemporary authors and young-generation newcomers who write part-time for the series. Pseudonyms are very rare. Because of the variety of authors, the style and aesthetic quality of

281

the Heftliteratur are uneven.

For the GDR readers, whom the editors assume to be educated male youth and young male adults, although not necessarily members of the intelligentsia, Heftliteratur provides relaxation and education; the readers are attracted by the characters and the reality-oriented plots (adventure and action in historic settings), by the relatively uncomplicated literary style, small and handy format, and the low price. For the political system of the GDR, Heftliteratur is a channel of socialization. For editors and writers, it is a means of literary expression as well as an educational contribution. And for non-GDR readers, brochure literature provides an additional window onto certain aspects of GDR society.

Notes

[1] See Frank Trommler, "Die Kulturpolitik der DDR und die kulturelle Tradition des deutschen Sozialismus," in Literatur und Literaturtheorie in der DDR, ed. Peter Uwe Hohendahl and Patricia Herminghouse (Frankfurt/M: Suhrkamp, 1976), pp. 13ff.

[2] Linkskurve, 3, No. 12 (1931), pp. 12-13.

[3] Potsdamer Forschungen, Reihe A, No. 15 (1975); Reihe A, No. 16 (1975); Reihe A, No. 21 (1976).

[4] Regina Kahsche, "Profil und Gestaltung der belletristischen Heftreihe 'Das Neue Abenteuer' von Verlag Neues Leben Berlin," Diss. Martin-Luther-Universität, Halle, 1978.

[5] Anita M. Mallinckrodt, Das kleine Massenmedium. Soziale Funktion und politische Rolle der Heftreihen-Literatur in der DDR (Cologne: Verlag Wissenschaft und Politik, 1984).

[6] Paul Lampe, "Du wirst schießen müssen," Meridian, No. 71 (1978), p. 49.

[7] Horst Szeponik, "Mord in Corleone," Tatsachen, No. 97 (1969), p. 10.

[8] Werner Reinowski, "Handstreich zwischen den Fronten," KAP, No. 101 (1970), p. 5.

[9] Friedel Hohnbaum-Hornschuch, "Funken im Rauch" Meridian, No. 73 (1978), p. 66.

[10] Herbert Friedrich, "Der Tod des Geigers," Das Neue Abenteuer, No. 383 (1978), p. 27.

[11] Alexander Andreew, "Die Dame mit dem Trick," Blaulicht, No. 115 (1970), p. 62.

[12] Heiner Rank, "Modell Traumland," Blaulicht, No. 121 (1970), p. 14.

[13] Horst Lohde, "Tatort Waldsee," Blaulicht, No. 184 (1978), p. 19.

[14] Ulrich Waldner, "Die Thorsteinbande," Das Neue Abenteuer, No. 301 (1970), p. 27.

[15] Susanne Günther, "Sabotage in Dabelow," Erzählerreihe, No, 232 (1978).

[16] Fred Ufer, "Am Nachmittag träumt man nicht," Blaulicht, No. 190 (1978), p. 4.

[17] Funktion und Wirkung. Soziologische Untersuchungen zur Literatur und Kunst, ed. Dietrich Sommer, Dietrich Löffler, Achim Walter, and Eva Maria Scherf (Berlin/Weimar: Aufbau, 1978), p. 533.

[18] Dorothea Kleine, "Einer spielt falsch," Erzählerreihe, No. 155 (1969), p. 8.

[19] See discussions of the political socialization process in Richard E. Dawson and Kenneth Prewitt, Political Socialization (Boston: Little, Brown, 1969), and Gabriel A. Almond and G. Bingham Powell, Jr., Comparative Politics: a Developmental Approach (Boston: Little, Brown, 1966), pp. 24, 52.

Recent Directions and Tendencies
in Linguistics in the GDR

James E. Copeland

My purpose in this paper is to comment on directions in GDR linguistics during the past few years,
more specifically, the directions reflected in the recently established journal <u>Zeitschrift für Germani-
stik</u>. But first it is necessary to discuss some developments in GDR linguistics in the 1960s and 1970s
which are important for understanding the more recent
trends.

For almost two decades, linguists in the GDR have
been on the forefront of international research in
generative linguistics. In recognition of this status, student demonstrators in the Federal Republic
carried banners in the open protest marches of the
1960s saying "WIR WOLLEN AUCH LINGUISTIK." This demand struck many West German academics as odd, since
<u>Sprachwissenschaft</u> in some form or other had been part
of the standard curriculum in universities all over
Germany since the eighteenth century, and because it
was, after all, precisely in the German-speaking area
of central Europe that the modern field of linguistics
had its early roots, developing out of the philological tradition of comparative studies represented in
the work of such early linguistic giants as Jakob
Grimm, August Schleicher, Johannes Schmidt, August
Leskien, Karl Brugmann, among others.

But what the West German student demonstrators
were demanding was something different; they wanted
the "new" linguistics: the kind of neo-structuralist
linguistics that was being researched and applied to
studies of the German language at the Akademie der
Wissenschaften in East Berlin under the leadership of
Manfred Bierwisch, Wolfgang Motsch, and Wolfdietrich
Hartung, that is, a linguistics which would, by impli-

cation, have a stronger orientation towards the social accountability of the discipline and towards an application to a broader scope of human problems than the older, largely historical approaches had had. Much of the abstract theoretical framework for research in the so-called "new" linguistics was being developed during that period in the United States, initially under the leadership of Noam Chomsky at MIT.[1] It was to be a linguistics, the expressed object of which was to explain systematically and in explicit terms the nature of human speech and its general importance for a more integrated understanding of humankind and, more specifically, of the nature of the human mind.[2]

By the early 1960s Manfred Bierwisch and other linguists in the GDR had become aware of Chomsky's model of linguistic structure and its initial promise. A group of outstanding linguistic scholars was assembled at the Akademie der Wissenschaften in Berlin, and work on analyzing German was begun by the group using Chomsky's theoretical paradigm. This early work at the Akademie der Wissenschaften had a twofold purpose: first, to provide a more complete structural description of the German language using and further developing the latest analytic tools; and, second, to examine the theoretical and methodological bases for the general development of the science of linguistics in an international context. Beginning in 1965, the majority of the work produced by this group was published in an excellent series of monographs under the general title Studia Grammatica by Akademie Verlag in Berlin. In 1969 the Zentralinstitut für Sprachwissenschaft was established at the Akademie der Wissenschaften to continue and promote this linguistic research.

The two decades of research by the Berlin collective resulted in 1981 in the publication of Grundzüge einer deutschen Grammatik, (GdG).[3] It is by far the most advanced reference grammar of the German literary language ever written.[4] The theoretical model used for the early research on the grammar was, with some modification, the standard mid-1960s version of transformational theory, but by 1981 the work of the collective shows a very marked departure from Chomsky's model (1965). The GdG model is much broader in scope, less closely tied to the structure of the individual sentence, and more eclectic in its perspective than either the most advanced versions of transformational grammar or of generative text linguistics. The book is not intended by the authors as an abstract contribution to linguistic theory as such, but rather as a basis for describing a wide range of facts about the structure and use of the German language in context. Some theoretical questions are intentionally left open, as a reflection of the state of the art: for example, the relation between the communicative-pragmatic component and the other major components of the grammar. Nor do the authors any longer defend the theoretical notion of "grammatical transformation" in a dogmatic way, but use it instead as a convenient metaphor for visualizing and expressing complex grammatical relations that are crucial to the overall description of the language. The collective demonstrated with this work a refreshingly non-arbitrary, eclectic but well integrated approach to the multifaceted phenomena of the German language that is of interest to scholars in and outside of the GDR, including linguists, communication scientists, literary critics, language teachers, sociologists, cognitive psychologists, mathematicicans, and computer scientists.

All of the volumes of Studia Grammatica written in the 1960s reflect a strong interest in American generative theory, particularly as applied to German morphology, syntax, phonology, and semantics. By the early seventies, however, it was becoming clear to GDR linguists that research in the 1960s had been limited by the overly narrow definition of the object of study in generative linguistics. [5] Following Saussure's strict distinction between langue and parole, Chomsky (in Aspects of the Theory of Syntax) had even further constrained the object of linguistic investigation to include only the inferred knowledge or competence of an admittedly non-existent, idealized speaker of a language, with no performance limitations, and in the absence of intersentential or extra-linguistic context. Thus, despite its initial promise of broadening the field of inquiry to include a psychology of language, generative grammar accomplished exactly the opposite. It removed linguistics even further from the study of what real speakers actually do with language, and of the way in which language actually functions in real psychological, social, and artistic contexts.

By 1973 linguists in the GDR were posing a new complex of questions relating to the nature and functions of human speech. [6] With the belated appearance in 1976 of the revised papers delivered at the 1973 workshop on "Probleme der Textgrammatik" at the Akademie der Wissenschaften, the Studia Grammatica series inaugurated a radical theoretical reorientation. In the place of a linguistics with a system-oriented competence grammar at its center there evolved a linguistics that indeed incorporated such a grammar, but was reoriented towards linguistic performance: a linguistics that stressed the dynamic side of language and viewed speech as a communicative activity rather than as just a static system of linguistic relations.[7]

To be sure, this reorientation of linguistics did not take place in isolation in the GDR; the developments are rather part of an international trend in linguistics in the 1970s toward investigating the empirical principle that the study of language can not successfully be abstracted from the context of its use by actual speakers. Focusing on language in this way necessarily forces the investigator to look beyond the scope of the sentence and to view language from the perspective of texts rather than of sentences exclusively, and from the perspective of its communicative functions rather than of its structural components alone. This emphasis is now very strong in most schools of linguistics in the international community, and even American structuralists trained within the generative school have adopted the goals of functional linguistics in ever growing numbers.[8]

The recent history of the discipline of linguistics has often been characterized as involving a series of incremental steps leading to the analysis of progressively more complex levels of linguistic structure. When the elements and relations of one level are sufficiently understood, the elements and relations of the next higher, more complex level become the object of study. A major heuristic tendency in linguistics has thus been to proceed from the more highly rule-governed to the more highly creative aspects of human speech. As early as the late 1960s linguistic science had reached the point at which the syntactic age was coming to an end, and the sentence boundary, as the highest size level of linguistic analysis, was thus ready to be abandoned in favor of text-sized units of analysis. For example, it was realized that the sentence:

(1) she did it in June.

as an opening sentence in a spoken discourse with no extralinguistic context was not an appropriate text, even though it was well-formed grammatically, whereas if (1) had occurred in a text after the sentence:

288

(2) Juli Kaiser moved west.

it would have been textually well-formed as well.
Sentence-oriented grammars had not been successful in
characterizing phenomena such as anaphora, article selection, functional word order, or intonation, and
their cognitive correlates, so that discourse grammars
had, in the course of the 1970s, become necessary on
internal grounds within linguistics itself.

Impetus for the increased participation of linguistics in textual analysis was also coming from outside the area of linguistics, particularly from literary criticism, aesthetics, and language teaching, as
well as other areas of applied linguistics such as
artificial intelligence and computer analysis of natural language.

For several decades two major functional theories
have been available to linguists for informing research in functional linguistics. Both theories were
formulated outside of linguistics, but both have at
various times been adopted by schools of linguistics
that were interested in viewing texts as being oriented towards some communicative purpose. The first is
Malinowski's ethnographic functional theory, with
its sociological focus,[9] and the second is the psy-
chologically based functional framework of Karl Bühler.[10] The major philosophical difference between the
two approaches is that while Malinowski is concerned
with what a speaker/hearer of a language can do with
language, Bühler approaches functionalism from the
point of view of what an individual speaker/hearer of
a language must know in order to perform communicative
functions. The two theories can thus be viewed as
complementary.

The Prague School of functional linguistics and,
consequently, also the Russian School, owe a great
deal to Bühler's initial formulation of a tripartite
framework of the cognitive, the appellative, and the
emotive functions of language in which a text is
oriented towards speaker, hearer, and other referents.[11] Roman Jakobson expanded the number to six
basic functions, adding the phatic, the metalinguis-
tic, and the poetic, but he clearly remains within the
Bühler tradition.[12]

In England, Malinowski's approach to functionalism was further developed by the Firth School[13] and in
recent years by M.A.K. Halliday,[14] who has successful-

ly continued this research under the rubric of systemic linguistics. Of all the linguists currently working on textual analysis and linguistic discourse, Halliday and his co-workers have been by far the most productive, and combined with the formalism developed by the American linguist Sidney Lamb in his codification of a stratified relational network system for modeling the encoding and decoding of linguistic discourse, [15] systemic linguistics shows the most promise of any functional, process-oriented framework being pursued in linguistics today.

The reorientation of GDR linguistics towards functionalism in the 1970s was based only in part on theoretical grounds; it also reflected changes in the political policies of the GDR state that followed in the wake of détente and which took the form of Abgrenzung from the West. For in spite of the parallels in current research in linguistics in the GDR and in the West, there has been a clearly noticeable decrease in the citation of the most recent research from non-socialist countries in the GDR publications since the mid-1970s. One example of this apparent neglect of linguistics from the West is that M.A.K. Halliday's recent work is seldom if ever cited, even though his work in systemic linguistics not only treats similar research interests but in some fundamental ways is clearly more advanced. [16]

The shift in the emphasis of linguistic research in the GDR was articulated by Jürgen Kunze and Wolfgang Motsch in their foreword to Studia Grammatika XI (1976). [17] The new directions were to reflect research activities resulting from increased collaboration with functional linguists in the Soviet Union and in the other socialist countries, particularly in Czechoslovakia and in Poland. In addition to the ongoing theoretical and descriptive studies on the structure of the linguistic code as an abstract object, future research was to be more applied in its orientation and was to be designed to develop a detailed conceptualization of language, according to which language could be viewed not simply as a formal system of relationships, expressed by rules, but primarily as an instrument of social activity. By establishing relationships between language, thought, and cultural activity, the discipline of linguistics could become a more direct servant of the evolving cultural-political system in socialist countries and would conform more closely to the ideals of Marxist-Leninist socialism. The larger goal of linguistics was thus to be the construction of a pragmatic linguistic theory, the purpose of which would be to facilitate the investigation of the relationships between linguistic structure and communicative social structures, as well as to create bridges of solidarity to neighboring disciplines. In this way, it would be possible to insure congruence between linguistic theory and the theories of the other sciences.

It was partially in support of these goals that the journal Zeitschrift für Germanistik, published by the VEB Verlag Enzyklopädie Leipzig, was established in 1980. The journal is devoted to the study of the German language and literature; and the mix of articles, reports, discussions, and reviews in the first four annual volumes indicates a concept of Germanistik that involves the close cooperative efforts of both linguistics and literature.

The ten numbers of the Zeitschrift für Germanistik that I was able to examine, including Number Three of Volume One (1980) through Number One of Volume Four (1983), contain a total of thirty-one articles on linguistics. Of those, only one article is on historical Germanic linguistics; two papers are on German dialectology; and two treat themes in German orthography. Next in statistical prominence are four descriptive articles on lexical semantics and/or lexicography, and four dealing with German syntax. Five papers develop notions in linguistic theory. There are six papers on applied linguistics and language pedagogy, and seven articles on linguistic investigations of poetic or other genres of texts. This characterization of the papers is intended only as a rough indication of the emphasis in subject matter, since many of the authors treat elements of linguistic structure and functions which overlap with more than one category, particularly in those articles dealing with the applications of linguistic research to language pedagogy.

Of all the recent developmental tendencies in GDR linguistics the so-called "Pragmatisierung der Sprachwissenschaft" is the strongest and most pervasive in the literature. Two major directions emerge with new emphasis in the new arrangement: linguistics as applied to the analysis of spoken and written texts, and contrastive linguistics as applied to an actively evolving language pedagogy. A third is marked for increased attention in the future: linguistic applications to the automatic processing of natural language.

Papers on the linguistic analysis of text in the Zeitschrift für Germanistik have treated primarily, but not exclusively, the approaches and contributions of linguistics to poetic texts. A frequent theme is that the common object of inquiry shared by linguists and literary critics is the text. However, a shared object of inquiry does not insure that the goals of the two kindred disciplines are the same. The primary goal of a text-oriented linguistics is to investigate the semantic, syntactic, and pragmatic principles and regularities which underlie the construction and construal of texts in general. But these regularities are of interest to literary critics only insofar as they can contribute to the understanding of the communicative effect of the poetic text on the reader and/or to the understanding of the expression of the communicative content of the text.

To further illustrate research on text within GDR circles I will comment briefly on the work of three or four currently active linguists who publish in the Zeitschrift für Germanistik. In a paper on "Textbezogene Sprachwissenschaft und poetischer Text," Inger Rosengren takes the point of departure that every text, including the poetic text, is the correlate of a communicative act between a sender and a receiver in a communication process.[18] She distinguishes three levels of analysis: the illocutionary level, the thematic level, and the syntactic-lexical level. Text results from the performance of the pragmatic and linguistic competence of the sender in the encoding of information in a situational and/or cultural context. Information includes both content and intention.

In their article "Zur integrativen Analyse poetischer Texte," Hans Georg Werner and Gerhard Lerchner formulate their position based on the author-text-reader relationship, in which the message of a poetic text is definable primarily from the point of view of the effect of the text on the recipient.[19] Accordingly, a text is a poetic text by reason of the interplay between the text and its function in poetic communication. Not so much the text, but rather the poetic effect of the text forms the basis for the congruence of literary and linguistic text analysis. In a review of the article Georg Michel criticizes Werner and Lerchner for their neglect of the author/speaker's intention as a producer of text.[20] For Michel the function of a text as a goal-directed, purposeful construct stands in relation both to the intention of the author and to the effect produced on the reader.

In this regard research in the GDR parallels current work in semiotics in the West. For example, in his recent papers on visual semiotics, Donald Preziosi points out as significant the discovery that the recognition of speech sounds as meaningful sequences is an act of perceptual discrimination, cognitive classification, and commutation on the part of the language user, i.e., hearer.[21] And it is noteworthy that at the same time that theoretical linguistics was beginning to take into account the perceptually discriminative activity of the hearer, the focus in visual semiotics was shifting from a fixation on the intention of the maker/designer of the built environment towards the processes of reception of the actual user of the artefact. A focus on the subject neither denies nor undervalues the fact that an object may be intended by the maker to mark a particular content or system of value. But by emphasizing the perspective of the individual user/construer it is possible for the moment to avoid the problematic nature of the notion of intention, in what has been referred to as the "intentional fallacy." It is in this new focus on the recipient that Preziosi sees the primary productive direction in semiotics at the present time.

Also Charles Fillmore's recent work on text semantics at the University of California/Berkeley focuses on the behavior of the hearer in the decoding/construal of ordinary language.[22] Both Hockett and Lamb had taken a similar position earlier.[23] Fillmore's reason for choosing the interpretive process as the primary object of study is similar to Preziosi's: the comprehension process is more studiable. In an empirical study, it is relatively easy to observe many interpreters' responses to a single language sample that is presented to them, but it is essentially impossible to examine many speakers' activities of producing the same text.

But the main lines of contact and collaboration for present-day GDR text linguists are, according to Viehweger,[24] directed toward the Prague School and current Soviet linguistics, i.e., traditions that combine the notions of system, structure, and functions of language into an integrated methodological framework. And, despite the apparent neglect of significant research with similar goals and methods in the West, work on text linguistics in the GDR will continue to command our attention.

The second very prominent area of linguistics in

the GDR is the use of recent developments in contrastive linguistics in language teaching pedagogy. Papers on applied linguistics and language pedagogy in the Zeitschrift für Germanistik address two related issues: first, the role of context in foreign language teaching as a strategy for producing communicative competence; and, second, the redefinition of the contrastive principle to include contrastive pragmatics as well as contrastive grammar. With the increasing projection of pragmatic knowledge onto linguistics in the 1970s came the necessity of a corresponding readjustment of didactic concepts in language instruction. No longer was it sufficient in language teaching to produce students with a code competence that insured an adequate internalization only of the grammar and lexicon in the target language. Such an approach, normally based on the excessive use of pattern drills, ignores context, both the cognitive context of situation and the more distant context of culture. But no utterance ever occurs outside of some context, and students who have acquired even a very high degree of code competence have difficulty in an actual communicative situation. By then they have usually erroneously learned in the classroom that sentences in the foreign language apparently have nothing to do with each other, to say nothing of having something to do with extralinguistic contexts. A communicative competence, then, necessarily includes the pragmatic knowledge of how a speaker of the target language makes choices in the encoding of information and in the creation of situational flow without communicative distortion. Also included is the knowledge of how the speaker packages information in order to aid the hearer in identifying the intended referents of events and participant roles in the utterance.[25]

The latter issue, namely the use of contrastive pragmatics in an attempt to minimize interference from the native language, relates more closely to linguistics than the first. Two principles present themselves in the GDR literature: first, the more closed the subsystem in the target language, the less the effect of interference from the native language. For this reason contrastive grammar is less vital than contrastive pragmatics in language instruction. The second principle is related to the first: only the subsystems of the target language in which there is the possibility of choice are subject to the interference of the native language in language learning, and thus require extensive contrastive treatment. Foreign language instruction in the GDR is constantly updated and enriched by the most recent findings in theoretical linguistics. Instructors are informed not only through the published literature, as in this case papers in the Zeitschrift für Germanistik, but also by participation in periodic workshops and symposia on linguistics and language teaching.

In summary: It is apparent that linguistics in the GDR has been moving away from the exclusive dominance of morphology, syntax, and phonology, i.e., the central subsystems of linguistic structure as defined by post-Saussurean structuralists, towards a linguistics with more directly pragmatic applications and concerns. Most significant are its contributions to interdisciplinary studies involving the application of linguistics to textual analysis and to the important field of foreign language pedagogy. In short, linguistics in the GDR in the 1960s was highly abstract, theoretical, and oriented towards research methodologies in the West. There was a drastic pragmatic reorientation of linguistics in the early 1970s resulting in increased collaboration with linguists in the other socialist countries, and in neglect of the literature from the West, despite parallel research of high quality. The restructuring of linguistics in the 1970s in the GDR was partly done on legitimate theoretical grounds within the field of linguistics itself, and partly as a result of political/ideological pronouncements and priorities from the outside. These developments and trends are documented in the GDR linguistics literature of the last two decades and are particularly underscored by the papers published during the last four years in the new journal Zeitschrift für Germanistik.

Rice University

Notes

[1] Noam Chomsky, Aspects of the Theory of Syntax (Cambridge: MIT Press, 1965). Subsequent references to this work will be cited as Chomsky (1965).

[2] Noam Chomsky, Language and Mind (New York: Harcourt, Brace, and World, 1968).

[3] Erich Karl Heidolph, Walter Flämig, and Wolfgang Motsch, eds., Grundzüge einer deutschen Grammatik

(Berlin: Akademie Verlag, 1981). The grammar was edited by Heidolph, Flämig, and Motsch but written by eight collaborating scholars.

[4] See Peter Suchsland, "Besprechung von Grundzüge einer deutschen Grammatik," Zeitschrift für Germanistik, 2, No. 4 (1981), 474.

[5] See Peter Porsch, "Zur Bestimmung des Gegenstandes der Linguistik bei Ferdinand de Saussure," ZfG, 2, No. 2 (1981), 188.

[6] See František Daneš and Dieter Viehweger, "Vorwort," in Jürgen Kunze and Wolfgang Motsch, eds., Probleme der Textgrammatik, Studia Grammatica XI (Berlin: Akademie Verlag, 1976).

[7] See Wolfdietrich Hartung, "Tätigkeitskonzepte in der Linguistik," ZfG, 3, No. 3 (1982), 389.

[8] See, for example, Charles Fillmore, "Lexical Semantics and Text Semantics," in James E. Copeland, ed., New Directions in Linguistics and Semiotics (Houston: Rice University; Amsterdam: John Benjamins, 1984), p. 122.

[9] Bronislaw Malinowski, Coral Gardens and their Magic, Vol. 2 (New York: American Book Company, 1935).

[10] Karl Bühler, Sprachtheorie (Jena: Fischer, 1933).

[11] František Daneš, "A Three Level Approach to Syntax," in Travaux linguistiques de Prague (Prague: Editions de l'Academie Tchecoslovaque des Sciences, 1964).

[12] Roman Jakobson, "Linguistics and Poetics," in Thomas A. Sebeok, ed., Language and Style (Boston: John Wiley and Sons, 1960).

[13] J.R. Firth, Papers in Linguistics, 1934-1951 (London: Oxford Univ. Press, 1957).

[14] M.A.K. Halliday, "Modes of Meaning and Modes of Expression: Types of Grammatical Structure and their Determination by Different Semantic Functions," in D.J. Allerton, et al., eds., Function and Context in Linguistic Analysis (Cambridge: Cambridge University Press, 1979); also M.A.K. Halliday, "Language Structure and Language Function," in John Lyons, ed.,

New Horizons in Linguistics (Harmondsworth: Penguin Books, 1970), p. 140.

15 Sydney M. Lamb, "The Semiotics of Language and Culture," in Robin Fawcett, et al., eds., The Semiotics of Culture and Language (London: Francis Pinter, 1984).

16 See, as a rare exception, Dieter Viehweger, "Struktur und Funktion nominativer Ketten im Text," in Wolfgang Motsch, ed., Kontexte der Grammatiktheorie, Studia Grammatica XVII (Berlin: Akademie, 1978), p. 149.

17 Jürgen Kunze and Wolfgang Motsch, "Vorwort der Herausgeber," in their Probleme der Textgrammatik, Studia Grammatica XI (Berlin: Akademie, 1976), p. 7.

18 Inger Rosengren, "Textbezogene Sprachwissenschaft und poetischer Text," ZfG, 4, No. 1 (1983), 53-64.

19 Hans Georg Werner and Gerhard Lerchner, "Zur integrativen Analyse poetischer Texte," ZfG, 2, No. 3 (1981), 334-37.

20 Georg Michel, review of "Zur integrativen Analyse poetischer Texte," ZfG, 2, No. 4 (1981), 451-53.

21 Donald Preziosi, "Subjects + Objects: The Current State of Visual Semiotics," in James E. Copeland, ed., New Directions in Linguistics and Semiotics, p. 179.

22 See Note 8.

23 Charles F. Hockett, "Grammar for the Hearer," in Roman Jakobson, ed., Proceedings of Symposia in Applied Linguistics, Vol. 3, 1960; Sydney M. Lamb, "Linguistic Structure and the Production and Decoding of Discourse," in E.C. Carterette, ed., Brain Function, Vol. 3 (Berkeley: Univ. of California Press, 1966).

24 Dieter Viehweger, "Semantische Merkmale und Textstruktur," in Probleme der Textgrammatik, p. 198, et passim.

25 See James E. Copeland and Philip W. Davis, "Discourse Portmanteaus and the German Satzfeld," in William Agard, et al., eds., Essays in Honor of Charles F. Hockett (Leiden: Brill, N.P., 1983), p.

214.

Theater Activity in East Berlin -   A Brief Report[1]

Laurence Romero

East Berlin is without doubt the theater capital of the GDR, with a good number of well-equipped theaters and a constant availability of good players. There are also large and mixed audiences: theatergoers from all over the Republic, students, workers, professional people, many foreigners, and a substantial contingent of critics writing in the country's major newspapers and journals. A career in GDR theater must at some time be tested in Berlin.

There are of course some disadvantages to this kind of ingathering. Concentrating major theater work in Berlin helps in certain aspects of control. Moreover, prestigious playhouses tend to capture most of the attention of critics and the media and thus to attract the largest crowds. Under these conditions, theater often begins to function merely as popular event; actors dominate in predictable roles; well-known authors and works have the best chances of being played, to the detriment of lesser-known classics and contemporary works. To a certain extent, these limiting conditions are abetted by a lack of small theaters promoting experimental works with innovative stagings, acting styles, and scenic design. Elsewhere in the Republic, smaller, regional theaters have become known for occasional stagings that are less conventional in content and form: in Rostock and Schwerin, where Christoph Schroth did his early work, in Karl-Marx-Stadt, where Piet Drescher started, and especially in Potsdam, where a number of younger directors have worked, including Rolf Winkelgrund, who recently moved to the Berlin Maxim-Gorki-Theater, where Drescher also currently directs. An example of this type of interesting provincial fare was the very popular 1983 production of Claus Hammel's ironic comedy, <u>Die Preußen kommen</u>, in Eckhard Becker's staging in

Potsdam. The play's subtitle is "Prüfungsanstalt für die Reintegration historischer Persönlichkeiten der DDR"--Luther and Friedrich II are intended.

In Berlin there were three well-known smaller, somewhat experimental stages, all linked to established theaters: the Studiobühne of the Maxim-Gorki-Theater, the Theater im Dritten Stock of the Volksbühne (where Heiner Müller staged his Auftrag), and the Kleine Komödie in the main complex of the Deutsches Theater (DT) in the Schumannstraße. Unfortunately, the Kleine Komödie was not retained in the newly renovated Deutsches Theater, which reopened in the fall of 1983 after having been closed for two years. The loss of this quasi experimental stage is serious, diminishing as it does the excitement of theater work in Berlin and limiting even more the chances of playing contemporary GDR and foreign dramatists. That there has been virtually no debate on this issue in the press is a fact which a number of GDR theater professionals regretted in private conversation.

The impetus for innovative theater in Berlin as elsewhere must ultimately come from the playwrights, the Intendanten, the directors, and players who find the courage to attempt stimulating new productions and then deal effectively with local Party officials. Since all new works in the repertory have to be approved by the Ministry of Culture--both the text and the director's planned staging conception--self-censorship often dampens the innovative spirit. As a result, many pressing social issues like feminism, the military, the school system, and the peace movement are not being dealt with in contemporary GDR drama. The conspiration of silence on these questions makes many new plays uninteresting to ambitious directors, who stage the classics instead and then overload them with messages more appropriate to a contemporary text. Even when provocative plays exist, they cannot always be staged and this too inhibits good playwriting. The persistent task of trying to determine the parameters of tolerance in the theater can itself be an intimidating factor. In the long process from new script or new staging conception of a classic to the final production on stage, the key link is often the director. At the close of the 1982-83 season in Berlin, there was a clear but publicly unspoken opinion that new, younger directors were needed to mediate between playwrights, Ministry, actors, and audiences. This is especially true given the fact that since the Biermann

300

expatriation in late 1976, a number of well-known GDR directors have moved to the West: Adolf Dresen, Jürgen Gosch, Manfred Karge, Matthias Langhoff, B.K. Tragelehn, and Fritz Marquardt, among others.

In the overall standing of theaters in Berlin, there has been a gradual shift in prestige and popularity in recent years. The Berliner Ensemble has become more and more the museum that Brecht wanted to avoid; this is partly due to persistent, unresolved tensions between the director, Manfred Wekwerth (newly elected President of the Akademie der Künste), and an influential group within the theater centered around Barbara Brecht and Ekkehard Schall. The Deutsches Theater and, to a lesser degree, the Maxim-Gorki-Theater have emerged as the most interesting houses in Berlin, producing the most consistently appealing stagings of both classical and modern drama.

Three relatively young directors have distinguished themselves in these two houses: Alexander Lang at the Deutsches Theater, Rolf Winkelgrund at the Maxim-Gorki-Theater, and Thomas Langhoff, who has worked in both places. In the rest of this essay, discussion will focus on the first two of these directors, and especially on Alexander Lang.

Originally from Bielefeld, Rolf Winkelgrund has lived in the GDR for more than twenty years, having begun his career as an actor in Cottbus. He gained attention as a director with his stagings of modern foreign authors, especially Lorca, O'Casey, Rozewicz, Kesey/Wassermann, and with several GDR premiers of Athol Fugard's works. In July 1982 he directed a guest production in the Gorki-Theater of Kesey/Wassermann's One Flew Over the Cuckoo's Nest and was subsequently invited to join the theater's staff of resident directors. In March 1983 he premiered Fugard's Dimetos at the Maxim-Gorki, with the accomplished Jörg Gudzuhn in the title role.

Winkelgrund's staging of One Flew Over the Cuckoo's Nest--with Gudzuhn as R.P. McMurphy--was a vigorous rendering of a potentially problematic text.[2] The issue of the psychiatric ward as a prison, and psychiatry as a means of dealing with non-conformists was carefully avoided, at least in the staging conception. The main theme was the tyranny of an authoritarian society over the meek, in other words, the crushing of the spontaneous, the poetic, the good in all of us by high-tech late capitalism. It was sug-

gested that these conditions could only exist in an
evolved, western consumer society and that Kesey had
used the psychiatric ward merely as a metaphor of suppression in his homeland. In principle, this was a
discrete way of presenting the play to a GDR audience
while avoiding the touchier side of the main subject.
In the actual playing, however, the vitality of the
actors led by Gudzuhn surpassed the limited focus of
the conception and gave clear indication that the action of the play was more than mere metaphor and that
the abuses portrayed could be endemic to any contemporary industrial society. In a sense, Spielen went
beyond Konzeption, a healthy phenomenon emphasizing
flexible, open playing, in part the consequence of ex-
actors becoming directors. In any case, Winkelgrund's
work here and his other stagings indicate that he is
capable of subtle and original interpretations.

At the Deutsches Theater, Alexander Lang stands
with Friedo Solter and Thomas Langhoff as a mainstay
director in this large national theater. Still in his
early forties, Lang was a very successful actor before
beginning to direct at the DT in the 1970s. Gradually
he has come to concentrate on directing because it en-
gages more of his skills, because there is always room
for talented directors in the GDR, and, as he admitted
candidly in our interview, directors wait less for
good opportunities than do actors. One of his most
noteworthy stagings in the DT to date was Dantons Tod,
which opened in April 1981 and, during the renovation
of the theater, played often as a guest production in
the Berliner Ensemble. Typically for an actor-direc-
tor, Lang insisted on Spielen in his staging of Büchner's text, the playing element being the central mod-
ality in transforming content into performance. Thus
the very gifted actor Christian Grashof portrayed both
Danton and Robespierre, and, in a consciously artificial mode, both men were shown as essentially helpless
at the later stage of an historical event that had
surpassed its creators. For Lang, the main point in
Dantons Tod is the failure of the Revolution to solve
the "stomach question," i.e., to provide bread for the
starving masses. In line with this interpretation,
Lang emphasizes the reaction--confused and hapless,
but at the same time humane and comic--of the people,
who are faced with the disappointment of their own
history and the trauma of the reign of terror. The
people are a central figure in the production, a kind
of Gegenspieler to Danton and Robespierre. In order
to portray the masses as an emerging class, Lang presented them not as an anonymous crowd, but as a sum of

individual personalities. In keeping with the theatricalization of the entire text, the people were represented by two popular actors, Kurt Böwe and Dietrich Körner, who reflected convincingly the strength and vitality of small people caught up in large events. In this sophisticated form of aesthetic abstraction--Shakespeare's clowns and Schweijk come to mind--the director challenged his DT audiences intellectually and assumed rightly that his staging would be understood as being in the tradition of a refined Marxist analysis. The reaction was overwhelmingly positive, although some more orthodox critics questioned the absence of real crowds and the wisdom of reducing the masses to two clowns.[3] Sensing the controversial nature of his production, Lang had Grashof read as a curtain-raiser a "letter" from Georg Büchner in which the author suggests that his dramatic text is not completed and as such is open to interpretation and debate.

In a discussion with the respected GDR theater critic Martin Linzer, Lang expressed his views on the function of the actor, especially in productions of the classics. For Lang, the actor on stage today must embody both his role and his time. It is through this double-playing that an accomplished actor can, say in a Shakespearian part, reflect both the spirit of the classical role and our contemporary temper.[4] Lang is himself an actor in the Komödiant tradition, a play-actor with a penchant for irony, subtle humor, and double-playing. As a director, he has consequently tried in his productions to react against declamatory and mechanical acting styles in favor of as much looseness as possible. To develop this type of playing, Lang prefers long, informal rehearsals which help the actors free themselves of fears and inhibitions they might have brought to their roles. Lang connects his ideas here to the derivation of the key word, Schauspieler: the actor plays (spielen) and, in giving corporeal form to his performance, he offers it to the perception of the spectator (zur Schau stellen). In the ideal theatrical exchange between player and spectator, the actor should be as fanciful and intuitive as a child at play, and the spectator's viewing should be generous and uninhibited.

In these reflections, the matter of acting space is important. In a recent issue of Bauten der Kultur, Lang described some of his experiments with actors playing in a very limited space, exercises provoked in part by Peter Brook's investigations in Paris and while on tour in Africa. The basic concern was to reorganize limited playing space in such a way as to simplify stage design and sets, to reduce as much as possible the void between the actor and his spectators and thereby to lessen the gap between stage play and audience understanding. "The actor stands at the center of the complex relationships between stage space and audience space. His body and its possibilities must determine the shape and mass of his playing space."[5] Alexander Lang's work in actor/spectator space is not as radical as similar efforts in the U.S. during the Living Theater movement in the 1950s and 1960s and in many productions since. He does not believe that the spectators should become involved in the stage action or even be completely absorbed in it. In his view, the ideal relationship remains essentially Brechtian: that the spectator be caught up in the action on stage but never more emotionally than intellectually. The ultimate theatrical experience-- also a Brechtian ideal--is the one which influences the spectator's thinking in his daily life and work in a positive way. In any case, the link between the stage and the spectator is the responsibility of the actor and director, both of whom must be prepared to stage and to play texts in surprising, provocative new ways and then let the rest work itself out: " . . . offer new ways of reading and seeing which engage the spectator who then accepts them--or rejects them."[6]

Alexander Lang's attitude toward staging the classics reflects a typical GDR position in its preoccupation with Zeitgeschichte, but he adds to that a more personal concern with biography. "The more I delve into the author's life and time, the more I find sudden, unexpected connections that influence my directing and my acting or my actors."[7] Classics should be staged en situation, where past and present converge. The script from the past is reenacted by actors reflecting their sensibilities, thus completing the dialectic between what Robert Weimann called "past significance and present meaning."[8] Typical in this regard was Lang's production of A Midsummer Night's Dream at the Deutsches Theater in 1980, after a twenty-five-year interlude during which this work had not been staged in Berlin. Lang's interpretation went against the Max Reinhardt tradition, i.e., against the large, romantic, colorful conception of the playful, pastoral, dream story.[9] On the contrary, here was a staging that insisted relentlessly on the bitter and the perverse, on trickery, deceit, manipulation, and black magic. Lang made it clear that his conception was not merely a reaction to the Reinhardt model but his way of denying any attempt at sugaring-over or avoiding problems and contradictions he and his post-war generation have had to face. In other words, this was the director's way of looking for the new (based on his understanding of the past) and, in the process, of linking the new with the traditional.

Alexander Lang's work as a director at the Deutsches Theater has been original, imaginative, and it has been successful. Along with Friedo Solter, he was invited to direct one of the two major productions for the festive centennial celebration of the Deutsches Theater in the fall of 1983. His staging of Brecht's little-known Rundköpfe und Spitzköpfe was positively reviewed in Theater heute, a major FRG theater journal which is often critical of GDR theater work.[10] Lang's directorial experience has been very broad, including both classics and modern works, German plays and foreign: Shakespeare, Büchner, Brecht, Heiner Müller, Athol Fugard, Ken Kesey, and the recent world premiere production of Christoph Hein's Die wahre Geschichte des Ah Q.[11] Reflecting on model productions of the classics in the Deutsches Theater since 1945, Martin Linzer included Lang's stagings of A Midsummer Night's Dream and Danton's Tod among those of such distinguished directors as Wolfgang Langhoff, Wolfgang Heinz, Benno Besson, Adolf Dresen, and Friedo Solter.[12] With his primary concern for actors and their craft, Lang has been able to attract to his productions some of the most talented actors, old and young, in the large ensemble of Deutsches Theater, some of them considered among the best players in the GDR today: Christian Grashof, Roman Kaminski, Johanna Clas, Inge Keller, Kurt Böwe, and Dietrich Körner, to cite but a few.

Is it not, finally, the mark of a first-rate theater director to have worked effectively in a wide range of dramatic texts, to have come to the fore as a highly respected director in a large and demanding national theater, and to have cultivated and maintained the best working relations with top actors and actresses? Alexander Lang is that kind of director and his presence enhances all of GDR theater.

Villanova University

Notes

[1] This brief review was written after three visits to East Berlin in November and December 1982, and in March 1983, during which there were discussions with directors, actors, and dramaturgs, especially at the Deutsches Theater. The most extensive exchange was with Alexander Lang in late March 1983.

[2] For more information, see I. Pietzsch, "Regisseure im Gespräch: Rolf Winkelgrund," Theater der Zeit, 36, No. 9 (1981), 23-24; and the program, Einer flog über das Kuckucksnest, Maxim-Gorki-Theater, Spielzeit 1981-82.

[3] On Lang's Dantons Tod, see Martin Linzer, "Modelle revolutionären Verhaltens," Theater der Zeit, 36, No. 8 (1981), 42-46; Inge Diersen, "Büchners Dantons Tod," Weimarer Beiträge, 27, No. 12 (1981), 170-175; and the program for the production, Dantons Tod, Deutsches Theater Berlin, Spielzeit 1980-81 (Editor: Ilse Galfert).

[4] From an undated, hand-corrected typescript of an interview with Martin Linzer, most likely from late 1981. Similar points are reiterated in the more recent interview with Ingrid Seyfarth: "Da ist immer die Lust am Entdecken - Über Kreativität im Inszenierungsprozeß, Sonntag, 22 May 1983, pp. 8-9.

[5] Alexander Lang, Bauten der Kultur, 8, No. 1 (1983), 7. This and all subsequent translations from the German are by the author.

[6] Lang/Linzer interview, p. 4.

[7] Lang/Linzer interview, p. 5.

[8] Robert Weimann, Literaturgeschichte und Mythologie (Berlin: Aufbau Verlag, 1974), p. 431.

[9] On this Shakespeare staging, see Martin Linzer, "A Midsummer Night's Dream in East Germany," The Drama Review, 25, No. 2 (1981), 45-49; also Lang's program for the production, Sommernachtstraum, Deutsches Theater Berlin, Spielzeit 1979-80 (Editor: Ilse Galfert).

[10] "Neues vom alten Brecht?" Theater heute, 24, No. 11 (1983), 34-35.

[11] See Andreas Roßmann's review: "Die Revolution als Geisterschiff. Christoph Heins 'Die wahre Geschichte des Ah Q," _Deutschland Archiv_, 17, No. 3 (1983), 232-33.

[12] Martin Linzer, "Ich bin ein Fan," _Theater der Zeit_, 38, No. 9 (1983), 16.